TROUPE OF THE COMMEDIA DELL' ARTE

Eighteenth-century engraving. Artist unknown

THE ITALIAN COMEDY

The Improvisation Scenarios Lives Attributes Portraits and Masks of the Illustrious Characters of the Commedia dell' Arte

By

PIERRE LOUIS DUCHARTRE

Authorized Translation from the French by

RANDOLPH T. WEAVER

With a New Pictorial Supplement reproduced from the "Recueil Fossard" and "Compositions de rhétorique"

DOVER PUBLICATIONS, INC.

NEW YORK

Published in Canada by General Publishing Company, Ltd., 30 Lesmill Road, Don Mills, Toronto, Ontario.
Published in the United Kingdom by Constable and Company, Ltd., 10 Orange Street, London W.C. 2.

This Dover edition, first published in 1966, is an unabridged and unaltered republication of the work originally published by George G. Harrap & Co., Ltd., in 1929. The Frontispiece and illustrations facing page 24 appeared in color in the original edition.

This edition is published by special arrangement with George G. Harrap & Co., Ltd.

This edition also contains a new Pictorial Supplement compiled from the *Recueil Fossard,* published by Duchartre and Van Buggenhoudt in 1928.

International Standard Book Number: 0-486-21679-9
Library of Congress Catalog Card Number: 66-23390

Manufactured in the United States of America
Dover Publications, Inc.
180 Varick Street
New York, N.Y. 10014

Translator's Note

M. DUCHARTRE'S admirable study of the Italian comedy is already well known in the original to those interested in the subject, particularly in Europe, and surely it deserves the wider attention and appreciation which a version in English can provide. The present volume offers several advantages over the two French editions of *La Comédie italienne*, in that the author has made extensive corrections and added fresh material to the text. He has been good enough to add also twenty-six entirely new illustrations, most of which have never before been published. It is worth mentioning in passing that nine of these, and two figures which appeared in the second French edition, are taken from a rare collection of sixteenth-century engravings called the *Recueil Fossard*, which M. Duchartre has recently brought out in reproduction with the imprint of his own publishing house, Duchartre et Van Buggenhoudt, of Paris. The *Recueil* is the result of " the unhoped-for discovery by M. Agne Beijer of a magnificent in-folio album which was in the uncatalogued reserves of the Museum of Stockholm." It was made by a certain M. Fossard for Louis XIV, and, so far as is known, it had never been published, nor had more than two of the engravings ever been found in any other work.

Among the illustrations are three drawings by Domenico Tiepolo which Messrs Victor Rosenthal and Raymond Bloch have courteously given us permission to reproduce. The drawing from M. Bloch's collection is here published for the first time.

With the permission of M. Duchartre the translator has added a number of footnotes, usually embodying the views of other writers, explanatory of certain aspects of the subject. In order not to encumber the pages the longer of these have been relegated to appendices. In this connexion grateful acknowledgment is made to the proprietors of *The Mask* for the use of extracts from that periodical, and to Mr Cyril W. Beaumont for the use of passages from his *History of Harlequin*.

No attempt, it should be added, has been made to reconcile the differing spellings of certain names of characters, etc., which exist.

The translator wishes to express his sincere thanks to Messrs George Vardy and Pierre Loving for much valuable assistance with the translation.

R. T. W.

PARIS
June 1929

Contents

THE ITALIAN COMEDY

Illustrations

THE ITALIAN COMEDY

ILLUSTRATIONS

ILLUSTRATIONS

THE ITALIAN COMEDY

ILLUSTRATIONS

THE ITALIAN COMEDY

I

The Commedia dell' Arte

ARLEQUIN and Columbine, Isabelle and Scaramouche, Pulcinella and Pantaloon, belong definitely to romance. Behind their names are heard the guitars of the *Fêtes Galantes*, the lingering echoes of shouts, applause, and robust laughter. Yet, as in a Watteau picture, the charm and gaiety of far-gone days die away on a minor key, for those who bore these names are long since dead, and with them all their joyous fantasy.

We are reminded of that bright, care-free company when, exploring some old bookshop, we come by chance upon a volume of Gherardi's *Le Théâtre italien*, or a stray print of Beltrame da Milano, of Harlequin, or of Riccoboni. The very contact with these relics gives us pause, and all at once the festive scenes of yester-year are evoked, the shadowy figures come alive, and we sense with a vague sharpness the distant glamour of pageantry and colour still vivid in the musty pages. But the illusion is too quickly lost, and we grow aware that these beauties of the past are asleep and beyond our reach, awaiting a new Molière or else some Charlie Chaplin of the Latin race to reawaken them.

Harlequin, Punch, Columbine, and Pantaloon were, in their day, used again and again in many forms and guises, and often so badly that in the end the Italian comedy scarcely served for more than gross farces, which were sometimes amusing because they were so inept, but more often were simply tedious and vulgar. The consequence is that comparatively little is known now about the true Italian comedy, the *commedia dell' arte* of the Renaissance and the seventeenth century, that world of fantasy peopled with quaint characters, conventionalized but full of life, rare personalities given to antics as picturesque as the costumes they wore.

George Sand wrote :

> The *commedia dell' arte* is not only a study of the grotesque and facetious, . . . but also a portrayal of real characters traced from remote antiquity down to the present day, in an uninterrupted tradition of fantastic humour which is in essence quite serious and, one might almost say, even sad, like every satire which lays bare the spiritual poverty of mankind.

Pantaloon and Brighella are eternal verities dealt with by poets rather than by psychologists or pedants. Their origin is ancient, and they will live for ever. The ancestor of Pantaloon, and his son Harpagon, is Pappus, the lecherous old miser of the *Atellanæ*. Their descendants are still with us, for Lelio is the charming *gigolo* of modern days, Isabelle his lovely feminine counterpart. Harlequin has lost his nonsense, and has exchanged his motley for the frock-coat of an ambitious Government official. The crafty Brighella has left his native Bergamo and Pantaloon has deserted Venice, and we have only to look twice to see them in the passing crowd.

I must insist that this illustrious family is far from being extinct. In the matter of antiquity few members of the aristocracy can boast a longer line than Harlequin and Punch. The cradle of the family was the ancient city of Atella, in the Roman Campagna, and the gallery of ancestors shows, among others, Bucco and the sensual Maccus, whose lean figure and cowardly nature reappear in Pulcinella. Next there is the ogre Manducus, the Miles Gloriosus in the plays of Plautus, who is later metamorphosed into the swaggering Capitan, or Captain. And there is also Lamia the Ghoul, who is the worthy patron saint of all go-betweens and scheming mothers.

The *Atellanæ* were comedies and popular farces, parodies and political satires. Whatever the plot or argument of the piece, the *rôles* kept the same character, further emphasized by the famous mask, without which the more important Italian comedians rarely made their appearance until the end of the eighteenth century. The dialogue at Atella, and later at Rome, was for a long time improvised from a plot-outline, or scenario, decided upon in advance. The actor who found himself at a loss for words, or in any other predicament, usually resorted to slap-stick. Harlequin's bat was a ready reply when all cues failed. And if the farces were often lacking in propriety they possessed, on the other hand, the more essential quality of life, as is witnessed by the ancient bas-reliefs and frescoes. The players drew freely upon the life of the day for their material, making use of the customs and frailties of all classes. And their tight-fitting masks, unchanging and inseparable from a given *rôle*, seemed in the end to be the only true countenance of the wearer.

And these are the elements which go to make great art.

If we pass over to the sixteenth century in Italy we discover the famous *commedia dell' arte* existing alongside the regular or legitimate theatre. It had retained the principal characters of the *Atellanæ*, but as it grew it proceeded to develop new types of its own. Bologna, with its old university, contributed the Doctor, who was as foolish as he was pedantic. Venice, the city of merchants and adventurers, evolved Pantaloon and the Captain. The two Bergamos—the Auvergne[1] of Italy—produced the sly booby, Harlequin, and the knave, Brighella.

Otherwise there was little change. "The scenario, which the actors consulted at the beginning of each scene, was posted in the wings." It appears, however, that Angelo Beolco (1502–42), better known as Il Ruzzante,[2] stimulated the development of local types when he wrote a comedy in prose (presented in 1528) in which each character spoke a different dialect. Another actor, named Cecchi,[3] won considerable renown by ridiculing popular prejudices in a play called *Assinolo*, supposed to be "perfectly new"

[1] A mountainous region in the south central part of France which is supposed to produce slow-witted people. The French often say of a dullard, "Oh! c'est un Auvergnat" ("Oh, he's an Auvergnat").—Translator.

[2] The name means 'sporting' or 'playful.' See *Ruzzante*, by Alfred Mortier, p. 80.

[3] "Cecchi, Giovanni. Born 1518; died 1587. Playwright. He wrote *La Romanesca* in 1585, and in the prologue to this play he extols the *Farsa* and pleads the cause of Romantic Drama against the canons of Aristotle. A translation of this will be found in *Shakespeare's Predecessors*, by J. Addington Symonds, p. 208."—*The Mask*, vol. iii, p. 126.

and treating of " an incident recently befallen in Pisa, involving certain young students and certain ladies of the town."

The elements of interest in contemporary events which Beolco and Cecchi introduced provided a fresh point of departure for the Italian comedy. The subject-matter of the plays was no longer limited to slavish imitations of Plautus, Terence, and Boccaccio, and began to include more and more the various aspects of everyday life.

It was then that the celebrated characters of the *commedia dell' arte* came into being, created by a welding of humanism and direct observation. The new characters not only became heir to the traditions of the theatre of antiquity, tracing their descent from classic prototypes, but they possessed striking traits which stamped them with distinct personalities of their own. They had, for instance, their own manner of speaking and gesturing, their own peculiar intonations and dress, and they were individual even to their warts and moles. In short, they represented people not of the dead and forgotten past, but of living and growing cities like Venice and Bergamo. We have little exact information regarding the early period of the formation and evolution of these characters as we know them to-day, but the theory is tenable that both the actors and public must have co-operated to a great extent in perfecting and standardizing the different types.

From the middle of the sixteenth century onward there was a constant proliferation of characters which the famous troupes of the Gelosi, the Confidenti, and the Uniti eventually made popular everywhere. Milan produced Beltrame and Scapin, brothers of Brighella and Meneghino ; Naples brought forth first Pulcinella and then Scaramouche and Tartaglia ; to Rome are due Meo-Patacca, Marco-Pepe, and later Cassandrino ; to Turin, Gianduja ; and in Calabria appeared Coviello, of whom Callot [1] made a charming engraving. In this way each town created a representative type which was its boast, and to which its jealous neighbours added a touch of caricature. And thus the various *rôles* became stylized.

With this impetus the *commedia dell' arte* entered upon a period of increased activity, for it was naturally destined to flourish in the soil of Italy, where " the theatre is so popular that most of the working men deprive themselves of food in order to have the wherewithal to go to the play," [2] and almost everybody has a talent for pantomime.

It must be understood from the outset that the *commedia dell' arte* was, of course, a *genre* of theatre quite distinct from any other. In France it was called *comédie à l'impromptu* and also *comédie improvisée*, though it never received any very exact definition, as the reader will observe later on. The term *commedia dell' arte* signifies, according to Dr Michele Scherillo, a form of comedy which, " in distinction to the written comedies, was not, and could not be, performed except by professional actors " ; [3] while Maurice Sand [4] spoke of it simply as being the " perfection among plays." In any case, the two viewpoints taken together constitute a fairly adequate definition.

[1] See Appendix A.

[2] From a manuscript of du Tralage (seventeenth century).

[3] *The Mask*, vol. iii, p. 113. This volume in particular contains several very interesting articles on the subject of the *commedia dell' arte*.

[4] " The son of George Sand. Born 1823 ; died 1889. Author and illustrator of *Masques et Bouffons* (Paris, 1862), a work

There is no end to the list of names given to the characters of the *commedia dell' arte* in documents dating from the Renaissance to the time of Molière. Yet, after they have all been sorted over, we find a limited number of fundamental types to which each actor, each locality, and the customs of each period made a special contribution. These characters are Pulcinella, the Captain, two old men, Pantaloon and the Doctor, and the two Zanni,[1] or valet-buffoons, Harlequin and Brighella, or Francatrippa, etc. All of them wore masks, which is a strong indication of their connexion with the theatre of antiquity. The troupes of the Italian comedy interpreted not only these fixed types, but also less comic and less conventional characters, the lovers.[2]

Women appeared late in the Italian comedy. They did not wear a mask like the other players, but only a little black velvet *loup* to protect their beauty. Nor did they impersonate clearly defined characters, but played Inamoratas (*Donna Innamorata*), servants (*fantesca*), *ingénues*, mistresses, wantons, and matrons, as the occasion required. The Lovers were in the same category. They had a store of expressions, speeches, and general dialogue which were varied and coloured by the personality of each actor.

The composition of a troupe was, within certain limits, entirely a matter of expediency. It might contain ten actors or twice as many, according to the period and the place. The Captain might supplant Scaramouche; and Pulcinella, who was indispensable in Naples, might not be so anywhere else.

We have tried to trace the life and characteristics of this celebrated family, which, although having its origin in Italy, eventually held sway over all Europe, taking root in Spain, Holland, Germany, Austria, and especially in France. We have sought to summon up its scattered members, masquerading under different names, so that their worthy line may not be extinguished by oblivion, and that we may be able to recognize their legitimate descendants around us.

The first troupes of Italian players came to France during the reign of Charles IX, at the instance of Catherine de' Medici, of whom Brantôme[3] wrote that "from her earliest years she took a keen delight in comedies, even those in which the Zanni and Pantaloon performed. During the performance she was wont to laugh until her sides ached, and in every way showed as much interest as anyone there."

The history of the Italian comedy in France is not unlike the incident in which Harlequin is driven out by the front door, only to steal in again through the window. Catherine de' Medici invited the Italian players to come to France, and Parliament, which was not only nationalistic but stubbornly prejudiced in favour of the Confrères

giving some idea of the figures of the *commedia dell' arte*. The illustrations, giving only his own idea of these figures of the *commedia*, captivate everybody except those who know the original sources from which he drew them."—*The Mask*, vol. iii, p. 127.

[1] The word, in its varying forms Zane, Zanne, Zany, or Zani, does not necessarily denote the *genre* of *rôle* only; it is employed also as a proper name, as in the *Recueil Fossard*, an important work of the seventeenth century (see Bibliography), where for example, Francisquina says: "Sweet lord Léandre, calm your fears, . . . but take care lest Zani, Harlequin, or some one else . . ."

[2] The lovers were known in Italian as *innamorato* and *innamorata*. For convenience the male *rôle* of wooer, gallant, etc., has been referred to as Lover throughout the present volume, and the female complement as Inamorata, in accordance with the English spelling of the word.—Translator.

[3] Pierre de Bourdeilles Brantôme (1535–1614), the author of *Vies des hommes illustres et des grands capitaines français*, etc. He was especially celebrated for his *Mémoires*.—Translator.

de la Passion,[1] so harassed them that they were unable to remain. Henri III then invited the troupe known as the Gelosi [2] to come to Paris; but they fared no better at the hands of Parliament than their predecessors. In the seventeenth century several of the celebrated troupes returned, this time with official recognition, but they presently had the misfortune to offend the prudish Mme de Maintenon, who, in 1697, forbade them to come within thirty leagues of Paris. She died at last; the French gave an "Ouf!" of relief—after the manner of Scaramouche, and the Italians re-entered the Palais Royal in triumph.

The Italian comedy had by this time begun to feel the effect of French influence, gradually becoming, as it were, entirely Gallicized.[3] The troupes began to present "French comedies adapted for the Italian theatre," and soon the most prominent French authors, such as Mangin, Boisfranc, Brugière de Barante, and Losme de Monchesnay, were writing plays for them. There were also Regnard, and Dufresny, whose "serious and comic entertainments" were featured in Montesquieu's *Lettres Persanes*, just as the famous Turcaret of Lesage was derived from the "duped merchant" created by Nolant de Fatouville, another of the group. Then came Marivaux, whose art gave a new distinction to Isabelle, Columbine, and Aurelio, and made them more engaging and more complex. Beneath his touch they gained in subtlety and delicacy, and, without losing any of their original vividness, took on the tone and colours of the eighteenth century. The French theatre, both at the great Paris fairs [4] and later at the Opéra-Comique, absorbed the Italian types entirely. Yet they lived on none the less as Jonah is said to have lived inside the whale—very much at his ease.

Meanwhile in Italy the traditions of the *commedia dell' arte* were for three centuries transmitted wholly intact in certain of the most representative troupes. One of these, which was directed by Sacchi,[5] played from scenarios written by Carlo Gozzi,[6] the bitter rival of the over-productive Goldoni.[7] In France the same conditions did not so easily obtain, owing to the steady pressure of new influences in a foreign land. But the popularity of the troupes was fully as great as in Italy, and this was remarkable considering that the players did not begin to employ the language of their audiences until 1668.

[1] Or Confrérie de la Passion (the "Brotherhood of the Passion"). See Appendix B.—TRANSLATOR.

[2] So called because they were "jealous of pleasing."—TRANSLATOR.

[3] It is interesting to note in this connexion that Molière took the opposite trend, being an advocate of Italian interpretation and influence.

[4] The *théâtres de la foire*. See Chapter IX.

[5] "Sacchi was the last of those worthy comic actors who went about Europe and maintained the reputation of the Italian comedy at Vienna, Paris, and London."—*Storia della Letteratura Italiana*, by F. de Sanctis, vol. ii, p. 298 (Frat. Treves, Milano).

"But of all these Harlequins Sacchi was indubitably the greatest artist. He was a Ferrarese, born at Vienna in 1708. He was noted also as the Capocomico of a famous troupe of comedians which included Agostino Fiorilli (Tartaglia), Atanasio Zannoni (Brighella), and Cesare Darbes (Pantalone). Sacchi's great period was from 1740 to 1770. He invented the Mask of Truffaldino, a specific type of Harlequin."—*The History of Harlequin*, by Cyril W. Beaumont, p. 63.

[6] Carlo Gozzi (1720–1806) was born in Venice. "With Gozzi it had likewise the effect of leading to a new style of comedy by the introduction of those fairy dramas which had such an astounding run during several years, at Venice, and which are now completely forgotten except by the Germans, who, on their revival, conferred upon Count Gozzi the title of first comic writer of Italy."—J. C. L. SISMONDI, *De la Littérature du Midi de l'Europe*.

[7] Carlo Goldoni (1707–93) was born in Venice. He studied for the law, but, soon discovering that his true *métier* was writing plays, he set himself to effect a revolution upon the Italian comic stage. He spent several years in wandering over North Italy, until in 1740 he settled in his birthplace, where for twenty years he poured forth comedy after comedy. In 1761 he undertook to write for the Italian Theatre in Paris, and was attached to the French Court until the Revolution. His collected works fill seventeen volumes.—TRANSLATOR.

Indeed, there is no explaining the immense vitality of the Italian comedy except by the fact that these improvisators possessed the genius and mastery of their art to a degree rarely equalled in the history of the theatre.

Sorel wrote :

> Because they make a strong point of gesture and represent many things through action, even those who do not understand their language cannot fail to understand the subject of the piece ; for which reason there are many people in Paris who take pleasure in their playing.

It is evident that the Italians brought into France a fresh element of sparkle, exuberance, and salient expression at a time when the French theatre was wasting away in vain subtleties, insipid emotions, and ticklish points of honour, as inflated as bladders and quite as empty.

From the fifteenth century to the period of the Scudérys and after, not to mention Ponthus de Tyard, who set sail in a ship of dreams for the haven of Sweet Nothings, a whole branch of French literature and drama was infected by a persistent preciosity ; and this preciousness, or excess of refinement, tainted even the virile Ronsard. However, the Italians, with their absurd and delightful stylized costumes, introduced a wealth of colour and atmosphere of fantasy which even French painting had long since lost.

Furthermore, the Italians revealed to the French the advantages of increased movement on the stage, inculcated a taste for music in the theatre which, together with elaborate costumes, served as an evocative aid to fantasy, and, lastly, encouraged a cult of the voluptuous, beribboned woman which was almost unknown in France before the eighteenth century. Even in the purely comic field the Italians provided something new, as Brantôme points out :

> The comedy such as they played was rare in France, for before that time it was customary to speak only of *farceurs*, the Conards of Rouen,[1] the Players of the Basoche,[2] and other merry-andrews of the same kidney.

The jovial and crude naturalism of the art of the Italians, in contrast to the French theatre, which inclined rather more to reason and logic, oftentimes seemed intolerably vulgar to many contemporaries, but the immense success of *Arlequin Empereur dans la Lune* went far toward modifying this prejudice, and even induced women to attend the performances. There was, moreover, ample choice for all tastes in the Italian and Franco-Italian repertory, which ran the gamut from coarse farces to mordant philosophic satires, and from the popular *parade* [3] to the most long-winded declamation—all sometimes combined in a single play.

[1] " A society of jesters and merry-andrews in Normandy, which every year at carnival time undertook to ridicule the vices and frailties of the day. A decree of the Parliament of Rouen accorded them the exclusive privilege each year of wearing masks and authorizing strangers to dress in costume.

" The Conards would elect an *abbé*, whom they then decked out with mitre and crosier and conducted through the streets of the town on Saint Barnabas' Day. At Rouen he was taken about in a chariot, at Evreux on a donkey."—*Les Sociétés Bouffonnes*, by Arthur Dinaux (Paris, 1868).

[2] See Appendix C.

[3] The word *parade* in French can, in the theatre sense, mean almost any sort of informal spectacle, from a little raree-show to a bevy of beautiful girls mincing down the run-way of a music-hall among the audience. Strictly speaking, it is used in connexion with the Italian comedy more in the sense of the little ' act ' or show given on the platform outside a theatre or tent, as the case may be, to attract the crowd and whet its appetite for the talent to be enjoyed within. In most countries the

THE COMMEDIA DELL' ARTE

For three centuries or more the *commedia dell' arte* had an enormous influence throughout Europe, not only in literature, as exemplified by Lope de Vega, Shakespeare, and Molière, but in music and painting as well. The example set by the Italian actors helped to cure their French *confrères* of what Molière called "the demoniacal tone," or the atrocious declamation which was the fashion at the old Théâtre du Marais [1] and the Hôtel de Bourgogne.[2] It was this very method of declaiming, in fact, which often gave the actor an attack of apoplexy while on the stage, thus occasionally 'killing its man.' Du Tralage wrote of Molière that "he held Scaramouche in great esteem for his natural acting. He often went to see him play, and Scaramouche was the model which Molière followed in training the best actors of his troupe." A further tribute to Scaramouche was written beneath a portrait of him engraved by Vermeulen, to the effect that

Il fut le maître de Molière
Et la Nature fut le sien.[3]

In 1697, on the occasion of the triumphant return of the Italian comedy to the Hôtel de Bourgogne, a phœnix was painted on the curtain of the theatre, together with the motto, "Je renais." And, indeed, the Italian comedy is for ever reborn, springs ever into life anew. For even in our own day it finds expression in such various forms as the Fratellini at the Cirque Medrano,[4] Grock, and the stuttering Se-Se-Serato (indubitably the brother of the Bergamask Harlequin), as well as Les Femmes de Bonne Humeur and the Pulcinella of the Russian ballet. At all times it has had numerous and distinguished devotees—Molière, Regnard, Verlaine, and Debureau, Pourbus, Bosse, Callot, de Geijn, Watteau, Lancret, Tiepolo, Xavery, Rosa, and even the humble woodcarvers of the Renaissance; and, again, Guérin, Picasso, Brunelleschi, Severini, Gris, Lombard, Mariano Andreu, Claude-Lévy—the list is incredibly long. But, famous or obscure, they all join hands across the centuries: they have become members of this ever young and joyous family upon whose banner might well be inscribed the device, "All *genres* but the tedious."

parade is most often seen nowadays at fairs either as a prelude or 'ballyhoo' to a 'side-show' or circus, or else as an independent spectacle in itself. During the Renaissance, however, the actors of the Italian comedy employed the *parade* in various ways wherever they had occasion to perform. See also Appendix D.—TRANSLATOR.

[1] See Appendix E.

[2] The theatre made famous by the Italian players in the seventeenth century. See Appendix F.—TRANSLATOR.

[3] "He was the master of Molière, and Nature was his teacher."

[4] A picturesque little circus in Montmartre of the sort painted so charmingly by Seurat in his *Le Cirque*. The Fratellini played there until 1925, and then went to the Cirque d'Hiver.—TRANSLATOR.

II

The Origins

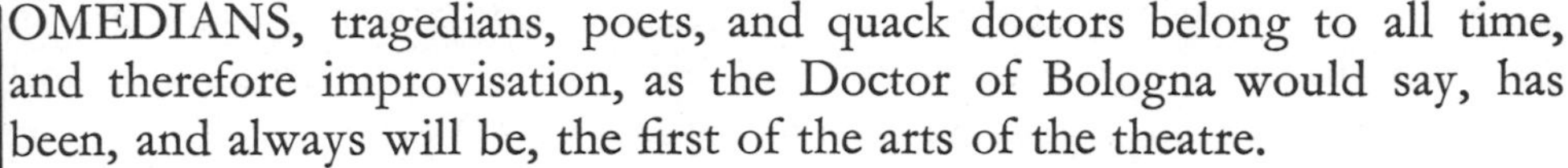

COMEDIANS, tragedians, poets, and quack doctors belong to all time, and therefore improvisation, as the Doctor of Bologna would say, has been, and always will be, the first of the arts of the theatre.

The first and last form of the theatre is a public performance (by mounting upon a barrel, a couple of planks, or a marble stage), and this performance must move its audience to laughter or tears or exaltation; or it must at least hold the attention. This fundamental necessity has thus created very ancient precedents covering every theatrical formula, whatever it might be. And it is this which basically relates the *commedia dell' arte* to Susarion, who, eight centuries before Christ, formed a band of comedians in Icaria and wandered throughout Greece; and likewise to Thespis, with his chariot-load of besmeared vagabonds who performed comedies with music.

The Cordaces, however, are more directly interesting because they gave spectacles interspersed with burlesque dances and pantomimes such as appear again in Callot's *Balli di Sfessania*.[1] Nor can we neglect, moreover, the mountebanks of Athens and Sparta, who, as early as the fifth century before Christ, attracted the crowd in order to sell their tawdry wares, because this form of art is precisely that of Tabarin, who with his " sleep-inducing " hat used to fleece the yokels of the seventeenth century.

The good actor of the *commedia dell' arte* also shows a close affiliation with the art of the crapulous Greek *ethologi*, parodists, obscene *cinaedologi*, and all the rest of the *simodi* or *lysiodi*, and *hilarodi* clad in white, who sang to their own accompaniments. For the skilled improvisator not uncommonly possessed all the tricks of the trade known to his ancient predecessors.

Like the *schoenobates* of Greece or the *funambuli* of Rome, the players of the Italian comedy were acrobats: while they did not leap upon gourds like the ancients, they were often tight-rope dancers and tumblers. Among the *phallophori*, daubed with soot and adorned with a phallus, as their name indicates, we find the origin of that astonishing detail of costume which later appeared frequently in pictures by Callot, de Geijn, and the sixteenth-century engravers.

All the actors of the classic theatre at that time performed close to the audience, without their buskins and masks and made up with colours inseparable from the particular *rôle* they were taking, a custom which gave rise perhaps to the traditional colour of the masks of the *commedia dell' arte*. Women were allowed to play and sing, and to mime interludes. The custom of giving women a share in the performance had its origin in

[1] Sixteenth century. See also Appendix A.—TRANSLATOR.

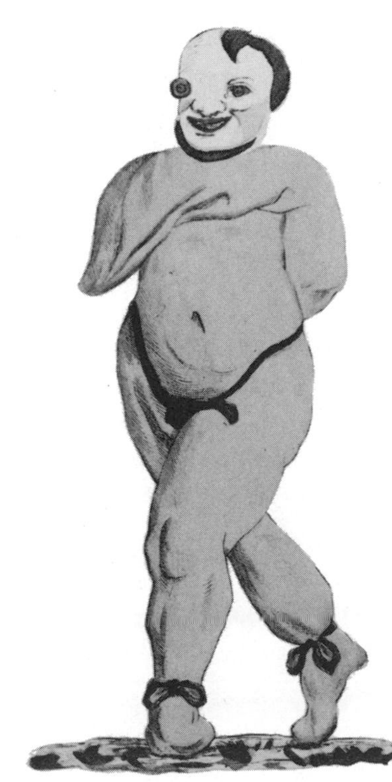

PAINTINGS AT HERCULANEUM

From an anonymous eighteenth-century collection

the Dorian countries, whence it passed over into Sicily, and thence to Rome. The Singer of the Italian comedy is probably a descendant of these.

Livy relates that even in his own time Oscan literature was studied as widely as Greek. The Etruscans taught the Romans a great deal about the drama; and their theatre at Tusculum was built of stone when those in Rome were still of wood. The ancient city of Atella, now known as Aversa, was one of the first to have a theatre, in fact. In the preceding chapter mention was made of the character and importance of the special kind of plays which the Etruscans originated. When performed in Rome they were called *Atellanæ*,[1] which became their accepted name.

COMEDIAN OF THE CLASSIC THEATRE
After Ficoroni de Larvis

The *Atellanæ* were improvised from scenarios, and enjoyed such success in Rome that they completely eclipsed the regular classic theatre. They were the special delight of the young patricians, and the actor who could play them well was granted citizenship and the protection of both the gods and the law. It was frequently the custom for one actor to recite while another acted the story. The story is told how Andronicus, having lost his voice owing to the number of encores he had received, resorted to miming while a slave recited his lines.

The Roman people had begun to tire of Greek tragedies, and turned with relief to pantomime, which the players of the Italian comedy were to exploit to such great advantage in a later day. The plot of the pantomime was either explained through singing or simply acted, and thus it was easily understood and enjoyed throughout the polyglot Roman Empire. During the reign of Constantine all foreigners professing the liberal arts were forced to quit Rome, with the significant exception of six thousand pantomimists. Nor was there any doubt but that the people preferred the *funambuli* to the works of Terence.

COMEDIAN OF THE CLASSIC THEATRE
After Ficoroni de Larvis

Only the Romans of the lowest classes had any particular liking for the 'art of the gesture.' This is borne out by the story that Cicero once issued a challenge to determine whether thought could best be rendered by word or gesture. The art of the gesture was called *saltatio*.

When the first Italian companies came to France they played in their native tongue, but they had of necessity inherited the traditions of their art to such a degree that they were able to make their Parisian audiences understand them without difficulty simply by virtue of their clever mimicry.

[1] They were later called *Exodiæ*, because they were often given at the end of the performance.

The troupes which retained the purest traditions of the *Atellanæ* during the first centuries of our era were probably itinerant companies which performed on platform-stages in the public squares, and led a career of the same sort as that of the actors of the regular theatre, of which, however, they were entirely independent.

It is relevant to point out that all forms of popular art have, as a general thing, been

BAS-RELIEF FROM THE FARNESE PALACE

regarded by men of letters and historians as unimportant and beneath their notice. For this reason it is easy to conceive why French *imagerie populaire*,[1] for example, which first came into being in the fourteenth century, in many cases persisted in the same spirit and character until well into the nineteenth century.

The Church fathers had always looked askance at the loose capers of the travelling

[1] Popular pictures such as children's picture-books, comic strips, caricatures of both politics and folk-lore, and the like. Pictures of this kind have always been more or less of a speciality in France, more so than in other countries, and the best known are the *Images d'Épinal*. Messrs P. L. Duchartre and René Saulnier have published an interesting book on the subject, called *L'Imagerie Populaire* (Librairie de France, Paris, 1925). M. Duchartre has also brought out a similar book, by Auguste Martin, entitled *L'Imagerie Orléanaise* (Duchartre et Van Buggenhoudt, Paris, 1928).—TRANSLATOR.

Comedians of the Ancient Roman Theatre

comedians, whose costumes and pleasantries smacked only too often of downright paganism. They had even gone so far as to place a ban on their entertainments as being nothing less than sacrilegious and blasphemous. The presence of women on the boards seemed to them equally immoral, and feminine *rôles* were in consequence gradually abolished. Then the Church itself took possession of the theatre, making use of it to present odd religious comedies, medleys of mysticism and farce, interlarded with sumptuous processions. During the great invasions many theatres were converted into fortresses and storehouses.

Meanwhile the theatre had taken so firm a hold in Italy that the ancient traditions persisted and survived in spite of many adversities. In 1224 St Thomas Aquinas speaks

COMEDIANS OF THE CLASSIC THEATRE
From a painting at Herculaneum
After Saint-Non (1730-91)

of the *histriones* and *histrionatus ars*—that is, pantomime, as we find it in the Italian comedy—as an art which had been in existence for centuries. The return of the Crusaders was responsible for widespread interest in mystery and miracle plays and farces based on themes taken from the Old and New Testaments, and the Italians were able to derive as much material for buffooneries from these new religious subjects as they had previously derived from mythology.

The fourteenth and fifteenth centuries brought with them the salutary winds of the Renaissance, and the theatre gradually revived and resumed its former position of importance. The *Atellanæ* then began to come back into vogue, and found equal favour with the patrician theatre, represented by such pieces as Bibbiena's *Calandria*, Machiavelli's *Mandragola*, and Tasso's *Aminta* (all got by heart), and the popular theatre made up of songs, dances, clowning, and improvisation. The regular written drama, ordinarily played by the 'Academicians,' was known as *commedia sostenuta*, while impromptu comedy, with the traditional masks, was called *commedia dell' arte*. The same troupes nearly always played both forms of entertainment, or else a mixture of the two, which resulted in what might be considered as a sort of extravaganza or revue *de luxe*.

And both the *commedia dell' arte* and *sostenuta* flourished side by side in Italy from the sixteenth century to the end of the seventeenth.

The chief traits which identify the characters of the Italian comedy with the theatre of antiquity are as follows :

Pulcinella was always dressed in white like Maccus, the *mimus albus*, or white mime ; but what is especially noteworthy about him is his extraordinary resemblance to an ancient statuette, which is supposed (rightly or not) to be a representation of Maccus.[1]

The Captain was almost a perfect duplicate of Plautus's Miles Gloriosus. There is also a remarkable analogy between Pedrolino and the slave in the comedies of both Plautus and Terence.

The name Zanni was given to the two masks from Bergamo, Harlequin and Brighella, because they were, according to Quadrio (*Storia e della Ragione d' Ogni Poesia*), descendants of the *sannio* of the *Atellanæ*.[2]

The head-bands or false scalps, which hid the hair of the actors, gave the effect of the shaved heads in vogue among the mimes in ancient times.[3]

The phallus was worn by Cerimonia, Smaralo, Scaramuccia, Spezza Monti, and Pantalone.

The valets in the Italian comedy wore short garments only, like the slaves of the *Atellanæ*, while long robes and capes were reserved for the nobles and old men. Almost all of the players wore the *tabaro*, a short cape in the classic style.

The slap-stick, or bat, belonging to Punch, Harlequin, and Scapin was the favourite weapon of ancient comic characters also.

Numerous other analogies of the same nature are described later when the masks, Pulcinella, Narcissino of Bologna, the Singer, and various other characters are dealt with.

It is true that Dr Michele Scherillo in *The Mask* has contested (and also, more recently, M. Constant Mic) the ancient origins of the *commedia dell' arte* with no little wit and learning ; but if we admit his point how are we to account for the fact that the Italian comedy was the only theatre in Europe which adopted the ancient custom of wearing the mask ? And how, moreover, explain the striking similarity between the traits and gestures of Punchinello in the seventeenth-century picture preserved in the museum of the Comédie Française and those of the statuette, supposed to be of Maccus, which was unearthed in the eighteenth century ?

[1] See p. 208.

[2] According to another opinion, Zanni is derived from Gianni, which means John (see *Ruzzante*, by A. Mortier, p. 80); or from Giovanni, which is the hypothesis put forward by C. Dati in the seventeenth century and resuscitated by Constant Mic in his work *La Commedia dell' Arte*, p. 209.

[3] " Sanniones mimum agebant rasis capitibus."—APULEIUS.

III

The Technique of the Improvisators

THE success of the *commedia dell' arte* depended almost entirely on the acting rather than on the scenarios. In the opinion of Gherardi[1] and Riccoboni[2] it was easier to train ten actors for the regular theatre than one for the extemporaneous stage. Moreover, a good improvisator had to practise a kind of self-abnegation and refrain from indulging his own conceit or overplaying his part to the detriment of other *rôles*. The actors of the Italian troupes of necessity developed a spirit of *camaraderie* in their playing, and they achieved such understanding and mutual co-operation as were not found in the companies playing ordinary drama or *commedie sostenute*.

PROBABLY ISABELLA AND THE GELOSI TROUPE
From a painting in the Carnavalet Museum, Paris

Listen to Harlequin himself, otherwise known as Gherardi, the gifted actor-author of the seventeenth century, who said:

> The Italian comedians learn nothing by heart; they need but to glance at the subject of a play a moment or two before going upon the stage. It is this very ability to play at a

[1] See Appendix G, and also paragraph on Flautino, p. 166. [2] See Appendix H.

moment's notice which makes a good Italian actor so difficult to replace. Anyone can learn a part and recite it on the stage, but something else is required for Italian comedy. For a

A Ve uolio Salludare á uanti che uada á la Velada

HARLEQUIN: "Hail! I wish to salute you before the curtain rises."
(Venetian dialect, seventeenth century.)

good Italian actor is a man of infinite resources and resourcefulness, a man who plays more from imagination than from memory; he matches his words and actions so perfectly with those of his colleague on the stage that he enters instantly into whatever acting and movements are required of him in such a manner as to give the impression that all that they do has been prearranged.

Riccoboni,[1] another actor-author, wrote in his *Histoire du théâtre italien* (1728):

Impromptu comedy throws the whole weight of the performance on the acting, with the result that the same scenario may be treated in various ways and seem to be a different play

ZANNI
From a drawing by de Geijn (seventeenth century)

each time. The actor who improvises plays in a much livelier and more natural manner than one who learns his *rôle* by heart. People feel better, and therefore say better, what they invent than what they borrow from others with the aid of memory. But these advantages are purchased at the price of many difficulties; the actors are pre-supposed to be clever, and they are also presumed to be of equal talent, for the drawback of improvisation is that the success of even the best actor depends upon his partner in the dialogue. If he has to act with a colleague who fails to reply exactly at the right moment or who interrupts him in the wrong place, his own discourse falters and the liveliness of his wit is extinguished.

[1] Riccoboni, like Gherardi, belonged to a line of improvisators, a fact which naturally adds weight to his opinion.

THE TECHNIQUE OF THE IMPROVISATORS

Even up to the second half of the eighteenth century the old traditions of the improvisators remained intact in some of the troupes like those of Sacchi, in Italy, and Colalto, who came to France in 1774. Grimm[1] wrote of Colalto in connexion with a piece in which he played three different characters :

> It is well-nigh incomprehensible how he is able to change his expression, voice, and personality, which he varies in scene after scene according to the demands of every *rôle*, and his interpretation surely leaves little to be desired.

And, speaking of the acting of this troupe, he repeated what had already been said in the sixteenth century :

> At every performance they also add the spice of variety to their discourses and their acting, and the unabating enthusiasm of the public for the play spurs the actors on to greater efforts.

Gozzi, who was the most inveterate and spirited defender of the old traditions of improvised comedy, has given interesting details in his *Mémoires* regarding the profession and methods of Sacchi and his associates. From a simple scenario posted behind the scenes grew the play.

Cicho Sgarra and Collo Francisco
From the "Balli di Sfessania" (1622), *by Callot* (1593–1635)

> These plays are never withdrawn on account of illness among the actors or because of newly recruited talent. An impromptu parley before going on the stage, as regards both the plot and the way in which it is to be played, is sufficient to insure a smooth performance. It often happens that in special circumstances, or because of the relative importance and skill of certain actors, a change in the distribution of the *rôles* is made on the spur of the moment just as the curtain is rising. Yet the comedy is borne along to a gay and sprightly conclusion. It is apparent that these actors penetrate to the very core of their subjects, establishing their scenes on different bases with so many varieties of dialogue that, with each performance, the interpretation seems to be quite new, yet inevitable and permanent.
>
> I have often heard these improvisators reproach themselves for having 'planted' the scene badly, and then they build it up again by excellent arguments in such a way as to motivate it and so prepare the ground for a new attempt.
>
> It is true that serious actors, and especially actresses, in this kind of comedy possess an extraordinary store of varied material which they exploit at will for pleas, reproaches, and moods of despair and jealousy. Yet, knowing this, it is none the less astonishing to see them improvising before the public and to observe how appropriately they select their material, always having the right quips ready and expressing them with such energy that they wring applause from the audience.

[1] Baron Friedrich Melchior Grimm (1723–1807) was a distinguished critic of French literature and a friend of Rousseau, Diderot, Mme d'Épinay, etc. See Sainte-Beuve's *Études sur Grimm*.—Translator.

> Such is the system of our improvised comedy, to which our nation only can lay claim. Nor has its verve been spent in the course of three centuries. . . . We realize this when, for example, it is possible for the capable Tartaglia, Agostino Fiorilli, to replace with ease the most excellent Doctor, Roderigo Lombardi ; for both are of an equal naturalness in their acting and both are able to renew each subject merely by the diversity of their talents. One new actor who is at all original suffices to quicken the originality of an entire troupe.[1]

President de Brosses,[2] who travelled in Italy during the middle of the eighteenth century, said of the improvisators :

> Their style may suffer from this method of playing *à l'impromptu*, but at the same time the action gains in naturalness and vividness. . . . There is always a happy blend of gesture and inflection with the discourse, and the actors come and go, speak, and act as informally as in ordinary life. Their acting gives a far different effect of naturalness and truth from what one sees in the French theatre, where four or five actors stand in a line like a bas-relief, at the front of the stage, and each declaims his discourse in turn.

We have seen above how Gozzi has limited the meaning and application of the word 'improvisation.' Certain it is that there never was such a thing as complete and absolute improvisation, nor ever can be. This held true of the *commedia dell' arte* throughout its entire career. Niccolo Barbieri [3] corroborates Gozzi by saying that his memory, like that of his associates, was "stored with phrases, *concetti*,[4] declarations of love, reproaches, deliriums, and despairs." Nor did this sort of preparation diminish in the least either the merit of the improvisators or the value of the *commedia dell' arte*. On the contrary, the importance of this equipment cannot be over-estimated, for it contributed to the perpetuation of the traditional language and gestures of the *rôles* which generations of actors interpreted. The actor never took any liberties in altering his *rôle*, and yet he was free to infuse into it all the life and colour of which he was capable.

And it is because of this that the career of each traditional character like Harlequin, or Pulcinella, or Brighella can be traced across the centuries. It is as if they were really living beings whose personalities evolved naturally through a number of reincarnations. The most individual actor was always careful not to dominate his *rôle*, but rather so submerged himself within it that he became an integral part of the character he portrayed. And, consequently, if the actor happened to be mediocre he risked playing his *rôle* little better than a marionette.

Thus the great improvisators did not cease to breathe life into the illustrious family of the *commedia dell' arte* ; they did not cease, moreover, to produce offspring and kin who became acclimatized in nearly every European country, and it is to be hoped that these merry and fantastic people will one day reawaken more lively and alive than ever.

[1] Gozzi, *Mémoires*. Translated from the French text.—TRANSLATOR.

[2] Charles de Brosses (1709–77), author of *Lettres familières écrites d'Italie en* 1739 *et* 1740 (Garnier Frères, Paris).

[3] "Beltrame (Niccolo Barbieri). An actor. Died about 1640. He invented the characters 'Scapino' and 'Beltrame,' assuming the name of this latter as his own. He wrote scenarios, his best play being, according to Mantzius, *L'Inavvertito, overo Scapino disturbato e Mezzetino travagliato*, which he wrote and published with dialogue complete, though it was originally acted as an improvised play. It is the prototype of Molière's *L'Étourdi, ou Les Contre-temps*, and he published the play to prevent it from being lost or spoiled by bad acting and by any improvisation inferior to that of the Gelosi and the Fedeli companies. He also wrote *La Supplica*, published in Bologna, 1836. It is a kind of *apologia* for the stage of his time."—*The Mask*, vol. iii, p. 126.

[4] Conceits—*i.e.* "conceits of happy love, or jealousy, or prayer, or contempt, or friendship, or admiration."—*The Mask*, vol. iii, p. 104.

Arlequin Soupirant

Arlequin pleurant

Arlequin Glouton

La Reveranse d'Arlequin

The Humours of Harlequin

Claude Gillot (1673–1722). *See Appendix I.*

The Lazzi

The *lazzi*[1] were one of the chief resources of the Italian improvisators. The word means ' turn ' or ' trick ' or ' Italian business,' and an actor would resort to *lazzi* whenever a scene began to drag or his eloquence gave out. For example, Harlequin would

An Italian Comedy Scene by Watteau

pretend to throw cherry-stones in Scapin's face, or to catch a fly on the wing and munch it with great gusto. When there was a scene in which the actors indulged in slaps and horse-play they would puff out their cheeks with air or water in order to heighten the comic effect. Many actors were acrobats, and could easily turn a somersault, walk on their hands, and do the *grand écart*, or ' split.' Some were as accomplished as the agile Scaramouche who, at eighty-three years of age, could box his fellow-actor's ear with his foot without the slightest difficulty. There was also Vincentini,[2] the celebrated Trivelin, who could turn a somersault with a glass of water in his hand and not spill a drop. He had another special trick of climbing along the boxes, and the public was always so agitated lest he fall and kill himself when he did this that he was at last persuaded to

[1] See Appendix J. [2] See Appendix K.

forgo his more perilous acrobatics. It required a great deal of skill, of course, to perform these *lazzi*. They formed a regular and important part of the entertainment, and served to keep the audience amused while the troupe took time for a breathing-spell. The illustrations throughout the present volume will aid the reader to obtain a fairly accurate idea of the 'postures' and mimicry characteristic of the acting of the Italian comedians.

AN ITALIAN COMEDY SCENE BY WATTEAU

Stage 'Business'

The Italian comedy teems with original devices and comic 'business.' In *Arlequin Lingère au Palais* Harlequin is a point-lace vendor, and "furnishes layettes for the children of the eunuchs of the Grand Harem." He is dressed half as a man and half as a woman. The scene is the lemonade-stall next door to a linen-draper's shop, presided over by a woman. Harlequin passes rapidly from one shop to the other, pivoting about so fast that Pascariel cannot tell whether he is dealing with the linen-woman or the lemonade-man. In the end Harlequin appears as a nurse with a child in her arms, and compels Pascariel to acknowledge it as his own. "Heartless father!" shrieks Harlequin. "To think of denying the child who has adored you from the cradle! The poor little brat! He runs up trustingly to every ass, pig, or ox he sees, thinking each time it is his dear dad. He was scarcely two months old when he first began to take after you. I never left him a minute but his little hands were full of cards. I even had to give him a pipe for a pacifier. And he'd never consent to suckle unless I rubbed my teats with wine." For answer Pascariel kicks Nurse Harlequin's bottom, and Harlequin howls, "Help! I'm murdered! He kicked me in the belly, and me big with child, already fourteen months gone."

HARLEQUIN ENTERS IN A SEDAN CHAIR, THE INTERIOR OF WHICH IS FITTED OUT AS AN APOTHECARY'S SHOP
From an engraving by Gillot

Disguises also played an important part in what to-day would perhaps be called theatrical 'hokum.' Harlequin appeared at times as Diana or as a giddy courtesan, Mezzetin as a pregnant woman, Scaramouche as a lady of quality.

Mezzetin is accosted by a young courtesan, who asks the way to the Place de Grève.[1] Mezzetin makes her a grave bow, and replies, "You've only to go on as you have started, mademoiselle, and you're bound to get there." But since the giddy-brained young woman is none other than Harlequin, they fall to blows, and a burlesque set-to ensues.

Harlequin sometimes makes his entrance as Mercury astride a cardboard eagle, let down from the flies. Again, he may enter in Neptune's chariot, or in a sedan chair, or

[1] Where executions once took place in Paris.

in a gondola, or in a gig, or else on a donkey. In another play Isabelle is alone in a garden full of statues; suddenly one of them sneezes and immediately all the statues descend from their pedestals, being, of course, actors in white make-up. In *Arlequin Esprit Follet* Mezzetin and Pulcinella are seated at table before a magnificent feast. As they are about to indulge their gluttonous appetites the tables suddenly rise and are whisked out of sight.

And, again, there is an elaborate stone fountain in full play in the centre of the stage. A gust of wind blows off the top and discloses four men holding sprinklers.

SCENE FROM "LE TOMBEAU DE MAÎTRE ANDRÉ"
From an engraving by Gillot

Scaramouche and Harlequin are plunged into a violent discussion. Presently Pascariel comes on inside a sack, and rolls up to Harlequin's feet. Harlequin, on spying him, says, "Here's a fine sack of coal on the way to market." Scaramouche asserts that, on the contrary, it is a bale waiting for inspection by the customs. Whereupon Harlequin peers into the opening of the bag, and immediately Pascariel pops out in the guise of the devil with three heads, which frightens the other two out of their wits. And so the first act ends.

In still another comedy four men representing statues support the ends of a mantel-shelf. At a signal from Harlequin two of the figures leave the mantel and seize Scaramouche, who chances to be strolling innocently by; the other two men carry over the mantelshelf, which they slip over him in the manner of a fish-basket, leaving only his head exposed. Later on Harlequin appears riding in a phæton followed by six mangy-looking horses hitched to an osier chariot which bears a tinfoil sun.

In the scene known as *Portrait d'Arlequin* the face of the betrayed Columbine takes the place of Harlequin's in the portrait and then disappears. Gherardi wrote :

> Those who have not seen the comic piece *Columbine Avocat Pour et Contre* will be at a loss to know how she comes into the portrait ; I shall therefore explain. There is a lifesize portrait of Harlequin upon a stand. The head is painted upon a loose flap of canvas that will yield to pressure from behind. Columbine, who has secret access to Harlequin's house through the Doctor's cellar next door, comes up on tiptoe behind the portrait, draws back the flap, and inserts her own head.

One of the tricks typical of the Italians for achieving a fine *dénouement* is described as follows :

> Harlequin, the thief, comes on disguised as a judge. He attempts to bring the court to order, but is unable to quiet the plaintiff and defendant. Of a sudden his chair turns into a frightful monster, which pours flames from its nose and mouth, terrifies the litigants, and so brings the act to an end.

Harlequin, in the guise of Mercury, comes flying through the air mounted on Jupiter's eagle. He perceives Jupiter disguised as a shepherd, and greets him with, " Adio, Signor Giove ! "[1]

JUPITER

How is it that I behold Mercury mounted upon my eagle ? Has he not wings on his heels to fly with ?

HARLEQUIN

Alas, Lord Jupiter ! My wings no longer bear me, for as I was passing down a street just now, a servant wench emptied a chamber-pot upon me and so did wet them that if I had not by good chance fallen upon a dung-pile, your Mercury would, certes, have broken his neck. As you see, I found your eagle on his accustomed perch in the stable and made use of him to carry out your commands.

JUPITER

Very good. I have something to tell you. Descend instantly and assume the form of a shepherd.

(*The machine disappears, and Harlequin is seen in his ordinary costume mounted astride a donkey.*)

[1] See Appendix L for original text illustrating the mixture of French and Italian dialogue ; see also p. 53 for a similar example.

IV

The Masks

T is hard to determine just how and for what purpose masks were first created. Whence did they come and what gave rise to the custom of using them? There is one theory that the masks were invented in antiquity to meet the requirements of the classic stage, where, owing to the great size of the Greek and Roman theatres, the faces of the actors could not be seen distinctly. But nearly all peoples, even the most ancient, conceived the idea of masks long before they thought of building a theatre or even a stage. Some authorities maintain, therefore, that the mask came into being in early times as the result of man's aspiration to a divine countenance, while others assert that it

originated merely from his desire to astonish or terrify his fellows. Or it may have been due to the curious longing which manifests itself in men of every race at some time or another to change, as it were, their skins as serpents do, or, in any case, the aspect of their faces. This impulse in its more elementary form appears in children when they invent some sort of mask in play; and it finds expression also in the annual carnivals held in many countries, which provide an opportunity for a change of personality at least once a year.

But men—at any rate, those who have neither much culture nor imagination—are less interested in novelty than in recognizing things familiar to them. People in general prefer the well-known actor in the type of *rôle* he has played a thousand times to a new face and personality to which they must grow accustomed. The mask, then, is one of the best and simplest means of giving an illusion of permanency to a favourite character. And in this spirit no doubt the traditional masks of the Italian comedy were conceived and standardized. The most uninspired lout, once he donned the black mask of Harlequin, would immediately lose his banality and become Harlequin himself. For the masks were not mere disguises of the face, but the full expression of a character itself. And it is the soul, in the Latin sense of *animus*, which stamps the features as surely as the thumb models the lump of clay.

ANCIENT ENGRAVED CORNELIAN

It is certain, therefore, that if an actor had not mastered the trick of 'playing the mask'[1] it would be an insurmountable obstacle to him and deprive him of all mobility of facial expression.

The masks of the *commedia dell' arte* neither laughed, nor wept, nor, unlike most of the classic masks and those of China and Japan, did they express any particular emotion. They wore an indefinable expression as full of possibilities as of impossibilities, like the *Mona Lisa*, which every generation interprets differently. We speak of the art of 'playing the mask' as though a precious stone were brought into play, because the feeling which each mask conveys varies according to the angle from which it is seen, and consequently it can range from the most extraordinary comic effects to the most disturbing or terribly tragic emotion.

The mask presupposes, furthermore, a constant and perfected play of the body which is an art in itself, requiring thorough study; in other words, the body must become a supplement to the mask—a new face, in fact. Nonnus of Panopolis said of the mimes of Theodosius' time that they "had gestures that speak a language, hands that have a mouth, fingers that have voices." It was by such art as this that Scaramouche, without uttering a word, was able to keep his audience in fits of laughter for more than half an hour in a scene in which he is frightened out of his wits.

ANCIENT ENGRAVED CORNELIAN

If the body was lacking in plastic eloquence the mask was meaningless. But if the body was subtle in its play the mask became a far more effective means of expression than the muscles. According to assertions of ancient commentators, the art of pantomime was developed to a high degree in Greece and Rome. In the present age, however, it has practically disappeared, and it would be sheer folly to attempt to revive the use of the mask while pantomime itself is a lost art; whatever

[1] The expression in French is "jouer du masque."—TRANSLATOR.

COMEDIANS AND THEIR MASKS
Lateran Museum, Rome

instinct for it still survives is found, not on the modern stage, but among the common people.

The stage masks of antiquity were of several kinds—namely, comic, tragic, and satiric—and they were called *personæ*.[1] The crudest and most vulgar of them, if not the oldest, were made of bark; others were of leather lined with cloth. They were

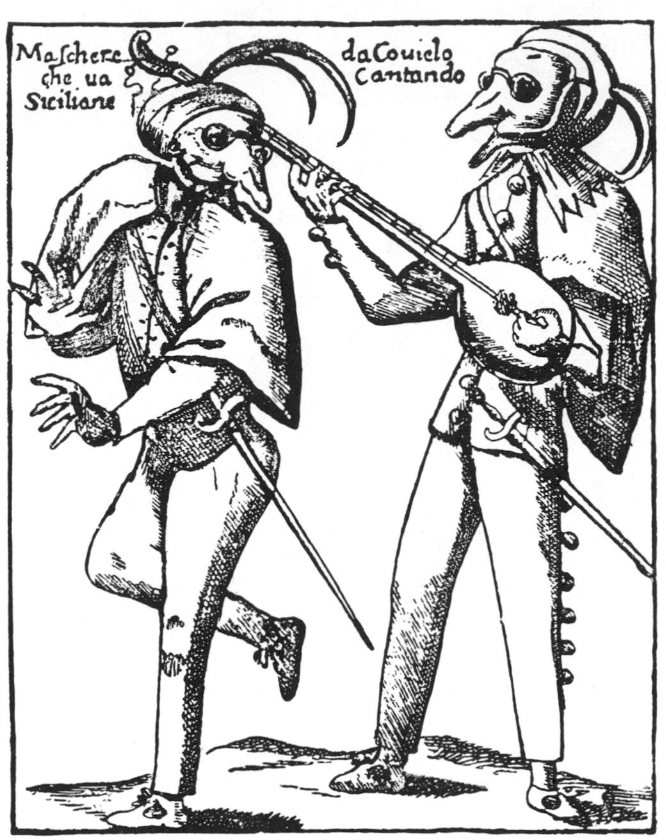

EXAMPLE OF MASK WORN BY COVIELLO
From the "Carnavale Italiane Mascherato," by Fr. Bertelli (Venice)

sometimes constructed of light wood in order to insure the preservation of the model. The mask was proportioned to the size of the amphitheatre so that it could be seen clearly even from the farthest rows of seats. The carrying power of the voice was augmented by strips of brass fastened inside the mask near the mouth, or else the lips of the mask were widened and exaggerated in order to form a sort of rudimentary megaphone. Seen at close range, all of the masks, even the most comic, had a terrifying look about them, but if they had not been so crudely fashioned they would have seemed quite featureless at a distance.

One of the most ardent champions of the mask was Carlo Gozzi, who was a

[1] Phædrus, Horace, Aulus Gellius.

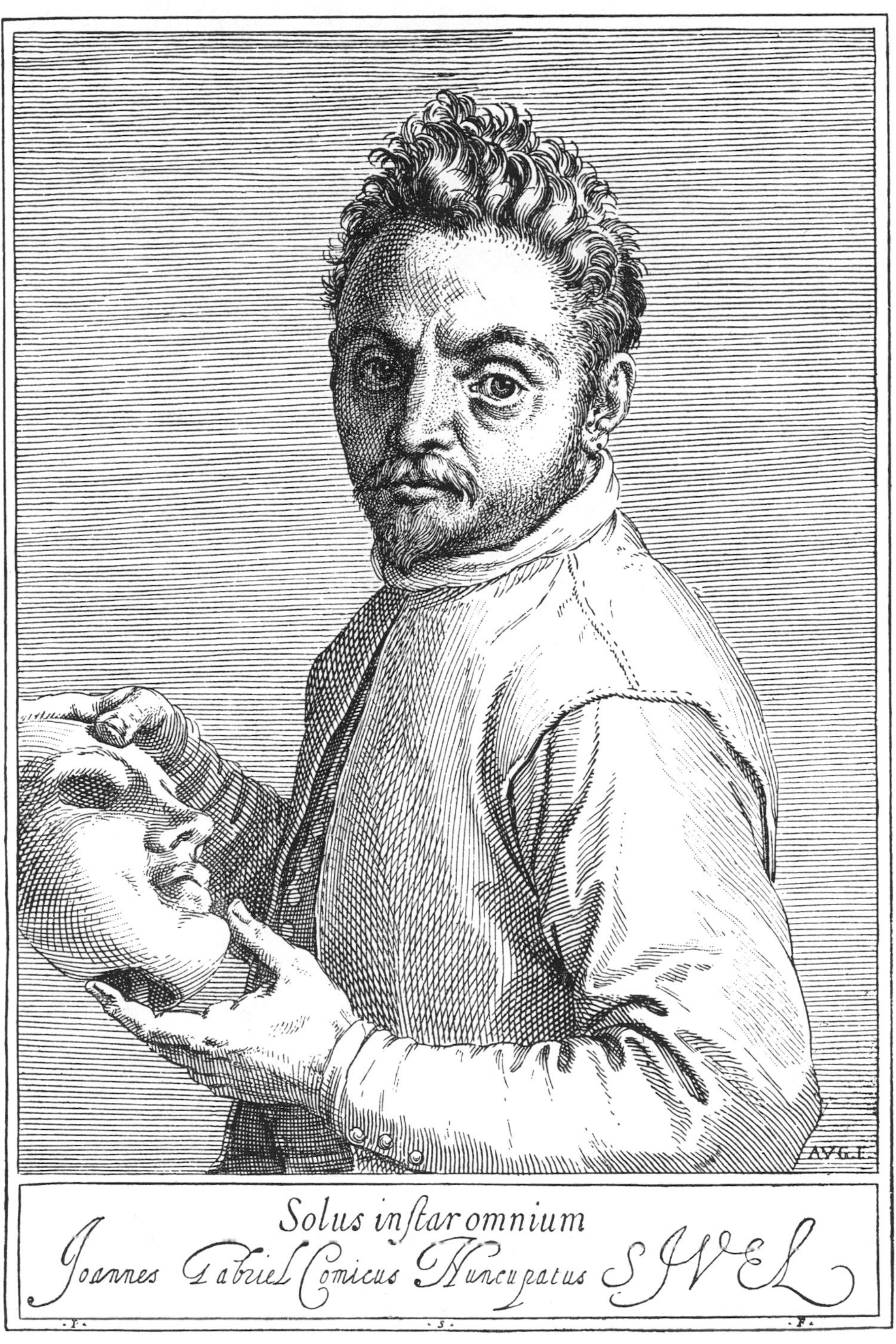

THE ACTOR JEAN GABRIEL WITH HIS MASK
Sixteenth century

traditionalist in all things. Goldoni, on the contrary, disapproved of them, and he says in his *Mémoires* that:

> The mask always interferes immeasurably with the actor's performance, whether he be interpreting joy or sorrow. Whether he be wooing, or ranting, or clowning, he always has

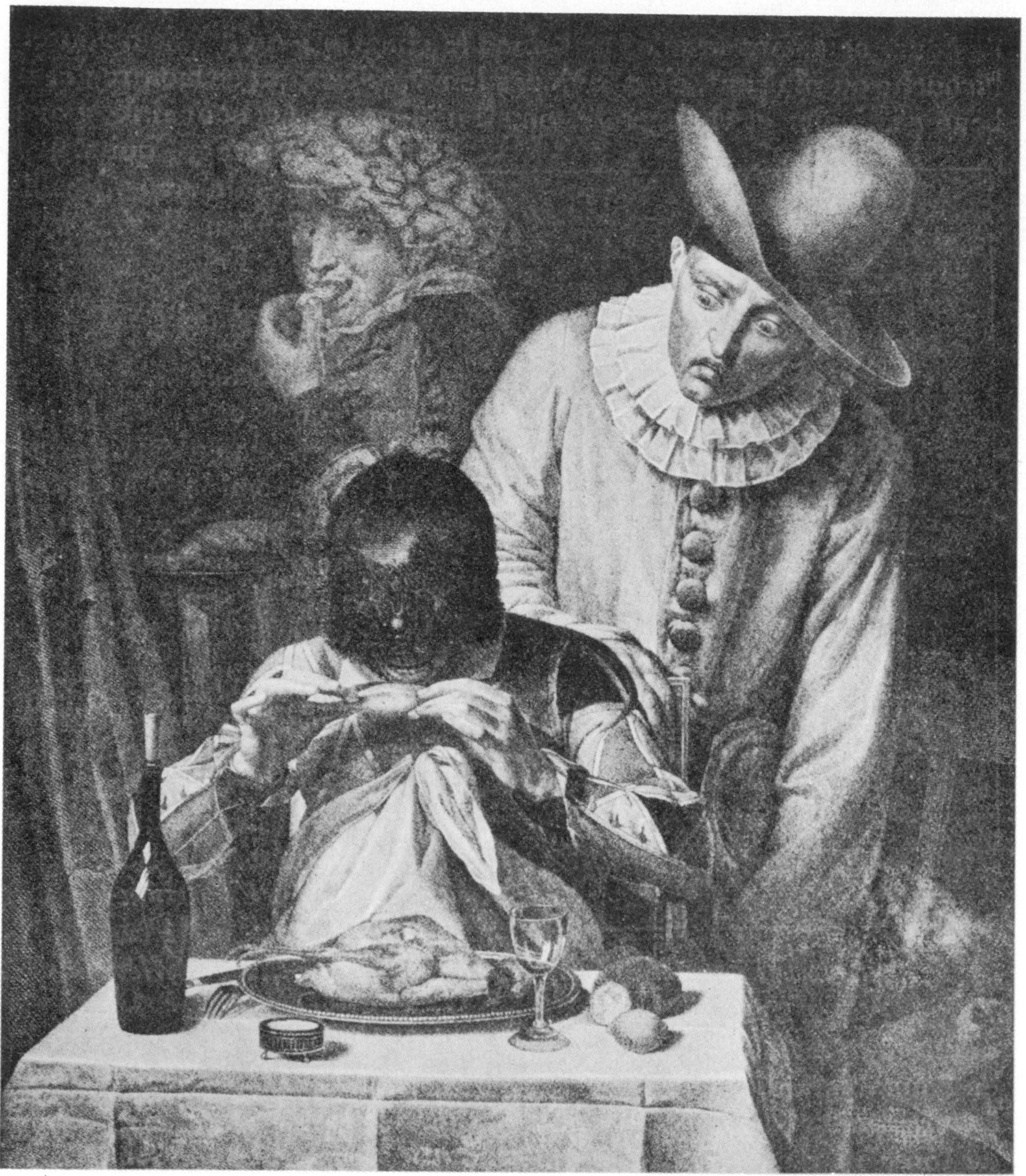

Sicardi pinx. "What Luck!" *Mecon sculp.*

> the same 'leather' face. He may gesticulate and change his tone as often as he will, he can never communicate by the expression of his face the passions that rend his soul. . . . The

Columbine, Harlequin, and a Venetian, with their Masks
After F. Maggiotto (eighteenth century)

masks of the Greeks and Romans were a kind of megaphone designed to carry the voice throughout the amphitheatre. In those times actors did not interpret the *nuances* of passion and sentiment that are in vogue at present; nowadays the actor is required to have 'soul,' and the soul beneath the mask is as fire beneath ashes. That is why I proposed to reform the masks of the Italian comedy and to replace farces by comedies.

The use of the words "soul," "passion and sentiment," together with the fact that the amiable Goldoni was a prodigiously fertile playwright, would seem to explain why he had so little liking for the masks and improvisation. He had neither vitality, force, nor art enough in his peculiar talent to enable him to stylize his characters. He dashed off his plays with the nonchalance of a Neapolitan street-singer twanging his guitar. His over-facility gave his work a fragile charm which has stood the test of time but badly. The masks of Pulcinella and Harlequin will always signify something vital and intense, for they are sculptured by both art and time to a semblance of humanity.

Italian Comedy Masks at a Carnival in Venice in the Piazza di San Stefano
Engraving by Giacomo Franco (about 1610)

However, Goldoni made an experiment which obliged him to recognize that, though he might see no good in the use of masks in plays, the Italian public was emphatically in favour of it. The actor Darbes, who was a promising Pantaloon, tried playing Goldoni's *Tonin, Celia Gracia* without the mask, and the piece proved to be a flat failure. As both author and actor were very much in vogue at the time they were completely nonplussed by such an unexpected reverse. Goldoni then wrote a new play for Darbes, which was neither better nor worse than the previous one. This time Darbes resumed his mask, and the play was an immense success. Darbes never played without his mask again, and with Goldoni's aid succeeded in becoming the most noted Pantaloon in Italy.

The mask never proved a hindrance to the expression of emotion if the actor knew how to wear it. Several authorities of different periods make mention of Harlequins whose acting with the mask was so extraordinary that they would often reduce their audiences to tears. One day the celebrated Garrick was watching Carlin Bertinazzi[1]

[1] See Appendix M.

as Harlequin play a scene in which he stood with his back to the public, rubbing his thigh and shaking his fist at some one who had struck him. Garrick was so impressed by the naturalness and finish of Harlequin's acting that he exclaimed, "Look how the very back of Carlin has expression!" [1]

The art of playing with the mask, then, is not conceivable without a perfect knowledge of pantomime. When once this is mastered all the muscles of the actor's body co-operate in his interpretation and perform the expressive function of the muscles of the face.

The masks of the *commedia dell' arte* were made of thin leather lined with linen. The corners were moistened, and so manipulated that they took the impression of even the finest lines of the mould from which they were made.

[1] Translated from the French. This speech attributed to Garrick is reported in *The Mask* (vol. iii, p. 106) as follows: "'Look,' said Garrick, the English actor, 'look at the character and expression in Carlino's back!'"; and in *The History of Harlequin*, by Cyril W. Beaumont (p. 60): "Behold how the very back of Carlin has a physiognomy and expression!"—TRANSLATOR.

V

The Scenarios

Il m'est souvent tombé en fantaisie de faire des comédies, ainsi que les Italiens, qui y sont assez heureux. . . .
Ils ont de quoi rire partout, il ne faut pas qu'ils se chatouillent.

MONTAIGNE

T is astonishing to think that, after more than three centuries of brilliant success and fame, the only material remains of the *commedia dell' arte* should be a mere handful of dry and brittle scenarios. Even as remnants they are disappointing, being, as it were, but a little heap of ashes left from a great and spectacular fire. Nor is there anything remarkable about them in themselves. Many of them make interesting reading to this day, chiefly on account of their historical value, but they would seem inane if produced on a modern stage. They belong to the period in which they were created. And since they are scarcely more than bare plot outlines, it is evident that their original merit lay not in the subject or text, but rather in the proficiency of the troupe that interpreted them. It would be quite futile, of course, for any playwright or theatre-director nowadays ever to attempt a revival of the repertory of the true Italian comedy unless he had at his command a company of actors well trained in the art of improvisation. Given the required talent and adequate interpretation, he would perhaps achieve some highly delightful results, but he would probably also find that modern scenarios written for the purpose would prove quite as effective as the old ones, if not more so.

Most of the improvisators of the *commedia dell' arte*, on retiring from the stage, wrote out the scenarios in which they had played,[1] in the hope of saving some part of their work from oblivion and at the same time providing a humble income against their old age. The famous Harlequin, Dominique Biancolelli,[2] a man of wit and culture as well as an actor of genius, wrote a great number of scenarios and caused them to be printed. Gozzi states that in his own time all attempts to revive them met with decided failure, "whereas the self-same subjects done by improvisation are still very popular on the stage." And this was the case in the second half of the eighteenth century, when excellent troupes of improvisators were still extant in Italy.

The form of the scenario did not differ greatly at any period, except in the matter of conciseness. Flaminio Scala,[3] or Flavio, who had travelled about all over Italy with the Gelosi toward the second half of the sixteenth century, left fifty scenarios, which were printed in 1611. The exact title of Scala's collection is rather verbose. It reads *Il Teatro delle*

[1] Often the actors were the original creators, not only of the *rôles* they interpreted, but of the entire scenario.—TRANSLATOR.

[2] See pp. 152-155.

[3] " Scala, Flaminio, actor and stage-manager. The dates of his birth and death are unknown. He was a director of the company of I Gelosi for some years. He published in 1611 (Venice) the first collection of scenarios, consisting of fifty pieces, . . . tragedies, comedies, and pastorals. The name of 'Pulcinella' is not to be found in any of these scenarios." —*The Mask*, vol. iii, p. 127.

THE SCENARIOS

Favole Rappresentative Overo la Ricreatione Comica, Boscareccia e Tragica, divisa in Cinquanta Giornate, composte da Flaminio Scala detto Flavio, Comico del Sereniss. Sig. Duca di Mantoua. In Venetia. Appresso Gio.-Batt. Pulciani. 1611.[1]

A letter from Francesco Andreini,[2] "detto il capitano Spavento," appears at the beginning of the volume. Forty of the fifty scenarios included are comedies, and the remainder are termed *opera regia,* or elaborate fantasies; only one, *La Forsennata Prencipessa* is a tragedy. All of the comedies are in three acts, and have one feature in common: they are based on love intrigues. Passion, sentiment, comic turns, and *lazzi* intermingled keep the movement of each piece at a rapid pace. Considered as mere texts, the scenarios seem to be of a dismaying dryness, but this fault is compensated by the lively action, the rapid forming and resolving of the scenes, the unexpected climaxes with which they abound, and which, indeed, were the chief qualities of the Italian type of plays. The principal value of the collection lies in the fact that it constitutes the best out of the repertory of the most famous of all the troupes of the *commedia dell' arte*, and offers at the same time the earliest exact information available on the subject. Those specialists who wish to pursue the matter further must be referred to Scala, of whom Riccoboni speaks in his *Histoire du théâtre italien* (1723) as follows:

> Flaminio Scala's plays are not in dialogue, but are set down in simple scenario form. They are not so concise as those we use and hang upon the wall of the theatre behind the scenes; neither are they so prolix that the actor can obtain the least suggestion of dialogue from them. They explain only what the scene is about, what the actor is to do, and no more.

The custom of referring to the scenario, thus posted behind the scenes as an aid to the memory, lasted in Italy well into the second half of the eighteenth century. Carlo Gozzi, the animating spirit of the company of the Harlequin Sacchi, states that

> The subject which serves as guide for these excellent players is written entirely on a small slip of paper and posted under a little light for the greater convenience of the troupe. It is astonishing to think that, with such a trifling aid as this, ten or twelve actors are able to keep the public in a gale of laughter for three hours or more and bring to a satisfactory close the argument which has been set for them.
>
> As an example of the kind of guide which serves to prompt our actors, I shall transcribe here, without adding or subtracting a word, a subject which I read by the glow of the little theatre lamp. It is entitled *Contrats Rompus*. We witness it several times a year, and always with pleasure.
>
> ACT I
>
> *Leghorn*
>
> BRIGHELLA enters, looks about the stage, and, seeing no one, calls.
> PANTALOON, frightened, comes on.
> BRIGHELLA wishes to leave his service, etc.
> PANTALOON recommends himself to him.
> BRIGHELLA relents and promises to aid him.
> PANTALOON says (in a stage whisper) that his creditors, especially TRUFFALDINO, insist on being paid; that the extension of credit expires that day, etc.

[1] Translated freely, *The Drama of Tales fitted for Representation upon the Stage; or, Comic, Tragic, and Bucolic Entertainments, divided into Plays for each of Fifty Days, and composed by Flaminio Scala, called Flavio, Comic Playwright to his Most Serene Highness the Duke of Mantua. In Venice. By Gio.-Batt. Pulciani.* 1611.

[2] See pp. 231–232.

At this moment:

TRUFFALDINO (scene of demanding payment).
BRIGHELLA finds a way of getting rid of him.
PANTALOON and BRIGHELLA remain.

At this moment:

TARTAGLIA comes to the window and listens.
BRIGHELLA espies him. He and PANTALOON pretend to be very wealthy.
TARTAGLIA comes down into the street. He goes through the 'business' of begging for alms from PANTALOON. In the end they agree to a marriage between TARTAGLIA's daughter and PANTALOON's son.

At this moment:

TRUFFALDINO again demands his money.
BRIGHELLA makes believe that PANTALOON gives it to him. He does this three times, and then all three go out.
FLORINDO tells of his love for ROSAURA. He complains of being excessively hungry. He knocks.
ROSAURA listens to his suit, desires to prove his love, and asks him for a present.
FLORINDO tells her that the moment is not suitable and that, moreover, he has no way of procuring it.
ROSAURA bids him wait and tells him that she will give him one. She goes out.
FLORINDO remains.

At this moment:

SMERALDINA enters with a basket, gives it to FLORINDO, and exit.
FLORINDO remains.
BRIGHELLA learns that ROSAURA has given FLORINDO the basket; he filches it and makes his escape.
FLORINDO follows him.
LEANDRO tells of his love for ROSAURA. He seeks a way to hoodwink PANTALOON.

At this moment:

TARTAGLIA goes out soliloquizing about PANTALOON's great wealth.
LEANDRO asks him for his daughter's hand.
TARTAGLIA informs him that she has been affianced to PANTALOON's son.
LEANDRO is amazed; he makes a scene, etc.

Out of this bit of text springs the comedy of the *Contratti Rotti*, and out of more than four hundred other formulæ, equally concise, are developed our *commedia dell' arte.* It would take too long to enumerate the four hundred odd themes which, by virtue of constant playing, are renewed both in scene and in dialogue. As each actor dies he is replaced by another equally talented, who contributes his own interpretation to the *rôle* and thus gives endless novelty to all these subjects.

Most of the time the director of a troupe assumed the task of composing and drawing up the scenarios; otherwise it was undertaken by one or more of the actors, among whom there were nearly always men of culture and imagination. This method enabled each player to revive scenes in which he could use his particular talents to best advantage.

Every troupe possessed a store of scenarios which it inherited from former troupes or pirated from rivals, and to this foundation it added material of its own.

Another reason for the remarkable homogeneity of the troupes of the *commedia dell' arte* was the fact that the players generally intermarried. Their children and grandchildren usually followed in the footsteps of their parents, and it was not uncommon for a man to inherit his grandfather's profession as well as his scenarios, his *rôles*, and even his stage 'business.'

THE SCENARIOS

" Every year," to quote Gozzi again, " the argument of the scenes is cut or expanded according to need, and the troupe has no difficulty in executing what is required of them on the shortest possible notice."

In addition to the plays improvised from scenarios and plays performed directly from text, there was a so-called *comédie mixte*, or mixed play, in which certain written passages were bound together by scenes of pure improvisation. The collections of plays of the French Italian comedy which Gherardi made in the seventeenth century are of this variety. Most of them are written partly in French and partly in Italian. The following extract from the *Mercure Galant* is a typical example :

ARLEQUIN (*au dieu* PAN)

Vous amoureux de Rosalbe ? Écoutez si je suis sincère. Rosalba è bella ; et vous, vous êtes admirablement effroyable. Rosalba ha una bella physionomie ; et vous, vous avez une physionomie patibulaire. Rosalba è ben fatta ; et vous, vous êtes fait comme un magot.

PAN *répond qu'il est beau et qu'il est le dieu Pan.*

ARLEQUIN

Cela est vray. Vossignora è il dio Pane, ma un panne bien bis, un pane bruno, plus propre à faire du biscuit pour les galériens, qu'à contenter l'appétit d'honnêtes gens.

PAN, *apercevant l'âne sur lequel* ARLEQUIN *était monté, demande à* ARLEQUIN *si cet âne luy appartient.* ARLEQUIN *répond qu'il est à luy ; que c'est un âne virtuoso, qui sçait faire le manège, qui corbette, qui joüe fort bien du clavessin.* PAN *lui demande s'il veut le lui prêter.* ARLEQUIN *y consent.* PAN *monte sur l'âne, lequel, après avoir fait quelques pas, se sépare en deux, laissant* PAN *par terre.* ARLEQUIN *se moque de luy et s'en va. Entre* ROSALBE, *etc., etc.* [1]

This form of improvised comedy mixed with text in varying proportions existed even in the theatre which was entirely Italian, from the time of Andrea Beolco in the sixteenth century until Gozzi's day in the eighteenth. It is interesting to note that the scenarios or printed libretti were subject to the " permission of superiors " in the sixteenth century and later on as well.

[1] This may be translated as follows:

HARLEQUIN (*to the god* PAN)

So you love Rosalba ? Listen to me, then, for I am a plain-spoken man. Rosalba is beautiful, and you are admirably frightful. Rosalba has a lovely countenance, and you are like a gallows-bird. Rosalba is well turned, and you are hung together like a baboon.

PAN *retorts that he is handsome and, what is more, that he is the god Pan.*

HARLEQUIN

That is very true. Your Lordship is the god Pan [It is impossible to render adequately into English the pun on the words *Pane, panne, pane,* and the allusion to biscuit which follows.—TRANSLATOR], but a scorched pancake, and more proper fare for galley-slaves than for honest folk.

PAN *asks* HARLEQUIN *if he is the owner of the donkey upon which he has been riding.* HARLEQUIN *replies that he is, and adds that the donkey is highly accomplished and knows the fine points of horsemanship ; it can also caracol and play the harpsichord.* PAN *asks* HARLEQUIN *to lend him the donkey.* HARLEQUIN *consents.* PAN *then mounts the donkey, which starts to trot away when it suddenly falls apart, and* PAN *is thrown to the ground.* HARLEQUIN *makes fun of him and departs. Enter* ROSALBA, *etc., etc.*

Guatsetto. Mestolino.

The Marvellous Malady of Harlequin

ILLUSTRATED DUTCH SCENARIO OF THE EIGHTEENTH CENTURY [1]

EXPLANATION OF THE PLATES

ACCORDING TO THE SCENARIO

PLATE I	*The Italian theatre is newly opened, and it is proposed to present the illness, pregnancy, and marvellous confinement of Harlequin as well as the education of his young son.*
PLATE II *Top of page*	*The curtain rises, disclosing Harlequin, who is ill. Piro comes to aid his master.*
PLATE II *Foot of page*	*The Doctor is unable to diagnose the case.*
PLATE III *Top of page*	*The Doctor makes an analysis of Harlequin's urine. Piro is uneasy.*
PLATE III *Foot of page*	*Piro hands a syringe to the Doctor ; Harlequin is unwilling to expose his posterior. Piro and the servant finally persuade him to, and he takes an injection. Mezzetin makes sport of Harlequin for submitting to the treatment.*
PLATE IV *Top of page*	*Harlequin is delivered of three boys, but only one survives.*
PLATE IV *Foot of page*	*The young mother Harlequin, aided by Piro, gives the child its first bath.*
PLATE V *Top of page*	*Harlequin gives suck to the child. Mezzetin gives good counsel.*
PLATE V *Foot of page*	*Harlequin now rocks the child madly. Piro washes the linen.*
PLATE VI *Top of page*	*Harlequin plays with the child.*
PLATE VI *Foot of page*	*The first steps. Harlequin is angry with Piro because he almost let the child fall.*
PLATE VII *Top of page*	*The Doctor pays a visit to the mother Harlequin, who complains of the difficulty of rearing the child.*
PLATE VII *Foot of page*	*Harlequin conscientiously combs the child's hair and rids it of lice. Columbine makes fun of him.*
PLATE VIII *Top of page*	*The first breeches. Piro the nurse prepares to take the little Harlequin out for a walk.*

[1] Designed by G.-J. Xavery; published by Petrus Schenk, Amsterdam.

PLATE VIII *Foot of page* — *Harlequin gives the child a vigorous whipping, which makes Columbine indignant.*

PLATE IX *Top of page* — *Harlequin threatens to repeat the punishment. Piro indicates that his master is a trifle mad.*

PLATE IX *Foot of page* — *The play ends with Harlequin's teaching the child to read.*

Het nieuw geopend
ITALIAANSTONEEL,
vertonende
de wonderlyke ziekte bezwangerheid
en baring van Arlequin
benevens de opvoeding
van des zelfs
JONGEN ZOON.
Getekend door G.J.XAVERY
t Amsterdam by PETRUS SCHENK
voor aan in de Warmoesstraat in Visschers Atlas

VI

The Theatres—The Stages—The Staging

HE actors of the *commedia dell' arte*, being organized, for the most part, in troupes which travelled constantly about the country, naturally could not hope to find a theatre in every town or hamlet they visited. Therefore, to guard against this exigency and assure their independence, they always carried about with them a simple portable stage structure which was housed in a cart together with the curtains, drops, costumes, and other properties. The life of the players, as well as their equipment, was, in many respects, similar to that of the itinerant mountebanks of the period. The platform used by the celebrated charlatans Mondor and Tabarin differed very little from the stages upon which the Italian comedians performed, except that they were smaller.

The stages were usually built high, so that the platform was on a level with the eyes of a man standing.[1] In this way even the spectators farthest removed from the stage had an unobstructed view of the proceedings, which was specially important, of course, in the case of the acting of the Italian players. The height of the platform assured another material advantage, for by dropping curtains to the ground on all sides a storing-place was formed underneath.

[1] At least it appears so in several of Callot's drawings.

The platform itself was divided into two unequal sections by a large drop-curtain suspended between two poles, making a back-stage and a fore-stage. The back-drop generally had painted on it a scene of some public square with houses and streets in perspective. Two or three slits cut in the canvas served for the entrances and exits.

The Theatre of Terrenzio di Trechsel
Fifteenth century

As a rule, there were two ladders, one placed at either side from the ground to the stage, and on the rungs of these one or two players, like Narcissino and the Songstress, would perch after having finished their turns in the performance.

In this use of the platform the Italian comedians merely followed the customs of the time. From the Renaissance to the seventeenth century, however, the more important

Stage-setting used in Theatres like that at Vicenza
Sixteenth century

companies played under altogether different conditions in many of the larger Italian towns. At Vicenza, for example, they were provided with the theatre built by Palladio, which was specially arranged to facilitate the kind of performance required by the scenarios Scala wrote. For Scala's plays were filled with *jeux de scène*, or scenic action, which would seem absurd, if not impracticable, on a modern stage; on the

FRONT VIEW OF THE STAGE AND SETTING IN PALLADIO'S THEATRE AT VICENZA
Sixteenth century
Photo Alinari

Palladian stage, however, it was possible for one character literally to go down the street in search of another, or for two characters to converse without being visible to each other, or for two groups to perform at the same time, yet independently, in full view of the audience.

The auditorium of Palladio's [1] theatre was constructed in a semicircle with tiers of seats, as in the ancient amphitheatres. The stage itself was divided into a main stage and proscenium platform, which extended out to the first row of seats. The main stage was

[1] There is an interesting book on Palladio entitled *Andrea Palladio, sa vie et son œuvre*, by G. K. Loukomski (A. Vincent et Cie, Paris, 1928).—TRANSLATOR.

then blocked off into three divisions by arcades which opened on streets in perspective lined with real wooden houses. Thus, no matter from what part of the auditorium they were seen, the streets gave an effect of distance. It is easy to imagine the immense possibilities inherent in such an arrangement and the liberty it gave to the staging. In such a frame the most intricate plots and intrigues became not only plausible, but

THE STAGE OF PALLADIO'S THEATRE AS SEEN FROM THE SIDE
Photo Alinari

entirely natural. While one group played on the proscenium the audience could see another group coming along the distant street. While Isabelle sat at the window Lelio serenaded her from below, and Brighella overheard their love-making from the shadow of the arcade. The spectator was able to follow every detail of the plot; Brighella was in full view of the audience and yet completely hidden from Isabelle and Lelio.

In the case of modern stage-construction it is always possible to anticipate where the actor will make his entrances and exits. He is like a rat whose hole has been discovered; he will return to it inevitably. In Palladio's theatre, however, the actor moved about as freely as in real life; he went along the street, entered his own house, came down into the audience, and played in the company of the other actors or independently of them, as he chose. Owing to the three stage distances, as many groups could enact different themes at the same time and yet were never out of sight of the spectator. There was also the added advantage of the fixed architectural setting, which was appropriate for nearly every sort of spectacle.

The Theatre of San Carlino

It cannot be denied, however, that this form of staging had its disadvantages, particularly in the lack of opportunity for local colour. Many of the scenes in Scala's scenarios, for example, were laid in different cities, but since there was no way of changing the scenery it devolved upon one of the actors of the troupe to recite a prologue to the audience, in which he stated that "the city for to-day is Ferrara, with the well-known river Po close by," and so on, giving a general description of the locality as the occasion demanded. In case the action took place in a house interior—such as in the scene where Cavicchio sings in his hut—a specially constructed set was erected in the foreground of the main stage.

Even during the Renaissance the elaborate stage structure was not always available, and in subsequent periods it became increasingly rare. In spite of this handicap, the various troupes made the best of whatever staging arrangements they found, as their engagements at Lyons, Blois, and Fontainebleau amply demonstrated. Improvising, as they did, from scenarios, they could take every liberty necessary, and also adapt themselves to the physical requirements of local stages without detriment to the action of the plays they gave. They were entirely accustomed to perform in ancient Roman theatres and circuses, as well as in countless other forms of auditorium. Thus two plays, *L'Assinolo* and *La Mandragola*,[1] were given at the same time in the palace of Leo X. One commentator described the double performance as follows:

> There were two stages, one at either end of the hall. After an act of *La Mandragola* had been presented on one, an act of *L'Assinolo* was given on the other, and so the two plays proceeded alternately to the end. In this manner each play served as an interlude to the other.[2]

[1] By Niccolo di Bernardo del Machiavelli (1469–1527). "In addition to his political and historical work he was a dramatic author. The finest of his plays is the *Mandragola*, which he wrote in 1504. Concerning this play J. A. Symonds wrote, 'It stands forth by itself, a sole inimitable monument of genius; peculiar and personal; accomplished by one single act of vigorous expression.' And Macaulay estimated it as superior to the finest works of Goldoni."—*The Mask*, vol. iii, p. 127.

[2] Guinguené.

COMEDIANS AND CHARLATANS IN THE PIAZZA SAN MARCO, VENICE
Engraving by Giacomo Franco (1610)

In France the Italians played at the Petit Bourbon, at the Hôtel de Bourgogne, etc. The accompanying illustrations show details of different scenes, which, after all, are not so dissimilar from those of the present day.

The Staging, Scenery, and Properties

During the Renaissance the Italians developed a taste for lavish and phantasmagorical productions, in which large crowds of supernumeraries figured as they do nowadays in cinema films like *Intolerance* and *Ben Hur*. These spectacles were called *opera*, or ‘works,’ in the original sense of the word, and they were produced with the aid of every sort of mechanical device and bizarre setting, as well as cavalcades, ballets, concerts, battles, and farces. The Italian comedy was also often included, and the troupe appeared either as an integral part of the performance or else as an interlude, there being no *entr'actes*.

TABARIN'S PLATFORM-STAGE (1630)

These *opera* eventually exercised a considerable influence upon the *commedia dell' arte*, and were responsible for much of its colour and fantasy and exotic character. The *Centaura* of Andreini, which was dedicated to Maria de' Medici, is an illustration in point, for in this piece there was a herd of centaurs

> which prance through the first act in a comedy; in the second they graze contentedly in a pastoral; and in the third they gallop and rear about under the stress of tragedy. Their adventures are numerous and picturesque and centre around the father, mother, and son centaurs, who engage in a war to recover the lost crown of the island of Cyprus. In despair because they are unable to realize their ambition they resolutely kill themselves. The tragedy is no sooner finished than the desired crown is brought to them. The little centauress, left an orphan, feels it her duty to accept the honour and mounts the throne at a gallop.[1]

The troupes of the Italian comedy adopted the vogue of elaborate stage effects to such an extent that they soon acquired almost as complete an equipment as a modern theatre. During the seventeenth century they rarely gave a performance, either in Italy or in France, in which they did not make use of a great variety of mechanical devices, numerous and sumptuous stage-settings, fireworks, and fountains. They never opened their ‘season,’ in fact, without a display of fireworks consisting of set pieces such as symbolical figures and cascades of light. Gherardi wrote, in the nature of a foreword to his plays, a long exposition of the pyrotechnical displays given by “the Royal Troupe of

[1] M. Sand.

Italian Comedians in front of their Hôtel de Bourgogne, on the occasion of the peace concluded between France and Savoy."

EXAMPLE OF THE KIND OF DÉCOR AND ARCHITECTURAL PERSPECTIVE EMPLOYED DURING THE RENAISSANCE AND THE BEGINNING OF THE SEVENTEENTH CENTURY
From "I Comici italiani," by Luigi Rasi

The following is part of a curious document concerning the staging of a piece played at the Petit Bourbon by a company to which the Scaramouche Fiorilli[1] and the Trivelin Locatelli[2] and his wife belonged:

> Explanation of the stage decoration and argument of the piece entitled *La Folle Supposée,*[3] Work of the celebrated Giulio Strozzi, the Right Illustrious Italian Poet, which is to be performed by the Grand Royal Troupe of Italian Comedians, maintained by his Majesty at the Palais Bourbon at the command of the Queen-Mother of the Most Christian King, and printed in the month of November of the year 1645.
>
> Flore will be interpreted by the charming and lovely Louise Gabrielle Locatelli, otherwise known as Lucille. . . . Thetis will be interpreted by . . . etc.
>
> This piece will be given entirely without music, which will not be missed because of the excellence of the production.
>
> The first act will end with a ballet by four bears and four monkeys which dance quaintly to the sound of little drums. . . .

[1] "Fiorillo, Tiberio. Italian actor born in Naples in 1608. He was one of the most celebrated comedians of the seventeenth century, and was for about fifty years the delight of his audiences under the name of Scaramuccia. According to his biographer, Angelo Constantini, he was the son of Silvio Fiorillo, but this assertion, when tested by dates, and viewed in the light of Constantini's erroneousness on almost all points of his hero's life, seems very doubtful."—*The Mask*, vol. iii, p. 162. See also pp. 237-242 of the present volume.

[2] "The next Harlequin of note was Domenico Locatelli. He would appear to have come to Paris about 1644. He played the character of Trivelino, a part analogous to Harlequin. . . . He was too much liked at Court. He composed in French the scenario of a piece entitled *Rosaure, Impératrice de Constantinople*, which was presented at the Theatre of the Petit Bourbon in 1658. Locatelli died on the 26th of April, 1671, at the age of fifty-eight."—*The History of Harlequin*, by Cyril W. Beaumont (pp. 51, 52).

[3] *La Finta Pazza*, in Italian.

Then ostriches will appear and, lowering their heads to drink at a fountain, execute a dance.

The argument of the last scene of the third act is something like this:

Nycomedes acknowledges Pyrrhus as his grandson. Meanwhile an Indian arrives. He makes obeisance to the king, and states that he has five parrots as part of the cargo of his ship,

Dalla *Veneziana*, Comedia di G. Batta Andreini sotto nome di « Sior Cocalin De I Coc da Torzelo » Academico Vizilante detto el Dormioso. (Venezia, Aless. Polo, 1619).

STAGE-SETTING FOR THE "VENEZIANA" (1619)

which has been driven into port by a storm. He offers them to the king, and they are brought to him in a cage. At this moment four Indians execute a Moorish dance. The parrots fly away from their owners, who are plunged into despair over losing them; after which the piece ends, and they all set out for the Trojan War.

A very natural conclusion, of course.

THE NUPTIALS OF THE HUMPBACK AND SIMONA

Sixteenth-century engraving

In connexion with this play Olivier d'Ormesson wrote that

> there were five different scenes. One represented three long cypress walks disappearing into the distance ; another, the port of Chio, in which the Pont-Neuf and the Place Dauphine were admirably depicted ; the third was a town ; the fourth, a palace in which you could see countless rooms and sumptuous apartments ; and in the fifth was a garden with a colonnade.

THE PREPARATIONS FOR THE WEDDING-FEAST OF ZAN TRIPUANDO
Doctor Gratiano may be seen at the left grating the cheese
End of the sixteenth century

> In all of them the perspective had been so admirably preserved that all the roads seemed to stretch out to the horizon, although the stage was but four or five feet in depth. . . . At the beginning Aurora rose lightly over the earth in a chariot and crossed the stage at a marvellous speed ; then four zephyrs appeared in the sky, and four descended and rose again with the same speed.

The staging of *Orfeo,* produced in 1645, comprised twelve settings which were changed without lowering the curtain. The cost of the mounting, including the mechanical devices and fanciful *décors* designed and executed by Giacomo Torelli, came to 500,000 livres. Some of the scenes were the siege and defence of a walled city, a temple surrounded by trees, the hall where the wedding-feast of Orpheus was held, a palace interior, the temple of Venus, a forest, the palace of the sun, a bleak desert, Hades, the Elysian Fields, a grove near the sea, Olympus and the heavens.

Du Tralage wrote :

> The sieur Angelo [1] told me that he had seen a play, or *opera,* at Parma which was truly extraordinary. The theatre was equipped with a mechanical device consisting of an arrange-

[1] The Doctor Baloardo of the Italian comedy in Paris in 1690.

ment of little wheels by means of which the stage mechanician rolled the floor of the pit, where more than a thousand people were seated, underneath the galleries without occasioning the least inconvenience to anyone. The musicians in the orchestra pit were next shifted under the stage by a similar mechanism. The space of the pit was then flooded with water to the

Stage-setting of the Seventeenth Century in France

depth of six feet, and a naval battle, after the manner of the Romans of old, was given forthwith. . . . The entire apparatus did not require more than twenty-four Swiss workmen to operate it.

Flaminio Scala and the Gelosi did not mount many of their productions in the extravagant fashion just described, but they nearly always employed the fixed architectural stage-set. They achieved their effects of fantasy and the fantastic by means of costumes and properties, a list of which Scala always gave in detail at the beginning of each of his scenarios. He would indicate, for example, " bats for beating ; numerous lanterns ; a live cat and a cock ; four hunting-dogs ; costumes for notaries, pilgrims, or travellers ; an artificial moon which rises," etc.

VII

The Actors and the Troupes of the Commedia dell' Arte

IT is a commonplace, perhaps, to say that the theatre has always been one of the great passions of the Italian people. Its fascination has been such, in fact, that it has often drawn its best actors from among men of culture and distinction, poets, nobles, and even priests. It has been pointed out in an earlier chapter that the vitality, influence, and success of the *commedia dell' arte* were due in particular to the unusual and special qualities of its actors. And since the technique of improvising required the most rare and varied gifts, an actor of the Italian comedy was obliged to be, among other things, an acrobat, dancer, psychologist, orator, and a man of imagination, possessing a thorough knowledge of human nature, so that he could adequately bring alive the character he interpreted.

The troupes of improvisators from the sixteenth to the eighteenth centuries contained a great many actors of this stamp, and it is interesting to mention a few of the more representative ones who contributed so much to the development and reputation of their profession. The name of Angelo Beolco, or Il Ruzzante, appears as practically the first of primary importance. He was a sort of Italian Shakespeare, an actor, writer, philosopher, and poet. Then there was the beautiful Isabella Andreini, who belonged to Scala's company. She was a member of several academies and a distinguished Latin scholar, and was honoured by Tasso as well as the princes of Italy and France. Her husband, Francesco Andreini, also achieved a reputation of some distinction.[1] He was born at Pistoia; he served as a soldier and was captured by the Turks. During his career in the theatre he played Capitano della Valle Inferna, and he was the creator of the Sicilian Doctor and Falcirone the Magician. He could play every kind of musical instrument, and he spoke Italian, French, Greek, Slav, and Turkish. He was a poet and writer, and a member of the Spensierati [2] of Florence.

His son, Giovanni Battista Andreini, was equally accomplished. He was an admirable actor, besides being the author of eighteen very obscene plays and a work called *El Teatro celeste*, a collection of twenty-three sonnets about actors who had won the martyr's palm.[3] There was also Valerini, a nobleman of Verona who lived during the second half of the sixteenth century. He was a doctor and a talented poet, and was well versed in Greek and Latin.

[1] He played about 1558.

[2] During the sixteenth and seventeenth centuries a great number of literary societies were formed in the principal cities of Italy. The Spensierati and the Accademia della Crusca were among the most representative of these.—TRANSLATOR.

[3] *I.e.*, actors who had become very religious and had consequently suffered martyrdom for their faith.—TRANSLATOR.

Examples of Scenes and Stage Effects of the Eighteenth Century
Engravings by J. M. Probst, after J. J. Schübler

The musicians were notably represented by Ottavio, who could play all sorts of instruments, including the flute, theorbo, harp, psaltery, cymbalo, hautboy, and organ. "He does not sing badly," adds a contemporary writer of the seventeenth century, "and, indeed, dances exceeding well."

The pretty Armiani of Vicenza, who played various *rôles* of Inamorata in Italy about 1570, was a poet, musician, and gifted *comédienne*. Diana Ponti, otherwise known as

EXAMPLE OF MECHANICAL DEVICE USED IN THE ITALIAN COMEDY
Seventeenth century

SCENERY AND STAGING OF "ULYSSE ET CIRCE"
Seventeenth century

Lavinia, was also a poet of some note. Brigida Bianchi, or Aurelia, the author of *L'Inganno Fortunato*, was a brilliant musician. Flaminia Riccoboni was a student of several languages, especially of Latin. Fabrizio de Fornaris,[1] who played Captain Cocodrillo, belonged to the nobility of Naples, and was celebrated for his wit and spirited humour. In 1585 he published a play called *Angelica*, which was given *à l'impromptu* in the residence of the Duc de Joyeuse.

Gherardi the Elder, or Flautino, imitated perfectly a variety of wind instruments with his voice while accompanying himself on the guitar. Tiberio Fiorilli, the great Scaramouche, was an acrobat of no mean worth. Nearly all the women of the theatre

[1] "Fornaris, Fabrizio de. An actor who recited in the second half of the sixteenth century in the famous company of the *Confidenti*. He was in France in the years 1571 and 1584, and while there he published the work *Angelica*, a prose play in five acts which has a certain value and interest as the work of an expert actor."—*The Mask*, vol. iii, p. 162.

could sing and dance and play the guitar and bass-viol. And so the number of examples is endless.

Over and above the special endowment of the actor, the custom of improvising with one or more colleagues lent additional vigour to the acting of an Italian troupe, which ultimately achieved a sort of unity of mind, each man having a perfect knowledge of the weaknesses of his partner.

STAGE DEVICE
Italian, seventeenth century

It was a common occurrence for the same *rôle* to be handed down from father to son through as many as three or four generations. The players, moreover, intermarried frequently, and it was not unusual to find that Columbine was Harlequin's wife in real life as well as on the stage. And these circumstances not only served to strengthen the cohesion of the troupe, but enhanced the naturalness of the acting.

During the Renaissance, and up to the beginning of the seventeenth century, the troupes of comedians led the nomadic life of the jugglers and tumblers. They travelled by wagons and barges, going about from town to town and from one province to another. As a rule each troupe was made up of about twelve members. The standard distribution of parts in the principal troupes of the Renaissance is given by Niccolo Barbieri as follows :

> The Lovers and women study history, fables, rime, and prose, and the conceits of language. Those whose part it is to make folk laugh rack their brains to invent new farces, not from any wish to sin, or to make others sin, nor to praise vice and folly in obscene words, but they strive to earn an honest living by arousing laughter with their covert quips and bizarre inventions. [Beltrame was pious.] The Captain inspires merriment by his extravagant boasts ; Graziano by his quotations ; the first valet by his intrigues, cunning, and ready replies, the second valet by his stupidity ; the Harlequins by their *cascades* ; [1] the Covielli by their grimaces and affected language ; the old men by their pompous airs and old-fashioned speech ; and thus the others in their fashion.

A troupe of players must have presented an amusing sight when travelling along the road with their heavy carts and paraphernalia. The old engravings on the subject show that the general appearance of these companies was much the same at the beginning of

[1] Italian, *cascate*. The term applies to " various kinds of jokes and pleasantries of more or less dubious taste, with which certain actors embellish their *rôles* when they feel particularly sure of themselves and of their audience. A *cascade* consists either of words or of ' stage business,' and is not usually employed except in comedies and farces."—*Le Dictionnaire du théâtre*, by Arthur Pougin, p. 148. The word also means practical jokes and byplay.—TRANSLATOR.

the Renaissance as in the eighteenth century. Goldoni gives a humorous description of them as follows :

> My actors were not like Scarron's ; however, this troupe in the *ensemble* aboard ship was a droll spectacle to behold. There were a dozen people—as many actors as actresses—a prompter, a stage carpenter, a property-man, eight men-servants, four maids, nurses, children of all ages, dogs, cats, monkeys, parrots, birds, pigeons, a lamb—it was a Noah's Ark.

The troupes were never able to settle for long in one place, because either the Church or the civil authorities were nearly always opposed to them ; at Paris the professional actors who inherited the privileges of the erstwhile Confrérie de la Passion saw to it that they were driven away by Parliament. The hostility of Parliament and the other authorities in France seems to have been due to self-interest, and also to a charge that the players were a menace to public decency. Things reached such a pass that the Italian actresses were treated like prostitutes and the actors like *mignons* or worse. In 1570 Parliament drove them out under the pretext that they were charging five and six sols, instead of two, for entrance fees. But, even had this been true, it is obvious that no one was compelled to attend the theatre unless he wished to. However, the official disapproval continued, and on the opening of the Seconds États at Blois in 1588 a remonstrance was made to the King to the effect that " the performances of the Italian strangers are a great evil which it is wrong to tolerate."

STAGE DEVICE
Italian, seventeenth century

In the sixteenth century the Parliamentary councillors, " even the youngest," claimed that the Italian comedy was good for nothing but to teach " lewdness and adultery," and that it was debauching the youth of " both sexes." The Gelosi were expelled, therefore, in spite of the King.

Barbieri wrote in his *Supplica* that, for the sake of making a scene more realistic, the troupes antedating the Gelosi did not hesitate to present " a naked man fleeing from a conflagration in the night or a woman stripped almost naked by brigands and bound to a tree by a transparent veil, and other things unfit to be witnessed by upright men." Indeed, it must be admitted that the Gelosi themselves were guilty of considerable laxity in these matters, for there are certain *dénouements* in some of Scala's scenarios, such as *Il Vecchio Geloso* and *Le Burle d' Isabella*, where the lovers make their appearance in the most scanty attire and enjoy the freest sort of adventures.

There is no doubt but that a spade was quite definitely called a spade in the Italian comedy ; yet in Italy the ladies and young girls of the Court were neither shocked nor astonished by such things, nor were they at the Court of France.[1] The *parades* devised by Gueullette, a sworn magistrate of the seventeenth century, were as crude as possible, yet neither great ladies nor young princesses took umbrage. Prudery and modesty are, of course, more a question of *milieu* than of epoch. The aristocracy and the general mass of people are, and always have been, freer of speech and more tolerant in this respect than the middle classes. It is a moot point whether the Italian players were more or less

STAGING OF " LE TOMBEAU DE MAÎTRE ANDRÉ "

PEGASUS BREATHING FORTH FLAMES
Seventeenth century

depraved than their contemporaries. Du Tralage in the eighteenth century maintained that:

> There are good and honest folk in every condition of life, but ordinarily the number is small. Although the actors are decried by various religious hypocrites, it is nevertheless certain that in my time—that is to say, during the past twenty-five or thirty years—there have been, and there are still, plenty of folk who live in a moral, regular, and even Christian manner, to wit:
>
> The sieur Molière.
>
> The sieur Poisson the Elder, and his wife. . . .

[1] *La Calandria*, which was written by Cardinal Bibbiena in 1490, while he was still secretary to Lorenzo de' Medici, had been given before sovereigns and princes and had not outraged even the pontifical ears. Yet it was not only licentious in language, but exceedingly frank in its situations and the customs it depicted. *La Mandragola* was another of the same feather.

Here a long list follows, and in it appear:

> Harlequin, deceased; his wife Eularia, and his two daughters, Isabelle and Columbine.
> The sieur Michel Fracasani, or Punch.
> The sieur Pierrot.
> The sieur Baron, a great gamester and satyr extraordinary toward pretty women.
> The wife of Molière, who has been the favourite of gentlemen of quality at various times; is separated from her husband, etc., etc.

VIGNETTES FROM GHERARDI'S "LE THÉÂTRE ITALIEN"

Not one of the Italian players appears in the list of the wicked, which continues at some length. Niccolo Barbieri wrote in this connexion in his *Supplica* that "stage crimes and improprieties are merely simulated and cannot sully the soul of the player who enacts them, for, in so doing, he is only conforming to the conventions of his profession." And elsewhere he says:

> When Captain Rinoceronte, Girolamo Gavarini, died on the second of October, 1624, there was found in his bed a very harsh hair shirt. . . . We must not risk speaking evil of the players too thoughtlessly, inasmuch as there have often been very upright men among them and, better still, great saints, such as Saint Genest, Saint Ardelion, Saint Sylvain, and San Giovanni Buono.

It is possible, of course, that poor Flautino, who languished for so many years in prison, and others like him, were not the saints they should have been.

Judging from the average of respectability just mentioned, it is not unlikely that Parliament's prudish accusations were due more to a basic hatred of foreigners than to anything else. However, foreign troupes were no rarer in Paris in the sixteenth and seventeenth centuries than they are now. An English troupe played there in 1609, a Spanish one in 1613, and in 1624 a Greek troupe, which gave comedies, farces, and ballets. From 1650 to 1672 two companies, one Spanish and the other Italian, were playing in town at the same time.

"La Fille Sçavante"

Harlequin, the Defender of the Fair Sex

The relations of the Italian players with the Church authorities were very unstable even in Italy, and varied according to the States and bishoprics. What obtained at Rome was, perhaps, the reverse at Parma, and so on. Beltrame da Milano, in his memoirs, gives us first-hand and curious information regarding the attitude toward the comedians in the sixteenth century:

> When I departed from my home in Vercelli in the year 1596 I chanced to encounter a clown surnamed Montferrin, and together we took the road just outside Aosta, a town in Savoy. There Montferrin asked permission of the chief authority of the place to put up his platform; but such a procedure was foreign to the customs of that country. The governor, therefore, not knowing what course to follow, betook himself to his spiritual adviser, who refused the permission instanter, saying that on no account should magicians be allowed in

the country. Montferrin was stupefied, and protested that since he did not know how to read it was hardly possible for him to make magic. The superior bade him be silent. "I know what you rogues do," said he; "I have seen mountebanks in Italy pass a ball from one hand to the other, and put a little piece of lead in one eye and make it come out of the other. I have seen them swallow fire and blow forth flames and sparks; thrust a knife through the arm and not suffer from the wound; and all this they do by enchantment and other works of the devil." Whereupon the superior sent Montferrin away, nor would he listen to his remonstrances, but threatened him with prison.

The superior was a theologian, but he obviously knew nothing of human ingenuity. And Beltrame, fearing lest he may not have convinced his readers, concludes:

> Many ignorant people do not know the etymology of *istrio*, or histrion, and think that by derivation *istrioni*, or histrions, means *stregoni*, or sorcerers, charmers, and men given to the devil. And it is for this reason that in some countries ignorant folk believe that the comedians can bring rain and a great storm at will. Little do they take into account that these poor starved conjurers have all they can do to charm enough money for their livelihood out of the skies; and if they had power to bring rain they would be chary in the use of it. For when it rains nobody will go to the play.

Happily for the comedians, not all of the clergy were disciples of St Bonaventure, who would have consigned them to the flames of hell without further ado. Charles Borromeo, one of the greatest saints in the Church, was kindly disposed toward them and proved his good-will when the actor Adriano Valerini and his troupe came to play in Milan. Valerini had given only a few performances when the governor of the city, being troubled by his conscience, forbade the actor to continue. Valerini protested, but the governor, fearing that he might be committing a mortal sin if he relented, referred the matter to Charles Borromeo, who was then archbishop, for decision. Borromeo received Valerini, heard his plea, and granted him permission to reopen his theatre on condition that all scenarios should be submitted for approval. He then took the trouble to go over the scenarios himself, and those he approved he signed with his own hand. That is why Diana Ponti, the daughter of Valerini, found in her inheritance a large number of scenarios signed by St Charles Borromeo.

Another interesting commentary on the customs of the Italian players and their relations with the Church is given by de Brosses:

> I must not forget to tell you of the astonishing incident which occurred the first time that I went to see a play in Verona. I had been watching the performance for some while, when I heard the town clock begin to strike. Immediately there was a great commotion behind me, and I thought that the theatre was tumbling down. Then I saw the players fleeing, and even the actress who at the time lay upon the stage in a faint, as her *rôle* required, arose and went out. It presently appeared, however, that the disturbance was due to the sounding of the Angelus and Pardon. The entire assemblage was kneeling in prayer facing the east, and even the actors behind the scenes were in the same position. Thereupon the Ave Maria was sung, and afterward the actress, who had lain in a faint, returned, made her reverence, resumed her *rôle*, and the play continued.

The persecutions of the Church and civil authorities had much to do, of course, with keeping the troupes constantly moving about. But there was still another reason for their peregrinations, namely, the necessity of finding new audiences. For it is obvious that one town alone could not support a troupe for more than a certain length of time, and the players were therefore obliged to take advantage of the patronage of some great lord whenever the occasion offered, or travel from one town to another, wherever there was a public celebration or annual fair. They usually departed as soon as the festivities were over, and oftentimes their expenses were guaranteed for a return engagement. They made it a rule, indeed, never to remain too long in one place. They were shrewd

Sketch of an Italian Comedy Scene by Gillot

enough to leave before their popularity began to wane, and, in consequence, the public was always sorry to see them go, and looked forward to their next visit. On tour the troupe naturally selected those towns and villages in which they were fairly certain to make money. Their admission prices varied according to the locality. The Gelosi charged a half-testoon[1] at Blois in 1577. At the Hôtel de Bourgogne the price was "four sols a head for all who came to see them play." The regular price for ordinary theatres was fixed at two sols by Parliament, but the Italians were obliged to charge more because of the cost of their scenery, costumes, and properties. Parliament overlooked the expense incurred in these productions, either unwittingly or deliberately, and

[1]An old coin worth about ten or twelve sous.—Translator.

the Italian companies were therefore often accused afterward of having exploited the public.

It is not here intended to give a complete history of the Italian comedy. That task has already been accomplished most satisfactorily by other hands. But, in order to understand the lives of the traditional characters, it is important to have some sort of perspective of the evolution of the *commedia dell' arte* throughout the length of its career both in France and Italy. It is equally necessary to know something about the *personnel* of the different troupes. The transference of actors from one troupe to another explains how the traditions attaching to each character were perpetuated, and how the personality of a Brighella or a Pantaloon was formed. The ensuing pages, therefore, are concerned first with a general account of the various companies of the Italian comedy, and then with a discussion of the famous characters themselves.

Owing to the roving habits of the troupes, the *commedia dell' arte* gradually achieved an international reputation. It eventually became widely known not only in Italy and France, but in nearly every country in Europe. The evidences of its influence appeared everywhere.[1] Thus we find that at the end of the sixteenth century, in Bavaria, two musicians named Orlando di Lasso and Massimo (one from Flanders and the other from Naples) wrote and played an improvised comedy, featuring Pantaloon, for the wedding festivities of Duke William IV. Again, in 1527, a troupe directed by Drusiano Martinelli, played in Germany and then in England. Shakespeare made the acquaintance of Pantaloon, and spoke of him in *As You Like It*. The Emperor Mathias of Germany raised the actor Pier-Maria Cecchini to the nobility on account of his brilliant interpretation of the character Fritellino. Ganassa and his troupe travelled about Spain, where they were widely successful and even won the approval of the dour Philip II. In 1530 the Pantaloon Pasquati and his companions played for the Emperor of Austria. There was a Coviello in Warsaw. Sacco performed at the Court of the Czar in 1730. And there was a troupe in Vienna during the reigns of Leopold, Joseph, and Charles IV which used not only the methods but the characters of the *commedia dell' arte*.

The Troupes of the Renaissance

M. Alfred Mortier has recently published a highly interesting work on Angelo Beolco, or Il Ruzzante,[2] of whom mention has already been made in an earlier chapter. Beolco was a person of signal gifts, being a poet, a writer of both dramas and comedies, an actor, and the director of a troupe. Although he performed all these functions with distinction and success, the scope of his activity and the importance of his contribution to the Italian comedy had never been duly appreciated before the appearance of M. Mortier's book, because the archaic forms of the Paduan dialect which Ruzzante employed had previously proved a stumbling-block even to the savants of Italy. M.

[1] The *commedia dell' arte* seems to have been known not only all over Europe, but as far afield as Japan. See the reproduction of an illustrated scenario published in Holland following p. 56, and the photographs of Japanese plates representing traditional characters on pp. 156, 221.—TRANSLATOR.

[2] See *Ruzzante*, by A. Mortier.

Mortier therefore deserves infinite credit for his work, which is likely to be a revelation even to the Italian public.

Ruzzante's art touched the *commedia dell' arte* at many points.[1] He made, for instance, the same use of dialects (notably Tuscan, Paduan, and Venetian) as did the Italian comedy ; he had the same interest in local types, as evinced by his Tonin, a Bergamask servant closely akin to the Zanni, Brighella and Harlequin ; and he laid great stress on making

Sketch of an Italian Comedy Scene by Gillot

the stage-action and characters as vivid, lively, and lifelike as possible. It appears that his *forte* as an actor was pantomiming, and there is every reason to believe that he often wore a mask when he played. Judging from the number and nature of his qualities, indeed, Ruzzante seems to have been a personality of the same order as Scala, Andreini, and all of the other troupe-directors, poets, and actor-authors who were the most notable exponents of improvised comedy in those days.

THE TROUPE OF ALBERTO GANASSA[2]

This troupe played in Mantua in 1568, when the company of Pantaloon (perhaps Pasquati) and Flaminia was also playing there. The Duke ordered the troupes to

[1] Ruzzante's connexion with the *commedia dell' arte* is discussed at length on p. 208 *sqq.* of the treatise in question.

[2] Written also Gavazza, Ganasse, and Albert Gavasse. Campardon, in *Les Comédiens du roi de la troupe italienne* (vol. i, Introduction, p. vi) gives " Gavazzi " as the authentic spelling of the name, but he fails to indicate his authority for this form.

give a comedy together. In 1570 Ganassa took part in the festivities held in honour of the marriage of Lucrezia d'Este at Ferrara. Ganassa came to Paris with his troupe for the first time in 1571, when Charles IX and his young bride made their entry into the city. On September 15, however, Parliament issued a decree forbidding the performances of the different troupes, under the pretext that they charged as much as five and six sols for admission : " an excessive sum never before levied for such purpose, and an imposition upon the poor." During the same year Ganassa and his colleagues received letters-patent from the King, permitting them " to perform publicly in this town both comedies and tragedies." But the King's word was not official until approved and registered by Parliament, and, inasmuch as Parliament was not in session at the time, the Provisory Chamber decreed that " this matter will remain suspended until St Martin's Day." [1]

Whatever the outcome of this decree may have been, it is certain that Ganassa was in Paris in 1572 to take part in the festivities held in honour of the marriage of the King of Navarre to Marguerite de Valois. His participation in the celebration is proved by a receipt from the King's Treasurer which states that he was paid " the sum of 75 livres in testoons of the issue of Tours at xii sols the livre, which the aforesaid lord presented both to him and to his companions in recognition of the pleasure they afforded his Majesty during the marriage." Afterward Ganassa departed for Spain, where he remained, it seems, at the Court of Philip II until 1577.

Vauquelin de la Fresnaye wrote in his *Ars Poetica* :

> . . . Ou le bon Pantalon, ou Zany dont Ganasse
> nous a représenté la façon et la grâce. . . .[2]

Elsewhere he is called the " good Ganassa."

There is some interesting information regarding the repertory and characters interpreted by Ganassa and his troupe in a Spanish document, quoted by Dr Scherillo, which states that the company played " Comedias Italianas, mímicas por la mayor parte y bufonescas de asuntos triviales y populares," in which were featured " las personas de Arlequin, del Pantalon, del Dotore." [3]

Apparently Ganassa was the first actor whose name has been preserved to play the *rôle* of the second Zanni, Harlequin. Furthermore he created in France the *rôle* of the Baron de Guenesche, a character who spoke a blend of Spanish and the Bergamask dialect.

After close inspection and study of a painting in the Museum of Bayeux, by Porbus, called the Elder, or by Frans Porbus,[4] I have an opportunity to correct certain portions

[1] *National Archives*, x, 1633 ; quoted by Campardon.

[2] ". . . Either the good Pantaloon, or Zany, whose manners and grace Ganassa has represented for us. . . ."

[3] " Italian comedies, for the most part in pantomime and treating chiefly of frivolous and popular subjects, given in a spirit of burlesque," in which were featured " the characters of Harlequin, Pantaloon, and the Doctor."

[4] According to some authors, Paul Porbus and Frans are one and the same painter ; others maintain that Paul never existed. In the Royal Museum at Brussels there is a picture attributed to " Paul Porbus, about 1510–84 " and Frans Porbus (1545–1581). The dates 1540 (or 1545) –81 are given also for Paul Porbus, which hardly makes the question any clearer.

In regard to the Bayeux picture M. Constant Mic in his recent interesting work on the *commedia dell' arte* writes : " Neither Porbus le Vieux (the Elder) nor his son Frans ever worked in France so far as is known." And further on he adds : " We can only surmise that the picture was executed by a little-known painter named Jacques Porbus, who resided, in 1571, in Paris, where he married, in 1578, a certain Nicolle Buffet." Armand Baschet, who had access to the archives in

of the text in the first edition of this book which treated of Ganassa, and at the same time I am able to offer new material of prime importance with regard to the history of the *commedia dell' arte*. The difficulties which confronted me when I set out to locate and identify this picture will show how slow and arduous is the approach to a solution of questions of this nature. It would require more than a lifetime to cover the ground. It must be said in this connexion that those who are merciless in their strictures of the mistakes of their predecessors are apt to forget that they profit by the work of all who have laboured before them; they might do well to consider that, although they may be more enlightened on certain points than others, there may be other points on which they are no better informed than the famous Doctor from Bologna.

In spite of prolonged and patient search, I have been unable to find the picture by Porbus the Elder of which Maurice Sand speaks in his *Masques et Bouffons*. Sand states that Charles IX is shown in the picture in the costume of Brighella, the Duc de Guise as Scaramouche, the Duc d'Anjou as Harlequin, the Cardinal de Lorraine as Pantaloon, and Catherine de' Medici as Columbine.

Moreover, Luigi Rasi corroborates Sand's analysis in his scholarly work entitled *I Comici italiani*[1] in these terms: "e sappiamo dal quadro di Porbus (1572) rappresentante un ballo alla corte di Carlo IX, che il Duca di Guisa (il Balafré) vi era in costume di Scaramuccia."[2] After extensive research I was successful in discovering in the Museum of Bayeux a picture entitled *Le Bal costumé sous Charles IX*, which corresponded to the description. It was listed in the museum catalogue by this fanciful title, which is incorrect, for, as the illustration on the next page shows, not one of the figures is dancing, nor is there anything to indicate a ball. However, it is fairly certain that the picture represents a troupe of the *commedia dell' arte* giving a performance in conjunction with the various Court personages, as indicated by numbers referring to a legend written in yellow paint at the foot of the painting. This legend is evidently of a later date than the scene it is intended to explain, for it reads in one place, "No. 5, the Duc d'Anjou, the King's brother, later Henri III." It was, therefore, evidently drawn up and added after the death of Charles IX and the marriage of Marguerite de Valois to the King of Navarre (1572). The picture is undoubtedly the one both Maurice Sand and Luigi Rasi had in mind, but it appears that neither of them had ever seen it. As a matter of fact, none of the members of the Court are in the masked character parts which Sand assigns to them; they are, on the contrary, playing the *rôles* of Lovers only, and there is no trace of a Scaramouche anywhere. The traditional characters of the *commedia dell' arte* are played by professionals, and we can distinguish Brighella at the left, making free with the maid behind the Inamorata (Marguerite de Valois), who is kneeling in front of her old father, Pantaloon, while two Lovers (Charles IX and Henri de Guise) are quarrelling over her. Beyond Brighella is a Zanni, wearing the

the house of Gonzague, tells us, on the contrary, that "the clever painter Porbus, a lodger in the house of Monsieur de Mantoue, dispatched and subsequently established in France . . ." We are at a loss to know to which Porbus he refers.

Although the history of the Porbus family is far from clear, it would seem of little use to unearth this husband of Nicolle Buffet, Jacques Porbus, of whom we know practically nothing.

[1] See p. 910.

[2] "We know from the picture by Porbus (1572), representing a ball at the Court of Charles IX, that the Duc de Guise (the Duke who was later stabbed) was dressed in the costume of Scaramouche."

mask with the hooked nose; his toque looks as if decorated with a fox's brush, which would suggest his being a Harlequin. In the foreground Pantaloon holds the

PICTURE BY PAUL PORBUS, CALLED PORBUS THE ELDER, OR BY FRANS PORBUS

Painted on wood about 1572 (dimensions, .85 × .85). It probably represents the company of Alberto Ganassa giving a performance in collaboration with various personages at the Court of Charles IX. Eleven of the twenty persons here represented are named in the legend inscribed in yellow letters on a black background beneath the painting. The legend reads as follows: " 1. Porbus, painter, and maker of this picture [at the extreme left]. 2. The King, Charles IX [to the left with arms extended]. 3. Henry, Duc de Guise [to the right of the kneeling woman]. 4. Catherine de' Medici, Queen Mother [toward the centre, behind Pantaloon]. 5. The Duc d'Anjou, the King's brother, afterward Henri III [in the middle background, wearing a sort of light-coloured turban]. 6. The Duc d'Alençon, the King's brother [holding the hand of Catherine de' Medici]. 7. Elisabeth, the King's sister and wife of Phillip II, King of Spain [to the right stroking a little dog]. 8. Claude, the King's sister, married to Charles II, Duc de Lorraine. 9. Marguerite, the King's sister, married to Henri IV, King of Navarre. 10. Charles, Cardinal of Lorraine [in the foreground to the right of Pantaloon]. 11. Marie Touchet, mistress of Charles IX [at the extreme right, in the background] "

Bayeux Museum

centre of the stage. His traditional phallic symbol has been effaced. Behind him stands his valet, who, judging from his motley costume, might also be Harlequin.

The picture was bequeathed to the Museum of Bayeux by Count Frederick d'Houdetot (1778–1859). The museum catalogue contains a note which construes this scene from the *commedia dell' arte* as a satirical allegory :

> 146. *A Costume Ball during the Reign of Charles IX* (1570). *Painting on wood. H.* 0.80 ; *L.* 0.83
>
> The scene represented in this picture is explained by a passage in the *Histoire des Français*, by Sismondi (vol. xix, pp. 97-99). The historian relates that Marguerite de Valois, sister of

SKETCH BY GILLOT OF A SCENE FROM REGNARD'S "LE DIVORCE"

> the King, Charles IX, desired in 1570 to marry the Duc de Guise ; but the King determined that his sister should marry Henri de Bourbon, Prince of Béarn and King of Navarre, in order to win him away from the Protestant party. Wherefore many violent altercations arose, and one of these clashes between brother and sister was depicted by the malicious brush of Porbus. Their dissension terminated in the marriages of the Duc de Guise to Catherine of Clèves and Marguerite de Valois to the King of Navarre, who repudiated her in 1599 and mounted the throne of France under the name of Henri IV.

Now it is to be noted that Sismondi makes no reference to Porbus, nor is any explanation given of the presence of Pantaloon and his fellows in the picture. The love scene represented, moreover, is typical of the *commedia dell' arte*, as a comparison with the Carnavalet picture on p. 30 will prove. It is evident, therefore, that Porbus depicted a troupe of Italian players, and there remains only the question of identifying it. Viewed from the standpoint of time, the troupe was certainly one of the oldest, and there is good reason to believe that it was Ganassa's company, which, as mentioned above, had taken part in the wedding festivities of Marguerite de Valois and the future Henri IV in 1572. The scene portrayed could not possibly have taken place later than 1574, as Charles IX, who appears in it, died that year. Moreover, the Gelosi did not arrive in Blois until 1577. Whether Porbus executed the picture from life or from memory is of no great moment; the point is that some troupe earlier than the Gelosi figures in it, and in consequence the painting stands as the oldest and most important document in the iconography of the *commedia dell' arte* now extant.

THE TROUPES OF ANTON MARIA, THE VENETIAN, AND OF SOLDINI, THE FLORENTINE

These two troupes, one composed of nine actors and the other of eleven, were in the service of Charles IX and Henri III from 1572 until 1578. They played alternately, giving comedies, acrobatic performances, and ballets. A record of the time notes: "To Soldini, the Florentine, and Anthoine Marie, the Venetian, comedians from the country of Italy, the sum of . . . in consideration of the plays and tumbling which they perform daily before his Majesty."

These troupes played both in Paris and Blois for the King's pleasure. They had been requested to perform at the celebration held in honour of the engagement of Marguerite, daughter of Catherine de' Medici, to Henri le Béarnais, but owing to the death of Jeanne d'Albret, the bridegroom's mother, the festivities were put off until the month of August; and the troupes were unable to remain. It is believed that Soldini went to Vienna.

GIOVANNI TABARINO

In 1568 Giovanni Tabarino was at Linz on the Danube; in 1571 he made a visit to France. He then became "comedian to his Majesty" in Vienna, where he probably remained till about 1574.

I COMICI CONFIDENTI, I COMICI GELOSI, I COMICI UNITI, I DESIOSI, I ACCESI

All these troupes were made up of individuals as remarkable for their culture as for their histrionic abilities, and their advent marks the climax of the *commedia dell' arte*. The period to which they belong was the golden age of their art and its interpreters. They rose into prominence during the second half of the sixteenth century, and their influence lasted well over into the first half of the seventeenth century. There was a frequent interchange of actors from one company to another, and the companies also often combined on special occasions. The reader will find the principal players and their talents discussed in detail in the chapters dealing with the characters they interpreted.

I COMICI CONFIDENTI[1]

The Comici Confidenti, after playing throughout Italy, came to France in 1571. In 1584 they performed at the Hôtel de Cluny, and probably in several provincial towns also, giving a repertory of comedies based on scenarios, as well as pastorals, tragedies, and *commedie sostenute*. Among the members of the troupe were:

Capitan Cocodrillo . .	FABRIZIO DE FORNARIS
Dottore Lanternone . .	BERNARDINO LOMBARDONE, an actor and author
Celia (Inamorata) . . .	The mother, perhaps, of Maria Malloni

I COMICI GELOSI[2] (1572–76)

There were a number of Ganassa's followers who did not go with him to Spain, and they, with other actors, formed a new troupe, called the Gelosi, which subsequently became widely famous. They were in Venice for the carnival of 1574, then in Milan for the festivities held in honour of Don John of Austria, and finally back again in Venice that same year. The Pantaloon Pasquati was with the Gelosi when they went, in 1576, to give their comedies for the Emperor of Austria. It would seem that their director at this time was Flaminio Scala, who belonged to the nobility and was a man of extensive culture and remarkably versatile as an actor. He played the various *rôles* of Lover in the troupe under the name of Flavio; he also left a collection of fifty scenarios, which were printed in 1611, and in spite of their general dryness, are interesting examples of the repertory of the Gelosi.[3]

Toward 1576 the Gelosi company was composed as follows:

Men

Innamorato (or Lover), then Capitano Spavento .	FRANCESCO ANDREINI
Dottor Graziano	LUCIO BURCHIELLA
Pantalone	GIULIO PASQUATI, of Padua
Zanne (Arlecchino)	SIMONE, of Bologna
Franca-trippa	GABRIELO PANZANINI
Flavio	FLAMINIO SCALA
Innamorato: Orazio	ORAZIO MOBILI, of Padua
Aurelio	ADRIANO VALERINI, of Verona
Zanobio da Piombino (old man)	GIROLAMO SALIMBONI, of Florence

Women

Prima Donna	LIDIA DE BAGNACAVALLO
Seconda Donna	PRUDENZA, of Verona

[1] "The comedians confident of themselves and of the public's indulgence."

[2] "The comedians jealous of pleasing."

[3] See the Bibliography and also Chapter V.

THE ITALIAN COMEDY

I GELOSI (1577–89)

The Gelosi were playing in Venice when Henri III requested them to come to Blois for the opening of the États, which were to be convoked on November 15, 1576. The États did not begin their sittings, however, until December 6. After considerable delay the troupe finally set out, and L'Estoile reported that

> In this month [February] the Italian comedians called Li Gelosi, whom the King had invited to come from Venice, paying their ransom after they had been captured by the Huguenots,[1] began to perform their comedies in the Salle des États at Blois; and the King permitted them to ask a half-testoon from all who should come to see them play.

And elsewhere he says:

> On Sunday, May 13, the Italian players surnamed Li Gelosi commenced their comedies at the Hôtel de Bourbon in Paris; and they collected four sols the head from all the French, and there came such a concourse of people that the four best preachers in the city of Paris together had not the like when they preached.

He further states that

> On Saturday, July 27, Li Gelosi, who were comedians from Italy, after having presented to the Court the letters-patent which they had obtained from the King, permitting them to perform comedies notwithstanding the prohibition of the Court, were finally sent away, and were forbidden to obtain or present any such letters again to the Court subject to the penalty of a fine of ten thousand livres in the currency of Paris, to be turned over to the poor. Notwithstanding the said prohibition they commenced their performances again the following September in the Hôtel de Bourbon as before, by the express command of the King. For the corruption of the time was such that players in farces, buffoons, prostitutes, and *mignons* had all the credit they wished with the King.

The Gelosi's greatest success was in a piece called *La Princesse qui a perdu l'Esprit*, with music and mechanical devices and a grand naval combat on the stage. In 1578 the Gelosi troupe returned to Florence. Under the direction of Flaminio Scala it had become the most unified of all the troupes of the *commedia dell'arte*. Scala worked out the characters more definitely than they had ever been presented before, giving them style and consistent form, and he established more order in the improvisation. It is due to him, also, that the fifty scenarios which made up the repertory of this company have been preserved intact. The emblem of the troupe was the two-faced Janus with an inscription which was a play on the word Gelosi, "Virtu, fama ed onor ne ser' gelosi."[2]

It was just at this time that Francesco Andreini succeeded Scala as director of the troupe. In 1578 Andreini married in Florence the celebrated Isabella whose beauty, intelligence, and cultivation were the talk and admiration of France and Italy. She was then sixteen years old.

In 1579 the Gelosi left Florence for the carnival in Venice; later they went to Mantua,

[1] Probably near Charité-sur-Loire.

[2] "They were jealous of attaining virtue, fame, and honour."

and in July proceeded to Genoa. They were in Milan in 1580, and then returned to Venice for the carnivals of 1581 and 1583. In 1586 they were again in Mantua, and there Prince Vicenzo favoured Isabella Andreini with the unusual honour of accepting her daughter Lavinia as his god-child. In January 1587 the Gelosi returned to Florence for

Engraving by E. Jeaurat, after Watteau (1728)

the marriage of Ferdinand de' Medicis and Christine de Lorraine; the company gave a performance of *La Pazzia* and other plays on May 13 of that same year.

The Gelosi came back to Paris once more in 1588, but a decree of Parliament, dated December 10, "forbade all comedians either French or Italian to perform plays, acrobatics, or any subtleties whatsoever under penalty of an arbitrary fine and corporal punishment." The Gelosi then departed, doubtless more frightened by the disturbances which ensued after the murder of the Duc de Guise than by the Parliamentary decrees. They reappeared in Florence in 1589.

I DESIOSI

Diana Ponti, the famous leading woman, seems to have taken over the direction of this troupe in 1582. The Desiosi were the *protégés* of the Cardinal Montalto. Diana Ponti transferred to the Confidenti so that she might be at Mantua to participate in the celebration held in honour of the marriage of Ferdinand of Austria.

THE TROUPE OF ADRIANO VALERINI[1]

Valerini left the Gelosi to become director of a troupe playing in Milan in 1585, in which the actor Braga interpreted the *rôles* of Pantaloon, and Pellesini those of Pedrolino. Valerini himself played the Lover under the name of Aurelio. It is of interest to note that Valerini belonged to the nobility of Verona; he was a Doctor of Philosophy, and wrote poetry in the vernacular, as well as in Latin and Greek.

THE TROUPE OF LAZARO

In the same year a troupe came to Paris directed by a certain Battista Lazaro. Very little is known concerning these actors except that their goods and equipment were seized because their director did not meet his obligations.

I COMICI UNITI

When this troupe appeared at Padua in 1584 it contained the following members:

Men	*Women*
Pedrolino	Franceschina (*rôle* played by a man, Battista da Treviso)
Magnifico (variant of Pantaloon)	Isabella (Giulia Brolo)
Dr Gratiano	
Lutio (Lover)	
Captain Cardone	
Flaminio (Lover)	
Grillo (Gio Donato)	

I CONFIDENTI

After a period of varying fortunes in Italy the Confidenti came back to France in 1584 and 1585 as *protégés* of the Medici. They performed for the Duc de Joyeuse, and among the plays they presented was an impromptu comedy called *Angelica*. The author of the piece played the *rôle* of Captain Cocodrillo, who spoke nothing but Spanish. The troupe also gave a presentation of a pastoral by Fabrizio de Fornaris. They were eventually expelled from the Hôtel de Cluny by the Confrérie de la Passion.

In 1590 an actress named Vittoria, as celebrated as the renowned Isabella, became director of the Confidenti during an engagement in Mantua. The troupe was thence-

[1] Possibly the Uniti.

forth also known as the Company of Signora Vittoria. While she was making a tour throughout Italy the Duke of Mantua invited her to come to his Court for the carnival. She accepted, and on May 6, 1589, gave a performance of *La Zingana* there. Several days later her professional rival, Isabella, appeared in the play *La Pazzia*. The occasion of these performances was particularly gratifying to the Duke, who was exceedingly fond of the theatre, and he had the rare privilege of being able to judge and compare the Gelosi and the Confidenti, the two most brilliant troupes of that day.

The Troupes of the Seventeenth Century

The history of the famous troupes of the Renaissance like the Gelosi might in some respects be cut short arbitrarily at the beginning of the seventeenth century. They were many times rehabilitated, disbanded, and reorganized, and they survived well into the seventeenth century—with varying success, it is true, but always retaining so clearly their individuality, vitality, and even their Renaissance costumes that they really should be listed as belonging to the previous century. For they had not the colour and style that suggests the seventeenth century. There was a period of transition which was best represented by the Fedeli. They inherited the traditions of the Gelosi by virtue of G. B. Andreini, the son of Francesco and Isabella Andreini, the celebrated interpreters of the *rôles* of Captain and Inamorata. After Isabella's death in Lyons in 1604 the Gelosi returned to Italy laden with honours and fame, and there the company was disbanded. In 1611 Scala wrote his scenarios, desiring to save from oblivion the gala performances of his colleagues. His collection of scenarios stimulates the imagination, causing us to speculate on their possibilities, but also giving rise to error on occasion because they are devoid of all colour and movement. The collection is the oldest and probably the most valuable one extant.

I GELOSI (1600–4)

After peace was signed with Savoy Henri IV recalled the Gelosi into his service about the time of his marriage with Maria de' Medici. They played at the Hôtel de Bourgogne until the spring of 1604. Among Henri IV's papers was found a memorandum which read, "I am sending you this note, Monsieur de Villeroi, to let you know that I am allowing the actress Ysabelle and her company to return to Italy." M. de Villeroi was the Governor of Lyons at the time Isabella died there of a miscarriage. Her funeral was marked by great pomp and ceremony. Francesco Andreini disbanded his troupe soon afterward, and devoted his time thenceforward to the publication of his wife's writings.

Composition of the Troupe from 1600 to 1604

Pantalone or Magnifico	Giulio Pasquati
Cassandro da Siena	?
Zanobio da Piombino	Girolamo Salimboni

Rôle	Actor
Dottore Gratiano Forbisoni	LODOVICO, of Bologna
Capitano Spavento della Valle Inferna and Dottore Siciliano	FRANCESCO ANDREINI
Flavio (Lover)	?
Prima Donna	ISABELLA ANDREINI
Burattino	?
Pedrolino	?
Arlecchino	SIMONE, of Bologna
Mezzetino	?
Servants: Franceschina	SILVIA RONCAGLI, of Bergamo
Servants: Lesbino	SILVIA RONCAGLI, of Bergamo
Servants: Ricciolina	MARIA ANTONAZZONI
Servants: Olivetta	?
Vittoria (' character ' *rôles*)	ANTONELLA BAJARDI
Pasquello or Pasquellina (old women *rôles*)	?
Claudione Francese (the French Claudion)	?
Cavicchio (a peasant)	?

THE ACCESI, THE TROUPE OF THE DUKE OF MANTUA[1]

This troupe was at the Court of France in 1599, and went to Lyons during the month of August 1600. It appears that Flaminio Scala and the actor Cecchini, who interpreted the character Fritellino, were both at Lyons at that time and were probably members of the company. Scala was also with the Accesi when they returned to Paris in October 1601. The Accesi then returned to Italy, in spite of the fact that the wealthy Countess de Boussu had invited them to come and give a season in Flanders and Brabant.

On November 10, 1606, Henry IV wrote to his cousin, Ferdinand de Gonzaga, asking him to use his influence with the Duchess of Mantua, who had promised to send the comedians back to France. The request was refused. But the troupe finally came in 1610, when the King and Queen acted as god-parents to one of Martinelli's sons. Later the comedians returned to their native land.

In 1608 there was still an Italian troupe in Paris which may have been Martinelli's, but it is not certain. Hérouard, the King's doctor, wrote that the young Louis XIII one day used the name of an Italian player, Colo, as a password in his games.

During the summer of 1613 the troupe of the Duke of Mantua set out for Paris, where it arrived at the beginning of September, after stopping at Lyons to give a performance on August 26. The company then went to Fontainebleau for a short period, and soon returned to town to play alternately for the public at the Hôtel de Bourgogne and for the Court at the Louvre.

[1] Also known as the troupe of Tristano Martinelli.

" MANTUA, DUKES OF. The Court of Mantua was hardly second even to that of Ferrara in the magnificence of its theatrical productions, and its Dukes, the Gonzagas, were famous for their liberality to actors and for the companies of these which they organized and maintained."—*The Mask*, vol. iii, p. 127.

In 1613 the cast was composed as follows:

Arlecchino	Tristano Martinelli
Pantalone	Federigo Ricci
Pedrolino	Giovanni Pellesini
Graziano	Bartolomeo Bongiovanni
Capitano Rinoceronte	Girolamo Gavarini
Leandro	Ricci, Federigo's son
Lelio	Gio. Battista Andreini Baldo Rotari
Florinda	Virginia Andreini Lidia Rotari

After their successful season in France Martinelli and his colleagues did not return again until the end of 1620. This time the actors Baldo Rotari, Pellesini, Bongiovanni, and the young Ricci were replaced by

Fichetto	Lorenzo Nettuni
Bernetta (a servant)	Urania Liberati
Inamorata	Giovanni Rivani

In 1621 the company played first at the Hôtel de Bourbon, then, from April 6 to 28, in Fontainebleau. In 1623 Martinelli was in Venice with the Fedeli. He died in 1630.

THE UNITI (1614)

The Uniti played for two months in Genoa. The female *rôle* of Franceschina was played by a man named Ottavio Bernardini. The company at this period contained the following members:

Men

Pantalone	Jacomo Braga, of Ferrara
Capitano Mattamoros	Silvio Fiorillo, of Naples
Young son of Mattamoros	Girolamo Fiorillo
Scaramuzza	Gio. Batta Fiorillo, son of Fiorillo
Trivellino	Andrea Frajacomi, of Bologna
Graziano	Michel Zanardi, of Ferrara
Flaminio	Gio. Paolo Fabbri, of Friuli
Curzio	Domenico de Negri, of Ferrara
Costelazzo	Hipp. Monteni, of Mirandola
Adriano	Andrea Mangini, of Genoa
Portinaro	Hipp. Agnella, of Ferrara
Portinaro (understudy)	Jacomo Filippo (called Savoncino)
Servants	Gherardi, Pennelli, Spadaretta, Alberti, and Anselmi

Women

Franceschina	Ottavio Bernardini, of Rome

THE COMICI FEDELI (1605–25)

The troupe of the Comici Fedeli was in the direct line of the Gelosi, from whom it had acquired several actors after the death of Isabella. It was directed by Giambattista Andreini, who took charge of it in 1604 or 1605, and, after being reorganized two or three times, enjoyed a prosperous career until 1652. In the latter year it was finally disbanded.

In the spring of the year 1608 the troupe participated in the festivities held in Mantua in honour of the marriage of Prince François to Marguerite de Savoie. The company came to Paris in 1613 at the request of Maria de' Medici, to whom Andreini had previously dedicated a religious play called *Adamo*. The Fedeli alternated with the French players at the Court and at the Hôtel de Bourgogne, giving the old repertory of the Gelosi and that of G. B. Andreini. The Fedeli travelled about through Italy from 1618 to 1621, and then returned to Paris, where they remained until the end of the carnival of 1623. Besides the plays based on scenarios, Andreini presented five or six of his own plays, which were printed there. It is worth mentioning, in passing, that these plays contained an extraordinary mixture of the Venetian, Bergamask, and Genoese dialects, interspersed with Castillian, French, and German. And it must be said that the combination did not delight the public to any extent. Andreini was in Paris again in 1624 and early in 1625.

An extract from a letter written by Maria de' Medici to Andreini will serve to show on what friendly terms the Italian players were with their royal patrons. The text has an informal style and homely flavour, and says in effect :

> Harlequin, I see from the letter which you wrote me anent the company of comedians that they have finally come to a decision to begin the journey hither, albeit they have waited a long while, and I had almost lost the hope of seeing them. They will, however, be well received, and each and all, I trust, will enjoy the journey. This will suffice to serve you as a passport. . . . Hasten then, as quickly as you may upon this my assurance and dispose yourselves to maintain the high reputation of Harlequin and his troupe, together with the other good *rôles* which you have recently added to it. The King, my son, and I await the pleasure and diversion that you always provide.

And from another letter :

> For your private ear, Harlequin. . . . You may be assured of the King's good graces. My son and I remember what you desire for the baptism of the child your wife is to bear, and shall have ready the golden chain which has been promised you. I wish to give it to you with my own hands without trusting it to any of my subordinates, for I know how ill disposed you are toward any intermediaries. The sooner you set forth, the greater will be your welcome. Come, then, with all speed. . . . At Fontainebleau, this twenty-sixth day of May, 1613.

Composition of the Fedeli Troupe from 1605 to 1652

Men

Flaminio (Lover)	Giov. Paolo Fabbri (formerly of the Uniti)
Beltrame of Milan	Nicolo Barbieri, director of the Fedeli in 1625 with G. B. Andreini

HARLEQUIN, PIERROT, PANTALOON, AND HANSWURST (JACK SAUSAGE), THE GERMAN AND AUSTRIAN COMIC VALET

Engraving by Philipp Haid, after Mathias Siller (eighteenth century)

Rôle	Actor
Harlequin Lelio (First Lover)	G. B. Andreini
Leandro (Second Lover)	Ricci, son of Federigo Ricci, who died about 1620.
Captain Rinoceronte	Girolamo Gavarini, of Ferrara
Pantaloon	Federigo Ricci
Pedrolino	Giovanni Pellesini (who still played with spirit and a high sense of comedy at the age of eighty-seven)
Doctor Graziano	Bartolomeo Bongiovanni

Women

Rôle	Actor
Florinda (Inamorata)	First wife of G. B. Andreini, whom she married in 1601. She died in 1627.
Lidia (Inamorata)	Second wife of G. B. Andreini, whom she married in 1652. He was seventy years of age at the time.
Second Inamorata	Margarita Luciani, wife of Gavarini

I CONFIDENTI (Seventeenth Century)

Flaminio Scala made his appearance again in 1611, this time as director of the Confidenti. The company played at Lucca in 1616, and in Venice in 1618. Giovanni de' Medici recommended them to the Duke of Mantua. The *rôles* were distributed as follows:

Rôle	Actor
Pantalone	Marc Antonio Romagnesi
Scappino	Francesco Gabrielli
Hortensio	Francesco Antonazzoni
Fulvio	Domenico Bruni
Amelio	Marcello di Secchi
Mezzettino	Ottavio Honorati
Beltrame	Nicolo Barbieri

THE TROUPE OF GIUSEPPE BIANCHI (?) (1639–48)

This troupe, whose director is thought to have been Giuseppe Bianchi (Captain Spezzafer),[1] came to Paris in 1639 on the invitation of Louis XIII. Tiberio Fiorilli, the famous Scaramouche, was probably by this time a member of the company. In 1644 the troupe performed various *opera* like *Achille à Scyros*, with mechanical devices arranged by Torelli and improvisations. In 1645 it gave Strozzi's *La Finta Pazza*, which has already been mentioned. It also played *Rosaura*, *Orfeo*, and *Ercolano Amante*, which were pieces interspersed with songs and dances. The troupe then left Paris in 1648 on

[1] See Appendix N.

account of the Frondist disturbances. The composition of the troupe from 1644 to 1645 was:

Men

Capitan Spezzafer	Giuseppe Bianchi
Scaramuccia	Tiberio Fiorilli
Trivellino	Domenico Locatelli
Horazio (Lover)	M. Romagnesi

Women

Aurelia (Inamorata)	Brigida Bianchi, wife of Romagnesi
Lucile	Gabriella Locatelli
Musicians and Singers	Diana Louisa Gabrielli (or Giulia) Margarita Bertolazzi

Composition of the troupe in 1648:

Men

Il Dottor Baloardo	Jean Baptiste Ange Augustin Lolli
Pantalone	The elder Turi
Virginio (Second Lover)	The younger Turi
Valet	Jean Doucet

Women

Diamantine	Patricia Adami, wife of Lolli

THE FIORELLI-LOCATELLI TROUPE[1] (1653–84)

Men

Harlequin	Domenico Biancolelli (called Dominique) (first played in 1661)
Brighella and the Captain	Spinetta (about 1675)
The Captain	François Mansac
Flautino	Giovanni Evariste Gherardi (taken on in 1675)
Valerio	Hyacinthe Bendinelli
Ottavio	Giovanni Andrea Zanotti
Cinthio	Romagnesi (taken on in 1667)
Leandro	C. V. Romagnesi (about 1675)

Women

Eularia	Ursula Cortezzi
Marinetta	Lorenza Elisabetta del Campo, wife of Tiberio Fiorilli (made her *début* in 1664)
Marinetta	Angelica Toscano, wife of Tortoriti (made her *début* about 1675)

[1] Later called the "Old Troupe of the Italian Comedy."

Colombina	CATARINA BIANCOLELLI, daughter of Domenico (made her *début* about 1675)
The Songstress	ELISABETH DANNERET (called Babet)

From 1660 onward this troupe played regularly in Paris. It left the Petit Bourbon for the Palais-Royal, where it played alternately with the company of Molière. Dominique, Scaramouche, and their colleagues attracted such crowds to the Italian comedy that the theatre *employés* were unable to control them, and frequently serious riots broke out in which many people were badly hurt.

In 1664 a pension of 15,000 livres was granted to Scaramouche. After Molière's death in 1673 the Italians followed his troupe to the Guénégaud Theatre, where they played up till 1680, then removing to the Hôtel de Bourgogne. In 1684 a regulation was made establishing a profit-sharing system of the gate receipts. The actors numbered more than the twelve which were originally stipulated, and the size of the troupe seems to have varied considerably from time to time. Up to 1680 the Italian players had remained wholly faithful to the traditions of the *commedia dell' arte*. After 1684 they began to make changes, interjecting French phrases into their dialogue and then interpolating entire scenes in French. Yet in spite of these radical innovations they were careful to preserve the traditional Italian character-types.

THE TROUPE OF THE DUKE OF MODENA (ITALY, 1673)

Men

Capitano Spagnolo	GIUSEPPE FIALA, of Naples
Gradelino	CONSTANTINO CONSTANTINI, of Verona
Pantalone	ANTONIO RICCOBONI, of Venice
Dottore	GIUSEPPE ORLANDI, of Ferrara
Finocchio	GIO ANDREA CIMADORI, of Ferrara
Orazio	BERNARDO NARISI, of Genoa
Florindo	DOMENICO PANNINI, of Naples

Women

Flaminia	MARTA FIALA, of Modena, wife of the Captain
Corallina	DOMENICA CONSTANTINI, of Verona, wife of Gradelino
Vittoria (? servant)	TEODORA ARELIARI

THE ITALIAN TROUPE ESTABLISHED IN PARIS IN MAY 1688

MICHAEL ANGELO FRACANSANO, Neapolitan (called Polichinello).
MARCO ANTONIO ROMAGNESI, or ROMANESE, of Rome (called Cinthio).
PLICITE (called Aurelio).
PATRICIA ADAMI (called Diamantina) (soubrette), of Rome.

URSULA CORTESA (called Aularia), wife of Arlequino.

DOMENICO BIANCOLELLI, or BIANCOLELLO, of Bologna (called Arlequino or Domenique).

CATHARINA BIANCOLELLA (called Isabella).

ANGELO LOLLI, of Bologna (called Il Dottore Balouardo).

TIBERIO FIURELLI (ninety years of age), from Naples (called Scaramouche).

(1685) BARTOLOMEO RANIERI, from Mount Ceni in Piedmont (called Aurelio).

(1682) ANGELO CONSTANTINI, of Verona (called Mezzetin).

(1687) CONSTANTIN DI CONSTANTINI, of Verona (called Gradelin).

GIOVAN BATTISTA CONSTANTINI, of Verona (called Ottavio).

JOSEPPE CHARLETON, of Ferrara (called Pierrot).

(1684) GIUSEPPE GIRATON.

(1685) JOSEPPE TORTORETTI, or TORTORITI (called Pasquarel), from Messina.

AURELIO was sent back to his native country in August 1689.

GIRARD EVARISSE, or the new Harlequin, the son of Flautino, was sent back in the month of October 1689.

EVARISTO GHERARDI (called Arlequino), from Prato in Tuscany, was sent back also in October 1689. He was the son of Giovanni Gherardi, surnamed Flautino.

Molière, Doctor Baloardo, and Scaramouche

It would be a digression to undertake here a discussion of the influence which the Italian players had upon Molière. The subject has already been most ably treated by other hands, notably Louis Moland, in his admirable book entitled *Molière et la Comédie italienne*. Suffice it to say, then, that Molière was indebted to the *commedia dell'arte* not only for the 'movement' with which he imbued his plays, but also for various plots, scenes, episodes, stage 'business,' intrigues, and characters. Du Tralage, the contemporary and friend of the comedians, wrote :

> Molière held Scaramouche in great esteem for his natural acting. He often went to see him play, and Scaramouche was the model which Molière followed in training the best actors of his troupe.

He continues :

> The Sieur Angelo (Doctor Baloardo) told me some time ago that the Sieur Molière, who was one of his friends, met him one day in the gardens of the Palais Royal, and, after having talked of the theatre, the Sieur Angelo said that he had seen a piece entitled *Le Misanthrope* played in Italian at Naples and that it might be a good subject to do at Paris. He gave an account of the play and mentioned several passages which had seemed especially remarkable. One of these treated of a shiftless courtier who spent his time spitting into a well and watching the rings he made. Molière listened attentively, and the Sieur Angelo was astonished fifteen days later when he beheld on the bulletins of the French comedians the notice of a new representation by M. de Molière called *Le Misanthrope* ; and three weeks or a month later the play was given. Thereupon I replied that I was amazed that a play of such worth and couched in such polished verse should have been written in so short a time. He answered that it might seem incredible, but there was no doubt about it, for he knew the play to be original ; and all that he told me was the truth, for he had no reason to disguise the facts.

One is inclined to agree with Dr Michele Scherillo when he says that " certainly the plays of Molière were the finest fruit of the *commedia dell'arte*, which found a second home in France."

THE TROUPE OF THE DUKE OF MODENA[1]

This troupe belonged to the end of the seventeenth century, and won honours of every sort wherever it went. It was first in the service of Alexander Farnese, then of the Duke of Modena, and subsequently of the Duke of Brunswick at Warsaw. The composition of the troupe in 1688 was:

Men	
Coviello	GENNARO SACCO
Lelio	ANTONIO TORRI
Leandro (Lover)	GAETANO CACCIA LUCA RECHIARI
Dottore	GALEAZZO SAVORINI
Pantalone	ANTONIO RICCOBONI
Truffaldino	M. A. ZANETTI
Guazetto	(?)

Women	
Armeltina (servant)	MADDALENA SACCO ANTONIA TORRI
Lavinia (Inamorata)	VITTORIA RECHIARI
Argentina (servant)	GAB. GARDELLINI

In Paris the Italian players reserved the right to use French on the stage, thanks to the wit of Biancolelli and in spite of the French comedians represented by the actor Baron. The acting and performances and jokes of the Italians appeared a trifle extravagant and licentious when rendered into French. And in this connexion the text of a letter states that

> the King being informed that the Italian comedians give indecent performances and utter much lewdness in their plays, his Majesty has commanded M. de la Trémoille to forbid them to do or speak such things in the future. And if they chance to present indecent postures or speak lewd words or do anything which may be against propriety, his Majesty will dismiss them and send them back to Italy.

It is evident from this that Mme de Maintenon was beginning to make her influence felt. Nevertheless it must be said also that customs in general and the mental attitude of the people were tending toward a greater sense of delicacy. The letter was dated 1696. The following year it was noised about in Paris that a novel entitled *La Fausse Prude*, aimed at Mme de Maintenon, had been published in Holland. The Italians then conceived the fatal idea of calling one of their plays *La Finta Matrigna*—that is, *La Fausse Prude*. The reaction was immediate. On May 13, 1697, M. de Pontchartrain hurriedly wrote instructions to the lieutenant of police to the effect that " The King has discharged his Italian comedians, and his Majesty has commanded me to write you to have their theatre permanently closed to-morrow."

At the time the troupe of the King's Italian comedians was dismissed the following members were listed in the company:

[1] Otherwise known as the Troupe of Gennaro and Maddalena Sacco.

Men

Mézetin	Angelo Constantini
Polichinelle	Michel Angelo Fracanzani
Arlequin	Evariste Gherardi
Pierrot	Jean Joseph Jératon
Octave	Giovanni Battista Constantini
Cinthio	Marco Antonio Romagnesi
Léandre	Carlo Virgile Romagnesi, of Belmont
Pascariel	Giuseppe Tortoriti

Women

Colombine	Catarina Biancolelli
Marinette	Angelica Toscano
Spinette	(real name unknown)
Babet-la-Chanteuse	Elisabeth Daneret
Mechanician and Scene Designer	Cadet

A short time after this crushing dismissal—which he may have ordered against his will—the King authorized Tortoriti, or Pascariel, and Cadet each to form a troupe of his own, but he forbade either of them to come within thirty leagues of Paris. The new troupes contained some of the actors listed above. The Italians did not appear in Paris again until nineteen years later.

Signor Bambinelli

VIII

The French-Italian Comedy, or the Italian Comedy in France

THE PLAYS OF THE HARLEQUIN GHERARDI, OR FRENCH COMEDIES ADAPTED TO THE ITALIAN THEATRE

THE REPERTORY OF THE ITALIAN COMEDY IN FRANCE (1682–97)

THE Harlequin Evaristo Gherardi,[1] son of Flautino, made a collection of forty or so scenarios in the Italian style, interspersed with text written by a dozen French authors. Each piece was a patchwork of French and Italian, and the *lazzi*, *cascate*, and set speeches inherited from the *commedia dell' arte* were combined with dialogue and repartee essentially French.

Some of the comedies were written by the improvisator Gherardi, the portrait of whose father in the *rôle* of Flautino appears later in these pages. The *commedia dell' arte* was, then, in Gherardi's blood from the very beginning, and as a consequence all of his plays are permeated with its traditions.

The principal French authors of the naturalized Italian drama were Regnard, Dufresny, and Nolant de Fatouville. There were also Boisfranc, Brugière de Barante, Mangin, Palaprat, and the satiric Losme de Monchesnay, who was a friend of Boileau.

Concerning Regnard and Dufresny, it is of interest to quote a vivid and amusing description by N. M. Bernardin :

> Regnard was a Parisian to his finger-tips. Born in the shadow of Les Halles,[2] he turned instinctively toward his native city in later life after he had grown weary of travelling for pleasure or profit. He settled down upon a bit of land where the Boulevard des Italiens now runs, and there he made a kitchen garden in which he cultivated lettuce, artichokes, and mushrooms. Certainly the air of the place must have had something very special about it, for Regnard possessed the *esprit* of a *boulevardier* long before the *boulevard* ever came into existence. His ready wit and fantastic humour flashes out in every line of the little plays which the future author of the *Légataire universel* and the *Folies amoureuses* was then writing for the Italian comedy. His dialogue is full of vivacity and malice, and it seems sometimes as though Regnard had been intoxicated by his own fresh and sparkling gaiety, as light and frothy as champagne.
>
> Some of these comedies were written in collaboration with Dufresny; the two poets were admirably suited to each other, both having a sly wit, a love of gambling, and an interest in gardens. Regnard, being the son of a merchant, had, despite his natural disorderliness, an

[1] See Appendix G.

[2] The great central market of Paris.—TRANSLATOR.

instinct for business ; he was a rich man to the end of his life and died of over-eating in his princely *château*. Dufresny was also a man of irregular habits and an incorrigible rake besides. He was a born Bohemian a century before Mürger had ever made the type popular. A great-grandson of Henri IV (who deserved the title of father of his people in more than one sense),

EVARISTO GHERARDI
Famous harlequin and author

he wasted the large fortune which Louis XIV and the Regent had bestowed upon him, falling at length into such a state of poverty that he could not even pay his washerwoman, Angélique. He married her in order to be quit of his debt, and though it is doubtful whether they were happy together, at least they had the good sense to wash their soiled linen at home.

It must be said in justice to Dufresny that he never had any luck ; he lost everything—his inventions, his ideas, and his first wife. It was his idea originally to make gardens luxuriant and picturesque instead of rigidly formal in the French manner ; and yet the irony of it is that the kind of gardens he favoured have since been called " English gardens." He also wrote

Evaristo Gherardi as Harlequin

a book, in which he jotted down the things that interested and amused him, and Montesquieu used his material in the *Lettres Persanes*, which won so great a success that it completely eclipsed the original. Again, Dufresny was so unwise as to show Regnard the outline of his *Chevalier Joueur*, and what did his unscrupulous friend do but dash off his own *Joueur* and produce it before Dufresny's play was ready. The climax came, however, when Dufresny surprised his wife in the arms of a law student. He gazed at the handsome young man lying in bed with his wife, who was ugly and over-ripe; then in a tone of bitter reproach he said to him: "And

ILLUSTRATIONS FROM GHERARDI'S "LE THÉÂTRE ITALIEN"

to think that you did not *have* to do it!" The *bon mot* is delightful, and there are many of the same character in Dufresny's work. There would have been many more if Dufresny, during his lean days, had not been obliged to sell Regnard a notebook full of his witticisms at one pistole each.

Surely there were never two characters more absurd or fantastic than these two authors, who seem as if they had come directly out of the *commedia dell' arte* itself. If we did not possess a record of their actual existence it would be difficult not to think that some one had imagined them.

As for Nolant de Fatouville, we learn that

he was a magistrate who had a horror of magistrates. He was a misanthrope, a pessimist, and he had a wilfully cruel sense of irony. He was a stodgy writer, yet a vigorous thinker, and

Illustrations for Two Comedies by Dufresny performed in 1688 and 1689

Comedy by Le Noble produced in September 1691

Comedy by Losme de Montchesnay produced in July 1689

Comedy performed for the First Time in July 1694

Comedy by Losme de Montchesnay performed during December 1693

Comedy by Gherardi performed for the First Time in October 1695

One-act Comedy produced in January 1695

he left behind him sixteen plays which in some respects are quite remarkable. His best work, *Le Banqueroutier*, in which he shows a revolutionary spirit considerably in advance of his day, was played at the Théâtre Italien. He never signed any of his comedies, and was therefore never very well known.

From 1682 to 1697 the repertory of the Italian comedy falls into two groups—buffoonery, *parades*, parodies, and satiric comedies filled with penetrating and often

COMEDY BY REGNARD PERFORMED FOR THE FIRST TIME IN JANUARY 1691

COMEDY BY REGNARD AND DUFRESNY PRODUCED IN 1696

caustic comment; comedies mid-way between the character comedies of Molière and the delicate and subtle plays, full of *nuances*, by Marivaux. The value of these comedies with their scenery and costumes is due as much to an unbridled play of imagination as to the now out-moded vulgarities of speech and humour.

IX

The Theatres at the Fairs[1]

Et cependant la foire fut ouverte
De Saint-Germain où ceux qui ont le cœur
Adolori d'amoureuse langueur
Vont, amoureux, d'une gaillarde bande.

RONSARD

AS early as the twelfth century the Fair of Saint-Germain was held yearly in the grounds belonging to the abbey of Saint-Germain-des-Prés. Toward the end of the seventeenth century it was the haunt of all the wastrels in Paris during the period between February 3 and Palm Sunday. During the month of July the Fair of Saint-Laurent[2] became the favourite meeting-place.

The fairs drew great crowds of people belonging to every station in life. There were great lords, marquises, lackeys, pages, rogues, honest and solid *bourgeois*, pretty ladies, and adventurers of all kinds who thronged to see the marionettes of Brioche and the two-headed cow; they danced the rigadoon and applauded Gertrude Boon, called La Belle Tourneuse, for her sword dance. Vendors went about selling Marseilles soap, Siamese bonnets, all sorts of Greek and Italian wines, and hot cream *ratons*[3] at "two liards."[4] Tooth-extractors blew horns to attract customers, and sharpers fooled the gullible with loaded dice. The air rang with the sounds of fights, disputes, laughter, and singing.

It was in this setting that Harlequin and Columbine, Scaramouche and Brighella, appeared after Madame de Maintenon had forced the regular theatre to close its doors to the royal Italian troupe. Here the players of the *commedia dell' arte* returned to their original practice of tight-rope walking and acrobatics in addition to their acting. In the heyday of the fairs there were two full-fledged theatres, one directed by the Alard brothers and the widow Moritz von der Beck, and the other by Bertrand, Dolet, and Delaplace. The members of these companies consisted of professionals, amateurs, carpenters, painters, and washerwomen; they performed amusing 'skits' and *parades* taken from the erstwhile repertory of Harlequin and Scaramouche. The entire history of the fair theatres is a long struggle between these unlicensed performers and the Comédie Française, which held the exclusive privilege of giving plays in Paris. Although the fair theatres were demolished time and again, they were rebuilt as if by enchantment. The actors at the fairs did what they could, of course, by way of self-defence, and brought forward a decree in their favour issued by François I, in opposition to the monopoly

[1] They were known in France as the *théâtres de la foire*, and the actors were called *forains*.—TRANSLATOR.

[2] Held on the site of what is now the Gare de l'Est.

[3] Small cakes which were extremely popular at that time.—TRANSLATOR.

[4] A quarter of a sou; figuratively, a farthing.—TRANSLATOR.

granted to the Comédie Française by Louis XIV. Forbidden to enact regular plays, they begged the question by giving monologues, pantomimes, and comic ballads. They were obliged, at the same time, to present their entertainments in several ways: Harlequin, for instance, acted the parts of several characters in a single scene.

"He began a scene and a discourse," wrote Demoncrif, the king's steward, "about a meal which he pretended he was eating at the Sign of the Cornemuse, and he gave an imitation of the waiters serving at table and of the manner in which the master paid his bill."

ALLEGORY OF THE CREATION OF THE OPÉRA-COMIQUE IN THE SAINT-LAURENT FAIR THEATRE (1730)

Again, they would enact a play in which one of the actors would speak for the rest:

> It befell that several actors and actresses came upon the stage in the dress of Scaramouche, the Doctor, and his servant. And he who was the Doctor spoke alone in the presence of the others, and they would reply in this fashion: they would feign to write their speeches with the right index finger in the palm of the left hand, and he who spoke would then read aloud what each one had answered; and thus they argued and discoursed.

Still another method required that each actor make his exit as soon as he had spoken his line. Their subterfuges were endless, and the more the players invented the more sympathetic and delighted was the public.

Following the example of the Italians with their Songstress, the performers at the fairs organized a form of *opera* in the early manner of the troupes which played by improvisation. They employed violins, bass-viols, hautboys, and even had changes of scenery. Lesage also invented "silent plays" for them with scrolls which Pantaloon and the Doctor would "unroll in turn and upon which the spectators read the cues."

In this fashion were given *Arlequin aux Champs Élysées*, *Les Aventures comiques d'Arlequin*, *Le Mariage d'Arlequin*, and Pellegrin's *Arlequin à la Guinguette*. To quote Demoncrif further:

> In this piece there was a scene in a tea-garden showing tables laden with pots and a company seated. One of the actors, dressed as a Spaniard, was dining with an actress. They were served by Harlequin, who drew first a salad, then an omelette, and then other dainties out of his breeches.

Thus the fair theatres had, to a large extent, retained the spirit of the gross but truly comical buffooneries of the Italian comedy.

Italian Characters at the Fair

Dutch engravings of the eighteenth century

In 1713 Lesage's *Arlequin Roi de Serendib* was produced at the Fair of Saint-Germain. It was a *parade* in the Italian style, and here again the actors made use of scrolls. At the end of the piece there is a temple scene in which Mezzetin is preparing to slay Harlequin

THE TOOTH-EXTRACTOR
Directoire period

A PARADE
Directoire period

as a sacrifice. Just as he is about to administer the fatal blow Mezzetin asks his victim what country he is from. The scroll displays the words :

" C'est à Bergame, hélas ! en Italie,
Qu'une tripière en ses flancs m'a porté." [1]

PERFORMERS GIVING A SHOW NEXT TO THE PUMPING STATION ON THE QUAI DU LOUVRE (1822)

At this moment Pierrot enters, and the three fall upon one another's necks with joy. Indeed, they are so moved by Harlequin's revelation that they decide to pillage the temple.

[1] " Alas ! it was in Bergamo in Italy that a tripe-seller bore me in her womb."

They try to carry off Kesaya (an idol), but it breaks and leaves only a sucking-pig in their hands. Next the pagoda tumbles in ruins as if the sacrilege had incurred the anger of the god. They all three flee; and so the play ends.

In addition to these different experiments in performing their comedies, the actors of the fair theatres tried singing the words of the play to old popular tunes, and the practice proved such a success that it developed into a distinctly new *genre* of entertainment, which eventually became the Opéra-Comique.

The next time the Regent invited an Italian troupe to Paris Lesage wrote the *Querelle des Théâtres*, in which Mezzetin, the Comédie Française, the Italian comedy, and the Opéra were personified and allowed to air their grievances.

But the theatres at the fairs began to languish under the strain of continual discouragement and opposition. Lesage and Dorneval in 1718 wrote *Les Funérailles de la Foire* as a fitting tribute to the passing of the fair:

La mort barbare
Détruit aujourd'hui tous les ris :
La Foire est morte ! [1]

And the Italian comedy and the Comédie Française replied with the song:

Elle est morte, la vache à panier.
Elle est morte, il n'en faut plus parler.[2]

Francisque, aided by Piron, known as that "joke-machine," put on *Arlequin Deucalion*, which scored a huge success. They produced several other plays, which earned Francisque a term in prison, and he was obliged to quit Paris as soon as he was released.

SCARAMOUCHE AS DIOGENES AT ONE OF THE FAIR THEATRES
Eighteenth century

[1] "Barbarous Death hath this day all laughter slain: the fair is dead!"
[2] "The old milch-cow has passed away. She's dead; there's nothing more to say."

X

The Revival of the Italian Comedy in the Eighteenth Century

THE closing years of the reign of Louis XIV had left a general feeling of gloom among the French, and, in order to dispel it, they turned avidly to gaiety and distraction. The public was quite in the humour to be diverted once more by the wit and antics of the Italian comedians and the droll and sprightly characters they portrayed. After the period of official mourning was at an end, therefore, the Regent undertook to procure a new Italian troupe to play in Paris. The actor Luigi Riccoboni, or Lelio, was assigned the task of forming it, and he chose the best actors from the troupe of Antonio Farnese, Prince of Parma, who consented to their departure on condition that they should " play with all modesty before his Majesty as well as his Highness, the Duc d'Orléans."

Riccoboni, like his predecessors Scala, Andreini, and Biancolelli, was a man of culture, as well as a distinguished actor and writer. His character revealed an odd mixture of contrasting qualities, for he was at once very liberal in his views and full of religious scruples. His wife, Flaminia, a worthy descendant of the famous Isabella of the Gelosi, was an actress of exceptional talent, an " eminent Latinist," and a member of several Italian academies. The two next most important members of the company were Mario, the elegant Lover, a brother-in-law of Riccoboni, and Silvia, who eventually became the toast of all Paris. Silvia was one of the most delightful actresses who ever interpreted Marivaux, and her spirit and charm were such that even at fifty she still gave a convincing impression of youthfulness upon the stage.

The company opened its season on May 18, 1716, at the Théâtre du Palais-Royal in the presence of the Regent and the Duchesse de Berry. The play selected for the occasion was *L'Inganno Fortunato, ou L'Heureuse Surprise*, from an Italian scenario in three acts, and it proved to be an immense success, due chiefly to the amusing *lazzi* of the Harlequin, Thomassin.[1]

In June the old theatre of the Hôtel de Bourgogne, from which Dominique's troupe had been banished, was rehabilitated, and on the curtain was painted a phœnix arising from the flames with the motto beneath, " Je renais."

The Italians then entered upon a period of extraordinary prosperity and triumph. But it was not to last very long. They soon met with as many difficulties as their compatriots had encountered before them. Their audiences first complained because the Italians played only in their native tongue; next the women considered that Pantaloon and Harlequin were growing far too vulgar; more fault-finding followed, and presently

[1] See Appendix K.

the career of the troupe seemed likely to come to a speedy end when Riccoboni in desperation conceived the happy notion of asking a friend named Autreau to write a play in French, using the traditional characters of the Italian comedy. The result was *Le Port à l'Anglais, ou Les Nouvelles Débarquées*, which won an immediate and overwhelm ing triumph, and so the company was saved.

Interesting to note is a curious inscription which was written at the beginning of the troupe's first register: "In the name of God, the Virgin Mary, St Francis of Paula, and the souls in Purgatory, we have commenced this day, May 18, 1716, with *L'Inganno Fortunato*." The invocation is charming, especially when one remembers that the company was given to playing the frivolous Marivaux, and that the lines were set down by the "merry *farceurs*."

In 1723 Louis XV granted a subsidy of 15,000 livres to Riccoboni and his colleagues, and on the Hôtel de Bourgogne, under the arms of France, was inscribed:

HÔTEL DES COMÉDIENS ORDINAIRES DU ROI
ENTRETENUS PAR SA MAJESTÉ, RÉTABLIS À PARIS EN L'ANNÉE MDCCXVI[1]

During the summer the troupe played at the Fair of Saint-Laurent.

Riccoboni's programme included a number of revivals, and in addition *Arlequin Sauvage* (1721) and *Timon le Misanthrope*, by Delisle. Later on he presented Marivaux's *Arlequin poli par l'Amour*, *La Surprise de l'Amour*, *Le Jeu de l'Amour et du Hasard*, *Les Fausses Confidences*, etc.

By this time the Italian comedy had become almost entirely French comedy, despite the names of Harlequin, Columbine, and Silvia, and certain traditions preserved intact in Pasquin and Harlequin. However, the Italian interpretation was still in force, in spirit at least, for it is evident that the inimitable fantasy and mimicry of the *commedia dell'arte* offered the only really suitable medium for bringing out the full flavour of the subtlety and supple wit of a dramatist like Marivaux.

Riccoboni left us his very valuable *Histoire du théâtre italien*, from which quotations have already been given elsewhere.

From 1716 to 1744 Riccoboni's company was composed as follows:

Men

Lelio (Lover)	LUIGI RICCOBONI
Mario (Second Lover)	BALETTI
Arlequin	VICENTINI, called THOMASSIN; later played by BERTINAZZI (1741)
Trivelin	PIETRO FRANCESCO BIANCOLELLI, called DOMINIQUE
Pantaloon	P. ALBORGHETTI (1744)
The Doctor	F. MATERAZZI; later played by BONAVENTURA BENOZZI (1732)
Scapin	J. BISSONI
Scaramouche	GIACOPO RAGUZZINI

[1] "Hostel of the Comedians Ordinary to the King, maintained by his Majesty, re-established in Paris in the year 1716."

Women

Flaminia (First Inamorata) . . .	Elena Balletti (wife of Riccoboni)
Silvia (Second Inamorata) . . .	Gianetta Benozzi (who married Balletti, or Mario)
Violette (Soubrette)	Margarita Rusca (wife of T.-A. Visentini)
The Songstress (Isabelle)	Ursula Astori
A Singer	Fabio Sticotti (husband of Ursula Astori)

Changes and additions in the Women's Rôles (1720–62)

Columbine	Teresa Biancolelli (1739)
Coraline	Carolina Veronese (1744)
Camille	Antonia Veronese (1744); also the following: Elisabeth Constantini (1730); Mademoiselle Belmont (1730); Mademoiselle Dehesse (1730); Maria Labora, of Mézières (1734), who became Madame Riccoboni; Colombe (1762); Madame Favart (1749); Madame Bognioli (1758)
Angélique	Mademoiselle Foulquier, called Catinon (1753); Mesdames Vesian, Bacelli, Zamarini, Billoni

The Italian Comedy and the Opéra-Comique (1756–62)

By the middle of the eighteenth century the art of improvisation had begun to deteriorate, and it became increasingly difficult to find actors sufficiently skilled in this *genre* of acting. As a consequence songs and music were introduced more frequently into the performances and soon took precedence over the dialogue. The Italian comedy in Paris then began to give comic operas and original plays written by Alainval, Laffichart, Legrand, Boissy, Delisle, Favart, Sedaine, Desportes, Lanoue, Fuselier, Anseaume, and Vadé. As time went on the French actors in the company outnumbered the Italians, and the Italian language was used on the stage but rarely.

In 1762 the Opéra-Comique (the erstwhile theatre of the Saint-Laurent Fair) was amalgamated with the Italian comedy. The resulting company was the last authentic Italian troupe to play in France, and the parts were distributed as follows:

Men

Harlequin	Carlin Bertinazzi
Scapin	Ciavarelli
Pantaloon	Colalto
First Lover	Baletti
Second Lover	Lejeune

Comic Lover	CHAMPVILLE
Valet	DEHESSE
Colas	CAILLOT
Cassandre	LARUETTE
Women	
Soubrette and Inamorata	MADAME FAVART
In the other *rôles* were	MESDAMES RIVIÈRE, DESGLAND, BAGNIOLI, LARUETTE, BÉRARD, BEAUPRÉ, CARLIN, and MANDEVILLE

In 1779 Grimm had occasion to write:

> After the new Italian comedy had obtained permission not to give any more Italian plays it replaced them by comedies from its former French repertory which had been entirely abandoned since its union with the Opéra-Comique. All our foreign actors have been dismissed with the exception of Carlin Bertinazzi and his understudy, who continue to play their Harlequin *rôles* in the French pieces.

In 1780 the theatre of the Italian comedy assumed the name of Théâtre des Italiens, although there was not a single Italian actor left in the cast.

CARLO GOZZI

In Italy Count Gozzi was the most ardent and ingenious partisan of the *commedia dell'arte*. As he described himself he was the champion of "the four masks of the old improvised comedy which our various cities have chosen to be their representatives."

Gozzi was greatly interested in assembling Sacchi's company, and he gave it all the encouragement and inspiration he could. He next set about writing scenario-plays of the kind used in former days, and he filled them plentifully with his caustic and malicious wit. Nor did he ever miss an opportunity in any of his prologues to attack and censure those actors who played without masks and learned their *rôles* by heart. It was not long before his barbed tongue and lively wit had completely captured the favour of the public, and his work became so popular that the theatre where the plays of his rival, the 'reformer' Goldoni, were being presented, was almost entirely deserted.

The scenarios Gozzi wrote for Sacchi's troupe were replete with material upon which the actor could draw and which he could elaborate at will without hampering the freedom of his improvisation in any way. Gozzi himself called his scenarios "children's stories," for he had a special fondness for fables and fairy-tales, which he embroidered with bits of poetry, burlesque, and drama, as in *L'Amore delle Tre Melarance*, *Il Corvo*, *Il Re Cervo*, *Turandot*, *La Donna Serpente*, *I Pitocchi Fortunati*, *Il Mostro Turchino*, *L'Angellino Belverde*, *La Zobeide*, *Zeim Re de' Genj*, etc.

At the height of his success Gozzi had the misfortune to become infatuated with Teodora Ricci, an actress entirely devoid of talent, and his passion proved his ruin. The trouble started when the other actresses in the troupe, who had far more ability than Ricci, grew jealous of her. Then the ageing Sacchi was smitten, and actually succeeded in becoming Gozzi's rival. Presently the rest of the actors took a hand in the affair, and a quarrel ensued, which terminated in the dissolution of the whole company.

It is curious to see what little humour or acumen Gozzi displayed as regards this episode. Had he been as intelligent as one would expect of such an author, he would perhaps have recognized the figure he cut as a lover, and he might, in consequence, have written a highly amusing scenario about himself. But he remained blissfully blind to the error of his ways and persisted obstinately in his obsession for the mediocre Ricci. He proceeded to place his creative gifts whole-heartedly at her disposal, with the result that the plays he contrived for her proved to be as insipid and artificial as the worst Goldoni ever wrote. Later on, however, he partially retrieved himself by writing a number of satires full of his old-time wit and zest.

GOLDONI

M. Moreau gives an interesting description of the gay Venetian playwright in his preface to the *Mémoires de Goldoni* (1822). He tells us that

> Goldoni began his career with little else but a good education and no sense of responsibility. His forbears had squandered the family fortune in unsuccessful theatrical ventures, and he himself finally turned to the theatre after attempting various other professions. He was a nomad even when he wrote and practised the dramatic art, travelling from town to town as had his father before him in practising medicine. He supported his wife and mother, and so was constrained to accept a pittance from theatrical directors, who exploited his fertile mind without mercy. Goldoni wrote more than a hundred and fifty plays, comedies and scenarios included.

This portrait of Goldoni allows us to understand him much better and excuse his more obvious shortcomings. The combination of financial pressure and an over-facile pen was often responsible for a tone of staleness and banality in his work. His comedies are instinct with a promise of great talent, which is never fulfilled. Goldoni's work must be studied and condensed before his persuasive, if slightly tarnished, charm can be appreciated. Nevertheless he always offers a pleasing blend of humour, truth, and sentiment, and there are often entire scenes of excellent comedy in his plays, evincing a gift for detail and naturalness.

Carlo Gozzi was at all times violently antagonistic to Goldoni. He overwhelmed him with epigrams and satirical sonnets which, unfortunately for Goldoni, were models of elegance and biting conciseness. Goldoni was at a disadvantage in not knowing the fluent phrases and expressions of the Florentine dialect, and Gozzi never lost an opportunity to ridicule his rival and expose his solecisms. Gozzi succeeded in prejudicing the literary academy of the Granelleschi against his victim, and Goldoni was thenceforth accused of having betrayed the *commedia dell'arte* and the national characters, which were still so much alive in Italy.

Goldoni never uttered a word in his *Mémoires* referring to the martyrdom to which he had been subjected and which, undoubtedly, was in part the motive for his eventual removal to France. His reticence is a fine trait, and it is fitting that he be given credit for it. The Italians considered Goldoni's style too Gallic to suit their taste, but this quality naturally made him all the more acceptable to the French. The Italian comedy produced several of his plays in Paris in 1762. Goldoni received a pension from the Court, and lived in the French capital until his death.

Troupes playing à l'impromptu in Italy in the Eighteenth Century

One of the most celebrated troupes of the eighteenth century was that managed by Sacco. It was especially known for its brilliant performances of pieces based on Gozzi's scenarios. The best actor of the company was Darbes, who made a great reputation for himself in the part of Pantaloon. Darbes had previously played in Goldoni comedies, and had at one time been associated with the Lapy troupe in the theatre of Sant' Angelo in 1769. Goldoni wrote chiefly for the Imer or Medebach troupe.

In addition to the two troupes just mentioned, in 1747 there appeared a company directed by a certain Domenico Giamelli, in which Rospizio de Antoniis and Elisabetha d'Affisio attracted considerable attention in their respective *rôles* of Pantaloon and Inamorata. There was also a troupe which played in the San Carlino Theatre in 1753, with Francisco Barese in the ever-popular mask of Pulcinella. Other troupes of the period worth mentioning were those of Edoardo Scarpetta, Pellandi, and Andrea Patriarchi, who had with him Giovanni Androux and his wife and daughter. With the exception of Sacco's company, all the others played regular comedies as well as those improvised from scenarios.

The Troupe of Improvisators at Vienna (Eighteenth Century)

As mentioned in an earlier chapter, there was a troupe of improvisators in Vienna during the reigns of Leopold, Joseph, and Charles IV. They played in the Italian manner, and adopted the traditional *rôles* of the *commedia dell'arte*, making new versions of some of them to suit the taste of the Austrian public. The masks were distributed in the following order:

The Doctor	WEISTERN
The Old Man *rôles*	HEINDRICH
Pantaloon	LEINHAUS
Hanswurst (a variant of Pulcinella) . . .	PREHAUSER
Il Bernadone (character not known in France)	
Il Burtino (a sort of Harlequin and Brighella) .	KURZ
The Village Idiot (a sort of Pedrolino) . . .	GOTTLIEB
Women's *rôles*	LA NUTIN ELINZONIN LA SCHWAGERIN

XI

The Marionettes

THE marionettes are so ancient in origin that there is no way of telling whether they were developed from the characters of the *Atellanæ* or *vice versa.*

The same question arises in the case of the *commedia dell'arte.* Lamia, the African ghoul, and Manducus, the ancient ogre, came into existence originally as marionettes; then Manducus was taken over into the Italian comedy and developed into the Captain. Burattino, originally one of the *commedia dell'arte* masks, became the leading character in the marionette theatre; so much so, in fact, that by the end of the sixteenth century all marionettes operated by strings and a wire were called *burattini*, instead of *bagatelli* or *fantoccini*, as they had been known up to that time. The marionette theatre developed parallel with the Italian comedy, and it is very probable that they continually borrowed scenarios and masks from each other.

At the Civic Museum in Venice are to be seen all the traditional characters very curiously costumed and stylized. They have an alert, uncanny look about them as though they were ready at any moment to dance merrily at the end of their strings, were they to be released from their glass sepulchres. Indeed, is not the marionette theatre nowadays the last vestige of the *commedia dell'arte* ?

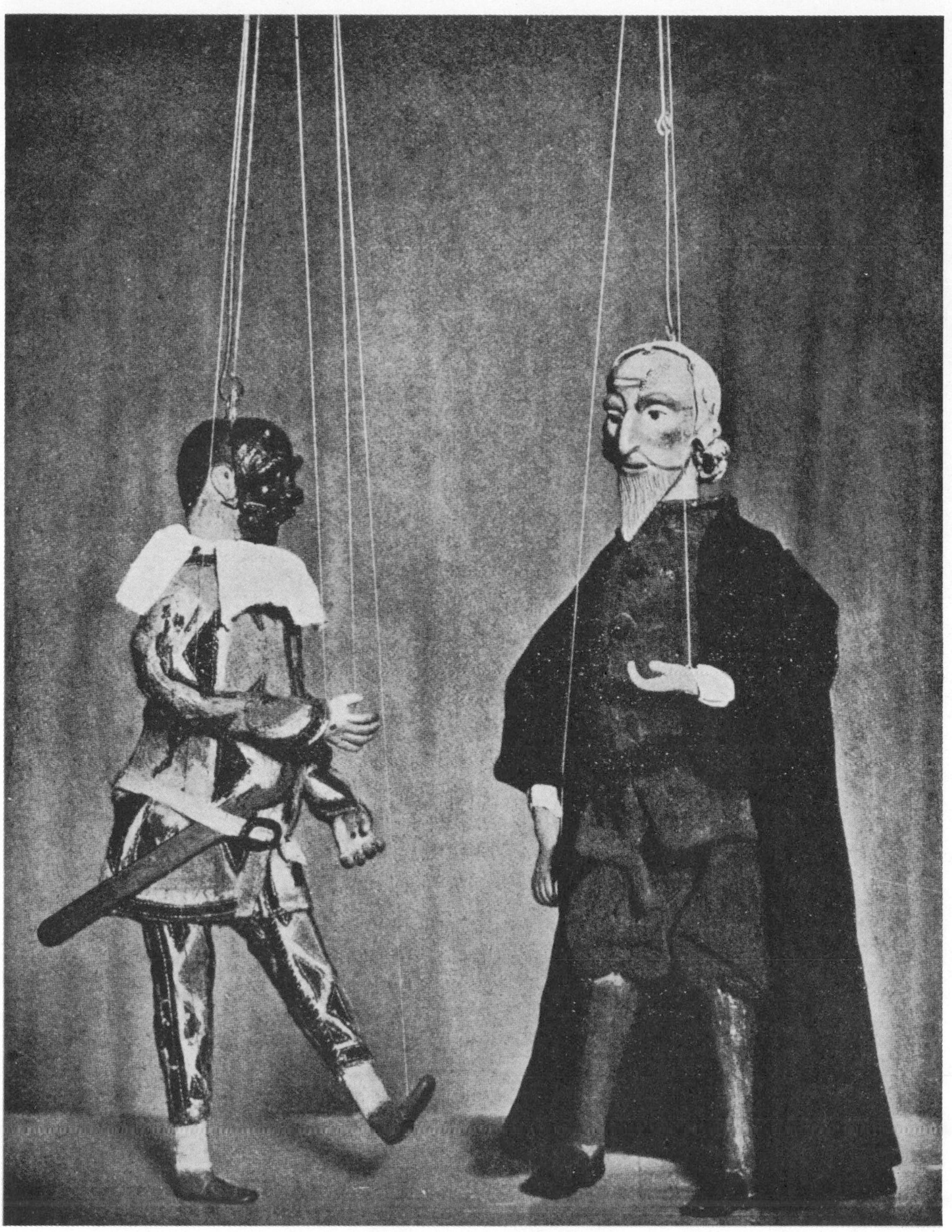

HARLEQUIN AND PANTALOON
Marionettes in the Civic Museum, Venice
Photo Anderson

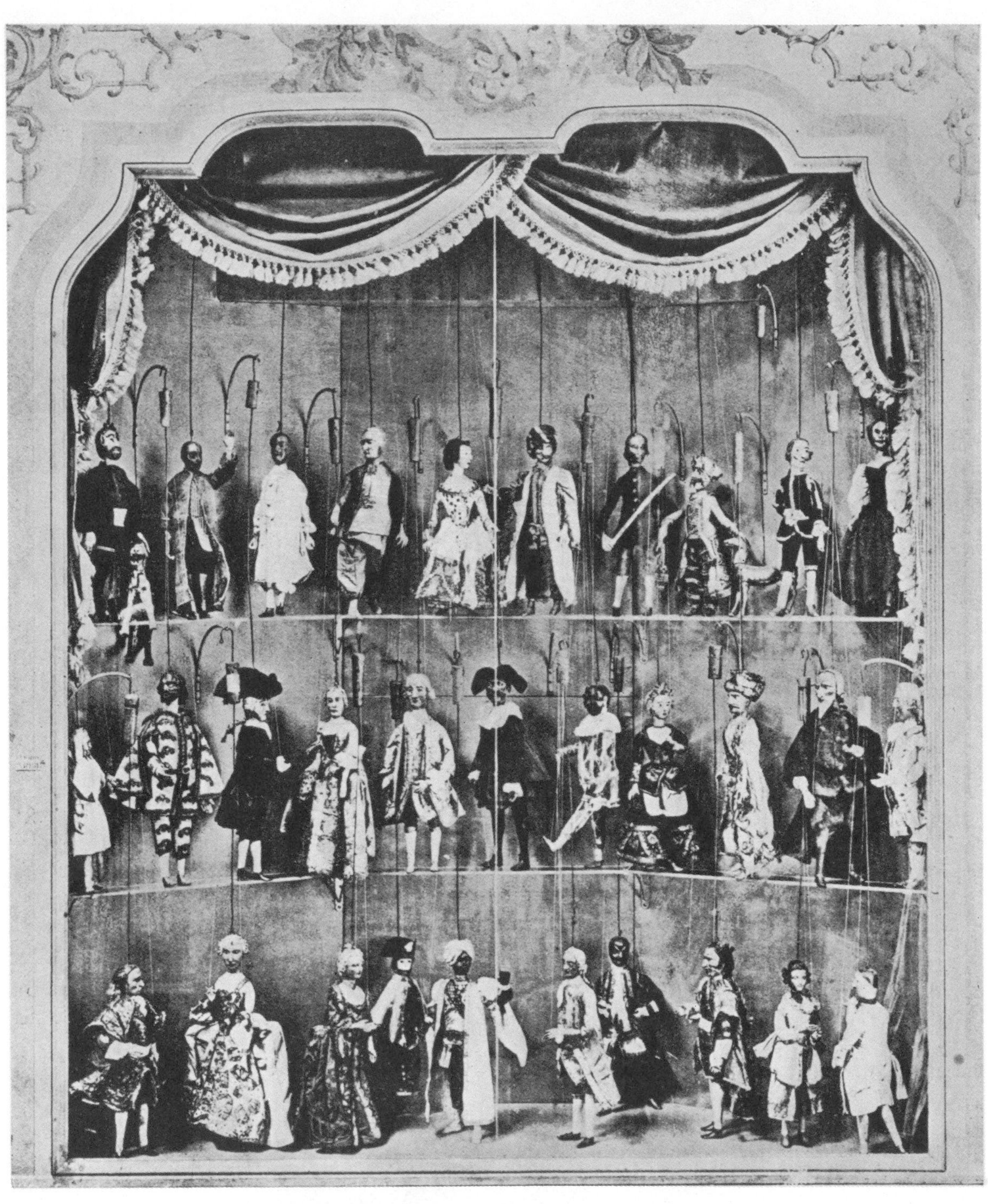

Marionettes in the Civic Museum, Venice
Eighteenth century

XII

Harlequin, his Ancestors, and his Family

TRIVELLINO, TRUFFALDINO, GUAZZETO, ZACCAGNINO, BAGATINO

Harlequin

IF Bergamo were ever to raise a statue to her illustrious son Harlequin the only appropriate material for it would be gutta-percha. Bronze and marble would be too rigid a medium for this quaint, paradoxical figure, this Harlequin who was both sluggish and full of bounce, impressionable and springy, a clown with a long reach and yet remarkably compact in person. Only rubber could do him justice in effigy, only rubber could receive the impress of his subtle spirit, created by the gods in a moment of incontrollable fantasy and bred by men of bold imagination.

HARLEQUIN (ABOUT 1577)
Possibly this is the actor Simone da Bologna
Detail from an engraving in the "Recueil Fossard"

Of all the traditional characters Harlequin is the most strongly individualized and yet the most enigmatic. Although he is one of the youngest members of the noted family, he seems in many ways far older than his own ancestors. He was called by many names, and no one can say which was rightfully and originally his. He remains intangible, for he is without doubt of divine essence, if not, indeed, the god Mercury himself, patron of merchants, thieves, and panders. These last, the *lenones* of the ancient satiric plays, wore the same sort of motley as Harlequin. It was their master's livery signifying poverty as well as "neither fish nor flesh," which indicates the diverse and dubious resources of Mercury's *protégés*. The *lenones*, or 'flat-feet,' of the Roman theatre are plainly Harlequin's ancestors, and likewise the phallophores who, their faces blackened with soot, played the parts of foreign slaves. By the same token Harlequin's mask was black, and some of the oldest documents on the subject sometimes show him wearing a phallus. But who can penetrate the mystery that is Harlequin? He has much of the divine in him, and, like all the gods, it has pleased him to remain aloof throughout the centuries which have enveloped him in a cloud of legends. The droll and whimsical god, the gliding, supple, and black Harlequin makes one think of a dolphin, appearing and disappearing in the sea, bounding and turning and capering. He is always volatile and elusive. Not until the end of the sixteenth century does he take definite shape.

THE IMPROVISATOR TRISTANO MARTINELLI
Lyons, 1601

Arlecchino, transformed into a citizen of Bergamo, made his appearance at the time when the ancient gods emerged from the fertile Latin soil. The town of Bergamo is built in the form of an amphitheatre, on the hills of the Brentano valley. It is said that the lower town produced nothing but fools and dullards, whereas the upper town was the home of nimble-wits. Therefore, Harlequin, having been born in the lower part, was a simpleton from the beginning, while Brighella, the other Zanni, his tyrannical crony, was born on the heights and was extremely crafty. It must be added, however, that Harlequin himself claims both the upper and the lower town as his birthplace.

Harlequin proved himself the prince of numskulls from birth, but his stupidity was intermittently relieved by flashes of shrewd wit. If the brain of the reincarnated Harlequin was woefully lacking in grey matter when he first reappeared in the Middle Ages, his body, nevertheless, has at all times been instinct with all the humour of the world.

Cicero seems to be describing his art when he said, referring to a mime of his day, that "even his very body began to laugh."[1]

Certain engravings of the sixteenth and seventeenth centuries show Harlequin leaping and dancing, walking on stilts, making love to an Inamorata, or executing *cascate*,

HARLEQUIN AS A GLASSWARE DEALER
From the "Recueil Fossard" (about 1577)

devilish capers and backward somersaults. At other times he is represented as expressing his personality and feelings in striking poses.

Riccoboni wrote that

> The acting of the Harlequins before the seventeenth century was nothing but a continual play of extravagant tricks, violent movements, and outrageous rogueries. He was at once insolent, mocking, inept, clownish, and emphatically ribald. I believe that he was extraordinary agile, and he seemed to be constantly in the air; and I might confidently add that he was a proficient tumbler.

The *Recueil Fossard*,[2] discovered by M. Agne Beijer in Sweden, gives additional proof of this acrobatic side of the acting of the early Harlequins.

There is a highly curious document in the Bibliothèque Nationale in Paris on the subject of Harlequin during the Renaissance. It is called *Compositions de rhétorique de M. don Arlequin*,[2] and it is embellished with drawings of unusual interest. The text

[1] "Quid enim potest tam ridiculum quam sannio esse? Qui ore vultu imitandis motibus, voce, denique corpore ridetur ipso?"—*De Oratore*.

[2] These documents have been published in reproduction in the same volume (Duchartre et Van Buggenhoudt, Paris, 1928).

is very amusing, and the extracts given below are typical. The wit of this Harlequin —Tristano Martinelli, the most celebrated of the early Harlequins—suggests and anticipates Dominique (Biancolelli), the foremost Harlequin of the seventeenth century. The document stands as proof that as early as the second half of the sixteenth century a keen and fantastic humour shone through the stupidity and grossness of the Renaissance Harlequin that Riccoboni depicted.

AL MAGNANIMO

Monsieur, Monsieur Henry de Bourbon, first burgher of Paris, chief of all the Messieurs of Lyons, Conte de Mommeillan, Chastellan of the fort of Santa Catarina, Governor of La Bressa, Pretender to the Marches of Saluces, Admiral of the Sea of Marseilles, Master of half of the bridge of Avignon, and good friend of the master of the other half,[1] Sovereign Councillor at the Council of War against the Plamontese, Most Gracious Ring-taker,[2] Captain General of France and of Navarre, Liberal Dispenser of Cannonades, the Terror of Savoyard and Spaniard, Colonel of the Soldiers in Savoy, Secret Secretary of the most Secret Cabinet of Madame Maria de' Medici, Queen of the Louvre, Grand Treasurer of the Italian Comedians, and Prince more worthy than any other to be engraved upon a medal, so much desired by me and many another;

HAIL
and to
MADAMA
Madame his wife, the same.

(*Page* 5)

Ha Reine, Colona	ROY Medaglia
Quantunque donné moy	per la morbin
Autrement m'en iray cert	in Itaglia.[3]

(*Page* 25)

ET HARLEQUIN DONNERA A. V. M.

Un mezo (C) Niente
Con un (O) Niente entiero
Accompagnato con un (R E).[4]

(*Page* 4)

Quantumque la chaine et la medaglia
Pour la monstrer à ces messieurs d' Itaglia.[5]

[1] Harlequin's humour consists in telling the King that he is his own good friend, for at that time both banks of the Rhone lay within the Kingdom of France.

[2] Doubtless referring to the game of skill in which the player on horseback removes rings with a lance or sword.—TRANSLATOR.

[3] "Ah, Queen and King, when will you give me the chain and medal? Otherwise [if you don't give them to me] I shall go back to Italy."

[4] "And Harlequin will give your Majesty a half (C) of *niente*, or nothing, with an (O) quite entire, accompanied by a (RE), or king."

By reading the letters in parentheses vertically the word *core* may be deciphered, which doubtless means *cuore*, or 'heart.' We may infer, then, that Harlequin will give *niente*, or nothing, if not his heart, in exchange for the medal. This kind of anagram is characteristic of the taste of the Renaissance.

[5] "And when [will you give me] the chain and medal to show these gentlemen in Italy?"

The medal and chain, or necklace, that Harlequin keeps asking for so facetiously constituted a present which was greatly coveted (such presents were often of solid gold) in those days, especially as it was a token of royal satisfaction. We find a proof of this, for example, in a letter written by Maria de' Medici at Fontainebleau on May 26, 1613, to G. B. Andreini: "And I shall have ready the golden chain which has been promised you. I wish to give it to you with my own hands, without trusting it to any of my subordinates, for I know how ill-disposed you are toward any intermediaries. . . ." (See also p. 94.)

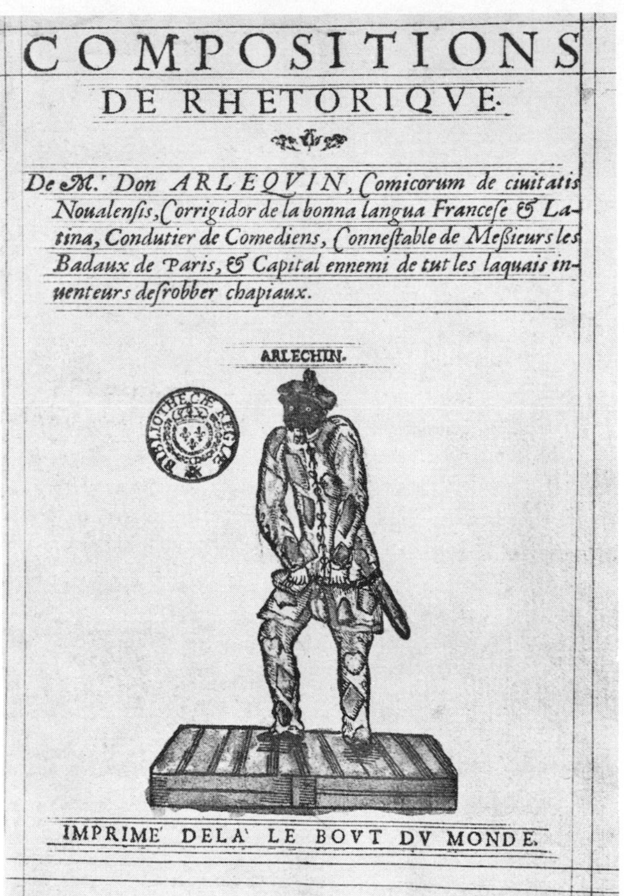

COMPOSITIONS
DE RHETORIQVE.

De M.r Don ARLEQVIN, Comicorum de ciuitatis Noualensis, Corrigidor de la bonna langua Francese & Latina, Condutier de Comediens, Connestable de Messieurs les Badaux de Paris, & Capital ennemi de tut les laquais inuenteurs desrobber chapiaux.

ARLECHIN.

IMPRIME DELA LE BOVT DV MONDE.

Lyons, 1601

25

LIVRE SECOND
DE RHETORIQVE.

Ha Rey & Reina donnez me la pesanta
Si vous voli que iour & nuict ie chanta.

48 COMP. DE RHETOR.

A Dieu mon Roy, & Reine, & mes Amis
Pour vous obeyr ie m'en vay a Paris.

Lyons, 1601

(*Page* 48)

A Dieu mon Roy, et Reine et mes Amis
Pour vous obeyr ie m'en vay à Paris.[1]

SCENE FROM THE COMMEDIA DELL' ARTE ABOUT 1577
From the " Recueil Fossard "

(*Page* 57)

SONGE

Ie me suis insomniato ce matin,
Qu'un fachin d'importanza
Me tiroit par la panza,
Et mi disoit, Monsieur Arlequin,
Habebis medagliam et colonam.
Ie respondis en dormant,
Si non me burlat opinio :
Piaccia à Iddio
Di farci vedere il matura parto
Di queste pregne speranze.
Per la mia foy en songeant au guadagno
Io parlo Toscolagno.[2]

SONET IN OTTAVA RIMA

Vient, void et vince, el grand Cesar Roman,
Casi ha faict Henri roy de Bourbon
Qu'a prins la Bressa, le Fort, et Mommeillan
Plus facilment, que manger maccaron.

[1] " To God, my King, my Queen, and my Friends ; to obey you I shall go to Paris."

[2] " The Dream. I dreamed this morning that an important-looking scoundrel seized me by the paunch and said to me, ' Mr Harlequin, you shall have a medal and chain.' I answered while still asleep : ' If I am not deceived [*i.e.*, if my opinion is correct], may it please God to show us the ripe fruit of these splendid hopes ! ' By my faith, in dreaming of my gain I speak Tuscan."

HARLEQUIN

Engraving by Giuseppe-Maria Mitelli (1634–1718)

A Moi, qui suis Arlequin Savojon [1]
Me semble bien qu'Henry à grand reson
De far' que Carlo li tienna parole
De luy rendre Saluse et Carmagnole.

Que venga la verole
A son conseil, qui l'a mal conseillé,
Qu'est causa qu' Arlequin est ruiné.

Ah sacra Majesta,
Fais moy doner tout astheure pour streina
La medaglia, attachée à una grosse chaina.[2]

There are several aspects of the foregoing document which make it notably important as a commentary on the customs of the time. The author is not named; he is simply "Arlequin" and speaks to King Henri IV in the Harlequin tongue in the manner he would ordinarily use in improvising on the stage. The *Compositions de rhétorique* is, of necessity, later than August 11, 1600, on which date Henri IV declared war against Charles-Emmanuel, Duke of Savoy, and took possession of "Mommeillan plus facilement que manger maccaron." [3]

In spite of this internal evidence, Martinelli, who is assumed to be the author of the tract, belonged more distinctly to the Renaissance than to the seventeenth century. The costume he wore was without doubt in use during the second half of the sixteenth century, and the interpretation he gave the character as well as the language he employed belong to the same epoch. This is substantiated, moreover, by the engravings in the *Recueil Fossard.*

It would seem, then, that although Dominique, the Harlequin who was so beloved of Louis XIV, contributed a vast amount of wit to the character which he impersonated, he rigorously abstained from altering the traditions of the Harlequin *rôle*. For in the sixteenth century Harlequin was supposed to possess above all a capacity for physical drollery, but he was a grotesque combination of other sorts of virtues and contrasting vices. Whatever else is characteristic of Harlequin, he is invariably resilient in both body and soul. And so he appears in the *Recueil Fossard*, in which he is given a place of primary importance.

In one comedy Harlequin, the valet of the miser Pantaloon, is going over his accounts, and each time that he comes to a nought he says, "You have no tail, but I'll give you one and make you a nine." Pantaloon revises the memorandum and murmurs aside, "You have a tail now, but you won't have one for long."

[1] It had always been thought in accordance with the data found in archives that Martinelli was born in Mantua; here, however, he himself states that he is from Savoy. Perhaps he did so because he had played at Turin before the Duke of Savoy a short time before, in 1599. Or perhaps his statement is intended as a witticism with reference to Henri IV, who was not on good terms with the Duke, having in fact just taken Montmélian from him. Or it may be simply that Martinelli actually was, or else considered himself, a Savoyard. In a letter dated 1613 Martinelli says that he is "de civitate Novalensis." There is a village of Novalaise in French Savoy, and also a village with the similar name of Novalesa in Piedmont, which was under the protection of the Duke of Savoy at that period.

[2] "Sonnet in Ottava Rima. The great Roman Cæsar came, saw, and conquered. Thus did Henri, King of Bourbon, and took La Bresse, the Fort, and Montmélian more easily than eating macaroni. It seems to me, Harlequin, who am Savoyen [of Savoy], that Henri is quite right in making Charles [Emannuel I] keep his word and surrender Saluces and Carmagnole. May the pox take his Council, which gave him bad counsel, which is the reason that Harlequin is ruined. Oh, Sacred Majesty, cause the medal with a gold chain attached, to be given me as a present immediately."

[3] "More easily than eating macaroni."

Seventeenth century

In spite of Harlequin's apparent cunning at figures, he is so absent-minded that he searches everywhere for the donkey on which he is mounted, like the old woman who is always hunting for the spectacles perched on her own forehead. And if we pass

ZANY AND HARLEQUIN ABOUT 1577
Note that the word 'Zany' is used as a proper name and not as a *rôle*.
Detail from an engraving in the "Recueil Fossard"

over directly to the eighteenth century we find Harlequin much the same booby that he always was.

Marmontel [1] wrote:

> His character is a mixture of ignorance, *naïveté*, wit, stupidity, and grace. He is both a rake and an overgrown boy with occasional gleams of intelligence, and his mistakes and clumsiness often have a wayward charm. His acting is patterned on the lithe, agile grace of a young cat, and he has a superficial coarseness which makes his performances all the more amusing. He plays the *rôle* of a faithful valet, always patient, credulous, and greedy. He is eternally amorous, and is constantly in difficulties either on his own or on his master's account. He is hurt and comforted in turn as easily as a child, and his grief is almost as comic as his joy.

[1] Jean-François Marmontel (1723–99). Born at Bort, near Gaillon. Known for his *Mémoires*.—TRANSLATOR.

There is another excellent description of Harlequin's personality to be found in the *Calendrier historique des théâtres* (1751):

> His character is that of an ignorant valet, fundamentally *naïve*, but nevertheless making every effort to be intelligent, even to the extent of seeming malicious. He is a glutton and a poltroon, but faithful and energetic. Through motives of fear or cupidity he is always ready

From the "Recueil Fossard"

> to undertake any sort of rascality and deceit. He is a chameleon which takes on every colour. He must excel in impromptu, and the first thing that the public always asks of a new Harlequin is that he be agile, and that he jump well, dance, and turn somersaults.

The primary point in the evolution of Harlequin's personality from the Renaissance to the eighteenth century is simply a change in the ratio between his physical and mental *esprit*. Although his companions were types drawn from society in general and subsequently standardized, the subtle and foolish Arlechino—"always in the air"—seems a strange personification of the fancy. He embodies a whole gamut of the imagination, now delicate, now offensive, comic or melancholy, sometimes lashed into a frenzy of madness. He is the unwitting and unrecognized creator of a new form of poetry, essentially muscular, accented by gestures, punctuated by somersaults, enriched with philosophic reflexions and incongruous noises. Indeed, Harlequin was the first poet of acrobatics and unseemly noises.

HARLEQUIN'S MASK AND COSTUME

The oldest-known costumes of Trivelin and Harlequin—for they are one and the same person—were very different from the decorative dress with which most of us are familiar. There were varicoloured patches, darker than the background of the costume,

HARLEQUIN THE JEWEL-MERCHANT

Arlequin Empereur de la Lune

HARLEQUIN AS DIANA
Second half of the seventeenth century

sewn here and there on the breeches and the long jacket laced in front. A bat and a wallet hung from his belt. His head was shaved in the same manner as the ancient mimes'. His soft cap was in the mode of Charles IX, of François I, or of Henri II; it was almost always decorated with the tail of a rabbit, hare, or fox, or sometimes with a tuft of feathers. This attire had much definite character in itself, and might be considered a conventionalized and ironic treatment of the dress of a tatterdemalion. It was not until the seventeenth century that the patches took the form of blue, red, and green triangles which were arranged in a symmetrical pattern and joined together by a slender yellow braid. At the end of the seventeenth century the triangles became diamond-shaped lozenges, the jacket was shortened, and a double-pointed hat took the place of the toque. The costume of the Harlequin of the Renaissance illustrates in general the later garb of the character, but there are many details about both which are still shrouded in mystery.

Sand observes with regard to the traditional adornment on Harlequin's toque: " This animal tail is another tradition from antiquity. A fox's brush or a hare's ears were attached to anyone who was the butt of ridicule." In the same connexion Goldoni tells us in his *Mémoires* that

> While going through Harlequin's country I watched everywhere for some trace of this comic character who was the delight of the Italian theatre. I discovered neither black faces nor small eyes, nor any of those ludicrous costumes in four colours ; but I did see hare-scuts with which the peasants of that district still decorate their hats.

One wonders whether the Bergamask people wore these tails in memory of Harlequin or if, on the contrary, Harlequin pinned the hare-scut on his toque in accordance with the tradition of the country. The second theory is more plausible. As for Harlequin's mask, to which Goldoni refers, there was scarcely any noticeable change in it during the entire time from the Renaissance to the eighteenth century. There is a story to the effect that Michelangelo restored an ancient satyr mask, which he adapted for Harlequin's use. But why it should be black is still another question. Perhaps it is because the ancient Harlequin was a phallophore ; and, inasmuch as some of the phallophores of the ancient theatre played the parts of African slaves, it is thought that Harlequin might be their direct descendant.

Another hypothesis is that there was a negro in Bergamo who served as model for the character, but this is scarcely probable. Goldoni offers yet another explanation of the colour of the mask, which is equally far-fetched. He says, " His tan mask (it is deeper than tan) represents the complexion of the inhabitants of those mountains burned by the fierce sun." It was also said in Italy that one Harlequin wore a dark mask to hide an enormous wen under his left eye, but it is an odd coincidence that the traditional mask has a wart on the cheek. When all is said and done, none of these conjectures is very convincing.

Harlequin's authentic mask [1] consisted of a half-mask and a black chin-piece. The eyebrows and beard were bushy and covered with stiff bristles. The forehead was strongly lined with wrinkles which accentuated the slightly quizzical arch of the eyebrows. The eyes were tiny holes beneath, and the *ensemble* gave a curious expression of craftiness, sensuality, and astonishment which was both disturbing and alluring. The huge wen under the eye, the wart, and the black colour completed the impression of something savage and fiendish. The mask suggested a cat, a satyr, and the sort of negro that the Renaissance painters portrayed. Indeed, the potentialities latent in the mask of Harlequin are various and without end.

According to M. C. Mic, " the Harlequin of the sixteenth and seventeenth centuries cannot be distinguished from the other Zanni except by his costume ; nor was the multicoloured garb his exclusive possession." M. Mic then offers in support of his assertion the copperplate engraving reproduced on p. 179 of *La Commedia dell' arte* in which Harlequin appears dressed in white. This proof seems insufficient for two reasons : first, that the figures portrayed are buffoons in the general sense ; and, second, that the picture itself belongs to a class of engravings the documentary value of which

[1] With the exception of those representing Martinelli, the oldest woodcuts and copperplate engravings reproduced in the present volume show Harlequin's mask so clearly that, seemingly, it is impossible to draw any other conclusion.

is uncertain and scarcely worth considering. At least, that is the opinion of those who have collected engravings of this kind or who have given them any study.

I am obliged to take issue with M. Mic again when he tells us that, "however, in Italy this character [Harlequin] was never more popular than the other Zannis." His observation seems somewhat of a paradox, at least so far as the sixteenth century is concerned, in view of the evidence provided by the *Recueil Fossard*, in which Harlequin is given a place of such great importance, as well as by the *Compositions de rhétorique*. Both documents are among the oldest known on the subject of the *commedia dell' arte*, and in any case belong to a period when the Italian troupes were only temporarily in France—that is to say, when the players were not subject to foreign influence as they were later on. It would seem very strange indeed that Martinelli, the favourite of Italian Courts who styled himself Dominus Arlequinorum (and therefore of a numerous race), should have triumphed for more than fifty years in the *rôle* of this Harlequin who was "never more popular than the other Zannis." And it would have been equally strange if Alberto Ganassa, the earliest known Harlequin, should, as director of the troupe in which he played, have chosen to interpret a mere secondary character.

ANOTHER ACCOUNT OF THE ORIGIN OF THE CHARACTER, COSTUME, AND MASK OF HARLEQUIN

The uncertainty surrounding Harlequin's origin, coupled with his immense popularity, has always drawn pilgrims to Bergamo in a vain attempt to probe the mystery. Dominique Durandy gives in his *Poussières d'Italie* a very curious version of the Harlequin question taken from a number of works on the subject preserved in the library of Bergamo, which he sums up as follows:

> Toward 1356 a French lord, the Count of Louvence, wishing to escape from the disturbances of his native land after Crécy and Poitiers, came to seek refuge in the Vale Bretano. He had with him a servitor charged with a thousand crimes, astute, shrewd, and uncouth of face, but insolent beyond all telling. This scarcely admirable person acted as porter and cobbler, and upon his door was hung the jocular and revelatory sign:
>
> "*Nacqui ad Arles, città della Provenza,—E pugnai Giovanotti à Povitiers:—Poi sazio di rapina et di licenzo,—Corsi à tentar fortuna altro sartiero—Ed offertomi al comte Lovenza—Quì il seguii in qualità di sua scudero—E come per comprar s'ingegnan' tutti—Faccio d'ogni mestier purché mi frutti.*"[1]

This fellow from Arles was obviously a man possessed of few scruples, being both ingenious and bold. He committed a theft one day, was caught, wounded in the face, and haled before a court of barons. He gave his name to the judges as Pietro, but he was called more specifically Pietro the Harlequin, and was sentenced to exile.

> Dressed in baize, with a wooden sword at his side, and covered from head to foot with as many patches as there are colours in the banners of those whose justice he had defied, he was placed upon a donkey and conducted to the frontier.

[1] "I was born in Arles, a city of Provence, and, as a youth, fought at Poitiers; then, satiated with rapine and debauchery, I sought my fortune elsewhere. Having offered my services to the Count of Louvence, I followed him here in the quality of squire. Every man needs his wits to get along, and I can do anything so long as I earn my living."

Thus the *cortège* passed through the country as had been ordered, to the immense satisfaction of the mountaineers come to enjoy the unique spectacle, and such was the general hilarity that the following year a band of rowdy drunkards took it into their heads to make themselves up like Harlequin, dressing grotesquely after the fashion of the valet of the Sieur Louvence with a wooden lathe and a black mask in imitation of the bandage which the condemned man had worn over his wound.

This ' historic ' version of Harlequin's origin is, of course, very illuminating, but it leaves several essential points still to be explained. For instance, it does not throw any

Italian Comedians in Austria
Seventeenth century

light on the inherent stupidity of the early Harlequins (Pietro Harlequin was more a rake and a rogue of the Brighella type) ; nor does it tell how the conventional mask, so special, intricate, and detailed, could have been developed from just a simple bandage.

HARLEQUIN'S NAME

Several authorities have maintained that the name of Harlequin originated as a sobriquet. It is said that a leader of Parliament named Hachille du Harlay became the patron of one of the actors in an Italian troupe, who was thenceforth dubbed Harlayquino. According to Johanneau and Esmangard, the name is supposed to be the diminutive of *harle*, or *herle*, a water-bird with variegated plumage.

The spelling of the name varies considerably. In Italy it was written "Harlequino," "Arlechino," "Arlecchino," and "Harlechino"; in a letter of Raulin's in 1521 it is spelled "Herlequinus." And in the *Compositions de rhétorique* both "Arlequin" and "Arlechin" appear on the same page.

HARLEQUIN
From a Dutch engraving (eighteenth century)

In the recent work of M. L. Sainéan, *Les Sources indigènes de l'étymologie française*, there is an article on dogs *à propos* of bird and animal hunts in which we find the following curious information regarding Harlequin:

> These popular traditions taken together reveal the predominance of the dog in this legend, which is entirely natural, since the subject is a hunt. Hellequin was in consequence interpreted as *hèlechien*, literally a 'dog-caller' (*chien*, or dog, taking the form of *quin* in the Norman dialect: a 'haloo-hound' let loose on the game).
>
> The result is:
>
> (1) That a legend relating to a certain Harlequin and his family was current at the height of the Middle Ages in the north of France; in the ninth century a priest named Gauchelin was visited (according to Orderic Vital) by a vision in which a member of this family Herlechini or Herlequin figured.
>
> (2) Starting from the thirteenth century, this legend underwent a great modification in

form and content, owing to the popular conception of the tradition which tells us at times of an army on horseback and at others of a hunting party.

. . . .

Literary language has also preserved a trace of the name *arlequin* (Harlequin) preceded by *harlequin* and *herlequin*, a name of French and not Italian origin (as the initial aspirate testifies). During the Middle Ages *herlequin* had the connotation of airy sprite, a will-o'-the-wisp, a dramatic character.

This form is therefore encountered in France before 1100, thus preceding the birth of the *commedia dell' arte* with its Arlechino by four centuries and a half. The Italian name is not certified before 1593, a date which is later than the Harlequin of the comedy. The people of Paris bestowed the name of Arlequin on a zanni of the Italian comedy at the end of the sixteenth century, and the name was carried from France to Italy and elsewhere.[1]

HARLEQUIN
Eighteenth-century engraving

I quote M. Sainéan's text not because I wish to accept all of his findings without reserve, but because he sums up from an etymological standpoint everything written so far about Harlequin's name. The interest of this sort of research does not lie in trying to establish a genealogy for Sieur Harlequin, as impressive as it is futile, but rather in endeavouring to find some trace of him before the time of Ganassa, the remotest Harlequin of whom we have any record. For Ganassa was not the creator of the famous character whose mask, costume, and personality overshadow all the other valets of the Italian comedy.

M. Constant Mic has been at no pains to show his contempt not only for this kind of investigation, but for " nebulous hypotheses " on the subject of Harlequin. This learned author and friend of certainties refuses to consider that there is anything enigmatic about either the mask or name of the character.[2] " We maintain that we know Harlequin's true name," he writes : " it is Zanni and nothing else." [3] Would it not be quite like saying, " We know the real name of this stork : it is a bird " ? And, again, what is the sense of the word Zanni, which is used at different times to designate a certain *rôle* (*i.e.*, first and second Zanni), or else the name of a character ? In the *Recueil Fossard* there is a picture with the words " Zany et Harlequin " written above the heads of two characters, which would seem to indicate in good French that the name of one is Zany, and of the other Harlequin. We can only conclude, then, that in the sixteenth century a distinction

[1] Otto Driesen, *Der Ursprung des Harlekin* (Berlin, 1904). The author explains the French source of the name and its passage from the world of mythology to that of the theatre. Its final phase in connexion with the theatre (which it went through in Paris between 1571 and 1580) represents the origin of the modern *rôle* of Harlequin which was adopted in Italy and elsewhere. *Cf.* also Martin Rhulemann, *Etymologie des Wortes Harlequin und Verwandter Wörter* (Halle, 1912). (Note by L. Sainéan.)

[2] We should like to know, however, what are the source and significance of this mask which represents neither a standardization nor a caricature of a pedant or of an old miserly merchant or of a social type or of a fixed character.

[3] *Op. cit.*, p. 50, 51.

was made between a Zanni and a Harlequin, just as between a Pantaloon and a Captain, a Doctor and a Francatrippa.

THE ORIGIN OF THE NAME OF HARLEQUIN AS EXPLAINED BY THE HARLEQUIN DOMINIQUE

(*Seventeenth century*)

(GIUSEPPE DOMENICO BIANCOLELLI)

CINTHIO (*to* HARLEQUIN, *his valet*)

By the way, ever since you've been with me I've never once thought of asking you your name.

HARLEQUIN

My name is Arlechino Sbrufadelli. (CINTHIO *bursts out laughing.*) Don't make fun of me; my ancestors were people of consequence. The first Sbrufadel was a pork-butcher by profession, but so eminent that Nero refused to eat any other sausages than those he furnished. Sbrufadel sired Fregocola, a great captain. He married a woman of so lively a temperament that she bore me two days after the wedding. My father was delighted, but his joy was short-lived because of certain complaints lodged against him by the minions of the law. Whenever my father would meet an honest man in the highroad by day he would never fail to lift his hat; and if it was night he would lift not only his hat, but his cloak also. The law took exception to this excess of civility, and issued an order to arrest its progress. But my father did not tarry long; he took me up in my swaddling clothes and, after putting me in a large kettle and the rest of his goods in a basket, he fled from the town, driving before him a donkey laden with his possessions and his heir. He beat the poor animal often and cried "*Ar! Ar!*" which in the Asiatic tongue signifies "Gee up!" As he went along thus he presently perceived a man following him. This man, seeing that my father was watching him attentively, went behind a bush and squatted down [*se messe chin*]. My father thought the fellow was a constable crouching in ambush for him. My father therefore beat the donkey and cried "*Ar-le-chin!*" which means "Gee up! He's lying in wait for us." He soon perceived his error, however, for the stranger who had frightened him so terribly proved to be only a simple peasant whose bowels were loose as a result of having eaten too many grapes. And so it happened that, as I was still unnamed, my father remembered the fright he had had and the words he had cried aloud so often, "*Ar-le-chin!*" and he therefore named me Arlechino.

HARLEQUIN'S WIT

(*Seventeenth century*)

OTTAVIO (*to* HARLEQUIN, *dressed as a beggar*)

How many fathers have you?

HARLEQUIN

I have only one.

OTTAVIO (*growing angry*)

But why have you only one father?

HARLEQUIN

Well, I'm a poor man, and can't afford any more.

(HARLEQUIN *dreams of marrying* COLUMBINE. *Absent-mindedly he counts the buttons of his jerkin and says at each button :*)

Columbine loves me; she loves me not; she loves me; she loves me not; she loves me; loves me not; loves me; —not; loves me; she loves me not (*he bursts into loud weeping*).

MEZZETIN

What's the matter? Why are you blubbering like that?

HARLEQUIN (*wailing*)

She—she—she—loves me not.

MEZZETIN

Who said so?

HARLEQUIN (*pointing to his buttons*)

The button-telling.

HARLEQUIN AS DOCTOR

(*The* CAPTAIN *has a toothache.*)

HARLEQUIN (*advising him*)

Take a pinch of pepper, some garlic, and vinegar, and rub it into your arse, and you'll forget your pain in no time. (*As the* CAPTAIN *is about to depart* HARLEQUIN *adds :*) Wait a moment! I know a better remedy than that: Take an apple, cut it into four equal parts; put one of the pieces into your mouth, and hold your head in an oven until the apple is baked. I'll answer for it if that won't cure your toothache.

HARLEQUIN, EMPEROR OF THE MOON

(HARLEQUIN *has just come down out of the sky. He states that he has no desire to be in the service of a comet which has a train two hundred leagues long.*)

HARLEQUIN

If I carried her train for her Madame Comet would reach home in time for dinner, but I should still have two hundred leagues to go, and there would be no food left by the time I arrived.

THE DOCTOR

Any news from the Antipodes?

HARLEQUIN

Oh, yes. (*He reads a letter.*) The people there are very anxious to know whether they or we walk about upside down.

THE ITALIAN COMEDY

HARLEQUIN'S ACCOUNT OF HIS TRIP TO THE MOON

THE DOCTOR

How did you manage to reach the moon?

HARLEQUIN

Well, it was like this. I had arranged with three friends to go to Vaugirard to eat a goose. I was deputed to buy the goose. I went to the valley of misery, made my purchase, and set out for the place of our rendezvous. When I had arrived in the plain of Vaugirard six famished vultures appeared, seized my goose, and tried to make off with it. But I held on to its neck for dear life, and the vultures carried us both away. When we had gone rather high a new regiment of vultures came to help the others. They threw themselves upon us, and in a moment neither the goose nor I could see the peaks of the highest mountains. . . . I fell into a lake. Fortunately some fishermen had stretched their nets there, and I fell into them. The fishermen pulled me out of the water, and, taking me for a fish of some consequence, loaded me on to their shoulders and carried me as a present to the Emperor. They put me on the ground, and the Emperor and all his Court gathered round to look at me.

"What kind of a fish is that?" they said. The Emperor replied, "I believe it is an anchovy, and let him be fried for me right away just as he is." When I heard that they were going to fry me I commenced to bawl and shout. I told the Emperor of the Moon that I was not a fish, and I related how I happened to arrive in his empire. He asked me immediately, "Do you know Doctor Grazian Balouard?" "Yes, my lord." "Do you know his daughter, Isabelle?" "Yes, my lord." "Well, I want you to be my ambassador and ask him for her hand in marriage. I shall send you to Paris in an exhalation of rheumatism, catarrh, inflammation of the lungs, and other similar trifles." "But, my lord," I said, "what will you do about Doctor Grazian Balouard? He is a man of no mean merit, and a scholar who knows rhetoric, philosophy, and spelling." "The Doctor! Ha, ha!" he answered; "I'm reserving one of the best places in my empire for him."

THE DOCTOR

Really! And did he tell you what it was?

HARLEQUIN

He did. He said that about two weeks ago the Scorpion sign of the Zodiac died, and he is thinking of putting you in his place. (HARLEQUIN *goes on with his description of the moon.*)

THE DOCTOR

And how do they live up there? Do they eat in the same way as we do here?

HARLEQUIN

Yes and no.

THE DOCTOR

What do you mean by "Yes and no"?

HARLEQUIN

Allow me to explain. When the Emperor is at table he has a line of twenty men on his right, each armed with a solid gold crossbow loaded with humming-birds, pork-sausages, little pasties, and other like delicacies. On his left are twenty other men with silver syringes, solid also, one filled with Canary wine, another Muscatel Champagne, *et sic de cœteris.* When the Emperor is ready to eat he turns to the right, opens his mouth, and *bing!* . . . the crossbowman shoots a little pasty directly at him. Then when he wishes to drink he turns to the left, and *whisht!* he receives a syringeful of St Laurent wine or good Canary or Normandy, accord ng to his taste.

Engraving by G. J. Xavery (Holland, eighteenth century)

THE DOCTOR

I understand perfectly, and that seems to me a marvellous method of eating, providing that the crossbowmen take good aim.

HARLEQUIN

Faith, there was an accident once, and since then no one is hired unless his aim has been tested first.

THE DOCTOR

What accident was that, pray?

HARLEQUIN

The Emperor once wished to eat some eggs fried in black butter. A clumsy crossbowman shot one at him, but, instead of aiming at his mouth, the fellow aimed at his eye, which was in a sorry mess for a long time afterward. The doctors feared that he might lose his eye, but luckily it did not prove dangerous, and his sight was restored after wearing a plaster for several days. And that is why the dish has been called poached eggs [1] ever since.

MUSIC IN THE MOON

HARLEQUIN

The people of that country have extremely long noses, which they put to good use by fastening a catgut string from one end of the nose to the other; then, placing the left hand on the lip and holding a bow in the right hand, they play the nose for you just as we play the violin.

THE DOCTOR

That must make a queer sort of harmony.

HARLEQUIN

Faith, it surely does. It gives an enchanting nasal twang. Ovid did it to perfection, and that is why he was named Ovidius Naso.[2]

HARLEQUIN'S DESCRIPTION OF THE BURNING OF TROY

Fire once had a serious difference with Troy; one day it wanted to attack the city, but just then a great rain came to the aid of Troy. The fire was thoroughly wet and retired furious. The story ended in a great smoke.

HARLEQUIN AS DEALER IN PRECIOUS STONES

(HARLEQUIN, *the merchant, comes in wearing a conical hat and a large sword. He cannot decide which of the two inns to visit.*)

HARLEQUIN

At the Sign of the Golden Sun would be the best. Listen, my friend, I would like a little room for myself and a large one for my sword.

FIRST INNKEEPER

Be careful about going to that fellow's place, sir. He is a rogue, and will try to make you take white wine for red.

SECOND INNKEEPER

I give lodging without taking people's silver.

[1] A pun in French derived from two meanings of the word *pocher*, 'to poach' (eggs) and 'to black' (eyes).—TRANSLATOR.
[2] From *Arlequin, Empereur dans la Lune* (1684).

HARLEQUIN

You don't take their silver, eh? And what the devil do you take, then?

SECOND INNKEEPER

I take only their gold, sir.

(HARLEQUIN *informs them that he is a dealer in precious stones. He puts his valise down on the ground, and takes out of it a little coffer filled with jewels.*)

HARLEQUIN

Have you ever seen more beautiful stones than these? See how well they are cut.

FIRST INNKEEPER

What is that stone there, sir?

HARLEQUIN

That is one that I removed from the bladder of the Grand Mogul. The one next to it is a lachrymal fistula from the King of Morocco.

(*As the* TWO INNKEEPERS *lean forward to examine them* HARLEQUIN *steals the purse of one and the watch of the other and makes his exit.*)[1]

HARLEQUIN'S SHADE

(HARLEQUIN'S SHADE *overhears* SCARAMOUCHE *boast of having stolen a purse containing a hundred gold louis. He goes up to* SCARAMOUCHE, *seizes the purse, and makes off with it.*)

HARLEQUIN

Learn, my friend, that I am the shade of an ancient thief, and by right of seniority it is my place to steal the purse, and not yours, for you are only an apprentice thief.

SCARAMOUCHE (*trembling*)

Ma—Madama l'Ombra, where did you leave your body?

HARLEQUIN

My body is in the galleys. I am its shade, and it is my business to cut purses to keep it alive.

* * *

(THE DOCTOR *declares that he is going to stop up every opening in his house to prevent his wife from deceiving him.*)

HARLEQUIN

But how the devil is your house going to breathe if you stop up all the holes?

HARLEQUIN ON LOVE AND MARRIAGE

(*He pays a compliment to* EULARIA *as she issues forth from the tomb.*)

HARLEQUIN

Lovely star of the coal-bin, sweet vessel of sorrow! Alas, how grief has changed you! Your cheeks, which were once of a vermilion as beautiful as the backsides of a newly whipped child, are now so pale and gaunt that they but seem like two dried codfish. (*He offers her some*

[1] From *Protée.*

Spanish wine.) Drink, drink—but do not drink all, or you will reduce me to tears. (EULARIA *sighs after she has drunk, and* HARLEQUIN *then says* :) It is good, madame, isn't it? (*He tries to take the bottle, but* EULARIA *clings to it and drinks again. He says* :) Good-bye, bottle. . . . Madame, you are a pretty little slipper, but, without a husband's foot, you are little else than down-at-heel. Oh, if I could deserve the honour of deserving some small portion of your desserts how I would love you, how I would caress you, how I would flatter you, how I would —beat you, madame!

THE IDEAL WIFE ACCORDING TO HARLEQUIN

HARLEQUIN

The girl I seek is a young child who has not yet left her parents' wing, nor ever looked a man in the eye.

(*Another time* HARLEQUIN *is in favour of marrying a one-eyed woman.* PASQUARIEL *asks him why.*)

HARLEQUIN

She'll die sooner than any other woman because she has only one window to close.

MADRIGAL FROM HARLEQUIN TO ISABELLE

I shall steep the gracious traits with which nature has endowed you within the porringer of memory.

HARLEQUIN'S DECLARATION TO ISABELLE

HARLEQUIN

Once more, mademoiselle, allow me to tell you that I am not the first rascal that love has made tolerable. I present you my heart larded with your graces, trussed up with your charms, and steeped in your attractions. Come, mademoiselle, it will mean nothing to you and everything to me if you will exchange an amorous glance with a poor devil greedy of your youth and beauty. Gaze upon me and observe how my passion shows despite the livery I wear.

ISABELLE

You are making fun at my expense, sir!

HARLEQUIN

Alas, if you but knew how deeply I am smitten. If you'd consent, so help me, I should be foolish enough to marry you.

HARLEQUIN ON THE MALADIES OF WOMEN

ISABELLE *and* HARLEQUIN, *as doctors*; COLUMBINE, *sitting upon a commode*; THE DOCTOR

HARLEQUIN (*to* ISABELLE)

You are too young to go poking about in the spleens of women as you would in the quarry of grief.

ISABELLE

Nevertheless, the area of melancholy——

Engraving by G. J. Xavory

HARLEQUIN

You are impudent with your melancholy. When a woman nurses some grief, do you suppose that her spleen is the cause of it?

ISABELLE

What else, pray?

HARLEQUIN

All you ignoramuses think that the spleen is the seat of the trouble. Now let us talk sense, for it is the only way we can understand each other. When a young married woman has but one tapestry in her room, and if looking at the green in the weave makes her ill, or if she wants a more costly one, does she look for it in her spleen?

ISABELLE

There is no answer to that question.

HARLEQUIN

When a jealous man keeps his wife under lock and key and forbids her to see anyone will she find company in her spleen?

ISABELLE

No, assuredly.

HARLEQUIN

When a miser refuses to give his wife a carriage and jewels and other indispensable conveniences is it her spleen or her husband she consigns to the devil?

ISABELLE

Pho! Her husband, of course.

HARLEQUIN

Yet, according to you, the spleen is the basic principle of grief. We may then conclude that in order to cure grief we must first rectify the true causes of the grief. It cannot be cured by the cassia and rhubarb which you ignoramuses give.

ISABELLE

By what, then?

HARLEQUIN

By a prescription suited to the malady in question. If a woman is grief-stricken because her home is badly furnished a doctor who knows his business will at once prescribe a damask bed and a tapestry full of charming figures. The prescription should then be folded and put into the hands of her husband.

ISABELLE

But suppose that the husband fails to carry out the doctor's orders?

HARLEQUIN

In that case the wife provides for herself. Furthermore, if husbands will play the fool, so much the worse for them.

THE DOCTOR

But if a young woman is vexed by an old man's jealousy what balm would you suggest for her cure?

HARLEQUIN

The best within your means. Prescribe a financier and a cavalier: one to provide money and the other to spend it.

THE DOCTOR

Let us return for a moment to my daughter, sir. How will you cure her?

HARLEQUIN, HIS ANCESTORS, AND HIS FAMILY

HARLEQUIN

When the fine qualities of a handsome boy are once lodged in the mind of a young girl there are certain membranes of affection which feel the prick of love. I don't tell every one that, by heaven! Love is a kind of alembic which drips in the soul incessantly; *gutta cavat*

HARLEQUIN
Engraving by M. Engelbrecht, after Wachsmuth (eighteenth century)

and all that follows. When love has once gangrened the soul reason flees as though her tail were on fire. It is then that the girl's spirit is aroused, and she thinks only of making the match of which her father disapproves. That is why, if it is within the realm of immediate possibility, *recipe matrimoniorum multorum fantorum*; otherwise, i' faith, neither cassia nor senna will get her out of the difficulty. There is no use trying to deceive you—the best senna for woman is man.

A SCENE OF DESPAIR[1]

(HARLEQUIN *plays the scene with many changes of voice, gesturing wildly and raging from one side of the stage to the other.*)

HARLEQUIN

Ah, unhappy me! The Doctor is going to force Columbine to marry a farmer; how shall I be able to live without Columbine! I would rather die first. Ha, idiot of a doctor! Ha, inconstant Columbine! Ha, knave of a farmer! Ha, wretched Harlequin! Let me die then, and it shall be recorded in ancient and modern history: Harlequin died for Columbine. I shall go to my room, tie a rope to the crossbeam, climb upon a chair, place the rope round my neck, kick away the chair, and ough! I'm hanged. (*He imitates a hanged man.*) It's done quickly; nothing can stop me; now for the gallows. . . . The gallows, did I say? Fie, sir, of what are you thinking? It would be a great folly to kill yourself for a girl. Yes, sir, but it is a vile trick for a girl to betray an honest man. Agreed. But when you are hanged will you be the fatter for it? No, I'll be the thinner, and I wish to have a fine figure. What have you to say to that? If you wish to be present you have only to come. Pho! as to that, no! You will not go. . . . But I shall go. You shall not go! I will go, I tell you. (*He draws out his knife and strikes himself with it. Then he says:*) Ah! There, I am delivered of that meddler at last. Now there is nobody to hinder me; let's off to the hanging. (*He makes as if to depart and then stops short.*) No. Hanging is an ordinary death; it's a death that can be seen any day, and I should scarcely gain much honour from it. Let me see—some unusual sort of death, an heroic death, a Harlequinic death. (*He muses.*) I have it. I'll stop up my nose and mouth so that no air can escape, and then I can die. Now. (*He stops up his nose and mouth with his hands and, after remaining in this position for some time, he says:*) No, the air comes out below; besides it is not worth the trouble. Alas, how difficult it is to die! (*To the audience.*) Sirs, if some one of you would die first, just to show me how, I'd be very much obliged. . . . Ah, I have it, by my faith. We read in stories how people die from laughing. I could die that way, and it would be a droll death. I am very ticklish. If I were to be tickled for any length of time I should probably die of laughing. I'll just tickle myself, and then I can die easily enough. (*He tickles himself, laughs, and falls to the ground.* PASQUARIEL *comes in, finds him lying there, and, believing him drunk, calls him, brings him to, comforts him, and leads him away.*)

HARLEQUIN IN THE EIGHTEENTH CENTURY

THE PRINCESS, HARLEQUIN, *and* HORTENSE

(HARLEQUIN *is lost in a palace and meets the* PRINCESS.)

PRINCESS

Art looking for thy master?

HARLEQUIN

Indeed, you have divined the truth, madame. My master talked with you a while ago, and since then I lost sight of him in this plaguey house, and, by your leave, I am lost also. I should be very glad if you would show me the way out. There is such a monstrous lot of rooms here—I've been wandering around for more than an hour and have not come to the end of them yet. Egad, if you let all this you ought to get a good rental from it. And there is

[1] Especially characteristic of the *commedia dell' arte.*

such a quantity of rubbish and furniture and finery ; why, a whole village could live on what it would fetch. . . . It is so beautiful, so beautiful that one hardly dares look at it. It frightens

Engraving by G. J. Xavery

a poor man like me. You members of the royalty are devilish rich ; and what am I in comparison ? I am impertinent to talk to you as I would to an equal. Your friend there is laughing ; I must have said something foolish.

HORTENSE

You've not said anything foolish. On the contrary, you appear to be in a good humour.

HARLEQUIN

Egad, I have enough to laugh at. I have nothing to lose by it. You people get pleasure out of being rich, and I out of being in good spirits. Every one ought to get his fun in this world.[1]

HARLEQUIN ON TRAVEL

(LELIO, *the great lord, asserts that he travels for the purpose of studying mankind.*)

HARLEQUIN

I' faith, it's a study which will teach you only of man's misery. There's little use in running about to study such rubbish. What will you gain from a knowledge of man? You will only find out the worst about him.

LELIO

Then I shall not be deceived any more.

HARLEQUIN

No, but you will be spoiled.

LELIO

In what way?

HARLEQUIN

You will cease to be honest when you have learned all there is to know about the race. For after you have seen so many scoundrels you will become a scoundrel yourself. Good-bye. Which way do I turn for the kitchen?

THE HARLEQUIN GIUSEPPE-DOMENICO BIANCOLELLI, OTHERWISE KNOWN AS DOMINIQUE (1640–88)

Dominique and Scaramouche were undoubtedly the best-known improvisators in France, if not the only ones known to the public in general. As regards Dominique, it has been remarked before that the brilliant Biancolelli always adhered faithfully to the precepts and traditions of the *commedia dell'arte*. He was strictly conscientious in subordinating his magnetic personality to the character he portrayed. In this respect he was no different from the rest of his colleagues, for the good improvisator so fused his own personality with the character he played that he practically recreated the *rôle*. If it had been otherwise each of the traditional characters would soon have grown stale and trite, and after a period of inanition they would have completely disappeared. Life, even in the theatre, is a process of rapid and constant transformation. And the Italian comedy and its characters were able to exist as long as they did only because, in spite of remaining fundamentally the same, they went through endless changes and renovations.

Dominique was, like so many players of the Italian comedy, the son of improvisators. Even in his early youth he was already considered one of the most promising actors in

[1] From the plays of Marivaux.

Portrait of Biancolelli, called Dominique

Italy. He was agile, supple, and well built, and he did not grow fat (as he appears in Bonnart's engravings) until he was well past his maturity. He had an alert and engaging expression. He was clever enough to know how to use even his defects to advantage, for he had a disagreeable, parrot-like voice which the public accepted and to which it became so accustomed that it refused to tolerate any Harlequin after him whose voice was normal. He was an athlete, a dancer, and a keen wit; and, above all, he was a superlative mime. Unfortunately for Dominique, the Spanish language was more popular in Paris in his day than Italian. Finding, therefore, that he could no longer achieve his comic effects by using the dialects of his own country, he was obliged to rely almost entirely on his skill in pantomime.

In 1654 Dominique was playing in Vienna with Tabarini's troupe when he received an invitation from Mazarin to join the Italian company in Paris, which was badly in need of new vitality. He accepted, and brought with him Ottavio, Eularia, and Diamantine. Locatelli continued to play the Trivelin *rôles*, while Dominique himself interpreted Harlequin.

Dominique's famous wit and *bons mots* endeared him particularly to Louis XIV. As an example of his cleverness there is the anecdote about the King and the dish of partridges. It appears that one evening, when the King was at dinner, he chanced to look up and noticed Dominique, who was present, gazing longingly at the platter of partridges which was being served. The King was touched by the actor's expression and said, "Let this dish be given to Dominique." "And the partridges also?" asked Dominique quickly. "And the partridges also," replied the King in high good humour. Incidentally, the dish was of solid gold. Again, the story is told that the King attended a performance of the Italian players *incognito*, and he afterward complained to Dominique that the piece had been dull. "Not a word to the King," replied Dominique; "he would have me discharged if he knew."

Dominique's troupe did not begin to score any marked success with the public until the actors were able to play with ease in the French language. Once this handicap was overcome their popularity was established, especially when they added memorized dialogues in French to the customary improvisation in Italian. The French comedians were very much perturbed by this increasing rivalry which threatened to do them a great deal of harm in time, and they forthwith made a complaint to the King. But Louis would not take any action in the matter until he had heard both sides. The Italians were represented by Dominique and the opposition by Baron, and the *Spectacles de Paris* published an account of the interview as follows:

> Baron spoke first on behalf of the French players. When Dominique took the floor he said, "Sire, in what language shall I address your Majesty?" "Speak in any way thou wilt," the King answered. "No more is necessary, then," said Dominique, "I have won my case." Baron protested vigorously against this unexpected stratagem, but the King maintained that it was entirely legitimate; that he had given his word, and would not gainsay it. And ever since the Italian comedians have performed their plays in French.

Dominique's character conformed to the popular superstition that all clowns are melancholy. It is said that he once went to consult the eminent Dr Dumoulin about what would nowadays be called neurasthenia. The good doctor did not recognize his celebrated patient, and told him that the only remedy possible was "to go and see Dominique play."

This great Harlequin died at the age of forty-eight as a result of his having become overheated while giving a parody of "the Sieur Beauchamp, dancing-master to Louis XIV and composer of his ballets. He danced before his Majesty in a very singular *entrée* which was exceedingly enjoyed by the entire Court." His death was, of course, a great loss to his company, and the theatre where he had played was closed for a whole month as a sign of mourning. "The death of the inimitable Dominique" was felt no less keenly throughout Paris. Below is a sample of one of the numerous verses commemorating the event.

Sur la Mort du Célèbre Arlequin

Les plaisirs le suivoient sans cesse.
Il répandait partout la joye et l'allégresse.
Les jeux avec les ris naissoient dessous ses pas.
On ne pouvait parer les traits de sa satyre :
Loin d'offenser personne, elle avoit des appas.
Cependent il est mort : tout le monde en soupire.
Qui l'eust jamais pensé sans se désespérer,
Que l'aimable Arlequin, qui nous a tant fait rire,
Deust si tost nous faire pleurer ? [1]

In 1662 Dominique married Ursula Cortèze, who played the *rôle* of Eularia, and had twelve children by her. Like their parents and grandparents, these children became Columbines, Isabelles, and Trivelins. One of them was a godchild of Louis XIV, and became a "director of the forts of Provence, a captain and chevalier of the order of St Louis." But though he did not follow the profession of the *commedia dell' arte* directly, he preserved his loyalty to it and left a number of scenarios which Gherardi included in his collection.

THE MOST CELEBRATED HARLEQUINS

1570 Ganassa
1578 Simone, of Bologna
1600 Martinelli
1605 Jean Baptiste Andreini
1624 Fremeri
1625 Belotti
1630 Francesco Girolamo
1660 Giuseppe Dominique Biancolelli
1689 Evariste Gherardi
1698 Babron (of the fair theatres)
1716 Antonio Vicentini
1720 Astori, of Venice
1721 Baxter (English Harlequin)
1730 Bertoli
1734 Ignacio Casanova, of Bologna
1739 Antonio Constantini
1740 Sacchi
1742 Carlo Bertinazzi, called Carlin
1777 Bigottini
1780 Golinetti
1792 Lazzari

[1] "Pleasure followed him unceasingly; he spread joy and gladness everywhere. Laughter sprang from beneath his very feet, and his ready satire offended no one, so merry were his quips. He is now dead, however, and every one is sad and cannot think of it without a heavy heart. Who would ever have thought that the gay Harlequin who once made us laugh so well should now so often make us weep ?" (August 1688.)

THE FAMILY TREE OF HARLEQUIN

THE CLASSIC THEATRE IN ROME

The *lenones*, the phallophores, who may have played the *rôles* of African slaves

TRIVELINO (?)
(The Tatterdemalion)

HARLEQUINO

Truffaldino — Guazzeto — Zaccagnino — Bagatino

ARLECCHINO
ARLEQUIN

Harlequin, as seen by an Oriental
Eighteenth century
Plate made for the Dutch East India Company

Trivelino

It is thought that Trivelino, whose name means 'tatterdemalion,' was the father of Harlequin, or perhaps this was the name by which the Harlequino of the fifteenth century was known. His costume, in which Domenico Locatelli played as late as 1653, is almost identical with Harlequin's oldest costume (p. 124), for Trivelin also wore a soft hat adorned with a rabbit-scut. He had, however, another kind of costume, decorated with stitched-on triangles, moons, and stars, which dates from the seventeenth century. His mask was a copy of the one worn by Harlequin.

THE CHARACTER AND RÔLE OF TRIVELINO

During the seventeenth century in Italy Trivelin was a very active rogue who never tired of badgering Harlequin and duping Pantaloon and the Doctor. Neither his character nor his *rôle* deviated greatly from those of Harlequin and Scapin.

Truffa, Truffaldin, Truffaldino

Truffa, the crafty, false, and boastful valet, first made his appearance in the sixteenth century. Truffaldino in the eighteenth century was a Bergamask caricature which had a close affinity to the Harlequin that Sacchi created. According to Gozzi, the *rôle* of Truffaldino was entirely improvised, and he says in effect that "no one could write the *rôle* of Truffaldino either in prose or verse. Sacchi had only to know the author's intention in order to improvise scenes which were unquestionably superior to any that a writer might outline for him." Nevertheless, during Gozzi's time the attempt was made with satisfactory results, as the reader will see from the following quotation.

THE STORY OF TRUFFALDINO, BY TRUFFALDINO

I came out of a foundlings' home. Allow me to go over my family tree. There is some probability that I am the son of a king, for I've always had a feeling of pronounced superiority in my blood. They tried to teach me to read and write in the home, but my ambitious soul could never stoop to such petty pursuits, and therefore, because of my royal ferocity, I was forced to break the head of the master. I ran away immediately afterward and have since been a mendicant, thanks to my heroism. [Truffaldino was captured by the corsairs and sold and resold a number of times. He goes on to tell about it.] The man who bought me tried me out in several different kinds of work, but he was soon aware of my regal contempt for all forms of labour, and in consequence sold me for fifty livres. My third master hitched me up with an ass. Thereafter I won such fame for my indifference toward any occupation except eating that my last master sold me for twenty-seven and a half livres. I was finally decorated with a meritorious kick in the behind, and was thus emancipated from slavery with honour and glory. I must say that I was as much out of place in a condition of servitude as a fish in a field or a piece of cheese in a library. After what I've told you you can easily see my proper vocation.

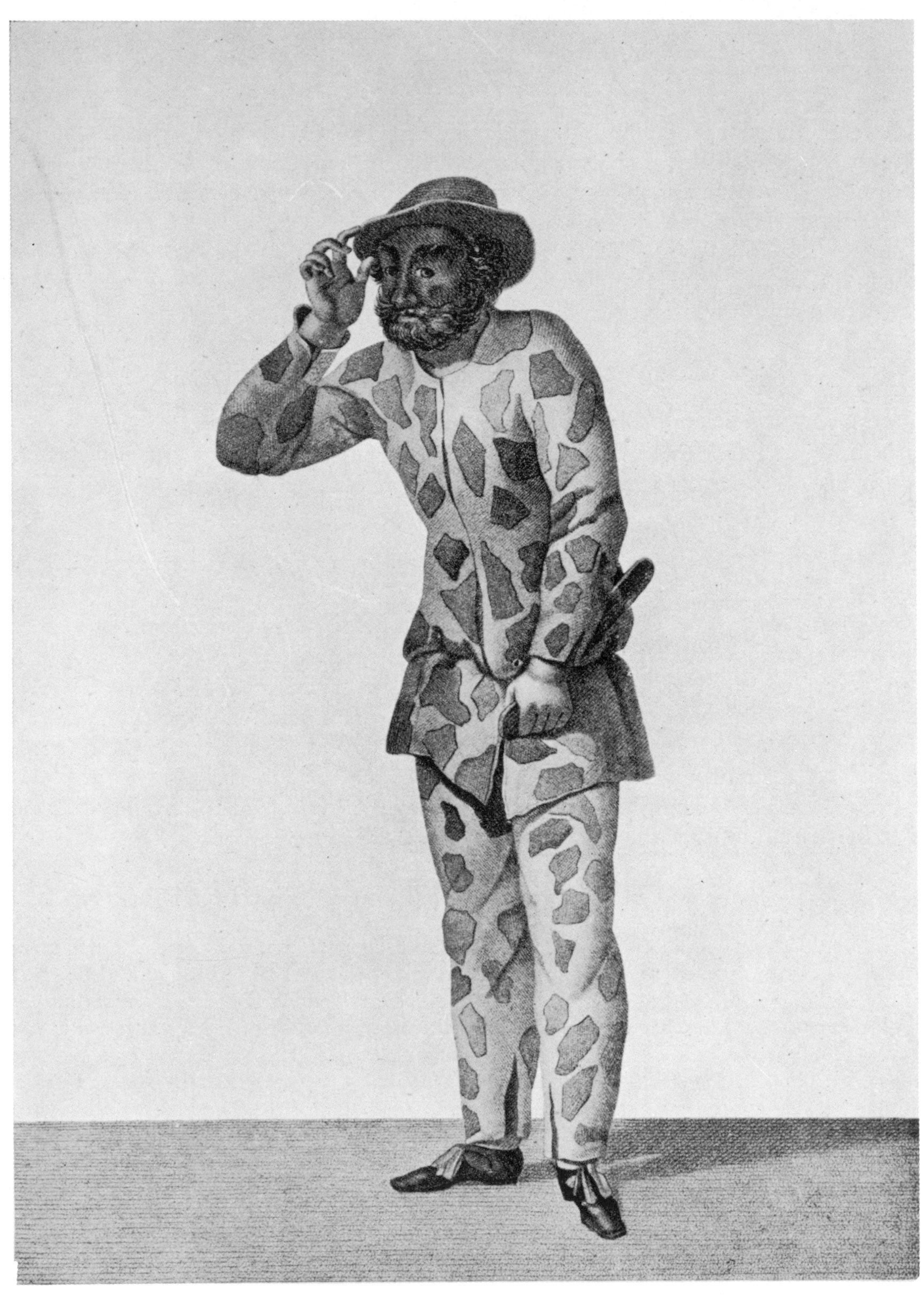

DOMINIQUE LOCATELLI AS TRIVELIN
Seventeenth century

Guazzetto[1]

In the *Balli di Sfessania* Callot portrayed a Guatsetto greeting Mestolino with restrained cordiality (p. 54). Guatsetto is shown wearing long, wide breeches, a loose jacket drawn tightly by a belt, in which is thrust a bat shaped like a scimitar. An enormous

ZANNY
Engraving by de Geijn

handkerchief is knotted about his neck like a fichu and falls over his shoulders. His head bristles with sharp points; he wears a pointed hat, feathers erect, a mask with a protuberant hooked nose, and a long, tapering beard as formidable as a sword. In a series of anonymous engravings of the seventeenth century Guazzetto is depicted as

[1] Written " Guatsetto " by Callot.

dancing and wearing a fox's brush in a certain place ; an enormous three-tiered collarette and a moustache differentiate him slightly from Callot's representation.

Guazzetto was a rollicking *farceur* closely related to Arlechino. One Guazzetto played the first Zanny in the troupe of the Comici Affezionati in 1630 ; there was another on the boards in 1650 named Giuseppe Albani ; and still another in the troupe of the Duke of Modena in 1688. In France there was a Guazzetto who played valet *rôles* similar to Arlechino in the Fedeli troupe.

Zaccagnino and Bagatino

The name Zaccagnino is found for the first time in 1496 in a letter from Ercole of Ferrara [1] to Francesco Gonzaga, of Mantua. In the sixteenth century an actor by the name of Francesco Ruino played the *rôle*, and Giulio Cesare Torri had it in the troupe of the Duke of Modena in the seventeenth century. Callot made an engraving of Bagatino, or the Little Juggler, making sport of the Capitan Spessa-Monti.[2] Both Zaccagnino and Bagatino are characters bearing close semblance to Arlechino.

[1] See Appendix O. [2] See plate facing p. 228.

XIII

Brighella and his Family

Brighella (The Intriguer)

OF all the characters of the Italian comedy Brighella is without doubt the most disturbing. The bizarre, half-cynical, half-mawkish expression of his olive-tinted mask once seen is never forgotten. It is distinguished by a pair of sloe eyes, a hook nose, thick and sensual lips, a brutal chin bristling with a sparse beard, and finally the moustache of a fop, thick and twirled up at the ends in such a fashion as to give him an offensive, swaggering air.

Brighella has only to thrust his head through the folds of the curtain, and the sweet discourse between Isabelle and Flavio is quickly hushed.

"I have a special weakness for quarrels," asserts Brighella. "And I always need at least two nice, tender young girls to satisfy me. And if murdering one man is not enough I'd just as lief kill two. You may remember, perhaps, the little tiff I once had when I gutted one man as easily as pricking a bladder, and broke the bones of another as I would crush a bean."

Like Harlequin, Brighella is from Bergamo, but there is little doubt that he soon emigrated to Naples, where he is still ubiquitous, for his progeny infest all railway stations and southern seaports to this day. He is of the sort who lie prone asleep in the sun along the waterfront until hunger brings them to life again. On awakening he stretches himself with the lithe ease of a cat, and rises to his feet in a gliding movement without apparent muscular effort. When he is standing up his slender figure casts a rod-like shadow. His quick and piercing eyes survey his kingdom with a look of interrogation, alive to every opportunity. Brighella does not walk in the ordinary sense; he prowls, rather, making a faint pattering noise with his sandals when he is not actually barefoot. A wharf or a modern railway station offers unlimited opportunities for the activities of a rascal of Brighella's type.

Whenever he is hungry or thirsty Brighella does not scruple to tap wine-kegs or poke into bales of goods on a wharf under the very eyes of the most vigilant watchman. Brighella's spine is so flexible that he can insinuate himself into any sort of nook or cranny and disappear completely, like his competitor, the rat. He is not restricted to the expedients of a mere thief; he is a man of infinite ingenuity, and he knows to within a hair's breadth how to make the most of every occasion—a quality which some people would be apt to call good luck.

A ship comes into dock, the gangway is let down, and Brighella watches the passengers disembarking. He surveys the slow-witted, Herculean labourers carrying enormous bales and cases on their shoulders, but he remains motionless. He is an observer and psychologist, and calmly continues to watch the flow of people, his hands clasped behind his back. Suddenly he spies a rich foreigner, the very one, in fact, he is waiting for, and, once having made his decision, he never abandons the pursuit of his prey until he has him in his power. He rushes forward and takes the stranger's luggage from him, calling him " Baron," " Marquess," or " Excellency " until his victim finally gives in good-naturedly. He suggests a dozen hotels; he offers to serve as guide to all the pleasures available in the town, forbidden or otherwise. He offers also to procure anything that can be had for love or money : his sister, the Governor's conscience—whatever his lordship desires. He demands ten times too much for his trouble, of course, and remains perfectly serene if the only payment he receives is a kick. He is sure to take his revenge eventually, either upon his aggressor or upon the nearest substitute.

BRIGHELLA
Sixteenth century

The guitarist who sings under the window in a mellifluous voice is also Brighella. Moreover, he knows how to dance. His natural apathy does not prevent him from being more adroit and lively than a monkey, and his wit is of the same mercurial character. Brighella is always on hand if there is any intrigue afoot, or secret to be laid bare, or debauch to be organized, or dagger to be planted between the shoulders of a political rival ; but it is best never to pay him until his work has been done and verified, for he owns not the slightest instinct of professional honour.

The moment Brighella has any money in pocket he ceases all work and enjoys life until the last penny is gone. He is never long absent from the tavern, and he drinks and roars and swaggers about, insulting and baiting old men—or any one, for that matter, who happens to be weaker than himself. But if some stronger man comes on the scene Brighella immediately fawns on him or else cunningly slips away. Women rarely like this strange scoundrel, but they fear and respect him. They tolerate his insolence because they are afraid of his claws and mischievous ways, and they yield only too often to his cajoling and his ingenious and persuasive eloquence. Nevertheless, they are well aware that once they do yield to him they must take the consequences. Brighella believes in no one but the hangman, he respects nothing and loves nothing but his own pleasure.

BRIGHELLA AND HIS FAMILY

Brighella is a Jack of all trades with no particular calling of his own. He will serve in turn as soldier, hangman's varlet, simple valet, or anything required of him, provided

Carlo Cantu as Buffet, one of the Variants of Brighella
Seventeenth century

that his baseness and rascality and knife-thrusts procure him money, for which, incidentally, he has the same cupidity as Pantaloon. Yet money for him is worth only the pleasure it provides, and in this respect he is more logical and human than the miserly merchant.

Such was the Brighella of the Renaissance, and his type is as ancient as Harlequin's. His costume during the sixteenth and seventeenth centuries was composed of a jacket and full trousers, adorned with a braid of some sort of green material along the seams, which gave it the aspect of livery. He wore the *tabaro*, or short mantle. His hat was a toque with a green border. Like his brother, Beltrame of Milan, Brighella always carried a large leather purse and a trusty dagger at his side, both significant symbols of his tastes and inclinations.

After the Renaissance Brighella gradually grew milder in temperament and habits. He remained a confirmed liar, however, as well as a perjurer, drunkard, and debauchee; but in later times he was not always so ready to draw his dagger. He became more of a valet and less of an adventurer. His costume went through an evolution similar in spirit to that of his character, developing into a white frock coat with a turn-down collar; but his vest and trousers retained the trimmings of green braid. The lower part of his face was shaved, and he sprouted a finer moustache. He also continued to wear the olive half-mask and the traditional toque.

Brighella's descendants in the eighteenth century were scarcely more than lackeys in the livery of the period and locality. The striped yellow and black, and red and black, vests worn by servants to-day in some European hotels represent almost the last remaining vestiges of Brighella's costume.

In 1671 Brighella was at the height of his popularity in France. The following verse is indicative of how his character was changing:

Brighella fourbe fait la figue,
A tous demesleurs d'intrigues.[1]

In the eighteenth century Brighella found able interpreters among the Italian troupes in such actors as Giuseppe Angeleri (1704–52) and Atanasio Zanoni, who died "on February 22, 1792, as he was coming from a magnificent dinner. He fell into a deep canal and died shortly after."

A FEW OF BRIGHELLA'S REFLECTIONS AND PROFESSIONS OF FAITH

(EIGHTEENTH CENTURY)

One should never say 'thief' but an ingenious calculator who finds an object before its owner has lost it. To commit a theft according to the rules one must be aided by three devils: one to teach you how to take objects, one to show you how to hide them when nobody is looking, and the last one to persuade you never to restore an object to its rightful owner. . . .

I am very garrulous because my father was a mute. He left me a patrimony of new words which have never been used. I am, furthermore, a bastard. . . .

The shirt I wear has become a sort of romantic story-book. It is full of knights-errant, and the washerwoman refuses to wash it for fear of polluting the river. . . .

[1] "Brighella, the knave, defies all those who try to unmask an intrigue."

BRIGHELLA AND HIS FAMILY

I am a 'well-rehearsed' convict. I am so busy, and I have so many affairs on hand, that I have not the time even to scratch myself. . . .

When I am compelled to travel—that is to say, to flee—I comfort widowed hens, I adopt young chickens and orphan ducks. I liberate purses and captive monsters.

THE GENEALOGICAL TREE OF BRIGHELLA

THE GREEK AND ROMAN THEATRE

Pseudolla and the slaves (?)

|

BRIGHELLA

Brothers of Brighella

BELTRAME, GRADELINO
SCAPIN, TRUCCAGNINO
MEZZETINO, FENOCCHIO (Chaff) (1560)
FLAUTINO, BAGATINO (The Droll)
SBRIGANI (a variant of the name Brighella, and occasionally his exact opposite)

PASQUARIEL

|

French and Italian derivatives

NARCISINO (seventeenth century)
TURLUPIN, GANDOLIN (1590)
GRATTELARD (1620)

The Comédie Française (seventeenth century)

SGANARELLE
MASCARILLE
LA MONTAGNE
FRONTIN
LABRANCHE

The plays of Marivaux (eighteenth century)

FIGARO

Beltrame da Milano

Beltrame was the wilfully blind husband and a rascal as crafty as Brighella. He made his appearance as a valet about the end of the sixteenth century. Riccoboni wrote:

> His costume is not extraordinary, and I believe it is a costume of his time or a little before. He had a mask similar to Scapin's. Beltrame, being a Milanese, not only preferred to speak the language of his own part of the country but to wear the native costume also.

NICCOLO BARBIERI

Barbieri was one of the most celebrated Beltrames, if not the creator of the type. He belonged originally to the Gelosi troupe, then to the Fedeli, and he finally became director of a troupe of his own. He wrote a highly curious work called *La Supplica: Discorso famigliare intorno alle commédie mercenarie: Lettura per que' galanthuomini che non sono in tutto critici, ne affatto balordi.*[1]

[1] *The Petition: Familiar Discourse concerning Low Comedies: Reading for Men of Worth who are not Prejudiced Critics nor Entirely Fools.*

FRONTISPIECE TO "LA SUPPLICA," BY NICCOLO BARBIERI
Venice (1634)

Flautino (The Flute-player)

The Tuscan actor Giovanni Gherardi in 1675 chose the name of Flautino for playing the *rôle* of Brighella. His versatility was such that he could imitate an entire orchestra. Giovanni Gherardi had the great misfortune, however, to continue the *rôle* of Brighella off the stage as well as on, and he eventually wasted away in prison on account of it. Nevertheless, he had time before his demise to beget the famous Harlequin, Evaristo Gherardi. There is a verse on an engraving of Flautino which gives a very pleasant explanation of the derivation of his name :

Sans flûte ni chalumeau,
Bref, sans instrument quelconque,
Merveille que l'on ne vit oncque,
Fait sortir de son seul gosier
Un concert de flûtes entier.
A ce spectacle, on court sans cesse,
Et pour voir, chacun s'empresse.[1]

FLAUTINO
Seventeenth century

Avec sa guitare touchée
Plus en maître qu'en écolier,
Il semble qu'il tienne cachée
Une flûte en son gosier.[2]

[1] "Without flute, pipe, or any instrument whatever, a miracle never seen, he brings forth from his throat a whole orchestra of flutes. The people flock incessantly to this entertainment, and every one hies to see him."

[2] "Plucking his guitar more as a master than as a pupil, he seems as if he had a flute concealed within his throat."

Joullain made a highly interesting engraving of Giovanni Gherardi, showing him in his Flautino costume. The expression of the mask is similar to that of Brighella, and the costume is the same to all intents and purposes. In the few proofs of this engraving still extant, coloured at the time they were executed, the background of the costume is done either in white or cream and the ribbons in maroon or green.

Fenocchio and Truccagnino

Fenocchio is Brighella's brother. He is given to playing pranks, and one of his tricks is to put a fierce tom-cat in the place of the birds which Harlequin is going to take to his lady love.

Fenocchio is at the service of Flavio, Leandro, and Celio in all their amorous intrigues. He devises a way for his rival Harlequin to see Olivette, whom Pantaloon has put under lock and key. " You play dead," he says ; " I'll put you into a coffin, carry you into the old apothecary's house, and pretend that I must have him make an autopsy on you. At night, after every one has gone to sleep, you can go and find Olivette."

Harlequin follows Fenocchio's instructions to the letter. Pantaloon rubs his hands in glee over the cadaver with which he has been provided, and is about to set to work when the corpse suddenly begins to scratch itself. Pantaloon believes that he is suffering from an hallucination and waves his scalpel wildly. Thereupon Harlequin jumps up and gives him a sound thrashing.

But the next time Harlequin is the victim of Fenocchio's wiles. He allows himself to be disguised as a pig intended as a present for Pantaloon. Once in Pantaloon's house the Harlequin pig is surprised making human gestures; he is obliged to flee and manages to escape, but only with the greatest difficulty.

Truccagnino is another name for the character Fenocchio.

Scapino

Scapino, like Brighella, is a valet-cicerone and general handyman ; but the resemblance goes little farther, for on occasions where his prototype would indulge in dagger-play Scapino is very well content to take to his heels. The name Scapino is derived from the word *scappare*, meaning ' to flee ' or ' to escape,' and Scapino never forgets the fact for an instant.

In temperament Scapino is very much like a starling. He skims away, swoops back again, twitters and warbles, pilfers right and left, flies off, but never fails to return.

Scapino is bereft of all sense of logic ; he makes confusion of everything he undertakes, and forgets everything except to hold out his hand for a gratuity. He is as amorous as the birds in spring, and for him it is spring the whole year round. He deserves some credit for his modesty, for he is not an ambitious Don Juan in his amours :

Scapino
Callot

he inevitably prefers to make off with a servant-girl rather than a king's daughter. He falls in love for the sheer joy of it, and, like a bird, flits from one love to another, never

SCAPINO AND CAPTAIN ZERBINO
From the " Balli di Sfessania "
Callot

becoming deeply involved and always obeying every impulse that enters his flighty head. He is a liar by instinct, but his lies, like himself, are of slight importance.

THE COSTUME OF SCAPINO

Engraving by Basset (eighteenth century)

Scapino's loose-fitting costume, as engraved by Callot, seems inappropriate at first glance because it makes him look like a romantic bandit, but it was the dress of people of his class at that period. Many of the valet *rôles* were played in this costume in Italy until 1630, notably by the actors of the Dionis company in Milan. At that time the mask was obligatory.

However, the best-known costume of Scapino (who later became Scapin in France and was made famous by Molière) is a combination of all the various styles of valet costumes which have come down from Brighella and the French men-servants. The alternation of green and white stripes is the only invariable rule.

Some of the more celebrated Scapins were :

Giovani Bissoni (1716). At first a clown in the service of a charlatan who sold unguents ; then he became a Scapin, and later *major-domo*. He eventually joined the Riccoboni company, to which he bequeathed all his worldly goods.

Alessandro Ciavarelli (1739). Known for his *lazzi* and grimaces.

Camerani (1769). Famous for his quips as well as his enormous appetite. (He died of acute indigestion contracted from secretly gorging *foie gras* late at night.)

Mezzetino (The Half-measure)

When Mezzetino came into existence in the sixteenth century he was the double of either Scapino or Brighella. Like Brighella he was a singer, a musician, and a ready dancer, but he had gentler manners than his prototype. His original costume, as shown by Callot, was even fuller than Scapin's. Like the slaves in Roman plays, he wore the *tabaro*, or short cape, about his shoulders, and he carried a wooden sword like the Zannys. At the close of the seventeenth century in France Constantini created a new costume and a new personality for Mezzetin, making free use of all the traditions of both Italian and French valets. He it was who established once and for all the use of red and white stripes corresponding to the green and white which Scapin wore. The personality of this character became as diversified as his costume. He was both a deceived and deceiving husband ; sometimes he accepted bribes and betrayed his master, and again he worked for him with blind devotion. In this respect he is like the other valets of the Italian comedy whom we have met so far, and he is akin also to the valets of the Molière comedies. Constantini, who had a remarkable talent for facial expression, played the part without a mask.

Ricuilina and Metzetin
From the " Balli di Sfessania "
Callot

SPECIMENS OF MEZZETIN'S DISCOURSE

A letter written by Mezzetin to Orpheus. From " The Descent of Mezzetin to Hades "

I have been told, my pretty boy, that you are a rare one for singing and scraping the catgut. Don't let it occur again or I'll make you howl in another key.

I should like to catch you with your instrument in hand! You are surely no better than a songster off the Pont-Neuf, and you ought to have been croaking with the frogs and braying with jackasses long ago.

Popular engraving of the eighteenth century

Mezzetin to Pluto

You have no idea how many little tricks are practised upon earth, Mr Pluto. Why, there's many a father who has never had a child.

This is very fine wine, and we must not take too much of it, because if the Captain gets drunk the whole company will fall out of line.

MEZZETIN'S PLEASANTRIES

What happiness to be the lucky tailor to measure such a charming figure! But I fear that the shears of my love—you understand?

* * *

MEZZETIN (*to* ISABELLE)

Come, my fair one, tell me truly: wouldn't you be charmed to be my better half? Haven't I an air about me and a fine manner? 'Od's life! it makes me rage when I see these little coxcombs at Court trying to play the rival with me.

ISABELLE

As if they'd the wit! They are little better than a pack of silly monkeys.

MEZZETIN

It is true that I have a rather large bottom—almost as large, indeed, as the chair-porter's; but my doctor has promised to rid me of it and has prescribed whey as a cure.

ISABELLE

Oh, that should be a sure remedy.

MEZZETIN

He told me that it came from an acrid humour seeping out through the diaphragm from the mesentery and falling on to the omoplate. But enough of that; let us talk of our future happiness.

Engraving by G. J. Xavery

ISABELLE

That's a calculation which often goes amiss, for one seldom attains the happiness one hopes for.

MEZZETIN

But I am a gentle, peaceful, and easy-going man; my disposition's as smooth as satin. Why, I lived six years with my first wife without ever having the least little contention——

ISABELLE

That is indeed remarkable.

MEZZETIN

Except once when I snuffed some tobacco and wished to enjoy my sneeze. She was stupid enough to interrupt me, and I nearly choked to death. I therefore took up a candlestick and broke her skull for spite. She died a quarter of an hour afterward.

MEZZETIN
After Sand

ISABELLE

Heavens! can it be possible! And are you not bitten with remorse for having committed so foul a crime?

MEZZETIN

I? . . . Not in the least. I have been quite used to bloodshed from childhood. During his lifetime my father fought at least a thousand duels and always killed his man. He was in the King's service for thirty-two years.

ISABELLE

On land or sea?

MEZZETIN

In the air.

ISABELLE

In the air? What do you mean? I have never heard of an officer of that kind.

MEZZETIN

I mean that he was exceedingly charitable, and whenever he ran across any poor fellow on his way to the gallows he hopped into the tumbril and helped the doomed man to die as best he could.

ISABELLE

How horrid!

MEZZETIN

If you had ever seen him at work he would have made you want to hang yourself.

ISABELLE

I can see only one slight obstacle to our marriage, and that is that I am already wed.

MEZZETIN

Already wed! and you think that an obstacle? So am I, but there is nothing easier than to get rid of one's mate. Five sous' worth of rat-poison will do the trick.

Constantini as Mezzetin

Gandolin and Turlupin

These two French descendants of Brighella wear a costume which resembles that of both their father and Harlequin. Gandolin adds to his livery a plumed hat, decorated with a rabbit-scut, and the Brighella mask. Gandolin was a *farceur* :

> Gandolin, par sa rhétorique,
> Nous fait la rate épanouir,
> Et, pour n'avoir pas la colique,
> Il faut seulement l'ouïr.
> Quelques fables qu'il nous raconte,
> Ont un si bel effet,
> Que chacun y trouve son compte
> Et s'en retourne satisfait.[1]

Turlupin was also a *farceur* of the sixteenth century. His name means ' unlucky.' The puns and improbable stories he tells in abundance are called *turlupinades*, and many of them were taken out of Rabelais. The following is a typical example :

> Dressed in *vert* (*de gris*) and wrapped in a mantle (of a chimney), he meets a woman decked out in a fine skin (of a calf), etc. He died of a waterfall.[2]

Belleville states that Henri Legrand was the creator of this *rôle*.

GANDOLIN (1595)

TURLUPIN (1650)

[1] " Gandolin makes us split our sides with his rhetoric, and hearing him talk is enough to banish colic. The moral tales he recounts are so effective that each of us gets what he wants from them and goes away satisfied."

[2] The play on words is difficult to render into English with any degree of success, particularly in the case of the calf-skin. The French of it is *fraise* (*de veau*), *fraise* meaning collar or ruff, and so translated has no sense at all.—TRANSLATOR.

Cucorongna.
Pernoualla.
12

Gian Fritello.
Ciurlo.

Franca Trippa.
Fritellino.

Smaraolo cornuto.
rsa di Boio

BRIGHELLA AND HIS FAMILY

Franca-Trippa and Fritellino

The character Franca-Trippa was originally created by Gabriello Panzanini, who came to Paris with the Gelosi company in 1577. He spoke the Bolognese dialect mixed with the Tuscan. In the *Recueil Fossard* (Plate XXXVII) he is seen standing on his head on

FRANCA-TRIPPA
From the " Costumi di varie nazioni," by Pietro Bertelli

the back of Captain Cocodrillo, and also (in Plate XXIV) on all fours " running like a water-spaniel," as his crony Harlequin tells him. Further on (in Plate XXIX) he is armed with a huge dagger with which he intends to carve up Harlequin, for the two have been quarrelling over Francesquina. This Franca-Trippa is probably Panzanini. He wears a brown mask with a long, sly, sensual nose, a beard, and long, pointed moustaches. His trousers are full and hang in folds, and likewise his blouse, which is open on his bull neck. His entire costume, including his hat with wide brims turned down over the eyes, is white. His blouse is drawn in at the waist by a slender twisted cord on which is hung a huge black purse. The character Gian-Fritello, or Fritellino, as interpreted by the actor Pietro Maria Cecchini, a member of the troupe of Tristano Martinelli when it performed at Lyons in 1601 on the occasion of the marriage of Maria de' Medici and

Henri IV, scored a great success in Germany. The Emperor Matthias[1] raised Cecchini to nobility by way of appreciation of his acting. In France the character went by the name of Fristelin in Tabarin's farces. One of the drawings by Callot in the plate facing p. 176 shows Franca-Trippa and Fritellino dancing together.

[1] Reigned 1612–19.

FRANCA-TRIPPA (ABOUT 1577)
Possibly this is the actor Gabriele Panzanini
From the "Recueil Fossard"

XIV

Pantaloon and his Family

Pantaloon

SONNET CXXXIII

Il fait bon voir (Magny) ces colons magnifiques,
Leur superbe arcenal, leurs vaisseaux, leur abbord,
Leur sainct Marc, leur palais, leur realte, leur port,
Leurs changes, leurs profits, leur banque, et leurs trafiques ;

Il fait bon voir le bec de leurs chapprons antiques,
Leurs robbes à grand' manche et leurs bonnetz sans bord,
Leur parler grossier, leur gravité, leur port
Et leurs sages advis aux affaires politiques.

Il fait bon voir de tout leur Sénat balloter,
Il fait bon voir partout leurs gondolles flotter,
Leurs femmes, leurs festins, leur vivre solitère :

Mais ce que l'on en doit le meilleur estimer,
C'est quand ces vieux coquz vont espouser la mer
Dont ils sont les maris, et le turc l'adultère.[1]

JOACHIM DU BELLAY

LTHOUGH du Bellay did not indicate specifically that he was writing about Pantaloon, the eminent citizen of Venice, his poem is an excellent portrait of the old merchant done to the life, indeed a portrait in the grand manner. The figure of Pantaloon with his long red legs, his loose black cape, or *zimarra*, his beard blown in the winds, his Turkish slippers, and his red woollen bonnet, was in truth as much a part and symbol of the prosperity of Venice as the Rialto or St Mark's. His personality is as old as mankind, of course, but it was Venice who individualized him with the stamp of her own particular colour and picturesqueness.

Pantaloon had long been a celebrated character in his native city before the single-piece breeches he wore had acquired his name and equal fame. Nor did the Venetians

[1] " Magny, it is good to see these magnificent columns, their superb arsenal, their vessels, the approach to the city, their St Mark, their palace, their Rialto, their port, their Exchange, their prosperity, their bank, and their transactions ;

" It is good to see the visors of their old-fashioned hoods, their wide-sleeved gowns, and their brimless hats ; their crude speech, their gravity, their bearing, and their wise participation in public affairs.

" It is good to see all their Senate vote, it is good to see their gondolas afloat everywhere, their women, their great festivals, and their island life :

" But the best spectacle of all is when these old cuckolds go down to wed the sea, of whom they are the husbands and the Turk the paramour."

ever spare him with their ridicule: they not only made sport of all the peculiarities he already had, but attributed to him as many more as they could think of.

Even his name was a jibe. It seems originally to have come from the phrase *pianta leone*, 'to plant the lion.' For the Venetian merchants in the old days were supposed to be consumed by a feverish passion to increase their wealth in every way possible, which was logical enough, considering their profession; but Pantaloon went to extremes,

PANTALOON (ABOUT 1577)
Possibly this is the actor Pasquati
Detail from an engraving in the "Recueil Fossard"

THE ACTOR PASQUATI (?) AS PANTALOON
Lyons, 1601

setting himself up as a conquistador and going forth to plant the flag of Venice emblazoned with the Lion of St Mark all over the world. His real or imaginary conquests (and even the most upright old fellow might have had his head a bit turned by thinking too much about money) therefore earned him the title of Pantaleone, or Plant-lion.

Another theory purports that he received his name from San Pantaleone, the old patron saint of Venice; but Pantaloon would be just as humiliated by this supposition as he would be if he were forced to take down his trousers in the middle of the Square of St Mark.

Pantaloon is always old and as a rule retired from active business. Sometimes he is rich, sometimes poor, sometimes the father of a family, and, again, an old bachelor. All his life long he has been engaged in trade, and he has become so sensitive to the value of money that he is an abject slave to it. And yet it is unjust to judge him without taking account of his side of the matter, for he has much to worry and discourage him. On more than one occasion he has had to wait month after month for news of his great-hulled ships laden with fine Syrian silks and perfumes. He watches the horizon for his brave ship with all the anxiety of a mother listening for the step of her errant son, estimating meanwhile, however, the profit he plans to make out of it. It happens only too often that an unfeeling storm or the more unfeeling Turkish pirate ravages, pillages, and destroys his coveted gains. Then Pantaloon tears his beard and spits into the sea, which in derision has wafted to his feet only a head of cabbage. But Pantaloon is seldom disheartened; he tightens up his belt after each reverse and sets to work to make his fortune over again, quite well aware of its greater cost and value. What difference if people call him "beggar," "skinflint," "calamity-howler," and "Pantalone dei bisognosi cagh' in aqua"?[1] He can afford to make light of their opinion when he lifts the great slab in his cellar that conceals old silver bullion, or when he rummages among the casks with false bottoms and the straw mattresses which he uses as strong-boxes for his beautiful ducats. It must be admitted that Pantaloon is excessively miserly. Ill-disposed gossips assert even that his most sumptuous feasts consist of dog or alley-cat soup, that he draws his wine from the fountain at the corner, and partakes of a duck egg as the chief dish of the banquet. Pantaloon himself eats the yellow of the egg, and gives the white to his wife and the watery part to his children, in order to spare them the rigours of stomach-ache.

Pantalone dupé
PANTALOON THE DUPE
Beginning of the seventeenth century

Pantaloon has an ancestor whom Plautus calls Euclio in his *Aulularia*. His slave Strobile says of him:

> He is so mean that when he goes to bed he ties up the neck of the bellows to prevent them from losing any air during the night. Some time ago the barber pared his nails, and he carefully picked up and carried away all the clippings, so that nothing would be wasted.

In punishment for his avaricious nature, which is evidently only an atavism, and which, after all, affects no one but his near and dear ones, the fates combine to rain down all manner of ill-luck and calamity on his venerable head.

If Pantaloon is married his wife is generally young and pretty, and, unaware of the

[1] "Poverty-stricken Pantaloon, spit in the water."

honour of being the wife of a reputable merchant, she deceives him at every turn. To add insult to injury, she makes fun of him because he coughs and spits, because his nose runs, and because he slavers a little.

If he happens to have any daughters, Isabella and Rosaura or Camille and Smeraldine, they worry their old father enough to drive him out of his wits. Even the servant-girls in his household, Fiametta and Olivette or Zerbinette and Catte, become doubly deceitful in order to let a lover into the house in secret or steal some of their master's silver. Or perhaps it is the old procuress who comes in and delivers a letter, sealed with a bleeding heart, to Isabella right before her father's eyes. Pantaloon's chalky face turns purple with rage, and he draws his poignard. But he never kills anyone. At heart he is a peace-loving man. He has a horror of blows, and yet he receives them—far oftener than he likes. And for this reason: Pantaloon has retired from business, and, having nothing better to do, has turned his attention to matters of State and the affairs of his neighbours. When he is sauntering along the sunlit street and overhears the beginning of a discussion he cannot refrain from offering the disputants the fine fruit of his long experience and the weight of his well-known probity. He interferes forthwith, and is immediately fired by his own eloquence; he swears by all the saints of Venice; he waves his hands. . . . But human nature seldom deserves the altruism wasted upon it, and so the honest Pantaloon is most often rebuffed for his good intentions and is usually the victim of most of the kicks and blows delivered at the close of the argument.

THE ACTOR ROTI AS PANTALOON (1754)

Poor Pantaloon's troubles in life rarely come singly. If he is not sufficiently tormented by his fellow-man the relentless Cupid appears on the scene and shoots his arrows into the centre of this old heart which every one judged dry and shrivelled as a bit of lemon peel. The woman he loves is almost always a maiden, "lovely as the parroquet that Aldo drew, fair as fine linen, light as a hare . . ."; or she is a mocking flirt who makes sport of him or continually demands gold in payment for her love, and still more gold. Evidently Pantaloon has no fear of ridicule, for we see him in Callot's picture as Trastullo down on his knees before the deceitful Rosaura, who mocks him the moment he is out of her presence as a "scurvy, gouty, catarrhous old beast." And she also adds: "A pretty object to be cuddling!"

It would never do, however, to waste much sympathy on Pantaloon's unfortunate amours; his passion is scarcely more than lust. He appeals to Prudenza, "the complete

Decoration in the Room of William V in the Château of Trausnitz

Decoration in the Room of William V in the Château of Trausnitz

atlas of all lusts," and invokes her aid in corrupting the most innocent of all innocent doves. On these occasions he is so mad with desire that he says, " If it weren't for my infirmities I could turn a dozen handsprings, and more."

But it seems a decree of fate that Pantaloon must always be the dupe of some one: either a rival, his own son, a servant wench, or a lackey. Harlequin often takes advantage of his addled brain by disguising himself as a fellow-merchant and presenting him with a bill in which are listed " Two dozen chairs of Holland linen; six cushions trimmed in truffles; two tents of spider-web bordered with fringes of Swiss moustaches," etc.

TRASTULLO, A VARIANT OF PANTALOON
Callot

Pantaloon's valet is either Grillo, Nane, Mantecha, or Harlequin; but, whoever it is, he is usually starved by his master until he hardly casts a shadow. Pantaloon engages Mantecha as an apprentice valet, and discharges the poor boy just at the dinner-hour. Tafalo, Mantecha's father, entreats Pantaloon to take his son back into his service. The master is obdurate at first, but finally consents on condition that Mantecha takes his meals at home. Such are Pantaloon's niggardly triumphs, but his victims plan their revenge and play him tricks which ought to send them to the gallows.

Sometimes Pantaloon forgets his famous probity and sells nutmeg as Mestre nuts, or a bit of dried earth from the bottom of a marsh as cloves, or a decoction of eels as snake-balm.

Occasionally Pantaloon is a rich and noble lord, and then his name is dignified by the title of " Don " or even " Magnifico." His clothes are cut in the Venetian style of the sixteenth century; ordinarily they are old and threadbare, but in his affluence he wears only silks and satins. Instead of attending to his own affairs, he much prefers to meddle with those of the State; and when his vanity suffers he forgets his habitual meekness and flourishes his dagger.

DEVELOPMENTS IN THE PERSONALITY OF PANTALOON

Riccoboni writes:

Toward the close of the seventeenth century he changed into a respectable head of the family, extremely particular about his word of honour and a strict disciplinarian of his children. He retains several of his more pronounced failings, however, for he goes on being tricked by every one he knows; he is still either duped into spending money that he does not intend to spend, or fooled into marrying his daughter to her lover in spite of other matches which he makes for her.

At the beginning of the eighteenth century the people of Venice undertook to introduce certain reforms in the country and used the character of Pantaloon by way of illustration. Thus he was seen sometimes as a husband, sometimes as a very jealous lover, or, again, as a rake and a bully, and so forth.

PANTALOON
Callot

THE REQUIREMENTS FOR THE RÔLE

The actor who assumes this *rôle* should have at his finger-tips a complete command of the Venetian dialect with all of its variations, proverbs, and phrases. He should be able to play a decrepit old man who tries to pass himself off as a youth. He should have a harangue ready for every occasion, such as when Pantaloon attempts to give his son convincing advice, or when he offers suggestions to princes and potentates, as well as compliments for the women he wooes, or any other discourse which may be necessary. He should try to provoke laughter at appropriate junctures by his self-importance and stupidity, and in this manner represent a man ripe in years who pretends to be a tower of strength and good counsel for others, whereas in truth he is blinded by amorous passion and continually doing puerile things which might lead an observer to call him a child, for all that he is almost a centenarian. The actor should also demonstrate how Pantaloon's avarice, common enough in men of his advanced age, is dominated by a more virulent vice, love, which makes of him a callow greybeard so lost to all sense of decency that it may well be said:

A chi in Amor s'invecchia, oltre ogni pena
Si convengono i ceppi e la catena.[1]

[1] "Anyone who falls in love when he is old should be put in the stocks."

Gillot

PANTALOON'S TRAVELS

The famous Pantaloon, a prophet in his own country, had only to go abroad to win the full measure of honours he deserved. He was acclaimed by the citizens of Bologna, as well as the Tuscans, Viennese, French, and Spanish. He crossed the sea and traversed many lands. Shakespeare knew him well, and wrote of him :

> The sixth age shifts
> Into the lean and slipper'd pantaloon,
> With spectacles on nose and pouch on side,
> His youthful hose well sav'd, a world too wide
> For his shrunk shank ; and his big manly voice,
> Turning again toward childish treble, pipes
> And whistles in his sound.[1]

Engraving by G. J. Xavery

[1] *As You Like It*, Act II, Scene VII.

PANTALOON'S COSTUME

Pantaloon wore a short, bright red jacket which was tight-fitting and buttoned in front, and close-fitting trousers of the same colour. Sometimes the turn-over collar of his shirt fell over the top of his jacket. He wrapped himself in the *zimarra*, or long black cloak with plain sleeves. Upon his head he wore either a brimless Greek cap or a black toque with rolled edges; his footgear consisted of either Turkish sandals or soft slippers. During the sixteenth century Pantaloon almost always carried a huge dagger and purse at his belt, while underneath the shameless phallus, doubtless a survival from the theatre of antiquity, was quite visible. This description is in accordance with the different engravings in the *Recueil Fossard*, dating about 1577. I should add that Pantaloon appeared at times in the trousers just described, and at other times in short breeches, with red stockings either secured by ribbons or else rolled at the top. The short breeches were worn as early as the sixteenth century. Toward 1660 the actor Turi played the part in a red *zimarra*; however, the oldest documents, contrary to all expectations, show the character in a black cloak.

PANTALOON'S MASK

He wore a brown mask with a prominent hooked nose, and, occasionally, round spectacles.[1] The moustache was grey and sparse. A white beard stretched from ear to ear, and came to one or two points well in advance of the chin, so that the tufts shook ludicrously as soon as Pantaloon began to talk.

PANTALOON'S PROLOGUE

There is an interesting prologue in the Venetian dialect which the noted Pantaloon Bruni recited at his performances in 1600. As a matter of curiosity it is given below in its entirety for the inspection of the reader, who must be assured that there has been no intention of trying to play a joke on him by leaving it untranslated. One respects Pantaloon too sincerely to betray him, and, besides, any attempt to render the delightful speech of the original in another tongue would only prove tame and inadequate. The only comment to be made, therefore, is that those who can understand the text will understand it, as our old friend Baloardo would say, and those who are unable to will, of course, turn the page.

Prologo da Pantalone

Se l'homo animal da do man (Magnifici, e Zenerosi Signori) è solo in questo mondo che vuol tegnir el mondo sotto de lù, e tutti i altri viuenti pi che sotto i piè, non desse alle volte in tel bestial noo ghe xe dubbio nigun chi el pareraue el padron de sta casa, el Principe de sta Republica, el Peota de sta Naue, el Mocarna de sto Impero e l'anema de sto corpo: daspuo che el monde xe vna Naue che altre volte se affondete in t'vn deluvio salvandose solo un

[1] *Recueil Fossard*, Plate XX.

PANTALOON
Watteau

battello. Una casa dove la natura vivi fa che habitemo in soffita, e morti la ne manda in magazen sotto terra. Una republica che el primo fondator ordeno che fina la bestie vivesse in libertà. Un imperio dozion o vicisitudini ne fa vegnir in cognizion razza real; e un corpo che per le sue alterazion o vicisitudini ne fa vegnir in cognozion delle sue infimitae. Ma per che co diseva l' huomo non cognosendo el so ben, contrastando alla so felicitae da si medemo se fabrica mille desgusti per viver in continue borasche. Considerè no ghe manca chi crede ch' el non haver robba sia una gran felicità, vordè quel balordo de Crate che butto via i so bezi, e Antippo che venduo tutta la so facultae la butete in mar per che sti balordi diseva che i ghe i ghe impediva i stuidij e nu altri per hauer occasion de studiar con tanta industria cer chemo de cavar soldi da vu altri; e moldi de vu cognosando che i soldi son de comodo e non descomodo, cosi mal volontiera i ne i da e cosi facilmente i ne stronza la paga. Altri dise che l'esser orbo è un gran contento; openion de quel filosofastro di Asclepiade, che vegnuo orbo ringraziette el cielo che per l' auegnir el faraue andà accompagnao dove prima l' andava solo, e non havevane abuo tanti impedimenti a i so studij. E vu, signori, chi non vorave haver cent occhi per veder in questa cittae donne cosi belle, fabriche cosi pellegrine, mercanzie cosie eccellenti, gentill'-huomeni cosi illustri. Poltroni recever pugni cosi eccelsi, e bravi correr cosi forte? Altri se duol perchè so mojer se troga spasso con un so vesin mantegnando uni opinion soi diabolica che le corne nassano al' homo quando se semini in tele vaneze della donna; senti cari Signori a consolazion de sti poveri homini. Se l' honor è un premio della virtù, perchè un homo che viva virtuosamente benchè so mojer sia poco manco che puttana non halo da esser premià de honor? E se l' honor xe un abito dell' anima di chi opera ben: com uodo le aggion d' un altro el pon far vituperoso? E se tutte le virtuose azzion d' una donna non puol far honorao un huomo infame per che la infamia d'una donna puo desonorar un huomo da ben? Altri han opinion ch' el non pagar i comedianti sia opera de carità, e nù haveno opinion che chi no paga . . . l' opinion xe brutta, non lo vogio dir; pero paghè che farè ben. Ma se anderave troppo in longo se de tutte le opinion eronee de l' huomo volesse trattar. Vegnemo solo alla considerazion che costu animal rasonevole se servi cosi mal della rason. L' huomo è un animal prodizioso composto de pezzi contratij, l' anema xe come un principe, el corpo come una bestia, con tutto zo queste do parte se abbrazza cosi ben tra loro, che i non puol vivere inseme senza verra, ne separarse senza dolor; podendosi con rason buttar in occhio l'un all' altra de non poder con ella ne senz' ella vivere. L' huom ose puo distinguer in tre parti: anima e spirito e carne: el spirito e la carne han tiolto in mezzo l'anema; el spirito per farmi intendere xe come el Principe nella republica: non spira e non respira che beni del ciel al qual sempre varda per contrario xe come la lega d' un popolo tumultuario e furfante, la scovazera e sentina dell' huomo, parte che cala sempre al mal. E l' anima nel mezzo xe come i principali del popular: è diferente tra 'l ben el mal, tralmerito e demerito; vien solecità dal spirito e dalla carne, e secondo da qual parte se butta la si fa spirituale e buona, o carnale e cattiva, come sarave a dir el nostro Portonier xe l' anemo, la cassetta el spirito, e le so scarsele la carne. Questa anima ha quei bezi in man la casseta el solicita a meterghei drento, le scarsele monstrandoghe l' util proprio prega per elle: segondo a quel che el se resolve el doventa, huomo da ben o laro. Da queste resoluzion dell' anema ne succiede i varij pensieri e stravagante opinion dell' huomo parte delle quali ne ho trattà cosi in compendio. Concludo dunque che l' huomo xe felice o misero, bon o cattivo segoudo che lu medesmo vuol. Pero se in potestà dell' homo xe d' operar ben e mal, che porà sforzar vu, signori, a criar adesso che xe tempo de star zitti? Chi pora sforzar la vostra modestia a non supportar i nostri marcamenti? Nigun; ste dunque zitti, che nu parla remo cercando con una bella commedia recompensar et premio abuo da vu Signori alla porta, e la grazia che receveremo del vestro silenzio.

PANTALOON AND HIS FAMILY

THE MOST CELEBRATED INTERPRETERS OF PANTALOON

1578	*Gelosi*	Giulio Pasquati of Padua
1580	*Uniti*	Il Braga
1600		Bruni
1630	*Fedeli*	Luigi Benotti of Vicenza
1645	*Mazarin's Company*	Ciulace Arrighi
1653	*At the Petit Bourbon*	Turi of Modena
1670	*The Company of the Duke of Modena*	Antonio Riccoboni, father of Lelio (Luigi Riccoboni)
1703	*At the fair theatres in Paris*	The Elder Colalto
1712	*The Company of Octave at the fair theatres*	Luigi Berlucci
		Giovanni Crevelli, who made his success under the name of " the Venetian Pantaloon "
c. 1716	*The Regent's Company*	Alborghetti of Venice
1732		Fabio Sticotti, gentleman of Friuli, husband of Ursula Astori (the Singer)
1744		Carlo Veronese, father of Caroline and Camille
1750	*Company of Medebach and of Carlo Gozzi*	Darbes
c. 1750	*In Venice*	Francesco Rubini; Corrini
	In Bologna	Ferramonti
	In Milan	Pasini
	In Florence	Luigi Benotti; Golinetti; Garinelli; Franceschini
1759		Colalto, author of *Les Trois Frères Jumeaux Vénitiens*, a play which had a "prodigious success," according to Grimm, who was not easy to please

Signor Gorgibus

PANTALOON'S LAST WILL AND TESTAMENT

I bequeath to my valet twenty-five sharp lashes with a good whip for having bored a hole in the bottom of my chamber-pot and made me wet the bed.

THE FAMILY TREE OF PANTALOON

ATELLANÆ
CASNAR and PAPPUS

|

COMEDIES OF PLAUTUS
THEUROPIDES, EUCLIO, DEMIPHO, NICOBULUS, DEMENETUS

|

COMMEDIA DELL' ARTE

PANTALONE
ZANOBIO DA PIOMBINO, FACANAPPA, IL BERNARDONE
(THE BARON) (Palermo), CASSANDRE (sixteenth century), IL BISCEGLIESE (Naples)

Commedia sostenuta	*French Farce*	*Plays of Gherardi*
COLLOFONIO, PANDOLFO, DIOMÈDE, DEMETRIO, COCCOLIN, BARTOLO, GERONTIO	GAULTIER GARGUILLE JACQUEMIN JADOT	PERSILLET BROCANTIN SOTINET GÉRONTE GAUFICHON. . . .

COMEDIES OF MOLIÈRE
ORGON, GORGIBUS, HARPAGON

Pangrazio the Bisceglian

As the name indicates, Pangrazio the Bisceglian originated in the little town of Bisceglia in Apulia—toward the end of the seventeenth century. The dialect of that region had a whining accent which never failed to delight all Italians, and the Neapolitans in particular, and it was for this reason that when a play was given at the San Carlino Theatre the placard nearly always read, " *Con Pangrazio Biscegliese.*" [1]

Pangrazio is an old man. Whether he be merchant, common citizen, or peasant, he is always the yokel come to the city on a holiday. He is eternally trusting and gullible, and in consequence is always being cheated. His excessive parsimony borders on avarice. And, what is most important, he is invariably astonished and shocked by everything he sees. " They don't do that where I come from," he says, or :

> It isn't as noisy in my town as it is here, and people don't keep pushing you out of the way. Back home everybody knows everybody else. Your Naples isn't so much, after all.

[1] " With Pangrazio the Bisceglian."

You ought to see Bisceglia, built high up on a big rock. There's a town for you! And a beautiful country with handsome villas, and wines and raisins that are famous the world over. That's more than you can say for your Naples. You don't see all the dirt and filth at Bisceglia that you do here. Once I finish my business you won't catch me staying long in all this uproar of fleas and beggars and loose women.

THE BISCEGLIAN AT THE SAN CARLINO THEATRE IN "LE JETTATORE"[1]

The three raps for attention had already sounded, and the little orchestra began the overture. Finally the curtain rose and Don Pancrace was revealed, decked out in all the known charms against bad luck. He had the ox horns and the coral hands, the rat made out of lava from Vesuvius, and the heart, fork, and serpent. He advanced to the front of the stage and, with a beseeching air, said, "Ladies and gentlemen, if I have forgotten anything I hope you will tell me. These horns which I carry under either arm save me from having my forehead decorated in a similar fashion. But to what purpose? It isn't in Dame Pancrace to be unfaithful to me. By turning this coral hand around so that the forefinger and little finger point outward I can escape the evil influence of suspicious-looking individuals. My equipment is complete, and I am told that I can now venture out upon the Via di Toledo without risk. It is very comforting to realize that an honest citizen is perfectly safe in Naples, for it is clear that he is in no danger if he conducts himself as he should. Nevertheless I am uneasy about a curious dream I had last night, and I feel that I ought to return to Bisceglia as soon as possible."

At this point Don Pancrace describes his dream and deduces from it all sorts of sinister omens. As a matter of fact, the poor fellow runs into one misfortune after the other that day. He first becomes entangled in his collection of amulets, and while he is struggling to extricate himself a thief comes along and steals his handkerchief; then another thief makes off with his tobacco-pouch, and a third his watch. Next Polichinelle disguises himself as a bailiff and charges him with an imaginary misdemeanour. Then a mischievous woman pretends that he is her long-lost lover who was kidnapped by pirates and taken to the Barbary Coast; she kisses him and badgers him with attentions. When Pancrace tries to flee he is knocked down by a cab and sent floundering into the mud. He picks himself up, uttering every known curse against his misfortunes as well as all the thieves and harlots in Naples. At that moment two pleasant young fellows, wearing yellow vests, watch-charms, gold chains, and eyeglasses, approach him and help him to brush himself. This fortunate encounter charms the poor Pancrace, and he goes into raptures over the courtesy and perfect manners of the young bloods of Naples. They go to an inn for refreshment, and, after rapping upon the table with their light canes, the young gentlemen order the waiter to serve Milord with all the richest and most expensive dishes, such as rice with peas, chops *à la Milanese*, soft-boiled eggs, big radishes, and cucumber salad. Pancrace prefers the macaroni to which he is accustomed. He is given a *rotolo* [roll] which he tears apart with his fingers and devours. Meanwhile the two dandies have been consuming the dishes which Pancrace refused. When they have finished they arise, take their hats, and after profuse good wishes leave. The old man cannot believe that he has been duped again. He entertains the audience by all sorts of far-fetched conjectures to explain the absence of the young Don Limones and finally pays the bill, though not without haggling over the price.[2]

[1] *The Witch-doctor.*

[2] Paul de Musset.

THE COSTUME OF PANGRAZIO THE BISCEGLIAN

Pangrazio dresses, in the fashion of the seventeenth century, in a doublet with very short sleeves and full breeches of black velvet. His sleeves and his skull-cap are red. Pangrazio Cuccuzziello (Pancrace Pickle), who is less ostentatious by nature, wears a red wig with a queue made of salsify. He wears a jacket in the Louis XV style, which is brocaded and figured. His stockings are red, and he wears buckled slippers. He has no mask.

Cassandro and Zanobio

Cassandro of Siena and Zanobio of Piombino were two sixteenth-century copies of the Venetian Pantaloon, with whom, in fact, they often made their appearance on the stage of the Gelosi troupe. Cassandro and Zanobio always played the part of a level-headed father, which served as a strong contrast to Pantaloon's eccentricities. Cassandro disappeared at the end of the Renaissance, and was not seen again until he was reborn in the eighteenth century as a rehabilitated Pantaloon in a straw-coloured wig and " rosy mug smeared with tobacco." This charming fellow was rich and mean, his mouth always hung agape, and he pretended that he was short-sighted and deaf, the better to deceive the world from behind his tremendous spectacles. His watch was so gigantic that his neighbours could hear it tick when he went along the street, and would say, " There goes Cassandro."

Cassandrino and Pasquale

These two characters are obviously one and the same person, and both are Roman. They are respectable burghers and full of years. But their age rests lightly upon them, they dress with impeccable taste, they are mundane and agreeable by nature, and very polished and witty. Cassandrino originated in the eighteenth century, and, because of the censorship of the time, became a member of the marionette theatre. Stendhal, after attending one of the performances at the Fiano Palace, described him as follows :

> The theatrical character most in vogue with the Roman people at present is Cassandrino, an old Lothario between fifty-five and sixty but still spry and on the alert. His white hair is heavily powdered and carefully arranged—almost like a cardinal's. Cassandrino is, moreover, a man of great experience, and he excels especially in his knowledge of the world. He would be a paragon of virtue if it were not for the fact that he has the misfortune to fall in love regularly with every woman he meets. You will admit that such a character is not a bad inspiration in a country where the Government is an oligarchic court made up of celibates, and all the power is in the hands of old men. Cassandrino belongs, of course, to the laity ; but I will wager that there wasn't a soul in the entire theatre who did not see in him a cardinal with a red hat, or at least a *monsignore* with violet stockings. As you know, the *monsignori* are the young men about the Papal Court, the councillors of this country, and that position leads to others more important. Rome is crowded with *monsignori* of Cassandrino's age who have missed preferment and console themselves as best they can while waiting for the coveted hat.

Facanappa and Bernardone

Facanappa is a sort of Pantaloon become sage and seer. He speaks only the most vulgar of Venetian dialects. His huge, hooked nose is adorned with green spectacles. He is short in stature, cunning, and imaginative. Facanappa wears a very long white frock-coat, a flat hat with wide brims, and a red cravat. He went by the name of Bernardone at the beginning of the eighteenth century.

The Baron

The Baron is a Sicilian lord who is the dupe of everybody in general and of his daughters and servants in particular. He was in high favour in Palermo ; he is, in fact, a Sicilian offshoot of the Pantaloon tradition.

Gaultier-Garguille

This name, which can be translated " Great greedy mouth," was adopted by a French comedian, named Hugues Guéru, who played at the Théâtre du Marais and later at the Hôtel de Bourgogne toward the close of the sixteenth century. Gaultier-Garguille is a Gallicized Pantaloon. M. Sand describes him thus :

> His body was emaciated, his legs attenuated, and his face broad. He wore a greenish half-mask with a long nose, a moustache of cat's hair, a thatch of stiff white bristle on top, and a pointed beard like Pantaloon's. He had a black skull-cap, black slippers, a black doublet with sleeves of red wool, black hose of the same material, a pouch, which hung at his belt, and a cane.

Signor Cascareth

XV

The Doctor

WHEN the eminent Baloardo came into the world, about the year 1500, in the city of Bologna—mother of letters and learning—it is said that, instead of wailing like an ordinary infant, his first utterance was a fine Latin quotation, slightly mutilated. Indeed, Gracian Baloardo was born a doctor as surely and naturally as other human beings are born with a facial blemish of some kind. No doubt the air of Bologna had something to do with it, saturated as it was with knowledge emanating from so many colleges of foreign nations and grave professors dilating upon " men and things " as they passed along the streets of the town. When the Doctor finally reached the stage in 1560 there was precious little he did not know. He was a philosopher, astronomer, man of letters, cabalist, barrister, grammarian, diplomat, and physician. Like Pico della Mirandola, he could talk *de omni re scibile*, and did. But his homilies often produced a singular effect, alas. For example, he undertook one day to use his vast learning in an affair which did not concern him in the least. It must be admitted, however, that no one could see a clear issue in the case but himself, and therefore, after he had launched forth upon his disquisition and was about to reveal the inmost truth of the matter, he discovered that the judge and jury had fallen fast asleep and that the audience had melted away.

The good Doctor is a member of every academy, known and unknown, and he is one of the brighter lights of the Accademia della Crusca. It is a curious fact that, although he spends his entire time with his nose in a book, it is always painfully difficult for him to give a Greek or Latin quotation without murdering it alive. He also confuses the Fates with the Graces. But, luckily enough, he is endowed with prodigious aplomb, which usually intimidates even the best instructed of his listeners until, unable to endure any more, they rise up and give him a sound beating. But even then the flow of his eloquence rarely ceases.

Some unfeeling folk say that the Doctor is " an eternal gas-bag who cannot open his mouth without spitting out a Latin phrase or quotation." And there is a verse about him which maintains that :

Quand le docteur parle, l'on doute
Si c'est latin ou bas-breton,
Et souvent celui qui l'écoute
L'interrompt à coups de bâton.[1]

It scarcely seems fair to maltreat so excellent a savant when he has spent his whole life learning everything without understanding anything.

1 " When the Doctor speaks one cannot tell whether it is Latin or Low Breton, and often his auditor interrupts him with a thrashing."

One fine day the Doctor was married, and his wife deceived him the following morning—if not on their wedding night, as some say. Later on he attempted to make up for lost time with his courting and play the gallant to the pretty women of the town, but they all responded rudely to his advances and called him by his own name, Baloardo ('Dullard'). His daughters and his servants made fun of him continually, and, to his own great astonishment, he even joined in the sport himself at times.

THE DOCTOR
Sixteenth century

The Doctor's chief consolation in life is his old friend Pantaloon, who occasionally makes the journey all the way from Venice to see him and converse with some one really worthy of his intellectual powers. As a matter of fact, these two greybeards possess more than one trait in common: they are of about the same age, they have the same fatal weakness for oratory, and they are miserly. They are constantly inviting one another to magnificent banquets, which, if the truth were told, would not keep a bird alive. The Doctor and Pantaloon present a highly impressive spectacle when they go out walking together, the one with his long, trailing robes, and the other with his long red stork legs.

Gracian Baloardo is only one of many names that the Doctor bears; he has others far more sonorous. Bianchi, the actor in the Gelosi company who played the Doctor *rôles*, announced himself as: "Plusquamperfetto Dottor Gratiano Partesana da Francolin." There are also other titles such as "Forbizon Spaccastrummolo," "Balanzoni," "Grazian de Violoni Scatalone," "Campanaccio," "Hippocraso," etc. Sand, in describing the Doctor, wrote that

THE DOCTOR
Seventeenth century

> The Doctor Balanzoni Lombarda wears a large hat turned up on both sides. He comes from Bologna, and, though chiefly a medical practitioner, he dabbles nevertheless in alchemy and other occult sciences. He is miserly, conceited, and unable to resist his sensual and gross appetites. When he goes to see a patient he chats about everything except the patient's malady. He becomes wholly trivial, wanders about the room, poking his nose into everything, breaks the ornaments, and finally takes the patient's pulse as a salve to his conscience, talking volubly the while about Columbine's rumpled hair or Violette's figure. The dying patient falls asleep at last, exhausted by the recital of the amorous exploits of which this Doctor, with his rubicund nose, pimply cheeks, and glistening

eyes, boasts interminably in lush and lisping tones. Once the patient is asleep the Doctor proceeds to ogle the maid-servant and act the young cavalier before the daughter or mistress of the house. There is no record of any case that he has ever cured, with the possible exception of Punch, who could not die if he would. With Punch, however, he had the most unexpected success, for it appears that some trouble once arose between them

THE DOCTOR
Seventeenth century
Engraving by de Geijn

THE DOCTOR ABOUT 1577
This may be either Luzio Burchiella or Ludovico de Bianchi.
Detail from an engraving in the "Recueil Fossard"

over a love affair—or perhaps it was gourmandizing. Whatever the cause, the effect was that Punch pretended to be ill, called in the good Doctor, and gave him such a reprimand as he was not likely to forget for many a year.

The following is a diverting description of the Doctor by a Columbine of the seventeenth century :

Properly speaking, the term 'Doctor' is but an empty word ; it is like an elaborate sign on a sorry tavern. The title of Doctor is no proof that a man is learned ; it only indicates that he should be. Averroës explained it best when he said that a doctor is, ordinarily, a

THE DOCTOR
Second half of the seventeenth century
N. Bonnart

kind of fowl which looks as if it might be flesh and turns out to be—fish! When a rabbit has a taste of broom-plant and wild thyme you may be sure that it comes from a real warren; but when it tastes of cabbage it is only a miserable little beast out of a hutch. You must smell a doctor with the nose of reason, and if he has the odour of *belles-lettres* he is a real doctor; but if he smells only of school and dialectics he is little better than a tame rabbit.

ROMAGNESI AS THE DOCTOR
Engraving by Gillot

The Costume of the Doctor

The costume of the Doctor in the sixteenth century and up to the beginning of the seventeenth was a caricatured version of the ordinary dress which the men of science and letters in Bologna wore both at the University and about the town. The Doctor was, with rare exceptions, clothed entirely in black. His footgear was black, and a short black gown fell below his knees. Above this he had a long black robe which extended to his heels. He also wore a small black toque. About 1653 this costume was modified by Augustin Lolli, one of the foremost actors of the *rôle* at that time. He wore an enormous black felt hat, a jacket cut in the style of Louis XIV, short trousers, and a wide, soft ruff about his neck. As may be seen by the illustrations, the costume varied considerably in detail in the course of three centuries, but never lost its basic character.

The Mask

The Doctor wore either a black or a flesh-coloured mask which covered only his forehead and his nose. His cheeks were smeared with red, according to a tradition

ROMAGNESI AS THE DOCTOR
Seventeenth century

which receives the support of Goldoni as well as of several others. Goldoni states, in fact, that "the singular mask which covers his forehead and nose took its form from a birthmark which disfigured the face of a jurisconsult of those days. It is one of the traditions still in existence among the amateurs of the *commedia dell' arte*." The earlier mask of the Doctor was set off by a short, pointed beard. The general aspect of the face conveyed an impression of foolish self-sufficiency, mingled with a gravity which bordered on severity, and the effect of these contrasts was comic in the extreme. It may be noted that the Messere Dotour of the *Recueil Fossard* (p. 198) does not wear a mask.

A Few of the "Cent et quinze Conclusions du Plusquamperfetto Dottor Gratiano Partesana da Francolin Comico Geloso et altre Manifatture et Compositioni nella sua Buona Lingua"[1] (by Ludovico de Bianchi, an actor of the Renaissance)

3. He who is always wrong is more right than anyone else.
4. A ship in mid-ocean is far from port.
9. A bandy-legged man and a humpback will never come straight.
13. A citizen of Ferrara is not a Mantuan.
22. Anyone who is sleeping has not yet awakened.
24. A person who is ill can say that he is unwell.

One of the Tirades[2] of the Doctor

(SEVENTEENTH CENTURY)

THE DOCTOR AND THE PHYSICIAN

THE PHYSICIAN

Yes, sir, I practise medicine out of pure love for it. I nurse, I purge, I sound, I operate, I saw, I cup, I snip, I slash, I smash, I split, I break, I extract, and tear, and cut, and dislocate, I dissect, and trim, and slice, and, of course, I show no quarter.

Doctor Strummolo (1610)

THE DOCTOR

You are a veritable avalanche of medicine.

THE PHYSICIAN

I am not only an avalanche of medicine, but the bane of all maladies whatsoever. I exterminate all fevers and chills, the itch, gravel, measles, the plague, ringworm, gout, apoplexy, erysipelas, rheumatism, pleurisy, catarrh, both wind-colic and ordinary colic, without counting those serious and light illnesses which bear the same name. In short, I wage such cruel and relentless warfare against all forms of illness that when I see a disorder becoming ineradicable in a patient I even go as far as to kill the patient in order to relieve him of his disorder.

THE DOCTOR

That is an excellent cure.

THE PHYSICIAN

I know no other. (*He talks himself out of breath before the* DOCTOR *can stop him.*) The jaundice, symptoms. . . . Itching, symptoms. . . . Gravel, symptoms. . . . The . . . the . . the . . . symptoms. . . .

[1] "Hundred and fifteen conclusions of the more than perfect Doctor Gratiano Partesana of Francolin, comedian of the Gelosi, and other fabrications and compositions in his own good tongue."

[2] Here used as a regular term of the theatre for any long speech or recital.—Translator.

THE DOCTOR

He's going to burst.

THE PHYSICIAN

The . . . the . . . the . . .

THE DOCTOR

He looks as if his spleen were swelling. Sir——

Fabio as the Doctor
Engraving by Gillot

THE PHYSICIAN

The spleen, you say? Ho! We shall require an anatomical chart for that. The spleen lies in the left hypochondria beneath the diaphragm between the ribs and the ventricles near the kidneys. On that side it is attached to the ventricle, the peritoneum, and the omentum.

THE DOCTOR

I wish you'd burst open, with all my heart.

Engraving by G. J. Xavery

THE PHYSICIAN

The heart is a muscle composed of membranes, flesh, tendons, etc.

THE DOCTOR

He's making my ears buzz.

THE DOCTOR

THE PHYSICIAN

The ear, you say? The skin that covers it adheres to the cartilage by means of a nervous membrane which makes it very sensitive.

THE DOCTOR

I'd like to bash in his nose. . . .

THE PHYSICIAN

The nose is divided into two nasal passages by cartilage, and communicates with the brain by the cribiform bone.

THE DOCTOR

I'd like to snatch out all his hair and leave him bald-headed.

THE PHYSICIAN

Hair comes from an excrement of the blood.

THE DOCTOR

If I had a club I'd break every rib in your body.

THE PHYSICIAN

The ribs are bent back, etc., etc.

THE DOCTOR (*pursuing him*)

Go to the devil; my head is splitting.

THE PHYSICIAN (*running off stage*)

Ignoramus, don't you know that the back of the head is called the occiput, and that is where the occipital bone is found? It fits together at the suture, and the summit, or top of the head under which is the suture, is called sagittal, and one part of the two parietal bones . . .

This scene out of the *Chevalier du Soleil*, though given in 1680, is nevertheless quite in the spirit and tone of a Renaissance tirade entitled *Le Docteur*, which is omitted here because it is written in Bolognese dialect mixed with Latin jargon, and therefore loses its comic flavour in translation.

THE PRINCIPAL INTERPRETERS OF THE RÔLE OF THE DOCTOR

1572	*In the Gelosi troupe*	LUDOVICO DE BIANCHI (DOCTOR PARTESANA)
1577	——	LUZIO BURCHIELLA
1578	——	LUDOVICO (OF BOLOGNA)
1570	*In the Confidenti troupe*	BERNARDINO LOMBARDI, a good actor and excellent poet. Author of a five-act comedy in verse called *L'Alchimista*

THE PRINCIPAL INTERPRETERS OF THE RÔLE OF THE DOCTOR—*continued*

1603	*The Duke of Mantua's troupe*	AGOCCHI (DOCTOR GRACIAN BALOARDO)
		BAGLIANI (DOCTOR FORBIZON), who played in Bavaria
1633	——	ANGELO AUGUSTINO LOLLI OF BOLOGNA
1694	——	MARCO ANTONIO ROMAGNESI
1690	*In Italy*	GIOVANNI PAGHETTI and GALEOZZO SAVORINI
1716	*The Regent's troupe*	FRANCESCO MATTERAZZI
1716	*In Venice and Vienna*	GANZACHI and LUGI OF VENICE
1732	——	BONAVENTURA BENOZZI, brother of the famous Silvia
1734	——	PIETRO VERONESE
1760	——	SAVI

THE FAMILY TREE OF THE DOCTOR

The ridiculous physicians of the Dorian mountebanks taken over into Roman farces

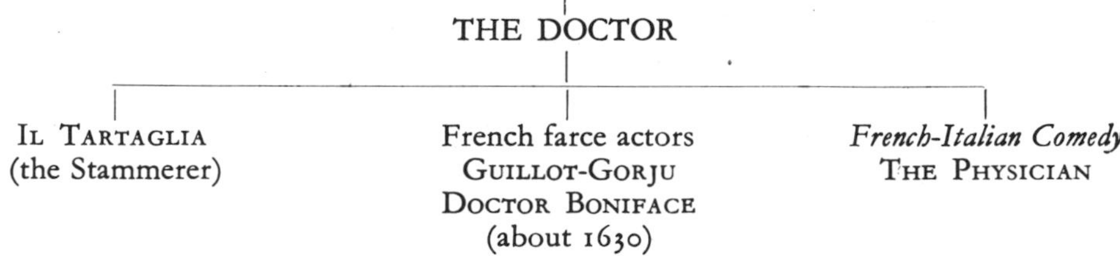

Guillot-Gorju

Guillot-Gorju, the Doctor in the old French school of farce (1634), was created by Bertrand Haudoin de Saint-Jacques, who seems to have been also the Dean of the Faculty of Medicine. "He was a tall, dark man, very ugly in appearance. His eyes were deep set, and he had a drunkard's nose, and, although he looked exceedingly like a monkey and really had no need for a mask upon the stage, he never failed to wear one." Guillot-Gorju, dressed in black from head to foot, wore the costume of the Doctors of the time of Henri IV. There is an engraving of him which bears the legend :

Guillot-Gorju, chacun admire
Et le savoir et le bien dire
Que tu débites en te moquant,
Et par ta haute rhétorique,
Le plus souvent tu fais la nique
Au plus docte et plus éloquent.[1]

[1] "Guillot-Gorju, every one wonders at the learning and eloquence you display when making fun of us. By your great rhetoric you often make mock of the most learned and the most eloquent."

THE DOCTOR

This former Dean of the Faculty and Doctor on the boards once thought of retiring from the theatre and going to live at Melun, but a "sadness overtook him" and he returned to continue his career at the Hôtel de Bourgogne. It was not difficult for him to interpret a grotesque character, for he had only to be his natural self. The little drawing below shows him in one of his *rôles*.

Guillot-Gorju

XVI

Pulcinella, his Ancestors, and his Family

CUCURUCU, MEO-PATACCA, IL SITONNO, BIRRICHINO, POLICHINELLE, PUNCH

Pulcinella

THE doom of duality was pronounced against Pulcinella even before he was born, for he had, it appears, the special privilege of having two fathers, Maccus and Bucco. Inasmuch as Maccus and Bucco were not in the least alike, Pulcinella was always drawn toward opposite poles by his dual heredity.

Maccus was quick, witty, impertinent, ironical, and a bit cruel; Bucco, self-sufficient, fawning, silly, timid, boastful, and, in short, a thief.

ANCIENT STATUETTE IN TERRA-COTTA (FRONT AND PROFILE) REPRESENTING ONE OF THE ACTORS IN THE ATELLANÆ

Compare with illustration of Pulcinella on p. 209.

Louvre, Paris. Photo Giraudon

By the same token the doom of duality worked its effect upon Pulcinella's personal appearance. Originally he was only slightly humpbacked; then, as a counterbalance, his pot-belly began to swell. The hump in turn grew larger, and the belly again followed suit.

From Maccus Pulcinella inherited his hooked nose, his hump, and his long, spindling legs, which gave him the look of a topheavy chicken when he walked. From Bucco he derived his great flabby cheeks and his enormous mouth.

BUCCO
From " De Larvis sceninis et figuricis convicis," *by Ficoroni* (1754)

PULCINELLA
Detail from the celebrated picture in the Museum of the Comédie-Française, representing French and Italian *farceurs* in the time of Molière

MACCUS
Ancient bronze statuette, discovered at Rome in 1727
From Ficoroni

It was from Maccus also that Pulcinella (one of the Neapolitan Pulcinellas) acquired the habit of peeping like a frightened chick—a sound which his father had exaggerated by means of a *sgherlo* or *pivetta* [1]—as well as a tendency to hop about and weary every one but himself. It is this very ' hen-step,' in fact, which gave rise to Pulcinella's name. Maccus was called ' the hen '—Pullus Gallinaceus, which developed into Pullicinello or Pulcino, and finally Pulcinella. This etymology, however, has not as yet been corroborated by Dottore Graziano.

The other Neapolitan Pulcinella [2] was extremely reserved in his gestures, like Bucco, from whom he likewise inherited a trait of slow, deliberate movement and speech. As the result of the various opposing elements in his temperament Pulcinella was often given to strange exhibitions of behaviour. Those lazy and sensual lips of his would whip out

[1] A sort of whistle, or squeaker.—TRANSLATOR.
[2] The duality of his nature was such that he finally came to have two different bodies.

a biting phrase at the most unexpected moments, or he would suddenly execute some curious acrobatic feat, in spite of his apparently stiffened joints.

It must not be supposed that these two Pulcinellas were different examples of the character at different periods. Riccoboni tells us that they often appeared together at the same time on the Italian stage, taking the place of Scapin and Harlequin. They were in effect the expression of Pulcinella's dual personality and thus paradoxically the son of both Maccus and Bucco.

Detail from Drawing in "La Vita di Pulcinella," by Domenico Tiepolo

From M. Raymond Bloch's collection

Pulcinella belongs to so ancient a house that the noblest of the noble barely keep their heads above the common crowd in comparison with him. In order to prove his lineage we have only to compare the little antique bronze figure which was unearthed at Rome in 1727 with the portrait of the seventeenth-century Pulcinella in the Museum of the Comédie-Française. Never was a case of direct descent more clearly established.

After his appearance in Rome in 540 there is no trace of Pulcinella until the sixteenth century, when the *rôle* was revived by a certain Andrea Calcese, otherwise known as Ciuccio. This Calcese was, according to the Abbé G. B. Pacichelli (1693), a jurisconsult, while Andrea Perucci (1699) said that he was a tailor and maintained that it was not Ciuccio who first reincarnated the character, but the actor Silvio Fiorillo,[1] who also played Captain Matamoros. It was Perucci's opinion that Calcese was responsible only for perfecting the *rôle* afterward.[2] Both Pulliciniello and Cucurucu are found at the beginning of the seventeenth century in the *Balli di Sfessania*.

The son of two fathers and doubly humpbacked, Pulcinella was born twice at the same

[1] "Fiorillo, Silvio. Italian actor born in Naples in the second half of the sixteenth century. He performed first under the name of Capitan Matamoros and later under that of Pulcinella. He wrote various plays and poems, of which *The Three Vainglorious Captains* was published at Naples in 1621. The date of his death is uncertain, but as he was already leader of a company in Naples in 1594, when he could hardly have been less than twenty years of age, and as the date of his last publication is 1632, when he would, according to the former supposition, have been nearly seventy, it seems probable that he died soon after that date. His son Giovan Battista was also an actor, performing under the name of Trappolino."—*The Mask*, vol. iii, p. 162. His name was spelled both Fiorillo and Fiorilli.—Translator.

[2] See "The Genealogy of Pulcinella," by Dr Michele Scherillo, in *The Mask*, vol. iii, p. 22.

Drawing from "La Vita di Pulcinella," by Domenico Tiepolo

From M. Victor Rosenthal's collection

time in different quarters of the town of Benevento, formerly the capital of the Samnites. Like Bergamo, Benevento is built on the side of a mountain, and the people

PULLUS GALLINACEUS (?) (ANCIENT ROMAN THEATRE)
Collection of the Abbé de Saint-Non (1730–91)[1]

of the upper town are entirely unlike those of the lower. The 'upper' Pulcinella is intelligent, sensual, sly, keen; in him the blood of Bucco predominates. The 'lower'

RAZULLO AND CUCURUCU
Callot

PULLICINIELLO AND LUCRETIA
Callot

Pulcinella is a dull and coarse bumpkin. Yet both of them have as much the same nature as twin brothers. According to G. B. Doni, who died in 1647, Pulcinella came

[1] *Choix de quelques morceaux de peintures antiques d'Herculanum, extraits du Musée de Portici* (4to, Paris).

Drawing from "La Vita di Pulcinella," by Domenico Tiepolo

From M. Victor Rosenthal's collection

from the district of Crifona, in the principality of Salerno; but other authorities hold that he came from Acerra.

Whatever his native town, it is certain that Pulcinella took solid root in Naples, where he became so thoroughly acclimatized that a writer in 1860 observed: "Only thirty years ago there was not a single individual in Naples who did not have a touch of

PULCINELLA
Seventeenth century
Engraving by de Geijn

Pulcinella somewhere in his character. The trait is not so prevalent these days as it once was, although it is still sufficiently in evidence." Indeed, his popularity rivalled that of Pangrazio, for there was scarcely ever a play given at the San Carlino Theatre in Naples in which Pulcinella did not appear in some *rôle*—alive or dead.

Pulcinella was never one to be bowed down by the cares and responsibilities of a profession. He was by turns a magistrate, a poet, a master, and a valet, but rarely a husband or father of a family. As a general rule he appeared as an old bachelor, an eccentric and selfish old curmudgeon strongly inclined to sensual and epicurean gluttony. As he possessed a great deal of wit, and his hump was chockfull of a sense of humour, his chief weapon of defence was to feign stupidity. Being self-centred and bestial, Pulcinella had no scruples whatever, and because the moral suffering from his physical deformity reacted upon his brain at the expense of his heart, he was exceedingly cruel.

PULCINELLA IS ILL FROM TOO MUCH EATING AND DRINKING, BUT CONTINUES THE SAME DIET

PULCINELLA: "For a certain terrible and hidden malady which has run through me from head to foot, seated in this chariot of pain, unhappy and out of sorts, I ought, by a fatal destiny, to send for the same doctor who gave me the disease."

PULCINELLA'S SON [*to the donkey*]: "By your long, elegant ears, Grillo, I beg you to save me from my father's trouble."

Engraving by F. Vasconi (1719), *after a drawing by Pier-Leone Ghezzi* (1674–1755). *By courtesy of M. Crescenzo Fornari*

But Pulcinella grew mellower with age, and lapsed into a sort of second childhood which softened his cruelty into mere teasing and his sensuality into coarseness. He became an honest citizen and waxed dull, though fortunately he never lost his wit entirely. He was always good for an occasional flare of repartee, which would start off well, only to die away abruptly. He could still manage a sharp quip or two now and then, but he eventually preferred to amuse himself by eating macaroni out of an enormous chamber-pot. Pulcinella was not endowed with the gay and lively imagination for vulgarity which saved Harlequin from obscenity. For all his cleverness Pulcinella was sadly lacking in delicacy, and he was epicurean only in the most popular sense of the word.

OTHER THEORIES OF PULCINELLA'S ORIGIN

Pulcinella, like others of the clan, has been responsible for many differences of opinion among scholars of both the past and present. Dr Scherillo has made one of the most important contributions to the literature on Pulcinella in his article dealing with the origin of the character published in *The Mask*.[1] It is his theory that a peasant actor

FRENCH ENGRAVINGS OF THE END OF THE EIGHTEENTH CENTURY

belonging to one of the numerous troupes which flourished toward the close of the sixteenth century once gave a caricatured imitation of the type of peasant living in Acerra. The parody was so successful that the comedian Silvio Fiorillo adopted it and created a character-*rôle* out of it for himself. Dr Scherillo also states that Pulcinella's blouse, which closely resembles the general style of dress favoured by the peasants of that region, was developed from the Acerrian custom of wearing the shirt over the pantaloons. And he suggests that the striking analogies between Pulcinella and his ancestors in the *Atellanæ* plays may be explained as due to heredity and the genius of race handing down characteristics.

But before discussing this point further, let us consider several other versions of Pulcinella's origin.

Riccoboni (1731), Ficoroni (1750), Flogel (1788), and many others seem to regard Pulcinella as the direct descendant of the Atellanian Maccus. G. B. Doni, a Florentine nobleman who died in 1647, maintained, on the other hand, that Pulcinella originated

[1] Vol. iii, p. 22.

" a few years ago " in a marshy district called Crifona in the Principality of Salerno, and he cited as corroborative evidence that the inhabitants of that region were fat and pale and given to speaking in a nasal treble. As previously mentioned, the Abbé G. B. Pacichelli (1693), of Pistoia, had declared that a certain Andrea Ciuccio created the part and was widely imitated in his interpretation, while Andrea Perucci affirmed that the *rôle* had been created by Silvio Fiorillo as a caricature of the peasants of Acerra.

The Abbé Galiani then contributed the following colourful legend regarding the genesis of the character :

> During the last century a troupe of itinerant comedians one day came upon a group of peasants gathering grapes in the vicinity of Acerra. Both actors and vintagers had drunk too deeply, and soon the two factions fell to baiting one another. One of the peasants, Puccio d'Aniello by name, a corpulent wag with a long nose and a ready wit, was particularly sharp in the exchange of repartee. At length biting words gave way to blows, and the Thespians were put to rout. But when both parties had finally recovered their tempers and good sense the comedians, remembering Puccio d'Aniello's clever tongue, invited him to join their troupe. He accepted, and straightway became one of their most popular members. And his costume when on the stage was none other than the same white linen shirt which he had always worn in Acerra.

POLICHINELLE
Seventeenth century
Fruijtiers (Dutch School)

Now, as to Pulcinella's title to antiquity, it must be pointed out that seventeen dark centuries elapsed between Maccus and Bucco on the one hand and Pulcinella on the other, and there is no record of any similar type having existed in the interim. The total lack of documentation is not surprising, however, if the fact is borne in mind that his type, like several others, was entrusted to the safekeeping of the illiterate common people during this period. One has, then, only to remember that the popular mind is capable of every sort of quirk and failing, and the consequences are obvious. I had occasion to encounter this not so long ago when M. René Saulnier and I set out to make a study of the traditional French *imagerie populaire*.[1] We found many examples which did not go back further than the beginning of the nineteenth century, but not one of them had been preserved either in the archives of the region where they originated, in the civic registries, or, much less, in the memories of the inhabitants thereabouts. It would seem that anything more than two generations old is likely to be a closed book to the common people, who make little distinction between a century and a millennium. It is not

[1] See footnote on p. 27.

unusual to find them employing customs and locutions of speech which have come down to them from remote antiquity, and yet they remain unaware of the fact that they are perpetuating traditions ; nor are they conscious of the real meaning underlying their words and habits. People still say, "I don't care a rap,"[1] and never take into consideration that a rap was a counterfeit halfpenny and that it has been out of circulation since the eighteenth century. If questioned on the meaning of the term the average person might say that it meant a slight blow across the knuckles. If a peasant of the Gâtinais[2] were asked why he calls the dog-brier *godon*[3] he would give the first reason that popped into his head without ever taking into account that these berries are of a reddish-orange colour similar to the footgear of the English who pillaged his country in the fifteenth century. If he were told the correct etymology of the word he would probably be convulsed with laughter. This is what took place, in fact, when I tried the explanation on several citizens of a certain village where an English arrow is still to be seen lodged in the wall of the belfry, an evocative proof that the enemy were there. And by the same token the legend which the Abbé Galiani championed must have originated in much the same way.

Pulcinella on and off Stage
Seventeenth century

It is true that Pulcinella's costume resembles the dress of the peasants of Acerra in many respects, but that fact does not necessarily restrict his origin to the sixteenth century ; there are numerous cases where costumes have remained practically the same for centuries, as in Brittany, for example, and it is possible that those in Acerra persisted from a period which antedated Pulcinella's first appearance. Furthermore, it is highly doubtful if the black mask which the character always wore was a part of the ordinary Acerrian garb.

In the last analysis it seems to me that all documents and evidence so far brought forward fail to refute definitely and beyond question the claim of Pulcinella to ancient

[1] The expression in the French text is *mener une vie de bâtons de chaise*, but as this has no direct counterpart in English the example of 'rap' may serve as a suitable equivalent.—Translator.

[2] That region of France lying between Fontainebleau, Sens, and Montargis.—Translator.

[3] Originally 'God-damn.' During the Hundred Years War the French nicknamed the English 'Goddams' because they heard their enemies using the oath so often.—Translator.

origin and lineage. In comparing the Pulcinella of the seventeenth-century picture in the museum of the Comédie-Française [1] with the antique bronze statuette discovered in 1727, the similarities between the two are at once so apparent and striking that it would be unreasonable to maintain that they are due to mere chance. The passage of time may have obliterated all trace of the connexion between the two characters, but the mystery surrounding it does not necessarily disprove its existence.

Yet the author who offers evidence pointing to the connexion between the *commedia dell' arte* and the *Atellanæ* does so at his peril. When it is a question of masks or the phallus or etymology his evidence is too uncertain, and the pedants are soon sent packing. I have taken the liberty of citing the obvious resemblance between the statuette of Maccus and Pulcinella, but here the facts are far too scanty to be given serious consideration. M. Constant Mic's verdict [2] on this subject is as follows:

> The only thing which militates in favour of the tradition thesis is the outward resemblance to be remarked between the Italian masks and the Roman mimes (there is an undeniable analogy, for example, between Pulcinella and the miniature terra-cotta figures of antiquity representing Maccus). But that is certainly not a sufficient proof; on the contrary, the resemblance between two types separated by several centuries only tends to prove the lack of any link or relationship between them. The early type would certainly have undergone some change over a period of centuries if it had continued to survive; it has been preserved as it is by the very fact of its death, for to live is to change. The direct thread connecting the celebrated Pierrots of Willette with the early Italian Pedrolino is perfectly evident, and yet what is there in common between the two types?

Quite so: to live is to change; but living also includes the reception and transmission of hereditary traits and signs; it means having high cheekbones or kinky hair if some Mongolian or negro once made love to one of your ancestors. Is it but a pedantic dream, then, to believe that one or more hereditary links could possibly exist between Pulcinella and Maccus, or between the Captain and the Miles Gloriosus of Plautus, all sprung from the same soil and the same race, simply because they were so ill-advised as to bear a definite resemblance one to the other?

THE ACTING OF PULCINELLA AND OF CHARLIE CHAPLIN

Though he may not be aware of it, Charlie Chaplin is undoubtedly one of the rare inheritors of the traditions of the *commedia dell' arte*. Mr Chaplin is not perhaps acquainted with the scenario called *Pulcinella the Brigand Chief*, in which the 'business' and certain comic and original effects of Pulcinella might seem to have been taken over bodily for the film *Shoulder Arms*. The reader familiar with the film may recall how Chaplin poses as a tree when he is pursued within the German lines, and how, when his ruse is discovered, he breaks away with an acrobatic feat of some sort only to freeze into another pose farther on. In the Italian scenario Pulcinella with the *carabinieri* at his heels pretends that he is a weathercock and whirls in the wind. When the police are

[1] See p. 209. [2] *Op. cit.* p. 211.

about to take aim at him he leaps to a neighbouring roof and from there into a garden, where he impersonates a milestone. Detected once more he hides under a winnowing-basket and makes for the woods, pretending that he is a tortoise. All the comicality of Pulcinella's and Chaplin's acting in these cases lies in the contrast between absolute immobility and sudden agility; but no one but a gifted madcap spirit would ever conceive the idea of trying to impersonate a tree or a milestone.

THE COSTUME OF PULCINELLA

Pulcinella's costume was probably copied from the attire in general use among the peasants of Acerra. His loose blouse was of white linen, and was caught in below the waist by a heavy leather belt, from which dangled a wooden sword and a fat wallet. He also wore wide and flowing pantaloons. About his neck he knotted a sort of scarf bordered with green lace, which served both as a short mantle (*tabaro*) and collarette, though it was not exactly either the one or the other. And on his head he sometimes wore a white skull-cap, and sometimes a grey hat with turn-up brims. His headgear when in Naples was, as a rule, a conical hat, either black or white.

During the seventeenth century in France the Pulcinella of the Italian comedy belonging to Mazarin's troupe adopted the red breeches and green-trimmed jacket worn by Jupille, the French Polichinelle of 1640. Toward the close of the seventeenth century Michel Angelo da Fracassano increased the size of the traditional hump and added cock feathers to his hat, and it was in this costume that Watteau painted him. It was said that when Pulcinella returned to Italy at the beginning of the eighteenth century he had become very Gallicized and wore a wide blouse, filled by his protruding stomach and fastened in front by large buttons. But, strangely enough, the new version looked remarkably like one of Pulcinella's earliest costumes, or, if not his, at any rate that of his brother Cucurucu. For it may be pointed out that Cucurucu was an onomatopœic name derived from the crow of a cock, and since Pulcinella's name was derived in precisely the same fashion, the relation between the two characters is very close. Indeed, the Cucurucu drawn by Callot in the *Balli di Sfessania* is certainly none other than the loud and bustling Pulcinella.

The principal changes in Pulcinella's costume eventually consisted of a starched ruff and the widening of the already exaggerated pantaloons, which, incidentally, were also shortened. The costume later underwent a further alteration in France in the short breeches, striped stockings, and conventional humps of the Punch with which most children are familiar.

THE MASK

The illustration on p. 221 gives an excellent idea of the kind of mask worn by the acrobatic Neapolitan Pulcinella. He was a cold and cruel rascal, and most often to be found in scenarios like *Pulcinella the Brigand Chief.* Pulcinella the dullard had a somewhat different mask, which was said to be older, though it is doubtful. It was adorned with a heavy moustache and beard. The nose was a humpback's nose, and was both witty and ridiculous, because of its great prominence.

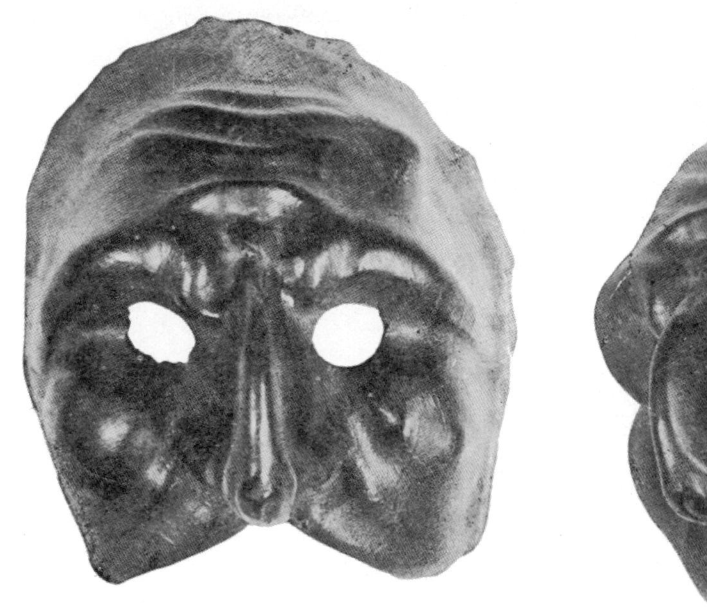
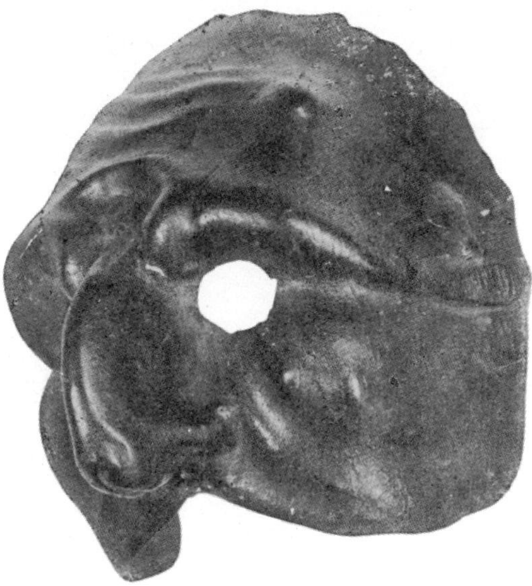

MASKS WORN BY THE NEAPOLITAN PULCINELLA
Mariano Andreu Collection

THE FAMILY TREE OF PULCINELLA

THE ATELLANÆ

MACCUS BUCCO

POLLICINIELLO

PULLICINIELLA (Naples)

PURRICINELLA (Bologna)

PULCINELLA

CUCURUCU
(*Balli di Sfessania*)

Italian Derivatives

IL SITONNO (1530)
BIRRICHINO
MEO-PATACCA (Rome)
MARCO-PEPE (Rome)

Foreign Derivatives

POLICHINELLE (France)
PUNCH and JACK PUDDING (England)
HANSWURST and PULZINELLA (Germany)
TONEELGET (Holland)
DON CHRISTOVAL PULCHINELLA (Spain)

THE PRINCIPAL PULCINELLAS

End of the sixteenth century	Silvio Fiorilli
	Andrea Calcese, called Ciuccio
First half of the seventeenth century	Argieri, called in Paris "the Roman Polichinelle"
1645 *Troupe of Mazarin*	Brabançois
1697	Michel Angelo Fracansano
Beginning of the eighteenth century	Coleson
1739 *At the San Carlino Theatre*	Francesco Barese
1753	Antonio Petito
1800	Celesi Balli
	Tomaso Fabioni
1803	Lucio Bebio
1805	Camerano

Pulcinella, as seen by an Oriental
Eighteenth century
Plate made for the Dutch East India Company

Meo-Patacca

Meo-Patacca is a Roman, living in the Trastevere part of the city. He is either the half-brother or the natural son of Pulcinella, the clever and cruel Pulcinella. Meo-Patacca uses his cudgel on all occasions. When his will is crossed he prefers to fell his victim with a blow rather than make an attempt at persuasion.

His profile is an exaggeration of the classic Roman features. In the drawings of Pinelli he looks astonishingly like M. Jacques Copeau.[1]

Meo-Patacca speaks the vigorous Roman dialect, saying "I want this," or "I want that" every other phrase. He suppresses the infinitive endings, and replaces the letter *l* with *r*.

At the close of the eighteenth century Meo-Patacca's disposition became more gentle. He wore the dress of the inhabitants of the Trastevere ; a jacket and velvet breeches with two rows of buttons, a wide cloth band around his waist, and a foulard handkerchief swathed about his bonnet, which descended to the nape of his neck and left his forehead bare. A later costume makes him look like a Pulcinella in rags.

There is a poem in praise of Meo-Patacca in twelve cantos written by Berneri in the *linguaggio romanesco*. It was printed in 1685.

Marco-Pepe

Marco-Pepe, also a Roman, was sometimes the dishonest rival and sometimes the partner, or even the victim, of Meo-Patacca. These two characters were inseparable. As a rule, Marco-Pepe aped the mannerisms of Meo-Patacca ; but he was a boastful coward at heart and afraid of his own shadow.

Il Sitonno

Il Sitonno was a young Neapolitan ruffian. He was always ready for a fight, and he never went out without his rattan. He was the 'holy terror' of the wine-shops, and he liked to expatiate on his exploits and pose as a dangerous individual, although in reality he was altogether harmless.

Birrichino

He was the Sitonno of Bologna. Birrichino was a nimble, frolicsome young fellow who, though not a knave, had nevertheless a horror of the representatives of law and order.

Polichinelle

The Polichinelle of the seventeenth century was much more like the Captain—a French Captain, and perhaps even a Gascon officer—than the Neapolitan Pulcinella. It is possible that there was no more than a general analogy between Polichinelle and his Italian prototype, for the chief resemblances between the two were the inflated belly, which ridiculed all similar monstrosities, and the hump, which symbolized the wit that the French have always attributed to the humpback.

The following song of Polichinelle would seem to serve as definite evidence that he

[1] Former Director of the Théâtre du Vieux Colombier.—TRANSLATOR.

was more or less of the Captain type, and it also indicates that the character originated during the reign of Henri IV :

Je suis le fameux Mignolet,
Général des Espagnolets.
Quand je marche la terre tremble ;
C'est moi qui conduis le soleil,
Et je ne crois pas qu'en ce monde
On ne puisse trouver mon pareil.

Les murailles de mon palais
Sont bâties des os des Anglais ;
Toutes mes salles sont dallées
De têtes de sergents d'armées. . . .

Je veux, avant qu'il soit minuit,
A moi tout seul prendre Paris . . .
Des langues des filles, des femmes
Saint-Omer je ferais paver.[1]

In the middle of the seventeenth century Polichinelle turned into a marionette, and every one knows the complete success he has had in this form. Neither the Roman nor the Neapolitan Pulcinella was ever very popular in France.

Punchinello-Punch

The Neapolitan Pulcinella found his way into England at the end of the seventeenth century, and there he proceeded to give rein to all the cold-blooded ferocity which he had stored up in his nature. His irony then took on an English tone, and he developed into a great seducer of the young girls of the people. A ballad of the eighteenth century affirms that his ardour became so intense that he required at least twenty-two women to keep him satisfied.

In *The Adventures of Punch and Judy* Punch, in spite of his hump, seduces a young girl, and has a child by her. Later he " keeps a woman." His wife upbraids him, and " he splits her head in two." He tosses the baby out of the window, kills his mother- and father-in-law, flees, seducing women as he goes, and finally knocks down the devil (Old Nick) with his cudgel after having hanged the executioner sent to hang him.

Hanswurst (Jack Sausage)

Hanswurst was a plump Pulcinella of the Renaissance. He kept his audiences amused by his extraordinary stupidity and his endless guzzling. He eventually borrowed many traits from Brighella, Harlequin, Hans Pickelhering, and other characters, both Italian and German.

[1] " I am the famous Mignolet ['little fellow'] who leads the Spanish troops. The earth shakes as I walk, and I direct the sun. I do not believe that there is another like me in all the world. The walls of my palace are made out of the bones of Englishmen, and all my halls are flagged with the skulls of army sergeants. I wish to capture Paris single-handed before midnight, and pave Saint-Omer with the tongues of women and young girls."

XVII

The Captain, his Ancestors, and his Family

SPAVENTO DELLA VALLE INFERNA, GIANGURGOLO CALABRESE, ROGANTINO, IL VAPPO, SCARAMUCCIA, CRISPIN

The Captains[1]

HE eyes of Captain Matamoros gleam like steel, his moustache bristles, and his huge nose and immense sword quiver with rage incessantly, somewhat in the same manner as a peacock's tail during the mating season. Nor is Spezza-Monti any the less impressive. That doughty hero always shuts his eyes so that he will not have to behold the victim he intends to carve and cut to ribbons. Again, there is Taglia-Cantoni all accoutred in tight-fitting uniform, with padded thighs and warlike crest standing erect. His rival is the terrifying Fracasso-brise-tout,[2] and when these two gentlemen cross swords they parry and thrust with such fury that not even the public square is large enough to hold them.

Captain Zerbino wears spectacles so that his flashing glance will not dim the sun's less ardent rays. And Cerimonia, the nimble, carefree swordsman, bows with such grace to Lavinia that surely he will break her heart as easily as he would a nut. The very infirmities of Mála-Gamba and Bella-Vita bespeak their notorious exploits. Whenever they encounter one another in the street they draw up proudly and exchange salutes like two men-o'-war loaded down with cannon, ready to open fire and manœuvring for position.

Every country teems with bold and swaggering Captains, of whom the most renowned are Sangre y Fuego, Cocodrillo, Escobombardon, Ariararche, Melampigo, the Captain of the black breeches, and Leucopigo, of the white breeches. Then follow Papirotonda, Rodomonte, Spavento della Valle Inferna—their names roll out like thunder—and with them their French prototypes, Boudoufle, Taille-bras, and Engoulevent.

The lordly band of Captains forgather in dazzling array. They come strutting in from Spain, from Italy and France. Each one wears a splendid uniform embellished with the turbans of infidels who have fallen by his sword. And each is also a gallant slayer of hearts : his coat of mail is a network of golden rings, the booty from the battlefields of love, the pledges wrested from the lovely army of princesses whom he has seduced. Ah, where is the woman who would not pluck worshipfully at the cloak of

[1] Sometimes written in French ' Capitan,' which has the meaning not only of captain but of a swaggerer and bully.—TRANSLATOR.

[2] " Fracasso-smash-all."

any of these doughty cavaliers as he strides down the street, or kiss in secret the noble device of the porcupine adorning his escutcheon? For there is scarce a maiden who does not know what the strange beast signifies. And as she thinks of it she seems

THE CAPTAIN AT THE BEGINNING OF THE SIXTEENTH CENTURY
This is possibly the actor Garavini

to see her hero emerging from the *mêlée*, bristling with arrows as thick as the bristles of a brush, or rather as the spines of the animal represented on his shield. Even Venus would be troubled by such a lusty gathering and blush rosily in her shell. Compared to her predicament, the Judgment of Paris were but a summer's game, for here are not just three to choose from, but a veritable multitude. Yet these brave officers protest their preference for Mars rather than the gentle Venus. Their bearing is of the sternest, and they are ready to wreak such havoc among mankind that they will set one half the world a-mourning for the other half, dash all the stars together, and fill the heavens with unholy uproar. But suddenly a nasal voice is heard crying from the wings: "Hand me my dagger, and I'll carve out their livers and lights!" There follows the clash of swords: it is Charles-Quint, with twelve thousand mercenaries at his back. The brilliant troop of Captains fall prone upon their stomachs. Is it a ruse? Fracasso scarcely winks, he lies so still. They all look as if they might be dead—or asleep.

Now Harlequin enters, armed only in his rags and tatters. He gleefully kicks each sleeper in the buttocks; but no one budges or opens an eye, for all the Captains are dead, literally frightened to death!

The Captain is a bombastic fellow and vastly tedious in his speech, but he manages to be amusing sometimes by virtue of his flights of fancy.

"As the wind drives the leaves or the puff-balls of the reeds," so does the braggart soldier of Plautus put mighty armies to rout. He is able to break the back of an elephant with a "gentle tap," and goddesses swoon by the dozen for love of him. Manducus, the ogre-captain of the *Atellanæ*, had a habit of eating babies, and he could overthrow an athlete by a mere twist of the wrist. It is undoubtedly from such valiant heroes as these that the Captain was descended. Yet his heaven-storming mentality is a trifle uninspired. His humour is far too heavy, if not downright obnoxious:

Tout m'aime et tout me craint,
Soit en paix, soit en guerre,
Je croquerai un prince aussi bien qu'un oignon.[1]

There is also a verse about one of the Spezzafers of the seventeenth century:

Ce Capitan fait grand esclat
Et sa valeur est si parfaite
Qu'il est des derniers au combat
Et des premiers à la retraite.[2]

It requires a high light indeed to show off the Captain in his proper colours, for he is like one of those pink or yellow villas on the Riviera which are so vivid that their charm is lost except when they are seen among olive-trees in the bright noonday sunlight.

Captains seem largely out of fashion nowadays. The age of machine-guns has altered and modified their manners, and perhaps changed them at heart as well. There have always been numerous Captains in every army, of course, and there always will be, but certainly the breed achieved its greatest and finest flowering during the Renaissance.

The type becomes much more plausible when one recalls the blood-curdling combats of the *condottieri*, in which, according to Machiavelli, the unexpected wheeling of a horse was sometimes enough to decide the issue of the struggle. It is obvious that these mercenary leaders, in fighting first for one party and then another, had no

[1] "Everybody loves me, everybody fears me both in peace and in war. I'd as lief chew up a prince as an onion."

[2] "This Captain makes a splendid show, and his valour is so great that he is the last to join the combat and the first to beat a retreat."

pecuniary or patriotic motive for annihilating their "human material," as it was called later on. By far the greatest number of warriors who died in battle died from suffocation inside their armour rather than at the hands of the enemy.

In this condition of affairs it was only natural that the civil populace of the time should have created an extravagant caricature of the *condottiere*, whom they had quickly

THE CAPTAIN
Engraving by de Geijn

learned to hate. For he was always their enemy, whether he was fighting for or against them. He lived by ravaging the country indiscriminately, pillaging to right and left, and roasting his prisoners to make them speak. And, since they were unable to revenge themselves upon him, they invented the character of the Captain as a substitute. His braggadocio was, therefore, never too outrageous to please them, nor were his fears too contemptible, nor the blows he received ever too numerous or too hard.

Cap.° Spessa Monti.
BaGattino

Cap Bonbardon.
Cap. Grillo.

Cap.° Mala Gamba.
Cap Bell

Cap. Esgangarato.
Cap.° Cocodrillo.

Cap. Babeo.
Cucuba.

Cap Cardoni.
Maramao

THE CAPTAIN, HIS ANCESTORS, AND FAMILY

When Callot came to engrave Malla-Gamba and Bella-Vita he represented them as pitiful and crippled, but he also showed them as burdened by all the 'horrors of war,' a theme which Goya was later to elaborate.

The first Captains were Italian, and belonged to the fifteenth century. Their cowardice knew no limits. During the Spanish domination in Italy the Captain acquired the name of Matamoros, and the Spanish conception of the character gradually superseded that of the Italians. The great warrior then dressed 'according to the country,' and mouthed Castilian. Although he never lost a whit of his ridiculous vainglory, his inherent cowardice appeared less often and came to light only when his bravado had wholly failed. Yet he had but to catch sight of Harlequin with his bat, and he was thrown into a frenzy of terror.

Of all the characters of the *commedia dell' arte* the Captain is, in some respects, probably the most difficult for us to understand, just as Tartarin is more or less incomprehensible to anyone who has not lived in the Midi. But the type has always been prevalent enough. The writer Scudéry revealed his Captain traits when, with a pen in one hand and a sword in the other, he solemnly defied Corneille to prove that *Le Cid* was a play of any value whatsoever. And the gallant Cyrano de Bergerac, with his cock-and-bull boasts (which had a certain courage behind them), is a superb example of the Captain.

Gaultier-Garguille once met Tabarin in Hades, and described the Captains of his day in the following terms :

> If you were still in the other world, my friend, you would laugh in open-mouthed wonder to see the braggarts of to-day with their pompous walk, *ita sati homines*, which means that they strut haughtily about with their hands on their hips, looking for all the world like wide-armed vases, and scorning every one they meet with a twirl of the moustache. Their dreadful swords have filled the cemeteries to overflowing ; but somehow all of their victims seem to be still alive and well. But the worst of all is that even Jupiter himself trembles at one squinting glance from beneath their shaking plumes. He is evidently only too ready to surrender his eagle and thunderbolts to be at peace with them—albeit the only victories they ever win are over the poor snails and flies and frogs.[1]

THE COSTUME AND THE MASK

The mask of the earliest Captains was flesh-coloured, and had a great menacing nose which served as the keynote to their character. It was also provided with fierce, bristling moustaches, which seemed like veritable iron spikes defending the entrance to a citadel only too ready to capitulate. The mask, in its general aspect, was intended to emphasize the contrast between a brave appearance and a craven nature. The war-masks of certain negro tribes were designed for the same purpose.

The history of the Captain's costume is much the same as that of military dress in general. The Captain followed the contemporary styles and changes of each period. The early Italian Captain wore a helmet, or morion, buff straps, and a long sword. His Spanish prototype was decked out in an immense starched ruff, a wide plumed hat, and

[1] *Opuscule Tabarinique.*

boots with scalloped edges at the top. His character was best delineated not so much by physical traits as by his pretentiousness and indigence, which always amused the poorer classes in particular.

Cap. Grillo.

THE ACTOR GIOVANNI DONATO
Engraving by Callot

At the beginning of the seventeenth century Abraham Bosse represented the Captain in tight-fitting, striped clothes and a plumed felt hat. The turned-up moustaches were sometimes replaced by a beard in the style of Henri IV. Toward the middle of the century Spezzafer is clad like a courtier in the king's palace.. He has a pourpoint and wide breeches, a thick ruff, and a little round hat with a feather in it. About 1668 the Captain dressed in heavy silk of bright yellow, and he wore his sword thrust through a buff leather belt During the eighteenth century in Italy his costume consisted of a coat, vest, knee-breeches, and a three-cornered hat; his sword, which he carried point upward, was quite as long as it ever had been.

CAPITAN SPAVENTO (FRANCESCO ANDREINI) (1550–1624)

Francesco Andreini had begun his career as a soldier before he became an actor, and one wonders if he did not create the character of Capitan Spavento as a sort of satirical

THE CAPTAIN MODELLED IN GLASS
Eighteenth century

tribute to his former profession. Soldiering had, to be sure, proved a hard life for him. The future Spavento had set forth bravely in the Tuscan galleys, and then was captured by the Turks. He escaped after seven years of slavery and succeeded in returning to his native land.

Andreini made his *début* on the stage with the celebrated Gelosi troupe, in the *rôle* of Lover. He created, besides Spavento, at least three other characters—the Sicilian Doctor, Falsirone, the Magician, and the shepherd Corinto. It might be said that the *rôle* of slave which the Capitan had played among the Turks was a servitude quite in the style of the *commedia dell' arte*. In any case, Andreini developed from a simple soldier into a poet, musician, and gifted linguist. His life reads like a tale out of a story-book. He married, at sixteen, the famous Isabelle, whose beauty and talents and virtue caused many a prince and poet to sing her praise in eager rivalry. He loved her devotedly, and was in turn beloved. He was made director of the Gelosi when the troupe went to France in 1600, and thenceforward his career was a succession of galas and honours at the French Court. He was, indeed, one of those rare and romantic adventurers who are born under a lucky star; nor had any evil witch out of a fairy-tale put a spell upon him in his cradle.

He suffered one misfortune, however, which proved to be the great blow of his life. As he was returning to Italy by way of Lyons in 1604 his beloved Isabelle fell ill and died. He composed and engraved her epitaph in Latin, and then retired to Venice, where he made a collection of all her letters and other writings.

In 1607 Andreini published the *Bravure del Capitano Spavento*, and later the *Ingannata Proserpina*, *Alterezza di Narsiso*, *Ragionamenti fantastici*, and in 1618 the second part of the *Bravure*. In the foreword to the *Bravure* there is a touching reference to the capricious fate that had taken Isabelle from the love of her spouse.

Spavento della Valle Inferna (Captain Fearsome of Hell's Valley) gave his credentials in this wise:

> Suzerain of the Devil, prince of cavaliers, bravest of the brave, arch-despot and killer, master and lord of the universe, son of the thunder and lightning, near relative of Death and close personal friend of the Great Devil of Hell. . . .

THE CAPTAIN AND THE LINENDRAPER

(SPEZZAFER *informs* HARLEQUIN *that he is in need of new linen.*)

HARLEQUIN (*addressing* SPEZZAFER)

Is it true, as they say, that you wear no shirt?

SPEZZAFER

Such indeed was my habit of old, and for this reason: I used to be an exceedingly fierce and violent man, and when I was made angry the hair which covers my body in goodly quantity stood on end and so riddled my shirt with holes that you would have taken it for a sieve. But I have lately come to control my temper like every one else.

(HARLEQUIN *leaves, and* SPEZZAFER *goes toward a shop*)

SPEZZAFER

Why, here is a linen-shop right before my eyes! I'll just go in and see if they have any shirts that would suit me.

THE SALESWOMAN

This way, sir. We have high-grade Holland linen and fine sweat-proof bed-socks.

SPEZZAFER (*taking up a shirt which he finds on the counter*)

It would be a pleasure to buy something from you. . . . (*Aside*) This wench is comely and well-favoured. She has such big blue eyes. (*To the* SALESWOMAN) This shirt would suit me well enough, but I think it's a bit too small.

THE SALESWOMAN

Too small? Why, not at all; it's three-quarters and a half long.

SPEZZAFER

How much do you ask for it?

THE SALESWOMAN

It will cost you ten crowns, and cheap at the price.

SPEZZAFER

Ten crowns!

THE SALESWOMAN

Yes, sir, and it's only right. I can't make more than one livre on the sou as it is.

SPEZZAFER

I'll give you thirty sous for it.

THE SALESWOMAN

Only thirty sous! You are not used to wearing shirts, that's clear!

CAPTAIN SPEZZAFER
Seventeenth century

SPEZZAFER

Come now. Here's a crown, and no more haggling. You don't want me to go elsewhere, do you?

THE SALESWOMAN

Very well, then. Take it; but on condition that you will do me the honour of coming back to see me. This is the Sign of the Virgin. I supply all the baby-linen for the babies of the eunuchs in the Grand Harem.[1]

THE PRINCIPAL CAPTAINS

1550–1624	FRANCESCO ANDREINI	Capitano Spavento della Valle Inferna
1560	FABRIZIO DE FORNARIS	Cap. Cocodrillo
1600	GIROLAMO GARAVINI	Cap. Rinoceronte
1618	MONDOR	Rodomont
1628	SILVIO FIORILLO	Cap. Matamoros
1639	GIUSEPPE BIANCHI	Cap. Spezzafer
1658	ANCATONI DIEGO	Cap. Sangue y Fuego

[1] Gherardi, *Le Théâtre italien* (seventeenth century).

THE FAMILY TREE OF THE CAPTAINS

ATELLANÆ

MANDUCUS
(The Ogre)

THE COMEDIES OF PLAUTUS

PIRGOPOLINICE

THE CAPTAIN
(fifteenth century)

SCARAMUCCIA IL VAPPO (The Blusterer) GIANGURGOLO ("Big-mouth," of Calabrian origin)	RODOMONT (*created by Ariosto*) SPAVENTO COCODRILLO (sixteenth century) RINOCERONTE SPEZZAFER (seventeenth century)	*The French Theatre* TAILLE-BRAS (1567) RODOMONT (1618) ENGOULEVENT SCARAMOUCHE CRISPIN	*The German Theatre* HORRIBILIBIFIBRAX

Giangurgolo (Big-mouth)

The combination of fear and a great sword, poverty and a vast hunger, a lively temperament and the ever-present dread of rivals, might have made life altogether intolerable for Giangurgolo, if it had not been that all these troubles were swallowed up in the sea of his silly self-conceit. Giangurgolo is the Calabrian offspring of the Captain. He is like one of those animals which, not being able to pursue their prey easily, have been provided with an elastic stomach by a benignant Providence. As the boa consumes a gazelle, so does Giangurgolo bolt down many a pot of macaroni. When he has wiped out the pot with the last piece of bread he gazes sadly at the bottom and sighs.

Giangurgolo is a thief, though not by inclination, for he has not the least vestige of courage, and therefore steals only from necessity. He never feels secure, even under the most favourable circumstances. His heart is always in his mouth. There is never any telling what may happen. The cat that just jumped out of the window may be on her way to inform the police. Giangurgolo does not like the police, and when the wind is from the right direction he sniffs and smells a *sbirro* at a hundred paces as easily as a hunting-dog scents a partridge.

Giangurgolo is the possessor of a dangerous temper, but he is careful about displaying it. Once he is sure that there is no one around more formidable than a woman or child or greybeard, he draws his sword and plays the insufferable bully.

Giangurgolo asserts that he is a nobleman. He made his first appearance during the seventeenth century.

THE COSTUME AND MASK OF GIANGURGOLO

The Giangurgolo here shown wears a scarlet doublet. His sleeves, jacket, and breeches are light yellow with bright red stripes. The half-mask required for his *rôle* covers only his forehead and his nose, which is always long and shapeless and often decorated by a wart tufted with fine hairs. Giangurgolo should be played as an ungainly lout.

GIANGURGOLO
Seventeenth century

GIANGURGOLO IN THE COMEDY "DISPERARSI PER SPERANZA," BY DR PIETRO PIPERNO (1688)

Rogantino

Rogantino is a Roman member of the Captain family. He is a corporal; he rolls his *r*'s like a regiment of drummers and possesses the true professional conscience. If he is ordered to arrest a malefactor he will seize the first-comer rather than return without a prisoner. Inasmuch as the mob always takes sides against him, Rogantino usually receives some pretty rough handling in the fray, but he emerges with a clear conscience at least, feeling that he has done his duty.

Rogantino also belongs to the marionette theatre.

Il Vappo, or Il Smargiasso (The Bully)

Il Vappo is another of the Captains. This time he hails from Naples. He swallows iron carts whole, and eats his enemies alive. The actor who plays Vappo must be a skilled pantomimist above everything. His acting consists of attitudinizing, threatening poses, quixotic gestures, and puffing out his chest.

He wears a uniform of a Captain of the eighteenth century.

Scaramuccia (Little Skirmisher)

(SCARAMUCIA, SCARAMUZZIA)

Born in Naples toward the close of the sixteenth century, Scaramuccia grew up into a Captain of the time, but he was a captain made for skirmishes only. He buzzed about with a long sword, stinging first this enemy and then that, like a bee darting from flower to flower. He is black from head to foot, like a bumble-bee, and it is to be noted that this colour was a feature which he retained without variation throughout the evolution of his character.

SCARAMOUCHE AND FRICASSO
Callot

SCARAMOUCHE AND FRICASSO
Callot

It is in *Le Sicilien* that Molière makes one of his characters say that the sky is wearing a Scaramouche disguise. By 1680 the Spanish Captain, who had supplanted the Italian one, had himself gone out of vogue, and Scaramuccia took over the succession and inherited all the braggadocio and cowardice of his predecessors.

The Scaramuccia Callot depicted fighting fiercely with Fricasso by turning his back to him belongs to this first type of Scaramouche. The character was played with a mask until the time of Tiberio Fiorilli,[1] who, being the "prince of grimacers," merely powdered his face.

[1] See p. 65 *n*.

Scaramuccia loves all women and bottles, provided they contain the semblance of love and wine respectively. He is usually the valet of an indigent gentleman, and he boasts not only of his master's ancient lineage, but also of his enormous riches, though in reality he has not a sou to his name. This black Scaramouche has a fondness for complicated intrigues of a non-political nature which generally consist of picking the pockets of some passer-by or else of his master. Strangely enough, he always manages to escape from these affairs without the least inconvenience or injury. He is exceedingly adroit, as slippery as an eel, and so clever at dodging that nearly every blow aimed at him falls on some poor innocent bystander.

The brutal and often cruel Pulcinella is Scaramouche's one great friend. The two are quite unlike, of course, and they are constantly quarrelling and falling out with one another, and making up again. But Scaramouche, with his sword, and Pulcinella, with his cudgel, like nothing better than to frighten peaceful citizens just to impress the women by their prowess. When he has had overmuch to drink Pulcinella enjoys hearing Scaramouche holding forth about his imaginary adventures; but when the black braggart goes too far Pulcinella clears the table with one sweep of his club, and Scaramouche does well to decamp as rapidly as possible.

Such was the character, in its general outlines, which Tiberio Fiorilli established in the seventeenth century. It is very likely that it was this same Fiorilli who inspired Molière to make the theatre his profession.

TIBERIO FIORILLI (1604 OR 1608 TO 1694)

If the famous Scaramouche Tiberio Fiorilli were to be judged solely by a book about him called *La Vie de Scaramouche*, we should not think him deserving of his reputation as a great actor and personality. For certainly the author, Angelo Constantini, or Mezzetin, one of his *confrères*, spared no pains to draw an unflattering picture of him, and at his best Scaramouche appears as no less than a highway bandit. But the book is, for the most part, unreliable, and is filled with unjust ridicule and heavy witticisms. It is likely that the laurels Scaramouche had won were thorns in the flesh of Constantini. Knowing no French, Constantini hired some one to write it for him, and, by way of good taste, the book was published by Barbin in 1695, immediately following the death of Scaramouche.

In the foreword to his *Théâtre italien* Gherardi, who had been an intimate friend of Scaramouche, wrote:

> I hope that every one who has ever spoken ill of Fiorilli or made puns or unpleasant jokes at his expense will be put to the blush and come at last to cast the light of truth upon the memory of this great man. . . . I excuse, however, the author of *La Vie de Scaramouche* in so far as he admits that his book is detestable.

Constantini's book has a certain value in that it gives a number of general facts about Scaramouche which are important even though they are coloured by the author's viewpoint. It seems, then, that Tiberio Fiorilli was the son of a cavalry captain who had not a few little encounters with the law. After a great many dubious adventures Tiberio

Scaramouche in Sixteenth-century Costume

became a member of a small theatrical troupe which was playing at Fano, and he immediately scored a huge success as Scaramuccia in a piece entitled *Il Convitato di Pietra.* The company then visited Mantua, where Scaramouche's acting attracted the attention of the

THE ENTRANCE OF SCARAMOUCHE
Seventeenth century

Duke, and later went to Florence and Naples. Scaramouche was remarkably strong, agile, and graceful. He had a superb voice and sang to his own accompaniment on the lute. The variety of his talents was, indeed, almost inexhaustible.

In Palermo Fiorilli met and married Lorenza Elisabetta, or Isabella del Campo, who played servant *rôles* under the name of Marinetta. The child he had by Marinetta was baptized in Rome by Cardinal Chigi, who represented Pope Alexander VII.

Meanwhile prosperity came to Fiorilli. He acquired a magnificent estate in Florence, over the entrance to which he inscribed the motto, *Fiori Fiorilli—Egli fu Flora il Fato.*[1]

SCARAMOUCHE
Seventeenth century

Wherever he went Scaramouche was acclaimed with the greatest enthusiasm. His success was tremendous. His fame spread into France, and he was invited by Mazarin

[1] This phrase cannot be suitably rendered in English because of the play on words. *Fiori* means ‘ to flower ’ and ‘ to prosper ’; *Fiorilli* means ‘ little flower ’ as well as the name of the man ; *Flora*, the name of a woman and of the goddess of spring, etc.—TRANSLATOR.

to come and perform at the Court. His popularity was soon as great in Paris as it had been in Italy, and he counted among his most faithful admirers not only Mazarin, but Anne of Austria and, later, Louis le Grand.

Engraving by G. J. Xavery

There is a well-known anecdote about Scaramouche by Riccoboni, which runs somewhat as follows:

Scaramouche and Aurelia were playing in Paris about 1640, during the reign of Louis XIII. This actress was noted for her wit, and was held in great esteem by the

Queen, who also admired Scaramouche. One day when both actors were in the Dauphin's chamber, in the presence of her Majesty, the little prince, then only two years of age, became very fretful and ill-tempered. He screamed and cried, and it seemed as if there were no way to stop him. Scaramouche then took the liberty of asking the Queen's permission to hold the Dauphin in his arms, saying that he felt sure that he could calm the child. The Queen consented, and the actor began to make such comic gestures and grimaces that the child not only ceased crying, but broke into a gale of laughter. Finally, after one of the most amusing bits of pantomime, which entertained the Queen exceedingly, the Dauphin suddenly gave rein to a natural impulse all over the hands and costume of Scaramouche, which thereupon increased the merriment of the Queen twofold, and all the lords and ladies in the hall laughed with her.

Scaramouche, a man of thirty-two or three at the time, was ordered to pay a visit to the Dauphin's rooms every time he came to Court, and he so diverted the child and gained his affection that he was included in every company that came from Italy. Louis XIV was fond of recalling to Scaramouche the scene of their first meeting, described above, and would laugh heartily at the faces the great comedian made as he recounted the story.

His Eminence Cardinal Mazarin and Anne of Austria (Queen-Mother and Regent of France) paid Scaramouche the signal honour—which was surely great for a man of his condition—of holding his and Marinetta's son at the baptismal font of Saint-Germain-l'Auxerrois. According to the baptismal certificate, the ceremony took place on "Thursday, the eleventh day of August, 1644."

The King required Tiberio Fiorilli to keep his troupe up to the highest standard possible, and gave him large sums of money so that he might go to Italy to procure the best available talent.

It is known that Scaramouche had at least three children by Marinetta, and he may have had more. While his wife was still living he had a son by Mlle Anne Doffan, and he named the child Tiberio François. Later he had a daughter, Anne Elisabeth, by Mlle Marie Duval, whom he married in 1688, when he was either eighty-five or eighty-seven years of age. Although Scaramouche had never set a very good example of rigid virtue himself, he went wild with rage, old as he was, when he thought that his wife had deceived him. He made her shave her head and sent her to the Convent of Saint-Lazare, then to Sainte-Geneviève-de-Chaillot, and finally to the Châtelet, where she died. In his old age Scaramouche went to live in Rue Tiquetonne in Paris, lonely and totally forgotten by all who had admired and applauded him in earlier days. Here death overtook him on December 8, 1694, and this time he was not able to give the tyrant a kick, as he did at the age of eighty-three.

SCARAMOUCHE'S EPITAPH

Las ! Ce n'est pas dame Isabeau
Qui gist là-dessous ce tombeau,
Ni quelque autre sainte Nitouche :
C'est un comique sans pareil.
Comme le ciel n'a qu'un soleil,
La terre n'eut qu'un Scaramouche.[1]

[1] "Alas, it is not Dame Isabeau who lies beneath this tomb, nor any other saintly dame, but a comedian without peer. As the heavens have but one sun, so the earth had but one Scaramouche."

THE CAPTAIN, HIS ANCESTORS, AND FAMILY

SCARAMOUCHE'S PANTOMIME

The stage represents Harlequin's room. Scaramouche enters, and, after putting everything to rights, sits down in an easy chair and plays his guitar while waiting for his master. Pasquariel comes up noiselessly behind him and beats out the time over his shoulders, which throws Scaramouche into a fright.

Of this Gherardi wrote :

> It is this scene of the incomparable Scaramouche, the ornament of the stage and example to all the famous comedians of his time, which served as a model for the difficult and necessary art of simulating all the passions, and expressing them solely through the play of the features. It was in this pantomime of terror, indeed, that he made his audience rock with laughter for a good quarter of an hour, without once opening his mouth to speak. He possessed this marvellous talent to such a remarkable degree that it is easy to understand how he could, by the mere promptings of his unaided imagination, wring the heart-strings more effectively than any orator could ever hope to do, even with all the resources of the most persuasive rhetoric at his command. A prince who once saw him play in Rome was so moved by the force of Scaramouche's art that he exclaimed admiringly, " Scaramuccia non parla, e dice gran' cose ! " [Scaramouche does not speak, but he says a great deal !] And as a mark of his esteem for the actor the prince sent for him after the comedy was done and made him a present of the coach and six horses in which he had been fetched.
>
> His talents were a delight to every prince who knew him ; nor did our invincible monarch ever tire of showing him high favour.

A TRIBUTE TO SCARAMOUCHE

There is a medallion which shows Fiorilli like some heraldic beast, surrounded with cabbages, pots, goose-eggs, dumplings, and mandolins ; beneath runs the inscription :

AL GRAN SCARAMUZZA
MEMEO SQUAQUERA

de civitate partenopensi
Figlio

DE TAMMERO E CATAMMERO
Cocumero cetrulo

E

DE MADAMA PAPERA TRENTOVA

E parente
De messere unze, douze, e trinze, et quiriquarinze
E de Nacchete, Stacchete, conta cadece
E de Tabuna, Tabella, Casella, Pagana, Zurfana,
Minossa, Catossa, e Dece Minece, etc.[1]

[1] Scaramouche calls himself all these names in one of his scenes.

THE ITALIAN COMEDY

Dedicatory Letter

This day entering the lists to obtain from this celebrated University of Francolin the crown of Doctorate, and having no obstacle to this ambition more fearful than the laughter of my audience, whom could I better choose as my sponsor than you who know so well how to change laughter into applause? Even though it appears that your jurisdiction is confined to comedy, I do not believe that even the scholars are outside your realm of influence, for their profession, as well as all the others which we observe, is no more than comedy, and the whole length and breadth of the world is only a vast stage where each plays his particular *rôle*. O Most Ridiculous Hero, cast a favourable eye upon this scholastic fray, and with your terrible grimaces defend me from the too critical gaze of the savants; for I am confident that with your protection not all the logic of these old wearers of the skull-cap and spectacles can make me answer one question correctly.

Conclusiones Morales

Première Conclusion

Il n'est rien de plus dangereux
Que l'estude et que la science,
Et rien ne nous rend plus heureux
Que la paresse et l'ignorance.

Seconde Conclusion

Ce qu'on appelle Valeur
Est une espèce de folie,
La vertu véritable est la Poltronnerie
Qui nous fait éviter la mort et la douleur.

Troisième Conclusion

Tout l'art de raisonner n'est qu'une invention
Pour nous surprendre avec adresse,
Mais la véritable sagesse
Consiste en l'Ostination.[1]

Has theses tueri conabitur ASINUS ASINONIUS de monte Asinorio. Die . . . Arbiter erit DOCTOR GRATIANUS CAMPANACCIUS, de Budrio.

PRO LAUREA
IN AULA FRANCOLINENSI

[1] *First Conclusion.* There is nothing more dangerous than study and science, and nothing makes us happier than laziness and ignorance.
Second Conclusion. That which is called Valour is a species of madness; the true virtue is Poltroonery, which enables us to avoid death and suffering.
Third Conclusion. The art of reasoning is but an invention to take us by surprise; but true wisdom consists in Obstinacy.

EXAMPLES OF SCENES PLAYED BY SCARAMOUCHE

OCTAVE, SCARAMOUCHE, *then* HARLEQUIN

(OCTAVE, *who has just arranged a meeting-place with the beautiful* ANGÉLIQUE, *wishes to give her an agreeable surprise. He asks* SCARAMOUCHE *to find a means of doing so, and leaves.* SCARAMOUCHE, *alone on the stage, ponders deeply.* HARLEQUIN *comes in, and* SCARAMOUCHE, *without telling him the reason for his request, sets him to thinking about ways and means.*

They walk up and down the stage without speaking, wrapped in thought.

Now and again they go up to each other and say :)

Egad, I have it !

(*They begin the same business again, saying :*)

No, that won't do.

(*Once more they begin the same business.* HARLEQUIN *turns round and faces* SCARAMOUCHE, *who says :*)

Oh, that is sure to do the trick !

(*And they both leave the stage without a word of explanation.*)

CINTHIO *and* SCARAMOUCHE

(CINTHIO *asks* SCARAMOUCHE *twice what his name is.* SCARAMOUCHE *replies :*)

Il mio nome, Signor, è Scaramuzza, Memeo Squaquera, Tammera, Catammera, e figlio di Cocumero et de Madama Papera trente'ova, e unze, e dunze et tiracarunze, e Stacchete, Minossa, Scatoffa, Solfana, Befana, Caiorca, per service à vossignoria.

CINTHIO

O che bel nome ! in verità non si puo far di più.[1]

(*He opens his purse.*) Here, this is for Scaramouche, this is for Memeo Squaquera, this for Tammera, this for Catammera, this for Cocumero, etc. (*He gives him a crown for each name.*) And whatever is left in the purse is for the rest of your names.

SCARAMOUCHE (*aside*)

Here is a fellow who goes big-name hunting.

SCARAMOUCHE AND MOLIÈRE

Mention has already been made of the excellent relations which existed between Molière and the Italian comedians. The anecdote about the origin of *Le Misanthrope* [2] is indicative, and it was on account of their mutual friendliness also that Molière's company played at the Palais Royal Theatre, alternating with the Italian troupe.

The importance of Molière's association with the foreign players cannot, of course, be over-estimated. They were not only interesting friends and fellow-workers, but they revealed to him the fact that an actor who lacks the gifts of pantomime and

[1] "What a fine name ! In truth one could not do better."

[2] See p. 99.

improvisation is no better than an elocutionist, or a mouthpiece which gives as much an impression of a human being as a pricked bladder. His work shows that Molière must have studied *unceasingly* the acting of these born comedians who inherited the

Engraving by G. J. Xavery

traditions of the *commedia dell' arte* just as naturally as a son inherits a goitre from his father.

Palaprat, who wrote frequently for the Italians, speaks of Molière's great intimacy with them:

> Who will ever bring back to us the marvellous art of Domenico (Biancolelli) and the charm of Nature herself revealed to us beneath the countenance of Scaramouche? This great actor [Molière] and ten times greater playwright lived in close intimacy with the Italians because they were all actors and honest folk; there were always two or three of them present at our suppers.[1]

In this connexion it is perhaps appropriate to quote once more the lines written under one of Scaramouche's portraits:

> Il fut le maître de Molière
> Et la Nature fut le sien.[2]

and another verse:

> Par exemple Elomire (Molière)
> Veut se rendre parfait dans l'art de faire rire:
> Que fait-il, le matois, dans ce hardy dessein?
> Chez le grand Scaramouche, il va, soir et matin.
> Là, le miroir en main, et ce grand homme en face,
> Il n'est contorsion, posture ny grimace,
> Que ce grand écolier du plus grand des bouffons
> Ne fasse et ne refasse en cent et cent façons.[3]

The above verses are from a comedy by Le Boulanger de Chalussay, entitled *Elomire, ou les Médecins vengés*. There is, in the rare copies of the play extant, a curious engraving by L. Weyer, which shows "Scaramouche teaching," with an eel's skin in his hand, and "Elomire studying" the facial play of his teacher, with a mirror in his hand. Another commentator on the subject wrote:

> It may be said of Scaramouche, who no longer appears on the stage: *Homo non periit, sed periit artifex*. He had the most perfect gift of pantomime of our time. Molière, the great French genius, never missed a performance of this original Italian.[4]

It is said that Molière took Scaramouche as model when he played Sganarelle in *Le Cocu Imaginaire*. It is sad to reflect that nothing remains, nor could remain, of the remarkable Scaramouche whom Molière so admired and honoured. When he left the stage Scaramouche passed into oblivion, even in the minds of his contemporaries. His name was scarcely ever mentioned again except by Mme de Sévigné and Tallement des Réaux, and then only most briefly. If it had not been for Molière, in fact, we should know little more of Scaramouche than could be learned from one or two engravings.

Pasquariello and Meo-Squaquara

Pasquariello Trunno and Meo-Squaquara belonged undoubtedly to a variety of Captains, acrobats, and dancers in vogue during the sixteenth century. They all wore

[1] Works of Palaprat (edition of 1712).

[2] See p. 23.

[3] "For instance, Elomire (Molière) desired to perfect himself in the art of making people laugh. How did the sly fellow accomplish this bold plan? He went to see Scaramouche night and morning, and stood, mirror in hand, before the great man; nor was there a posture or grimace that this great pupil of the greatest buffoons did not perform in a hundred different ways."

[4] *Menagiana: Notes posthumes de Ménage* (Baudelot, 1693).

swords. Callot adds "Trunno," which means 'terrible,' to Pasquariello's name. The name Squaquara rattles like the beak of an enraged heron; its owner must have belonged at one time to the family of Captains, otherwise Scaramouche would not have included him in the list of his own ancestors. Only Pasquariel was known in France. He was a tight-rope performer like Tortoriti, and acted as valet or else as double for Scaramouche and Scapin, though he had no particular character of his own. The Pasquariel of the

PASQUARIELLO TRUONNO AND MEO-SQUAQUARA
Callot

seventeenth century was clad in black velvet, and his costume was sometimes enlivened by bright red socks.

In *L'Avocat pour et contre* there is a forceful scene of rather cruel comedy in which Pasquariel plays a part:

PASQUARIEL *and* HARLEQUIN

(PASQUARIEL *enters. His top-vest is of many colours. He hobbles in grotesquely on crutches, his eyes almost closed.*)

HARLEQUIN (*spying him*)

This fellow is the painter from the Invalides. He is paralytic, and he'll paint me all lop-sided.

(PASQUARIEL *tries to take off his hat and salute* HARLEQUIN, *but he trembles so violently that he cannot hold himself up, and falls against* HARLEQUIN, *saying:*)

At your service, my master.

HARLEQUIN

Help! I'm crippled for life. Pierrot, help me to get this fellow on his feet again. (*To the* PAINTER, *after lifting him up:*) Between ourselves, my dear sir, you would do better to go away and die. You can come back and finish my portrait afterwards.

(PASQUARIEL *sits down on a chair, puts on very large spectacles, and mixes some colours on his palette with an unusually big brush. He smears paint all over the face of* PIERROT, *who stands by watching him work.*)

PIERROT (*weeping, his face covered with paint*)

Ye gods, take care, sir! I am not the picture! (*He leaves.*)

HARLEQUIN (*incensed*)

He is quite right. Pay attention to what you're doing. It seems to me you are trying to be a bit too funny, daubing my secretary like that!

(PASQUARIEL *looks at* HARLEQUIN *attentively without saying a word, then drops to his knees and crawls toward* HARLEQUIN *in this position, still holding his brush in his hand.*)

HARLEQUIN (*sees him coming toward him*)

What's the meaning of this?

PASQUARIEL (*answering him*)

I am going to paint your worship.

HARLEQUIN

Go over to my picture then.

(PASQUARIEL, *trying to turn toward the picture, which is on his right, sprawls full length on the ground.*)

HARLEQUIN

Now, there's a broken-down artist for you! I suppose I'll have to pay for him, too. Pierrot was right when he said he was only a glass-painter.

(PASQUARIEL *picks himself up, wishes to take leave of* HARLEQUIN, *totters feebly, and ends by falling against* HARLEQUIN, *who tumbles to the ground with* PASQUARIEL *on top of him.*)

HARLEQUIN (*rising*)

Fool of a painter! In trying to make a copy you have maimed the original.

(PASQUARIEL *picks himself up and exit.*)

Pasquino

The term 'pasquinade'[1] is in itself a sufficient explanation of Pasquino's character. Says Pasquino:

> Having left Rome at the point of a boot, I've gone about from inn to inn at this game of hunt-the-slipper with no other means of paying my way than to malign those who have fed me. Here I am, without a penny, hungry as a wolf, and no way of appeasing the famished wails of my weary guts.

Pasquin and Pasquariel are as much alike as twin brothers. Pasquariel is, in fact, little more than a sort of half-hearted Brighella.

Crispin

Crispin is the French son of Scaramouche. The creator of the part was an actor named Raymond Poisson, who presented the character in a highly imaginative costume, which later became more and more insipid as Crispin deteriorated into an ordinary valet. An engraving by Bonnart shows the first Crispin bearing an "astounding rapier" fixed in a baldric much too large for him, and wearing boots with funnel tops, one of which is

[1] *I.e.*, Lampoon.

turned up high and the other down very low. He also has spurs with immense rowels, and his head is swallowed up by a ruff in the shape of a half-moon. Underneath the engraving is written the following ingenuous verse:

> Crispin, dont tu vois la figure,
> Est un pauvre musicien
> Qui n'entend rien en tablature
> Si ce n'est qu'il entonne bien.[1]

Raymond died in 1690. But an entire dynasty of Poissons played Crispin up till 1753. And that is the end of the history of all those who began as Captains and eventually dwindled into mere valets.

[1] "Crispin, whose face you see, is a poor musician who understands naught of the score save that he intones well."

XVIII

Pedrolino and his Family

BERTOLDO, PIERO, PAGLIACCIO, GIAN FARINA, PEPPE NAPPA, GIGLIO

Pedrolino

PEDROLINO, Pierro, and Piero are one and the same person. The character dates from the second half of the sixteenth century, and not the second half of the seventeenth, as is generally supposed. Pedrolino was originally a valet, but he differs radically from the other valets of the *commedia dell' arte*: he is a young, personable, and trustworthy individual who can be a charming lover if necessary, like Lelio and Flavio, although he usually confines his attentions to the soubrettes. He cannot be considered, strictly speaking, a substitute for the other valets, for whom he doubled occasionally; he played in his own right in all the principal troupes of the sixteenth century, including the Gelosi, and appeared on the stage along with Bertolino and Burattino or Harlequin and Francatrippa or other pairs of Zannis. The sixteenth-century Pedrolino has such engaging simplicity and elegance that one is tempted to think of him as having sprung from the charming fantasy of Watteau or of Marivaux. In the pieces where Pedrolino is in love with Franceschina, which were created by Flaminio Scala, there is a tenderness and sensitiveness more characteristic of the lovers in the aristocratic pastorals of the period than of the kind of companions to whom Pedrolino was accustomed.[1] He was, none the less, a comic character. When Franceschina deceives him outrageously he shoulders the blame and dissolves into tears of self-reproach for sins he has never committed. And when Pedrolino is induced by Harlequin to play tricks on Pantaloon or the Doctor he is inevitably the only one ever caught and punished. Although he is often beaten by his masters, his hardships never have much effect upon his appetite. One day Harlequin brings a dish of macaroni to Pedrolino, saying that it is a present from the Captain. Pedrolino devours the macaroni, though weeping copiously at every mouthful. Harlequin is touched, and he too begins to eat and blubber. Burattino joins them and takes part in their feasting and lamentations. Racked by sobs they eat the last morsel of the tear-drenched macaroni. After it has disappeared they weep more loudly than ever. Pedrolino makes Harlequin promise to "kiss the hands of the Captain" in gratitude, and then departs. Burattino follows him. Harlequin, left alone, leaves the stage still weeping and licking the plate.

[1] That is my opinion, at any rate. M. Constant Mic (*op. cit.*), however, seems to think otherwise. "Although Pedrolino gave rise to the French Pierrot," he writes, "no distinction was made in Italy between him and the other Zannis."

In some of Scala's scenarios Pedrolino seems more like the other valets. He imitates the Captain, cuts capers, undertakes intrigues, and pretends that he is a mute; yet these touches do not alter the fundamental traits of his character to any extent. Pedrolino and Pierro often appear as valets in the scenarios of several authors between 1547 and 1604. The French Pierrot is a direct descendant of these two, and not an original creation of

QUINSON AS PIERROT
Eighteenth century
Gillot

GERATON AS PIERROT
About 1673

Molière's.[1] Indeed, he bears so close a resemblance to Pedrolino that it is impossible to believe that all trace of Pierrot's traditional character was lost between 1604 and 1665.

The actor Giratone, who revived the *rôle* of Pedrolino at this period, accentuated his simplicity and *naïveté* and awkwardness in order to make him more like the early Bertoldino.

Pierrot's costume is, of course, too universally familiar to require description here, but it must be noted that it was very similar to Pulcinella's, except that it was tighter and fitted more neatly.

Pedrolino was heavily powdered, and played without a mask.

[1] *Don Juan, ou Le Festin de Pierre.*

Peppe Nappa

He is a Sicilian Pedrolino. He dresses in blue, dances, leaps high into the air, is double-jointed and always active. He does not powder his face. He should have great play of facial expression.

PIERROT
After M. Sand

Pierrot
(Tableau parlant.)
Beginning of the nineteenth century

THE PRINCIPAL PEDROLINOS

1605 GIOVANNI PELLESINI
1673 GIUSEPPE GIRATONE, of Ferrara
1729 ANTONIO STICOTTI
1707 PRÉVOT

At the Fair Theatres

1712 HAMOCHE
1715 BELLONI
1721 DUJARDIN
1741 PIETRO SODI, of Rome

Giglio, Gilles, Gilotin

The Giglio of the sixteenth century, who played the part of an amorous valet in the Intronati company, was as much like Pedrolino as Pierrot was like Gilles and Gilotin, between whom there is apparently no difference whatever. Giglio dressed in white flannel, and wore white shoes and a head-band of the same colour.

GILOTIN
Seventeenth century

THE PRINCIPAL GIGLIOS

1531	*Intronati*	An anonymous Giglio
1700	*In Naples*	Filipo
		Fabienti
1702	*At the fair theatres in France*	Maillot (Gilles)
1780	*At Vauxhall*	Carpentier

Bertoldo, Bertoldino, Cacasseno

These three characters, father, son, and grandson, were distinctly plebeian in their origin and manners. They were to be found in certain troupes which played during the latter part of the sixteenth century.[1] Their *rôles* were those of valets. They were rustics to the marrow, and were possessed of an incredible *naïveté* combined with the rough simplicity and cunning of the peasant. Bertoldo had a disconcerting habit of stepping forward from time to time during the course of the comedy and expounding some embarrassing and unexpected truth with all the gentleness of La Fontaine's bear. Bertoldino and Cacasseno have not as much sense as their father; their excessive stupidity, in fact, is one of their most comic assets. The three are of literary origin, which is rare in the Italian comedy, and their history runs as follows:

There was a lusty blacksmith born in 1550, named Giulio Cesare Croce, who, after begetting fourteen children, awoke one fine day with the conviction that he was a poet. He had beaten with a mighty arm upon the red-hot iron for many a year, but he suddenly decided to quit his smithy and hammers and set forth to wander the streets of Bologna, improvising songs as he went to the accompaniment of a *lira*. Little by little he created and perfected a hero of his imagination, whom he called Bertoldo. Presently every one in Bologna began talking about Bertoldo. They never grew tired of hearing about him. Then Croce was obliged to invent a wife for him, named Marcolfa, and afterward Bertoldino, their offspring. The worthy blacksmith had so effectively hammered his characters into the popular imagination that even after he died Bertoldo's family continued to grow and prosper. And thus it was that Cacasseno, Bertoldo's grandson, was created by Camillo Scaligero.

Croce published, before his death, a *Vita di Bertoldo* and then a *Vita di Bertoldino*, which had a tremendous success. The *Vita di Cacasseno* was equally well received. During the seventeenth and eighteenth centuries many painters and engravers vied with each other in immortalizing Bertoldo, who thenceforth became a national hero and acquired

[1] I have in my possession two prints from wood-blocks representing comedians performing on platform-stages. Just above the actors are written the names Bertoldo and Bertoldino. One of the scenes is of a beating administered in the presence of two characters, one crowned and the other with horns; the other scene shows Bertoldo trying to pass through a low Roman door in a screen, while Bertoldino exposes his posterior to a woman wearing a crown. The type, and especially the frames, of the two pictures seem to indicate that they belong to the end of the sixteenth century.

the imagined qualities of most heroes of the kind. Bertoldo's reputation finally became so great that ordinary prose was no longer considered an adequate medium for his praise,

Engraving by G. J. Xavery

and therefore twenty-six poets of Bologna, Lombardy, and Ferrara united to compose a Bertoldian epic in twenty cantos, which was published in a *de luxe* edition in 1736, by the Enseigne du Renard at Bologna.

PEDROLINO AND HIS FAMILY

PORTRAIT OF BERTOLDO

(*After the popular poem of Croce Della-Lira*)

In the sixth century under the reign of King Alboin, that clement and righteous sovereign, there lived in Bertagnana, in the province of Verona, a poor peasant named Bertoldo, whose appearance was indeed ridiculous.

His head was as large as a pumpkin, his hair reddish and lank, his ears enormous, and his tiny eyes peered out from under turned-up lids ; his huge mouth ran from ear to ear, and he had but two teeth, which looked like the tusks of a boar. From his chin hung a thick and matted beard. His body was scarcely any comelier than his face, for his hands were hams, his legs stocky and bowed, and his hide calloused and hairy. But his mind was keen and penetrating, and his judgment sound ; he was, in short, the most agreeable man in the village of Bertagnana, where he lived. His fellow-citizens preferred his philosophy and instruction to the teachings of their priest. He settled their disputes with far greater wisdom than lords or judges could have done, and he was the cause of more laughter and merriment than all the charlatans and clowns that passed through the village.

A FEW SAMPLES OF BERTOLDO'S WIT

Bertoldo once sat down in the audience-chamber of King Alboin, and when some one reproached him for his lack of decorum, he replied :

" Well, I sit down in church, and that is the house of the Lord."

" But don't you see that the King is set above all the rest of us ? "

" But he isn't set as high as the weathercock on the steeple of the church in our village ; and a weathercock can tell what the weather is going to be."

King Alboin asked Bertoldo what sort of wine he considered the best.

" Whatever kind you can drink at another man's house, providing that it costs you nothing."

The jester of King Alboin, Fagotto, grew jealous of Bertoldo and tried, so they say, to beat him at his own game. One day he asked : " How would you go about catching a running hare ? " " I'd wait," Bertoldo answered, " until it was run through with a spit."

Fagotto and Bertoldo were always quarrelling. The latter once asked the King for permission to spit. It was granted him on the condition that he should select the least important place in the palace for the deed. After looking about Bertoldo caught sight of Fagotto and forthwith spat on him. Bertoldo waged war against the women of the Court, and was put in a sack to be drowned. He escaped, and was again captured and sentenced to the gallows, but he always managed to save himself in the nick of time, thanks to his nimble wits.

Bertoldino, Cacasseno, Pirolino, Bigolo

If the frogs keep Bertoldino from sleeping he pelts them with the gold pieces that have just been given him. He makes the great discovery that he is larger than a hen, and therefore concludes that he ought to be able to hatch more eggs at one time than the whole hen-yard put together. He proceeds to heap the eggs under him and succeeds in producing an omelet. Whenever Bertoldo is annoyed by flies he simply brushes them off with nettles.

Bertoldino is the despair of his mother, Marcolfa, and also of King Alboin, who sends him back to his native village.

Cacasseno, son of Bertoldino, is as ingenuous as his father, and even more timid and greedy.

Pirolino (Little Pill) and Bigolo (Noodle Soup) are other versions of Bertoldino and Cacasseno.

One of the first Bertoldinos was played by the actor Nicolo Zecca, who was a remarkable dancer and so agile that, according to Beltrame (Nicolo Barbieri), he could outdistance the swiftest hare in a race. In 1630 Zecca was still a member of the Fedeli troupe.

Pagliaccio (Chopped Straw)

Pagliaccio, the valet, was a sort of 'side-show barker,' a low comedian given, as a rule, to coarse burlesque. He was awkward, stupid, and heedless, and it was he, in fact,

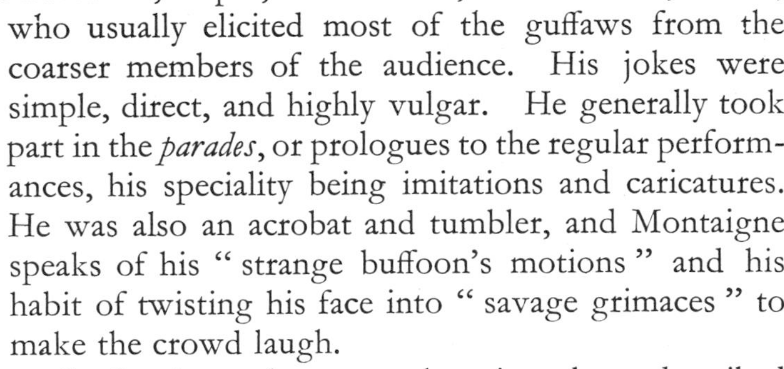

who usually elicited most of the guffaws from the coarser members of the audience. His jokes were simple, direct, and highly vulgar. He generally took part in the *parades*, or prologues to the regular performances, his speciality being imitations and caricatures. He was also an acrobat and tumbler, and Montaigne speaks of his " strange buffoon's motions " and his habit of twisting his face into " savage grimaces " to make the crowd laugh.

In the sixteenth century there is a clown described as wearing a soiled shirt, a skull-cap, and a high hat set off by cock feathers.

PAGLIACCIO (1600)
After M. Sand

THE COSTUME AND THE MASK

Pagliaccio wore a mask in spite of the fact that he powdered his face. His blouse fitted him very loosely, hung in folds, and was fastened together by large buttons. His costume was completed by a white hat which could be formed into any shape desired.

The best-known Pagliaccios were Zaniazi, who flourished about 1670, Natocelli, about 1770, and Martini, about 1803.

Paillasse

In France Paillasse was no more than an actor in *parades*, like Pagliaccio. At the end of the eighteenth century there was a Paillasse in the theatre directed by Nicolet, who was, according to all accounts, an excellent comedian. In one of the many adaptations of *Le Festin de Pierre* Paillasse, reduced to penury, clothed himself in a mattress cover, and performed juggling and acrobatic feats. The cover was red and white, with blue and white checks, and thereafter became the conventional costume of Paillasse.

PAILLASSE
Nineteenth century

Gros-Guillaume (Robert Guérin, called Lafleur)

"This is my valet, Guillaume le Gros [Big Bill]," Gaultier-Garguille would say, "and I can always tell him by his clothes striped like the Swiss Guard of Francis I, and his gourd of a belly."

Robert Guérin was indeed excessively corpulent. He was French and plebeian by birth, and he created a type for himself after the Italian fashion. He dressed entirely in white, and, with his unmasked face heavily powdered, he could make grimaces that were a wonder to behold. We are indebted to Tallement des Réaux for a most interesting account of Gros-Guillaume:

Once the King held him [the Maréchal de Roquelaure] between his knees while Gros-

Guillaume played the farce *Le Gentilhomme Gascon*. At every turn the Maréchal made as though he wished to leave him and go and thrash Gros-Guillaume, saying, " Coz, don't be angry," and this he did to amuse his master. After the death of the King the actors no longer dared play in Paris, so great was the general mourning, and they went away on a tour of the provinces, finally arriving at Bordeaux. The Maréchal was the King's representative in that place, and the players found it necessary to ask his permission to perform. " I grant it you," he said to them, " on condition that you give the farce of *Le Gentilhomme Gascon*." They thought that they would be soundly beaten as soon as they had left his presence, and so began to make excuses. " Do as I tell you," he commanded. The Maréchal attended their performance, but the remembrance of his good master caused him such grief that he was constrained to leave the theatre in tears just as the piece commenced.

Pierrot-Deburau

Deburau was, during the nineteenth century in France, the most authentic descendant of the old French and Italian comedians. Baudelaire, Théophile Gautier, and other distinguished contemporaries have all made mention of his genius for improvisation and pantomime. Like Trivelin, Scaramouche, and many others, Deburau was gifted with extraordinary agility, and his ingenuity was such that he would invent a new dance almost every evening, sometimes eccentric, sometimes burlesque, but always charming. There, in the dim candle-glow of the noisome little Funambules Theatre, he would move his audience, varied as they were, from laughter to tears and back again, without so much as uttering a word. His entertainments were a mixture of pantomime, harlequinade, and extravaganza which belonged quite definitely to the old school of the Italian scenarios. He even used the traditional names of Isabelle, Léandre, Harlequin, and he himself took the name of Pierrot. But he differed considerably from the *commedia dell' arte*, playing neither Pedrolino nor Pagliaccio, but interpreting a thousand characters in one—Deburau.

Eighteenth century

It would be futile to attempt to trace his affiliation with any of the characters in the Italian comedy. His white costume without collar, the loose blouse, and the black skull-cap made Deburau as much like Pagliaccio as Pierrot, and unlike either, except that he wore a white make-up as they did. Deburau-Pierrot, " pale as the moon, mysterious as silence, supple and mute as the serpent, straight and tall as the gallows," died in 1846.

PEDROLINO AND HIS FAMILY

THE FAMILY TREE OF PEDROLINO

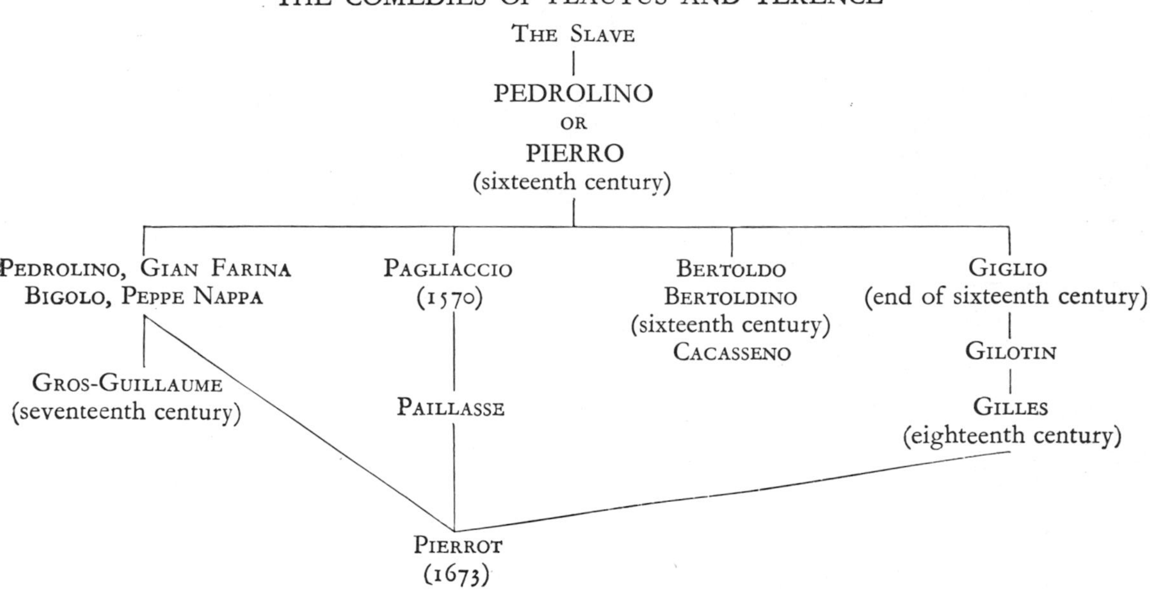

XIX

The Women of the Commedia dell' Arte

THE CANTARINA, THE INAMORATA, THE SOUBRETTE, FRANCESCHINA, ISABELLA

THEIR very names are redolent of dreams, the gracious names of these Inamoratas, some of whom were tender, some false, some modest servant-maids, and some wantons.

To mention them is to evoke the glamorous Italy of bygone days, the Italy of Casanova or of President de Brosses,[1] for they recall old chronicles of Renaissance splendours in which the charm and loveliness of these women of the Italian comedy have been captured and preserved for ever. Their gentle memories bear us far away back into the past, to villas at Baiæ or at Capua, to revels and sumptuous pageants which some have since been pleased to call Roman decadence. We think of these women as being both voluptuous and exquisitely cultivated, such women as belong to every age in which hypocrisy does not usurp the place of innocence.

Until the beginning of the Renaissance the Church was beset by an ever-present fear that the great pagan revels might be revived, unloosing once more the furious pleasures of the flesh and the devil, and it was perhaps due to this fear that for sixteen centuries throughout the Christian world all women were prohibited from acting in the theatre. When they began to reappear upon the stage in the sixteenth century, in the more important troupes like the Gelosi, the ban against them was lifted in several of the Italian states.[2] With the exception of three legations, however, the exclusion lasted in the Papal States far into the eighteenth century.

With regard to women in the theatre, there is an amusing anecdote concerning Casanova and the actor Bellino. It is said that one time Casanova was very much disturbed by a strangely tender feeling which he had for the comely Bellino. But his mind was soon set at rest when he discovered that Bellino was a woman who had been compelled to adopt a male disguise so that she would be permitted to play female *rôles* on the stage. And in the *Mémoires* of Goldoni there is a reference to this same subject:

> There was a company of actors in Rimini which seemed to me very good indeed. It was the first time that I had ever seen women upon the stage, and I found them a piquant novelty. Rimini lies in the legation of Ravenna, and, as women are allowed on the stage there, female *rôles* are not taken by beardless youths or clean-shaven men, as at Rome.

[1] See p. 34, *note* 2.

[2] In 1558 Pope Sixtus V issued a new edict forbidding women to appear on the stage.

THE WOMEN OF THE COMMEDIA DELL' ARTE

In France and England young striplings enacted the parts of leading women and soubrettes until about 1762. It is easy to imagine the joy of the Parisians when they first saw women on the stage in the different troupes of the Italian comedy. Parliament was so bewildered by the innovation that it accused the women of dressing and undressing

An Inamorata
Engraving by Callot

on the stage, and of giving " instruction in lewdness and adultery." In fact, one of the engravings (about 1577) in the *Recueil Fossard* shows Harlequin caressing Francesquina in a manner far from discreet.

Now it was due to this absence of women from the stage for so long a time that the female *rôles* were not developed to any great extent in the *commedia dell' arte*, and hence never became as important characters as Pulcinella, Harlequin, and the others, who had a long tradition behind them. The history of Isabelle, Francesquina, Flaminia, Columbine, or Zerbinette was rather that of the actress who played the *rôle* than of the *rôle* itself. A *comédienne* was required to be pretty as well as charming. She had also to be an accomplished dancer and musician, and to possess a good voice. La Cantarina, or the Songstress, was the only one of the women of the Italian comedy who inherited her *rôle* from an extremely ancient tradition, which managed somehow to survive sixteen centuries of obscurity. The proof of her antiquity can be found in paintings and engravings, as testified by comparing, for example, the Songstress of Herculaneum with Callot's Franceschina or the eighteenth-century drawing of Camilla Veronese.[1]

The Costumes

The costumes of the women of the sixteenth century,[2] and even later, belonged just as much to the persons who wore them, Isabelle, Columbine, or Zerbinette, as they did to the *rôles* of Inamorata, servant-maid, or bawd, as the case might be. Never did women indulge their fancy for magnificent and intricate dress more than during the Renaissance. They revelled in bodices and ruffles embroidered in gold and silk, jewels of every description, earrings of pearl or of gold thread in rings and twisted strands. The most beautiful of the costumes were, of course, those of the Inamoratas and Courtesans. In the *Anconitana*, by Ruzzante, the sprightly Isotta declares :

> I know how a lady should dress. I know just what clothes go best with the devices and liveries of various stations, and what colours signify love or hope or jealousy or any of those things. I know how *faldigie*[3] should be worn, and how to make a fringed headdress show to best advantage. I know all the different styles of corsets, and which one will make the throat look fine and delicate, or reveal just enough of the breasts. I know how a woman should walk, how she should laugh, how she should droop her eyes and curtsy, and just what gestures show that she is both winsome and innocent.

Every time a play was given in which, according to the taste of the time, goddesses and nymphs appeared as a divertisement, or when there was a scene representing some purely imaginary place, the costumes of the women were *à l'antique*—that is to say, entirely fanciful and having no particular relation to the subject or setting of the play in question.

Rabelais wrote a delightful description of a Diana in a divertisement given in Rome in 1569 :

> Diana wore upon her brow a silver crescent ; her blond hair fell loosely about her shoulders, and was caught up in plaits about the crown of her head by a garland of laurel intertwined with roses, violets, and other fair flowers ; she wore a tunic and undergarment of crimson damask richly embroidered, together with fine Cyprian linen shot with gold and curiously folded like the surplice of a cardinal. This dress extended just below the knees, and over it

[1] See the illustrations on pp. 268, 269.

[2] See the two illustrations in the chapter on Harlequin (pp. 125, 129) showing the costumes of " La Nimphe " and " La Dona Cornelia," both of which belong to the second half of the sixteenth century.

[3] *Faldigia*, a headdress consisting of a veil and ribbons.—Translator.

An Inamorata of the Renaissance
Probably Isabella Andreini, of the Gelosi company
Carnavalet Museum, Paris

was draped a costly leopard-skin which was fastened at the left shoulder by huge gold buttons. Her gilded boots were cut away and tied with thongs of silver. Her quiver, which hung from her right shoulder, was studded with pearls and was secured by large cords and tufts of white and rose silk.

Apart from these fantastic creations, which lasted until the eighteenth century, the women never had specific ' character ' costumes. The dresses in which Harlequine and Pierrette usually appeared were merely modifications of the Harlequin or Pierrot costumes, dating from the close of the seventeenth century.

The Masks

Properly speaking, there were no masks for the women in improvised comedy because the real mask was the standardization of a character, and no matter how frequently or how variously the Inamoratas, soubrettes, or matrons were introduced, these Flaminias, Sylvias, and Fiamettas changed in character and personality as often as different actresses were found to interpret them. This fact is particularly worthy of note, for it serves to throw additional light on the ancient origin of the traditional masks.

There is yet another reason why the women did not wear masks—namely, that no mask could ever approach the enchanting effect of a lovely woman's face, whose beauty was obviously the chief requisite of her *rôle*.

The tiny black velvet mask, or *loup*, which the women of the *commedia dell' arte* sometimes wore cannot be considered a true mask, for it was used outside as well as inside the theatre. The *loup* was as much a part of a woman's dress as her brocade and lace. Brantôme says that the women of his day took to wearing *loups* in the street, and even at home, because it gave them the ' pearl and nacre ' complexion which was so much prized at the time.

Youths in Women's Rôles

In connexion with the female *rôles* as played by youths, it is of interest to quote from an amusing essay on the subject by Niccolo Barbieri (Beltrame da Milano), who apparently wrote with great seriousness :

> These young men do not know how to dress themselves in the attire of the other sex, and they must therefore dress at home with the aid of their wives or some feather-brained maid with whom they make free and lively ; and he whose passions are not cooled by the years or by serious work runs the risk of becoming an insufferable coxcomb. These lads pass openly through the city, chatting and romping together, and often they arrive at the theatre so completely dishevelled that their friends or teachers must needs comb their hair again, refurbish their paint, and rearrange their finery. One may be content if they manage to arrive in time ; furthermore, they must be flattered and cajoled for encouragement. Indeed, they are enough to exhaust the patience of those who have the care of them.

Beltrame concludes his account with the opinion that only women should play women's *rôles*, and that any other custom is frankly indecent.

A Ballerina of the Seventeenth Century

The Cantarina and the Ballerina

Properly speaking, the *rôles* of Cantarina and Ballerina belong to the same category, for almost every Songstress in the *commedia dell' arte*, as well as in the later French-Italian comedy, could dance and sing, and even play a number of musical instruments. This idea of the *rôle* of a Songstress is an important detail from an historic point of view, since it is the only link between the women of the Italian comedy and a very ancient tradition. As has already been mentioned, a comparison of the Songstress of Herculaneum with Callot's Franceschina and the eighteenth-century drawing representing Camilla Veronese reveals the most salient features held in common. In spite of the passage of so many centuries, these two seem to be precisely the same woman; even their gestures are the same.

A Songstress of the Ancient Roman Theatre
Herculaneum

The Ballerina, or Dancer, of Herculaneum, like the Songstress of the troupes of the Renaissance, was accustomed to come forward to the apron of the stage and sing the story of the play. She took part in the comedy also, and at intervals would sing, dance, or play a fragment of instrumental music. Her entrances and exits, in fact, often served no other purpose than to add variety and movement to the performance, and were accepted as an ordinary stage convention.

It must be borne in mind that in ancient times there were no *entr'actes* during the performances, even in the case of the *Atellanæ*. It was quite usual, therefore, to fill in the necessary pauses with various kinds of divertisements such as *farceurs*, a comedy, a ballet, a play with songs, or impersonation or balancing 'acts.'

President de Brosses wrote:

> The Italians are more fond of the theatre than any other nation, and, inasmuch as they love music equally well, they seldom separate the two, with the result that for them all tragedy and comedy and farce tend to become opera.

The Italians have, of course, been noted always for their passion not only for music, but also for dancing, at which they are particularly adept.

FRANCISCHINA AND GIAN FARINA
Beginning of the seventeenth century
Callot

Some of the Italian Cantarinas included acrobatic dances in their repertoires, and some also played the viol while performing on a tight-rope. It was in this form of entertainment that they showed their relationship to Scaramuccia and Trivellino. During a festival given by the Prince of Calabria in 1492 a Songstress, impersonating Joy, sang to her own accompaniment on the viol, and then danced while her handmaidens played the flute and rebeck. Was not this actress a spiritual sister of Rosalie Astraudi,[1] who danced, sang, and played the violoncello, and also interpreted various *rôles* of Inamorata and soubrette? Machiavelli, in writing to a friend about the Florentine Songstress Barbera, who went about from town to town playing interludes, said: "I recommend her highly to you, for she interests me more than the Emperor himself."

CAMILLA VERONESE
Eighteenth century

The young bloods of the sixteenth century went to Italy to learn how to *baller*, or dance. Nor had the art deteriorated there in the eighteenth century; de Brosses wrote that

> What astonished me most was a young woman dancer who could spring as high and nimbly as Javilliers. She executed twenty *entrechats* in sequence without pausing for breath, and clicked her heels eight times at each leap; and she did the same for all the *entrepas* for which our masters are so admired. Indeed, compared to her supple grace La Camargo seems but a block of stone.

The companies of Italian players which came to France included both the Cantarina and Ballerina. In Gherardi's collections of scenarios there is always a

[1] She made her *début* in April 1744, at the age of eleven.

little music designed for the Songstress, and the text contains numerous couplets in Italian from old operas as well as French lyrics and rigadoons, and even songs composed especially for the scenario in question. One of the most typical examples of Cantarina in the seventeenth century was a young woman named Elizabeth Danneret. On the stage she was known as Babet la Chanteuse, and she made her first appearance in the Italian comedy in 1694, in a piece entitled *La Fontaine de Sapience*. She was dressed as a shepherdess, and, holding out a cup of magical water, she sang:

Elizabeth Daneret
Seventeenth century

"Qui goûte de ces eaux ne peut plus se méprendre
Quand l'amour lui demande un choix;
Buvons-en et mille fois;
Quand on prend de l'amour, on n'en saurait trop prendre."[1]

She came on again at the end of the play, and, while the swains and shepherdesses disported themselves in dances, she sang:

"Amando,
Penando,
Si speri, si, si;
Che baste sol un di,
Un' hor, un momento,
Per render contento
Un misero cor."[2]

Babet scored a sensational success in every *rôle*, whether she played as a shepherdess or a naiad, as Bellona or a sibyl or an Egyptian.

Elizabeth Daneret was small and well formed, and she had a pretty face and a very agreeable voice. After the death of Gherardi, by whom she had a son, she entered the company of the Opera.

The most celebrated Cantarinas in France during the seventeenth century were Margarita Bertolazzi, Luigia-Gabriella Locatelli, and Jiulia Gabrielli.

Ursula Astori, the daughter of a Venetian clock-maker, was the Cantarina in a company which came up from Italy to play in Paris about 1716. She married the Pantaloon Fabio Sticotti; she died in 1739. Her principal *rôles* were in *Le Stratagème*, which had music by Pagliardi (1716); and in a sort of parody called *Alcyone* (1741), with music by Blaise; and in a revival of Pergolese's *Serva Padrona*.

Among the most celebrated Cantarinas in Italy were Catarina Martinella, at Rome; Franceschina Caccini, Julia and Victoria Lulle, La Moretti, Adriana Baroni, of Mantua; Checca della Laguna, Margherita Costa, Petronilla Massimi, and Francesca Manzoni.

[1] "Whoever drinks of this water will never mistake when love requires a choice; let us drink then and a thousand times, for, in partaking of love, we never take too much."

[2] "Loving, striving, hope, hope always; the wretched heart needs but a day, an hour, a moment, to rest content."

THE WOMEN OF THE COMMEDIA DELL' ARTE

The Inamorata (Prima and Seconda Donna Inamorata)

The Inamoratas of the sixteenth century went by such names as Cornelia, Isabella, Lucinda,[1] Flaminia, Lucrezia, Lavinia. The rustic maids were known as Fiorina, Dina, and Ghetta. The types, like the names, ranged from the most noble, innocent, and tender lover to the loose apprentice wench, who is saved just in time by virtuous love, and the worldly courtesan whose good as well as whose naughty deeds always cause her to be clapped into prison.

AN INAMORATA
Beginning of the seventeenth century
Callot

At the beginning of the seventeenth century the Inamoratas were called Renemia, Lucia, Pandolfina, Virginia, Diana, Rosaura, Rosalinde, Ortensia. The name Flaminia, which Agate Calderoni (an Inamorata) adopted, became hereditary in her family. Her granddaughter, Virginia Baletti, the wife of Riccoboni (Lelio), played the same *rôles* as her grandparent under the same name. And it was in a similar fashion that the Andreini family retained the name of Isabella. This custom of keeping the stage names of the women as well as of the men is another interesting instance of the fidelity to tradition which was so strong among the Italian players.

A COURTESAN AND BURATINO
End of the sixteenth century

FIORINETTA

Fiorinetta was a cultivated and passionate courtesan. Placido, the father of Flavio, who is Fiorinetta's lover, says of her:

> Fiorinetta is not a nun, thank Heaven; if she were she would be the most dangerous kind of mistress. Neither is she a married woman—which is also a risk, especially if the husband is of a jealous nature. Nor is she a vicious woman who might undermine my son's health. On the contrary, she is a charming young girl who has taken my son for her first lover, and she loves him so much that she cannot abide another man near her. But I confess I do not know just how their little household is prospering at present.

[1] The first three names figure in the *Recueil Fossard* (about 1577).

Her mother is a *ruffiana*, and wants to sell her daughter to the rich old Polidoro because my son has no more money to give her. Neither have I, for that matter. My wife keeps every last sou under lock and key, and her steward refuses to be bribed. You must find some way of robbing me, my dear Truffo [his valet], without my wife's discovering it, so that my son may have enough money to live another untroubled year in complete possession of his mistress.

Tut, tut, I want to be my son's best friend and do as much for him as my father once did for me.

Farther on Fiorinetta asks her mother, the *ruffiana* Celega :

Would you have me love every one who comes along as I love Flavio ?

CELEGA

I don't care whether you love them or not so long as you pretend to.

FIORINETTA

Mother, dear, that would make me too unhappy. I can never do the opposite of what I feel or what my heart commands.

A little later Fiorinetta tells Flavio :

No, my heart is not for sale like so much goods on a vendor's stall.

And so, after first selling herself to Flavio, Fiorinetta falls desperately in love with him and eventually marries him. This so-called redemption is a far cry from romanticism, presented, as it is, in a series of burlesque and realistic scenes in which there is no quibbling about calling a spade a spade.

ISABELLA (YSABELLA, YZABELLA, ZIRZABELLE)

The name of Isabella speaks of tender and devoted love as Scapino's speaks of out-and-out rascality.[1] In the sixteenth century there was an Inamorata by the name of Isabella, the actress Vittoria degli Amorevoli. It fell to the lot of Isabella Andreini, however, to have the honour of bestowing her name permanently upon this idealized type of woman in love. This remarkable actress has already been mentioned in these pages, but it must be said further in her praise that she was " as celebrated for her virtue as for her beauty, and she brought such glory to the profession of acting that the name of Isabella Andreini will be held in veneration as long as the world shall endure and unto the end of the ages."

During her lifetime she was fêted and honoured and admired throughout both France and Italy ; and it is easy to understand why her son, Giovanbattista, wrote, with just pride, that Ariosto, Aretino, Giraldi, Guarini, Marino, and numerous other men of distinction had voiced their praise and admiration of her. There is a sonnet of Tasso's which begins

Quando v'ordiva il prezioso velo
L' alma natura, e le mortali spoglie,
Il bel cogliea, si come fior si coglie,
Togliendo gemme in terra e lumi in cielo.[2]

[1] In the *Recueil Fossard* (1577) Francesquina and Donna Cornelia are portrayed in rather indecent postures, but Isabella always remains dignified and modest.

[2] " When fostering mother nature fashioned the fair veil of her physical graces she sought out beauty and gathered it as a flower, taking jewels out of the earth and stars from the heavens."

The closing lines of this tribute are

> Felici l' alme e fortunati i cori,
> Ove con lettre d'oro Amor l' imprima
> Nell' imagine vostra, et in cui s'adori.[1]

ISABELLA (ABOUT 1577)
Possibly Vittoria degli Amorevoli or Isabella Andreini
Detail from an engraving in the "Recueil Fossard"

Maria de' Medici and Henri IV also held her in high esteem. On her departure from Paris in 1604 a charming poem was written to Isabella by du Ryer:

A ISABELLE, COMÉDIENNE

> Je ne crois point qu'Isabelle
> Soit femme mortelle ;
> C'est plutôt quelqu'un des dieux
> Qui s'est déguisé en femme
> Afin de nous ravir l'âme
> Par l'oreille et par les yeux.[2]

[1] "Happy those souls and blessed those hearts in which Love has been stamped in letters of gold after your image, and is thus adored."

[2] "I do not believe that Isabelle can be mortal woman. She must be one of the gods who has assumed woman's guise in order to ravish away our souls through our eyes and ears."

In 1578 Isabella had, at the age of sixteen, been enrolled in the troupe of Flaminio Scala at Florence. She subsequently married Francesco Andreini. When she died in childbirth in Lyons the entire city turned out to pay her last honours. The civil magistrates sent their mace-bearers to the funeral, and the guild of merchants marched in the procession, carrying torches.

End of the seventeenth century

Isabella Andreini was, as previously stated, an exceedingly cultivated woman. She knew Latin perfectly, and she was a poet of considerable talent. She wrote a *Pastorale de Myrtille*, as well as many sonnets and songs. Almost the only trustworthy proof of her beauty still extant is the picture of her reproduced at p. 265. It is not absolutely certain that the portrait is authentic, but it is the only existing copy which bears the least resemblance to an engraving made in 1607, which was printed as a frontispiece to the *Lettere*. Oddly enough, neither shows her as beautiful as she was reputed to be, and the engraving represents her as even less lovely than the painting. The medallion in the Bibliothèque Nationale shows a woman of heavy features and rather bovine expression. There are two other portraits purported to be of her, which do not resemble any of the others. They are woodcuts, and were executed in 1588 and in 1601 respectively. The illustration at p. 273 from the *Recueil Fossard* also possibly shows Isabella.

An Inamorata of the Italian Comedy
Engraving after a drawing by Watteau

The stage character of Isabella had been fully developed by the end of the seventeenth century: in any case, it was completed by Françoise Biancolelli. Isabella was now not so much of a tender, loving woman as a flirtatious young miss, ruling both her parents and admirers with a rod of iron. She possessed, moreover, a somewhat masculine turn of mind and a lively, picturesque wit similar to that of Ninon de Lenclos.

SILVIA, FLAMINIA, CAMILLE

As mentioned in the chapter dealing with the renaissance of the Italian comedy, *Arlequin Poli par l'Amour* was the first of Marivaux's comedies which the Italian players presented. In his plays nearly all of the Inamorata *rôles* were enacted by Rosa Zanetta

ROSAURA
Eighteenth century

Benozzi (the Silvia of *Arlequin Poïi par l'Amour* and of the *Amante Romanesque*), who had made her *début* in 1716, and in 1720 had married Baletti, the Mario of the Regent company. It cannot be said that Silvia interpreted a type character, in the strict sense of the word, because she played Marivaux; nevertheless she must have been well versed in all the tricks of the Italian trade to be able to give a finished performance of Marivaux's comedies, so full of *nuance* and allusiveness, without missing anything in his graceful and swiftly moving text. She played Inamorata *rôles* for over forty years and never counted a single failure.

Flaminia, Riccoboni's wife, also played leads along with Silvia. She was another woman of great cultivation, like Isabella, besides being an excellent actress. She was, moreover, a writer of merit, and her *Lettres de Fanny Butler* is a book still worth reading.

Antonia Veronese, or Camille (see illustration at p. 269), was already an accomplished dancer at the age of nine, and by the time she was twelve she began playing various *rôles* as Inamorata. Favart said of her, with reference to the ballet *Pygmalion*, in which Camille represented a statue :

> The art of her pantomime is beyond praise, especially when the statue comes slowly to life : she depicts her surprise, her curiosity, her budding love, all the intangible and ripening impulses of her nature, with an effect never before imagined. One might say of Camille that she dances even in her thought.

The quotation is especially interesting because, although it was written as late as 1760, it indicates how the spirit of the old Italian comedy of the days of Andreini, Dominique, and Scaramouche was still in force among the descendants of these men, at a time when the main stream of current drama was supposed to have turned, for the most part, to treacle.

THE MOST CELEBRATED INAMORATAS

About 1570 *Valerini troupe*	Flaminia	Vincenza Armiani	
1572	Celia	Maria Malloni	belonging to the Confidenti and Gelosi
	Lidia	L. de Bagnacavallo	
About 1578	Isabella	Isabella Andreini	
		Vittoria degli Amorevoli	
About 1580	Lavinia	Diana Ponti, actress and poet	
About 1593	Aurelia		
Confidenti troupe	Valeria	Austoni	
1601 *Gelosi troupe*	Florinda	Virginia Ramponi, wife of G.-B. Andreini	
	Clarice	Mme Alborgezzi	
	Angela	Mme Armelini	
	Graziosa	Andreoletti	
1624 *Fedeli troupe*		Margarita Luciani, wife of Girolamo Garavini (Captain Rinoceronte)	
1630	Diana	Mme Aspontini	
1635	Lidia	The second wife of Andreini	
About 1640	Aurelia	Orsola and Brigida Bianchi	
1652 *Fedeli troupe*		Eularia Coris	
About 1660	Ortensia	Francesca Allori	
	Florinda	Orsola Corteze	
About 1670	Flaminia	Agata Calderoni	
About 1700	Flaminia, Silvia	V. Baletti, granddaughter of Agata Calderoni	
About 1720	Servant-Inamorata	S. Baletti, Rosalia Astrodi, mentioned by Casanova in his *Mémoires*	
About 1760	Prima donna	Teodora Ricci, in Gozzi plays	

The Soubrette (Servetta or Fantesca)

The servants of the sixteenth century went by such engaging names as Francesquina, Licetta, Tiffia, Gitta, Betta, Gneva, and Nina.[1] We meet the two frolicsome maids, Francesquina and Licetta, in the *Recueil Fossard* (about 1577). Licetta seems to be a country girl and very indulgent toward the amorous Harlequin, whom she feeds with porridge with a spoon. She is far from timid about showing her breasts. Francesquina yields to Harlequin's passionate gestures without restraint. She regains the path of virtue, however, by marrying her seducer. Pantaloon joins the hands of the happy couple. Presently, in another engraving, we find Francesquina in Pantaloon's arms while Harlequin creeps up behind them, dagger in hand.

Besides these buxom wenches there were the " fresh and frisky " servant-*confidentes*, who were sometimes crafty and nearly always of doubtful morals. In Italy this type was called the *servetta birichina*, or artful servant-maid. There were also Olivetta, Fiametta, Nespola, Spinetta, and Columbine, the maid who waited upon Isabella. In the seventeenth century appeared Diamantina and a galaxy of Columbines, of whom the most celebrated was Catherine Biancolelli, the daughter of Eularia and the Harlequin Dominique. She married the actor Le Noir Sieur de la Torilière, of whom du Tralage wrote so admiringly :

> He loved gaiety and good cheer, and, to please his rich friends, he induced his sister to accord them her favours. His wife, Columbine, the principal actress of the Italian players and daughter of the late Harlequin, is an admirable manager, but la Torilière spends more in one day than his wife can save in a month.

The grandmother of Catherine Biancolelli had been a Columbine, as was her daughter after her. The Columbine they interpreted, in fact, became the standard type : she was rather French in character and was noted for her coquetry. She was the constant friend and companion of Harlequin, eternally in love either with the rascally valets or with Lelio, and by her keen and active wit was able to hold her own in every situation and emerge with ease and dignity from the most involved intrigues.

EPISODE OF COLUMBINE'S BETRAYAL

(*From the plays of Gherardi*)

ISABELLE, HARLEQUIN, *and* COLUMBINE, *later* PASQUARIEL *and the* DOCTOR

(HARLEQUIN *has deserted* COLUMBINE *in Venice and then proceeded to Paris, where he is courting* ISABELLE, *having first assumed the name of the Marquis de Sbrufadelli.*)

HARLEQUIN (*to* ISABELLE)

If you must know, I've been commissioned first colonel of the Limoges Regiment.

ISABELLE

Does not the present state of peace limit your activities as colonel, dear Marquis ?

[1] In the troupes of the Intronati and Gelosi, about 1630.

HARLEQUIN

Upon my word, I thrive in times of peace! I am the man who keeps all the masons on the jump building the walls of the great park at Versailles.

HARLEQUIN AND COLUMBINE
Eighteenth century
Engraving by G. J. Xavery (Holland)

(COLUMBINE *comes to Paris disguised as a maid, and wishes to enter the service of Isabelle.* HARLEQUIN *does not recognize her and discourages her project.*)

HARLEQUIN

But you are mad, my dear, utterly mad. Come live with me, and be adored.

COLUMBINE

So that is the kind of suitor you are! A girl would be flighty indeed to give ear to a man who is about to be married.

HARLEQUIN

Ah, but that is the proper time, my pet. As soon as I have my part of the dowry I'll get you a room newly furnished from top to bottom; I'll hire a lackey for you, and I'll give you the finest clothes you've ever dreamed of. Come, come, good fortune is not to be laughed at. I assure you I am the most generous and lavish marquis in France, and I say so without conceit or exaggeration.

COLUMBINE

I'd be mad to trust you. After what happened to a girl named Columbine I would not take a man, not if they were as plentiful as raindrops.

(*In the end* COLUMBINE *tells* HARLEQUIN *who she is, and cries:*)

Perfido, traditore, m' avrai negli occhi, se non m' hai nel core! [1]

(*She leaves*)

HARLEQUIN

Hoimé! Aiuto! Spiriti! Demoni! Larve! [2]

(*Some time later* HARLEQUIN *sets out to buy a Moorish slave-girl for* ISABELLE. PASQUARIEL *has told him that he will find one at an inn where some Turks are staying.* HARLEQUIN *goes to the inn and is confronted by a Gascon servant, who in her native patois tells him the sad story of poor* COLUMBINE. HARLEQUIN *jeers at her dialect. The Gascon woman, who is none other than* COLUMBINE, *reveals her identity and cries once more:*)

Perfido, traditore, m' avrai negli occhi, se non m' hai nel core!

HARLEQUIN (*running away*)

Help! Help!

(PASQUARIEL, *disguised as a Turk, and two Moors and a Moorish slave-girl who accompany him dance in a ring around* HARLEQUIN *and play the guitar. They sit down in a circle with* HARLEQUIN *in the middle and next to the slave. He haggles over the price of the girl with the slave-trader, and then asks the slave how old she is.*)

THE MOORISH SLAVE (*pulling* HARLEQUIN'S *beard*)

Sturta, burgia, curgia; mi abir quindici ansia, quindici auna.

HARLEQUIN (*rising*)

That's a tale for the devil. If she were forty I wouldn't have a hair left in my beard.

(CINTHIO *arrives and picks a quarrel with* HARLEQUIN, *who is about to get the worst of it when the Moorish slave runs over and seizes* HARLEQUIN'S *sword; she then rushes at* CINTHIO, *who departs, saying:*)

There is no honour in fighting women.

HARLEQUIN (*overjoyed at what the slave has done, goes up to* PASQUARIEL)

Sir, you have a veritable jewel there. Why, she's saved my life! There's nothing on earth I wouldn't give for her. See here, I'll give you forty sols.

[1] "False, fickle wretch! I'll haunt your sight, if not your heart."

[2] "Alas! Help! Spirits! Demons! Ghosts!"

(*The slave takes off her veil, revealing* COLUMBINE, *who clutches* HARLEQUIN *by the arm and points the tip of her sword at his belly. She says :*)

HARLEQUIN AND COLUMBINE
Eighteenth century
Engraving by G. J. Xavery

Perfido, traditore, m' avrai negli occhi, se non m' hai nel core!

(*She departs with* PASQUARIEL. *The two Moors return and play the flute as they pass by* HARLEQUIN.)

(*When* HARLEQUIN *goes to look at himself in a mirror he sees reflected in it the face of* COLUMBINE, *who is standing behind him. She disappears before he has time to turn round.* PASQUARIEL, *disguised as a bandy-legged artist, comes to finish a portrait of* HARLEQUIN. *During the sitting he knocks* HARLEQUIN *down twice; and is driven out of the room.* HARLEQUIN *then steps over to the portrait and discovers* COLUMBINE'S *head there instead of his own.*)

MADEMOISELLE HARLEQUINE

About 1695

HARLEQUIN

Ah ! poveretto mi ! Columbine's head even in my portrait ! (*He looks again at the portrait and sees it in its original state.*) What ? Am I going blind ? I thought I saw Columbine on that canvas. (*He inspects the portrait again, and* COLUMBINE'S *face reappears in it.*)

COLUMBINE (*in the portrait*)

Perfido, traditore, m' avrai negli occhi, se non m' hai nel core ! (*She goes.*)

HARLEQUIN (*fleeing*)

Help ! Help ! Have mercy ! The fiends are after me !

(ISABELLE *has just shown the* DOCTOR *the written promise of marriage that* HARLEQUIN *once gave to* COLUMBINE. *The* DOCTOR *thereupon vows to take vengeance and send* HARLEQUIN *to the gallows.* PASQUARIEL *hastens to tell the news to* HARLEQUIN, *and adds that he knows a doctor who can save him. The new* DOCTOR *appears and consults with* HARLEQUIN *about* COLUMBINE *and* ISABELLE.)

THE DOCTOR

Have you given Columbine your word of honour? Have you both exchanged a solemn troth?

COLUMBINE IN DISGUISE
Seventeenth century

HARLEQUIN

In all truth we have, sir, at least a thousand times, but there is no love affair that can withstand the lack of money, and if it were not for the thirty thousand crowns that have come between us I swear by all the gods——

THE DOCTOR (*taking off his mask and revealing* COLUMBINE)

Perfido, traditore, m' avrai negli occhi, se non m' hai nel core! (*She departs.*)
(HARLEQUIN *in terror attempts to flee, runs into* PASQUARIEL, *and they both fall down.*)

THE COSTUME OF THE SOUBRETTE

According to the *Recueil Fossard*, the Soubrette in the sixteenth century wore a large, wide apron, and her personable figure refused all persuasions of a corset. Her costume was that of a woman of the people. In other documents it is difficult to distinguish the costume of the maid from that of the mistress, particularly during the seventeenth century, when the *servetta* wore a similar bow in her hair and left off her apron. In her cunning she was often prompted to make use of every possible sort of costume and disguise, and she would appear as a cavalier, as a doctor, as a barrister, and even as Harlequin. The maid, Columbine, was almost always the wife or mistress of Harlequin, and eventually she turned into Harlequine. Her costume in this *rôle* dates from the close of the seventeenth century, or, to be more exact, from 1695, at the time when the *Retour de la Foire de Bezons* was first produced.

SOME OF THE MOST CELEBRATED SOUBRETTES

About 1570 *The Gelosi*	Franceschina Lesbino	The actor BATTISTA DA TREVISO The actress SILVIA RONCAGLI, of Bergamo
1593–1639	Ricciolina	ANTONAZZONI
About 1673 *Troupe of the Duke of Modena*	Olivetta	V. TEODORA ARCHIARI
About 1633 *Troupe of Dominique*	Diamantina	BEATRICE ADAMI
About 1683	Colombina	CATHERINE BIANCOLELLI, daughter of the Harlequin Dominique
About 1697	Spinetta	(?) Sister-in-law of Constantini-Mezzetino
About 1716	Violetta	MARGHERITA RUSCA
About 1744 *Plays of Goldoni*	Corallina	ANNA VERONESE, daughter of the Pantaloon Veronese
1745–69 *Plays of Gozzi*	Smeraldina	

Eighteenth century

La Ruffiana, La Guaiassa, The Go-between,[1] *The Gossip*

Fiorinetta has the misfortune to love the bankrupt Flavio, and her mother, Celega, talks to her in this wise:

You little fool! You don't know half the trouble that is in store for you. Just remember that if you go on in this stubborn way, loving a man who hasn't a sou to give you, you will certainly get nothing from any other man. Don't you realize that our entire welfare depends on creating some sort of rivalry among your men? I've told you what to do a thousand

A Ruffiana of the Renaissance

times, if I've told you once. The moment one of them gives you a necklace or ring or any kind of present don't lose any time showing it to the rest, for there's not one of them likes to appear poorer than the others or be outdone by them. You must learn how to lead each one on and make him believe that he is the one you love best. . . .

If you go on doing just as you please you'll be a poor nobody to the end of your days; but if you take my advice you'll soon be a rich and fine lady. Now, look at Nina. Not long ago she was making the rounds of the taverns and dives in her rags and bare feet. And now look at her, I say; she has more silk dresses and pearl necklaces than she knows what to do with, not to speak of a whole troop of servants to run about and wait on her.[2]

The Guaiassa is a Neapolitan type. She is an old woman of the people, trifling, garrulous, extremely limited, but good at heart. Her quips reek of garlic.

[1] All these titles have analogous meanings of go-between, procuress, scandal-monger, etc.—Translator.

M. C. Mic asserts that the Go-between is a character which belongs more to the regular or legitimate stage than to the *commedia dell' arte*. It is interesting to note, however, that she appears in the fresco by Trausnitz (see p. 182), in the engraving reproduced below, and in various documents of the sixteenth and seventeenth centuries.

[2] Angelo Beolco, *La Vaccaria* (sixteenth century).

XX

The Lovers

THE lovers and wooers of the *commedia dell' arte* were always dapper and engaging and just a trifle ridiculous. Whether their names are Flavio, Ottavio, Orazio, Silvio, Leandro, or Cinthio del Sole; Federigo, Lelio, Mario, or Fulvio—all reveal a fatal trace of fatuity. Though their protestations would melt a heart of stone, there always seems to be a comic side to everything they say. One wonders if the explanation does not lie in the fact that love often robs the lover of all sense of his own absurdity, even though he may be the most rational of living men under ordinary circumstances. Perhaps in this case the reason is that in the days of the Renaissance the god of love was no longer as formidable as he used to be, but had deteriorated into a mere little practical joker. Or, again, it may have been simply that in a theatre devoted to comedy it was impossible to take anything seriously save farce.

THE ACTOR ZANOTTI AS FABIO
Callot

Whatever the names of the Lovers in the *commedia dell' arte*, they had no other trait as 'characters' than that of being in love. Their function was to depict a state of mind rather than to paint a personality. The Lover had to play with dash and be able to simulate the most exaggerated passion. He had to be young, well set up, courteous, gallant even to the point of affectation—in short, a blade and dandy. He used perfume and was "prolific of sonnets." He was the *gigolo*, the '*matinée* idol' of his day. He was at times a sort of servant-cavalier, discreetly 'kept' by some female admirer, and sometimes a man of precious cultivation for the entertainment of well-born women.

In the *Recueil Fossard* Il Segnor Orazio is depicted striding, sword in hand, up to Harlequin, who falls to his knees in fear. Orazio then cries:

"Je te tiens, je te tiens, ô traître, ô inhumain !
Tu m'as pris mon habit, pour aller par ruse
Violer une dame, où mon amour s'est mise.
Sus, sus, c'est à ce coup tu mourras de ma main." [1]

[1] "I have thee, I have thee, O traitor, O cruel wretch ! Thou didst take my coat in order, by this ruse, to violate a lady in whom my love is placed. This time, then, thou shalt die by my hand."

Another engraving in the same collection shows how Segnor Leandro, in spite of his gaudy orange hose, has few compunctions about an occasional *amour* with a kitchen wench. His declaration is in the grand manner, although the object of his passion is only a prosaic servant-girl :

> " Francisquine, mon cœur, j'ai trop temporisé
> A vouloir découvrir l'amour que je vous porte,
> Qui me fera mourir d'une étrange façon
> Si je ne suis ce jour de vous favorisé." [1]

However, this sort of ridicule is indicated but slightly in most Lover *rôles*, and at times is hardly perceptible.

THE LOVER AND THE SOUBRETTE (ABOUT 1577)
Detail from an engraving in the " Recueil Fossard"

During the second half of the seventeenth century a new style of lover was developed in Orazio, who throws money right and left, flies from duel to duel and from one woman

[1] " Francisquina, my heart, I have delayed too long in disclosing the love I bear you. I shall die in a strange fashion if you do not this day accord me your favours."

to another. He courts the Servetta as well as Isabelle. This hardy and passionate young man has for his ordinary diet a lavish combination of gold, blood, tears, declarations, and dangers. Cinthio del Sole[1] follows in Orazio's footsteps, although he is rather more cold and calculating. Leandro il Bello is a caricature of Ottavio, and resembles the Captain to a remarkable degree.

Poets, men of birth and position, and even the director of the troupe often played the *rôles* of Lover in the *commedia dell' arte*. The importance assigned to this part arises from the fact that it could be played fittingly only by an actor of intelligence, cultivation, and imagination. Flaminio Scala, for example, not only was the director of the Gelosi, but played the principal *rôles* of Lover as Flavio. He was also the author of the collection of comedy scenarios called *Il Teatro delle Favole Rappresentative*, which has already been mentioned in an earlier chapter. G. B. Andreini, or Lelio, son of the famous Isabelle and Andreini, and director of the Fedeli, was also an author. Besides his celebrated *Teatro Celeste*, he wrote a great many obscene comedies to suit the taste of the times. He was a man of wit and cultivation and exceedingly well read. In the eighteenth century the type was represented by Luigi Riccoboni, another Lelio. He too was the director of the troupe in which he played many of the Lover *rôles*. He was the author of the well-known *Histoire du théâtre italien*, as well as of numerous comedies. In spite of the fact that he had a large following in the Italian comedy, he left it for the legitimate stage.

Since the chief asset of the Lovers was their comeliness, they played without a mask, like the Inamoratas. They had no particular costume, but dressed in the latest fashion of the period to which they belonged.

THE PRINCIPAL LOVERS

About 1556	Leandro	(?)
About 1576 (*Gelosi*)	Flavio	Flaminio Scala
	Cinthio	Cinthio Fidenzi
	Fulvio	Domenico Bruni
About 1605 (*Fedeli*)	Lelio	G. B. Andreini
About 1645	Orazio	Marco Romagnesi
About 1653	Virginio	Turi, son of Pantaloon
About 1660	Ottavio	Andrea Zanotti, of Bologna
About 1668	Ottavio	G. B. Constantini, of Verona
About 1680	Aurelio	Bartolomeo Ranieri, of Piedmont
About 1694	Cinthio del Sole	Mario Antonio Romagnesi
About 1716	Lelio	Luigi Riccoboni
	Mario	Joseph Baletti
About 1725	Lelio	G. A. Romagnesi
About 1726	Lelio	Francesco Riccoboni, of Mantua
About 1759	Lelio	Zanucci

[1] *C.* 1667.

XXI

The Caratterista[1]

STENTARELLO, MENEGHINO, GIANDUJA, ZACOMETO

STENTARELLO, the simpleton, would come on stage and go off without the slightest regard for plot or action, making jokes, in the Tuscan dialect, on prominent men or events of the day, taking off one of the actors, and playing the clown in general. This part of lone cavalier was performed by Meneghino in Milan, by Gianduja in Piedmont, and by Zacometo in Venice, each speaking his own respective dialect. The Italians called these *rôles caratterista*, because they belonged to a particular region, and had nothing to do with the play itself.

STENTARELLO
About 1751

[1] *I.e.*, 'character' *rôles*.

The Caratteristas do not seem to have come into vogue before the eighteenth century. They were popular types and very variable.

Stentarello was given to frequent changes of costume, preferring always the loudest and most delirious colours he could find. As a rule, one of his front teeth was missing. He was lazy, absent-minded, and fidgety, a glutton and a blackguard; but, in spite of his many defects, he was usually content with little or nothing in the way of money and keep.

Meneghino, Zacometo, and Gianduja are types quite similar to Stentarello. They possess all the flavour of their respective localities, and resemble shoots from the same vine planted in different parts of the country.

XXII

A Few Anonymous, Forgotten, or Little-known Characters

Coviello

NICCOLO BARBIERI states that "the Coviellos [provoke hilarity] by their grimaces and silly speech." And Salvator Rosa tells us that

> Coviello is keen and subtle. He is sly, adroit, supple, and conceited. He has the accent of his birthplace, and wears the native costume, which consists of a jacket and breeches of black velvet, edged with silver braid. He wears a mask which has flaming cheeks and a black nose and forehead.

But neither Callot's Coviello nor the one whose picture appears in Bertelli's *Carnavale Italiano Mascherato*[1] answers this description in the least.

Callot

Cavicchio, Cicciabuccia, etc.

Cavicchio[2] and Cicciabuccia were two peasant servants. Fichetto was a clumsy valet, inclined to be restless, timid, and pedantic. Stephanel Bottarga—a character unknown, I believe, except for Ganassa's *lamento* which was addressed to him—is repre-

[1] See p. 44 of the present volume. The author is indebted to M. Bragaglia for facilities in regard to this reproduction.

[2] Peg.

sented in the *Recueil Fossard* as a type akin to Pantaloon. There are almost a hundred other characters of the same kind, but it would be quite superfluous to name them here, since the majority were short-lived and soon forgotten. Every notable family has

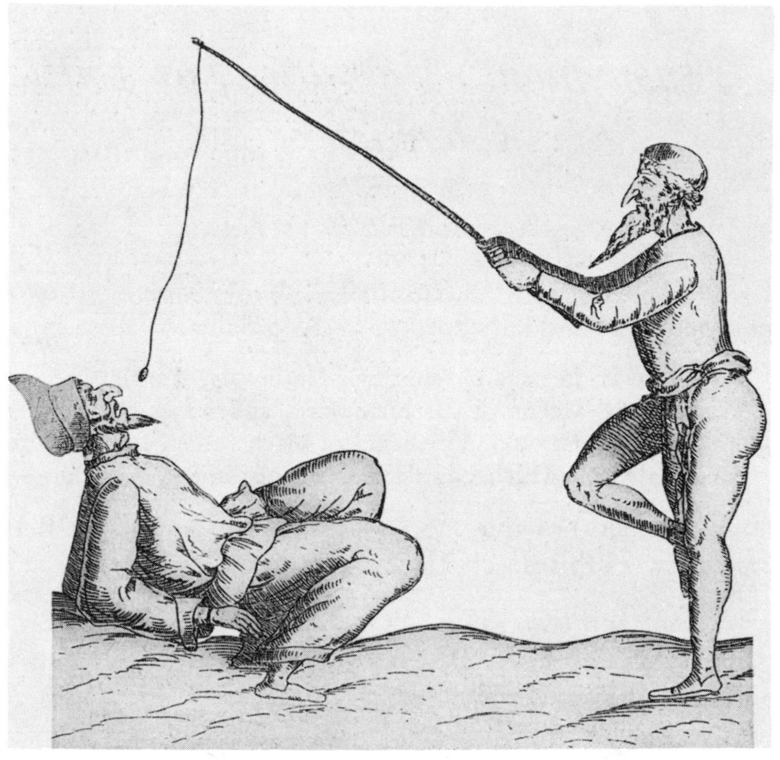

Unknown Actors
Engraving published in Rome by Lorenzo Vaccaro, c. 1560–80. From the " Recueil Fossard "

its poor relations, and the *commedia dell' arte* is no exception to the general rule. But who can say that one of them might not unexpectedly reappear some day, having returned from a well-rewarded quest to the Indies, rich now and honoured and sought after by all men.

XXIII

Overtones

To

CHARLES DULLIN

in memory of our comrade Marcel Levinçon

HE *commedia dell' arte* has, from its inception, always exercised a mysterious power over the minds of men of spirit and imagination. It has borne a glamour, an eerie fascination, compelling yet intangible, much the same as those distant isles of melodious and seductive names which men dream of but hardly ever reach. For they are places invisible upon the blue expanse of the world's surface; they lie for ever veiled, just beyond the horizon, haunting, alluring, and unvisited.

The Italian comedy, then, is, in its way, a sort of shadowy country, a Thélème [1] of the fancy filled with many strange and delightful people: characters and personalities whose conversation is as subtle as their antics are unexpected. They are, of course, our closest friends, nor do they ever grow tiresome, because their faults are at once too numerous and amusing. They live a charmed life, for they are secure in their ultimate good fortune. Their every enterprise and adventure is destined to a happy end. Even the traditional jealous lover turns out to be a gay and sympathetic character, for he is willing to dissipate his rage in clowning and appear at the last covered with flour and confusion. He really bears no malice, and his deepest-dyed malevolent designs never lead to anything more than a giddy song and dance in which he trips it with the best of them.

Neither Hamlet nor Othello is to be found in that happy land, nor is there any Phædra or Chimène, or others of their nature, with minds darkened and overburdened by tragic and grotesque passions. True, Harlequin is often extravagantly coarse, but his very manner of uttering a greeting seems somehow to redeem his worst offences against delicacy. It must be confessed also that Brighella is rather an ugly ruffian at times; yet he disarms us when he plays the theorbo, the flute, and the psaltery. And then, the blood he spills by his knife-play is, after all, only a little wine or quite innocent red ink.

The *commedia dell' arte* is a kind of enchanted Cytherea where lovers never lose their happiness, and are never troubled by domesticated love or by the communion of souls or deficits in the household budget. All the inhabitants of that land lead a care-free, sprightly, and fantastic life to the accompaniment of quaint, seductive music. And they

[1] The earthly paradise described by Rabelais in *Gargantua*.—TRANSLATOR.

are swayed now by impulses as swift and precipitate as rockets, now by a mood of fleeting melancholy, and now by a wild spirit of farce as irresistible as a typhoon.

The *commedia dell' arte* is, in short, a world by itself where each can find his level and field of activity. Poets, musicians, writers, and painters of the most diverse talents and temperaments are brought together by their common devotion to it. They have been drawn to it as were the great princes of Italy and France, over whom it exercised such

Costumes for Sganarelle and his Wife, by Yves Alix
Théâtre du Marais, Brussels

fascination that they would summon back their favourite comedians absent in other lands, and themselves cross the mountains to meet once more these actors whose art they found so perfect and delectable.

Other men of distinction have done them honour in various ways. The Duke of Parma presented his coach and equipage to Scaramouche as a mark of his esteem. Verlaine paid homage to the Italian comedy in his *Fêtes Galantes*, a magnificent gift indeed, and one that carried with it immortality, for if one but listens to these exquisite and fragile poems—as it were to a sea-shell—one may easily catch the distant sound of voices and gaiety and the strumming of guitars.

It may be that some day the lovely Isabella will leave the obscure grove where all the bright, masked figures are at rest, and for the thousandth time return to earth to marry Lelio. It is amusing to imagine the widespread interest she would awaken. Her

PERFORMERS AT THE FAIR
Mariano Andreu

wedding would loom as an event of signal splendour and importance, and a vast crowd would flock to the ceremony. The church would be filled with the oddest assortment

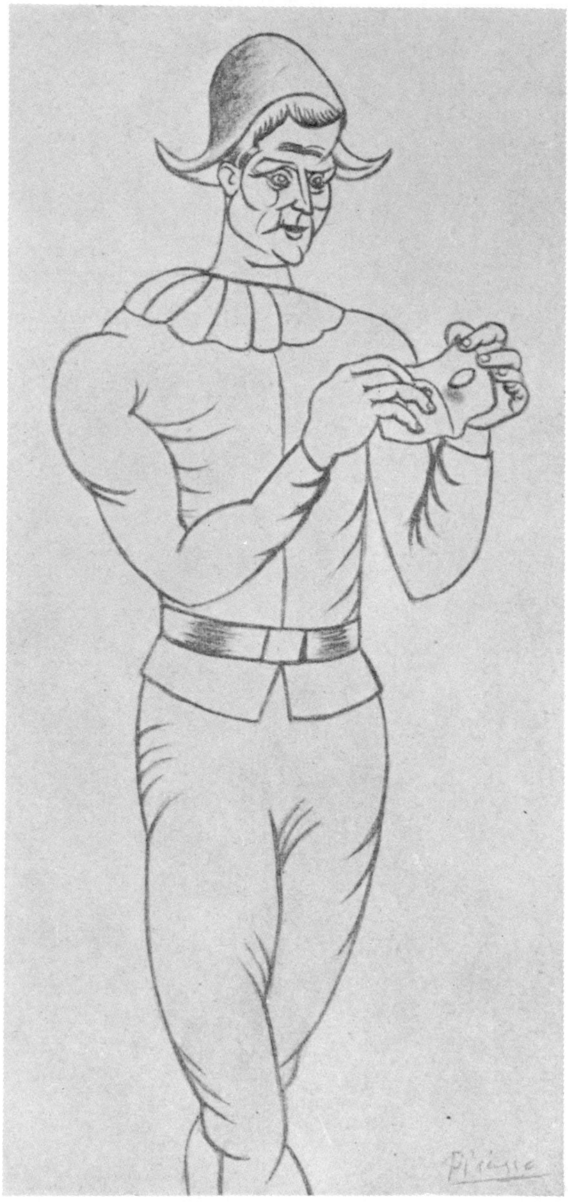

DRAWING BY PICASSO
Photo Paul Rosenberg

of famous personages, recruited from the dead and the living, that ever gathered together under one roof. Among the notable guests would be the jovial Rabelais, and with him Montaigne; then would come Max Jacob and Apollinaire, as well as Gillot, Molière, and Marivaux. Close by Callot would be Aloysius Bertrand, and de Geijn might be seen gossiping with Picasso. And after these would follow Gordon Craig, Baudelaire, Saint-Simon, and George Sand; Watteau, de Brosses, Lancret, Cézanne, Pater, Tasso, Shakespeare, Giovanni Battista Tiepolo, Gérard d'Houville, Brunelleschi, Georges

HARLEQUIN
Cézanne. Photo Librairie de France

Barbier, Goldoni, and Gozzi, the last two having finally decided to make peace for a while. Verlaine would be in the company of Charles Guérin, his ever-faithful friend. Regnard would make a witticism for the special entertainment of the wedding-procession. Roland Manuel would preside at the organ and play his *Isabelle et Pantalon* from the repertory of the Trianon-Lyrique theatre. One may picture the Captain acting as beadle, and the Fratellini brothers as altar boys, whirling their censers in the most amazing fashion. Then would come the guild of scholars and painters and decorators, while outside the inimitable Charlie Chaplin would delay his entrance by skating about upon the church *parvis* as if it were coated with imaginary soap. The church would be packed to overflowing with all those who had ever loved and enjoyed the inimitable foolery of the Italian comic actors. The throng would contain every condition of folk of every race and age, the great mixing with the humble, princes with baker-boys, staid burghers with country louts, proud ladies with proud courtesans.

CARTOON FOR A TAPESTRY
Alfred Lombard

I have a friend of rare and original tastes who once conceived the notion of making a collection of furniture in the Italian comedy style. It turned out, however, that he was not able to proceed very far with his idea; he told me that the Italian comedy really had no existence outside the imagination. Nor is his statement hard to believe when one thinks of all that the *commedia dell' arte* produced, either directly or indirectly. But it might be more just to say that all this world of colour and fantasy which the actors of the Italian comedy bequeathed to us, all these gardens of the Hesperides planted in the richest soil of the imagination, make a generous and fertile heritage which will be for ever fruitful.

Jacques Copeau, Delacre, Dullin, and many other directors of theatrical companies who still put their faith in the nobility of the actor's profession, have had a profound and unwavering respect for, and interest in, the *commedia dell' arte*. It has made known to them the rich values inherent in the art of acting, and chiefly the value of improvisation.

For the improvisator is, in truth, the only complete actor. And to create a company of improvisators would be a hazardous undertaking foredoomed to many set-backs and disappointments.

One of the primary difficulties, of course, would be to find the right kind of actors for such a company. There are so few nowadays who have any genuine talent for improvisation. Furthermore, the actor required for this sort of venture would of necessity have to be endowed with numerous other gifts. He would, in fact, have to be a man of cultivation and imagination, supple of mind and body ; and he would have to know how to dance, sing, and impersonate supremely well.

Painting in the Spirit of the Italian Comedy
Claude Lévy

Nevertheless, the idea is worth trying. At least, that is the conviction of Charles Dullin,[1] who has had the courage to establish a special course of his own in the art of improvisation. And it is my sincere hope that his stubborn will to overcome all obstacles, together with his talent and the mastery of his art, will enable him to realize his ambition to the fullest extent.

Dullin already has one triumph to his credit in the training of the late Marcel Levinçon, a comedian whose aptitude for improvisation was little short of extraordinary.

[1] Actor-director of the Atelier, one of the more progressive experimental theatres in Paris.—Translator.

Levinçon, a cabinet-maker in civil life, was a small, wizened fellow with a profile like the plaster-cast head of Dante so often seen in art schools. He and his two friends,

Painting by Georges Barbier
Meynial, publisher

"Tuture" and Bonnat, had always made themselves conspicuous by their incredible adventures, their original pranks, and their ability to keep themselves supplied with all the necessities of life—wine in particular. Levinçon was endowed with unusual manual dexterity, as well as exceptional wit, and during the War he had plenty of opportunity to employ both to good advantage. For instance, whenever the gunsmith of the regiment had any repairing to do and found a piece of mechanism beyond his skill Levinçon would take it in hand and have it in working order in the twinkling of an eye. He always carried about with him a little bundle of tools, which contained numerous files, screw-drivers, and keys, and he had also a two-litre can, which he could enlarge to any size simply by firing his gun point-blank into the mouth of it.

Levinçon was a master of cold and penetrating irony; his movements and expressions were rather deliberate and measured, but were none the less irresistibly droll, and he spoke vividly and picturesquely without ever becoming vulgar. Generally he displayed good humour and was ready for any kind of nonsense; no one could play the 'silly ass' better than he whenever he was in the mood for it. To this day I am convulsed with laughter whenever I think of his absurd remarks and clowning every time we came out of the trenches.

He was a natural acrobat, and seemingly had no joint or bone in his body. He could walk with the whole upper half of his body bent back, as though his spine were broken, forming a right angle with his legs, and he also had a trick whereby he could increase his height by several inches. He was the constant despair of disciplinarians and representatives of law and order. The Burattino in the illustration is almost the very image of him.

BURATTINO
See p. 120.

It was while they were at the Front that Dullin undertook to make a pantomimist and improvisator of Levinçon. Dullin persuaded his friend to play in 'skits' to amuse the soldiers during the rest periods, and it goes without saying that their entertainments never failed to be tremendously successful. At many of their performances a soldier would sing from the wings of the little makeshift stage some popular air such as *Nina Cruelle*, or *On l'appelait la Panthère*, or *C'est la Femme aux Bijoux*, while Levinçon would stand in front of the audience and interpret the words of the song entirely by means of his facial expression. It was the most impressive bit of acting I have ever seen. He could tell the complete story without speaking, in the same manner as the great Scaramouche. Dullin also persuaded him and two of his friends to enact improvised comedies, and their performances were witty and subtle, and truly amazing. If Dullin ever succeeds in organizing a real company of finished improvisators I shall be willing to mount the heights of Montmartre on my knees, if necessary, just to be allowed the privilege of seeing them perform.

Once after an attack Levinçon raised his canteen, saying, "They didn't get me that time." The next instant he crumpled up with a bullet through his brain.

Were it ever possible to create a troupe of such engaging souls as Levinçon, we might at last envisage a new form of theatre, the product of the *commedia dell' arte*, yet by no means a copy of it. The original group of characters would be replaced by modern types, speaking their everyday language and exhibiting all the idiosyncrasies, vices, customs, and characteristics of their various callings and stations in society. Nor would it be long before appropriate masks would be devised for them. For the stuff of human

Sketch by Charles Guérin for the "Fêtes Galantes"
Helleu and Sergent, publishers

nature is as provocative nowadays as it ever was. And the shopwalker, the business man, the manufacturer all hark back to Pantaloon, the epitome of the Venetian merchant. The Doctor is eternally ubiquitous and powerful, despite the fact that radium is now more fashionable than the humble syringe. The sublime Charlie Chaplin has originated a character far more popular and universal than was Harlequin. And there are the puppets in the "Noce à Nini Patte en l'Air"[1] at country fairs the world over. But we have yet to see a new and complete group of 'masks' capable of representing properly in standardized forms the great range of human types to-day. Who can say when they will appear?

[1] *I.e.*, The Wedding of Nini Foot-in-the-Air. The French title has been retained here in order to avoid any confusion which might possibly arise from the fact that in England the game is known as Aunt Sally and in America as Hit the Nigger Baby. It is so named in France on account of the fact that the puppets represent a wedding-party with the bride and groom and guests all done in stereotyped caricatures. It is said, however, that this particular set of puppets is not now seen so often as it was before the War. But the game is still as popular as ever, and goes by the more general name of *Jeu de Massacre*, in which the characters are of any type which happens to please the showman's fancy.—Translator.

Appendices

A

Callot, Giacomo or Jacques. Engraver born at Nancy in 1592. He lived a short, adventurous life, . . . the life of an artist, accompanied, his biographer tells us, *de misère et de joie.* When scarcely twelve, being opposed by his parents in his desire to become a painter, he ran away from his home, and, having no resources, joined a company of gipsies or players bound for Italy. He reached Florence and there began to study, but, being recognised by some merchants, he was sent back to his father. This happened more than once until he at last obtained permission to remain in Italy. He returned later on to Nancy in the service of Henry, Duke of Lorraine, and this prince's favour, added to his own talents and charm of character, quickly won him success.

After the capture of Nancy he was urged to engrave a souvenir of this conquest, but replied proudly that " he would sooner cut off his thumb than do anything contrary to the honour of his prince and country." Louis XIII, admiring the artist's fine spirit, accepted this refusal and even offered him a pension of five thousand francs to enter his own service, but Callot, preferring liberty to all else, refused.

His works are far too numerous to name, but those which have a peculiar interest for the student of the theatre are his *Balli di Sfessania* (many of the figures from which appear in this and the preceding number of *The Mask*) and illustrations of pageants and scenes from plays. He died at Nancy on March 27, 1635, at the age of forty-two.—*The Mask*, vol. iii, p. 161.

B

It must be said that the members of the Confrérie de la Passion, or Brotherhood of the Passion, a society which was famous in the fifteenth century, were truly the fathers of the French theatre. The details regarding this curious organization are still very vague and confused, and little more is known about them to-day than was known fifty years ago, when the worthy and conscientious Beauchamps wrote his book, *Recherches sur le théâtre de France*, in which he says of the Brotherhood :

> A number of burghers of Paris had chosen the borough of St-Maur as a place to give representations of the Passion of Our Lord. The prevost of Paris, on learning of this enterprise, issued an edict forbidding all inhabitants of Paris, St-Maur, or any town within his jurisdiction, to present any kind of plays with characters drawn from the lives of the saints, or otherwise, without leave of the King, on pain of incurring his displeasure and wrath. Thereupon they made an appeal to the Court ; and to make their society more acceptable, they formed a brotherhood which they named The Passion of Our Lord. The King desired to see their spectacles, and accordingly they performed several pieces, which pleased him, and they were granted certain letters patent on the fourth of December, 1402, for their establishment in Paris.

It is clear from this account that even as early as the year 1398, that is to say, before the end of the fourteenth century, they who were to be known as the Confrères de la Passion (Brothers of the Passion) had made their first essays in the presentation of scenic spectacles, but four years were to pass before they succeeded in forming a regular organization. We shall see presently how they came to occupy the Hôpital de la Trinité, where they constructed a theatre which was undoubtedly the first of the kind ever to be seen in France. To quote further from Beauchamps :

> Once provided with these letters, the Brotherhood sought a suitable place to give their performances. Now it had been but two hundred years since two German brothers, Guillaume Escuacol and Jean de la Bassée, nobles by birth, had purchased two acres of land outside the gates of Paris towards St-Denis, and there they had erected a large building for the housing of pilgrims and poor travellers who chanced to arrive too late to enter the city, whose gates were closed at nightfall in those times. In this building there was a great hall, twenty-one and a half fathoms long by six fathoms wide, raised three or four feet from the ground, and supported by arches in order to make it more healthy and commodious for the poor who were received there.
>
> After the death of the founders, the good work was abandoned. The Brotherhood found the great hall vacant and fallen in ruin ; they rented it and converted it into a theatre where they presented their plays and spectacles, which they called neither tragedies nor comedies but simply moralities.
>
> This first theatre continued for nearly a hundred and fifty years on the same footing. François Ier confirmed its privileges by letters patent in the month of January 1518. The public grew weary of these solemn spectacles. The players therefore enlivened their performances with farces taken from profane subjects, which were vulgarly called *poix pilés* (lit. ground pitch), doubtless an allusion to some ridiculous scene to which the name applied. This mixture of moralities and buffoonery was in turn found displeasing, for what had seemed edifying under Charles VI was considered scandalous under François Ier. Therefore, by virtue of a decree of Parliament of the 30th of July, 1547, the Maison de la Trinité became an hospice again in accordance with the original spirit of its foundation.

The Brotherhood of the Passion gave mystery and miracle plays such as the *Mystère de la Passion* (their first production), the *Mystère de Sainte Geneviève* . . . etc. But . . . it is certain that under their pious guise nothing could have been less moral than these performances.

> Following the trend of the theatre of those times [says M. Paul Lacroix], a great number of scenes in the Mystery of the Passion and analogous mysteries were dragged in the mud of obscenity, and the dialogue of the secondary characters contained a great quantity of licentious allusions and bawdy words borrowed from the popular speech of the day.

However that may be, the success of the Brotherhood of the Passion prepared the way for the growth of two other theatrical societies, namely, the *Clercs de la Basoche* and the *Enfants Sans Souci*, who had much to do with stimulating the interest of the Parisian public in scenic productions. After the Théâtre de la Trinité had been closed by a decree of Parliament the Brotherhood set about procuring another theatre. Beauchamps tells us again that :

> Deprived of their establishment, the Brotherhood, which had meanwhile acquired considerable wealth, found itself in a position to purchase the erstwhile hotel of the dukes of Bourgogne, which had fallen into complete ruin. They divided it into a reception room, a theatre, and out-buildings, which are still to be seen to this day (1735). They were permitted by a decree of Parliament of the 19th of November, 1548, to occupy the place on condition that they would present licit, profane, and decent subjects only ; but they were forbidden to present mysteries of the Passion or any other sacred mysteries whatsoever ; those were the terms of the decree. Furthermore, their privileges were re-confirmed ; and all others were forbidden to perform any plays whatsoever, either in the town, *faubourgs,* or suburbs of Paris except in their (the Brotherhood's) name and to their profit.
>
> This new establishment was confirmed by letters patent from Henri II in the month of March 1559, and likewise by Charles IX in the month of November 1569. The Brotherhood recognized finally that the exclusive privilege of playing upon the stage was not in keeping with their religious garb, and they therefore rented their hotel to a troupe of players which had recently been formed, reserving for themselves and friends two boxes, which were set apart from the others by railings and were called " the boxes of the masters."

From that time forward the Brotherhood of the Passion ceased to exist, and its place was taken by the Hôtel de Bourgogne, which was the first regular theatre Paris ever had.—*Le Dictionnaire du théâtre*, by Arthur Pougin (Paris, 1885), pp. 238–240.

C

THE Basoche du Palais was nothing more or less than an association of the clerks of Parliament, organized to regulate all differences arising among the clerks, and to safeguard their interests and administer all affairs relating to the corporation. It is difficult to know just how or when this corporation first came to form a dramatic society; indeed, it is practically impossible to ascertain with any degree of precision. It is known only that this society was almost as old as the Brotherhood of the Passion, and that it originated probably during the first years of the fifteenth century.

> These clerks [wrote Léris] had attracted much favourable attention for some time on account of their poetry. Stimulated by the success of the Mystery plays, they (the clerks) sought permission to perform their own works; but in this they were prevented because the privilege of giving performances belonged to the Brotherhood exclusively. They therefore bethought them of some other means of interpretation and hit upon a plan of composing pieces called 'moralities,' in which, by personifying the Vices and the Virtues, they proposed to render the former as odious as the latter were desirable. Then on one of their *fête* days they presented their pieces with as much splendour and ceremony as possible.
>
> The applause they received encouraged them to continue. . . . They seized every opportunity available to give their performances and thus celebrated every entry of a king or queen, victories, birthdays and marriages of princes and princesses, etc.

The Clerks of the Basoche gave performances everywhere. . . . They were audacious and insolent from the very beginning and indulged freely in satire, so much so, indeed, that at the end of one of their plays, Charles VIII, being exceedingly displeased, ordered five of them to be imprisoned. . . .

> In its theatrical representations [says M. V. Fournel] the Basoche preserved its special aspect of a judiciary corporation, and at first did not go beyond satirizing the people connected with the Palais. Clerks, bailiffs, lawyers, even the judges, one and all were the target of their mordant ridicule. They censured the inconsistencies and abuses of Dame Justice. . . . And these little clerks, upstarts, and scribblers were protected by the privileges of their society as a whole. They thus became folk to be reckoned with, acquiring, in their heyday, rights as extravagant as those of the slaves of ancient Rome, who, during the saturnalias, were able to take revenge with impunity in unlicensed speech upon the tyranny of their masters. The range of their attack gradually widened, and presently the farces and moralities of the Basochians included the entire human comedy—or at least as much of it as could be conveyed by the mocking, comic, but naïvely coarse spirit of these Thespians of the French theatre. One can truly say, however, that they contributed directly and actively to the development of the dramatic art in France.

But the time came when the audacity of the Basochians exceeded all bounds. They were not content with caricaturing the people of the Palais, nor did they limit themselves to mere criticism, farces, and moralities. They were pleased to chafe and ridicule publicly many persons of high degree by means of masks, costumes, and expressive symbols. Not even the highest dignitaries in the country escaped their satire. On several occasions they were forbidden to make use of anything in their farces which might reflect upon the reputation of citizens or offend against public morals. Then they received an order not to present any piece whatever without first submitting it to Parliament for examination and approval, which marks the origin of theatre censorship. And finally, after many successive permissions and prohibitions, they were forbidden in 1547 to perform again any play, spectacle, or representation whatsoever. From this time forward nothing further was heard of them, and it is evident that the dramatic career of the Basoche thus came to a definite and drastic termination.—*Le Dictionnaire du théâtre,* by Arthur Pougin (Paris, 1885), pp. 181–183.

D

THE *parade* is a comical and often coarse burlesque scene which the mountebanks and performers at our fairs give gratis outside their booths in order to draw the attention of the public and provide a foretaste of the show which is to take place within, and so persuade the onlookers to buy tickets and enter.

The *parade* is very old in France, where it grew out of the morality and mystery plays and *soties* which were given in the early days of our theatre, and later in the time of the Clerks of the Basoche, the Brotherhood of the Passion, and the Troupe of the Prince of Fools. It did not disappear when the rules of comedy were established because, its character being popular, it became the forte of clowns and acrobats, who employed it as a bait to entice the crowd of unreluctant spectators.

It is really a sort of elementary farce with neither rules nor restraint, and is ordinarily composed of *lazzi,* cock-and-bull stories, puns, and vulgar stage ' business ' to amuse the public. It harks back to the old *commedia dell' arte* in that those who perform the *parade* give free play to improvisation and embellish each in his own way the scenario which serves as the underlying theme. In the eighteenth century the performers at the Fairs of St-Laurent and St-Germain always interpreted a certain set of characters known as Le Vieux Cassandre, La Gentille Isabelle, Le Beau Léandre, Le Placide Pierrot, Harlequin, and a Candle-snuffer. A collection of the *parades* containing these characters was published under the title of *Théâtre des Boulevards* (Bauche, Paris, 1756, 3 vols., 12mo). The individual titles of these platform farces are as curious as they are amusing: *Léandre Fiacre*; *La Confiance des C—*; *La Chaste Isabelle*; *Le Doigt Mouillé*; *Caracataca et Caracataqué*; . . . *Le Marchand de M—*; *Ah! voilà qui est Beau. . . .*; *Isabelle qui est Grosse par Vertu*; etc., etc.

Later, during the period of the Revolution, the Boulevard du Temple became the popular centre and developed into a sort of permanent *kermis,* which supplanted the erstwhile celebrated fairs. The charlatans, acrobats, and other performers lost no time in setting up their booths and contributing to Parisian gaiety. The *parade* then underwent a decided change owing to the advent of two celebrated comedians who displayed an amazing talent for witty, comic, and vulgar nonsense. The pair were named Bobèche and Galimafré; one was the complement of the other, and their success was prodigious. It was not long before their *confrères* began to imitate them, and from Bobèche were evolved Janot, Jocrisse, and Paillasse, who were all similar types. The characters of the old pantomime, with the exception of Cassandre, gradually disappeared. Cassandre survived alone with Paillasse, whom he served as a sort of interlocutor and so facilitated his partner's *lazzi* and somewhat *risqué* foolery.

The *parade* at this period became far more a species of entertainment than it had been heretofore, on account of the very real cynical spirit it proffered as well as the clever coarse jokes which up to a certain point equalled the *esprit* of regular actors. But when the booths of the famous Parisian mountebanks began to leave the Boulevard du Temple to make room for legitimate theatres, when the last performer had given his last performance . . . the *parade,* with all its liveliness, its grotesque and crude hilarity, succumbed for all time. The only practitioners of the *parade* nowadays are the acrobats at country fairs, and since they lack the real Parisian spirit and inspiration . . . they have retained its superficial aspects only and have lost the secret of its vigorous gaiety and sprightliness, its comic and carefree earthiness.—*Le Dictionnaire du théâtre,* by Arthur Pougin (Paris, 1885), pp. 580–581.

E

About the time a permanent company of actors took possession of the Hôtel de Bourgogne two other companies made an attempt to establish themselves in Paris and built two theatres, one in the Collège de Reims, and the other in the Collège de Boncourt. Several troupes from the provinces, one of which rented the Hôtel de Cluny, also tried to gain a foothold in Paris. But these tentatives were without result chiefly because the actors of the Hôtel de Bourgogne, who had been given special privileges and brooked no competition, never rested until they had driven away every possible rival.

Nevertheless in 1600 they were unable to prevent a troupe of comedians from the provinces from securing permission to turn the Hôtel d'Argent, in the Rue de la Poterie, into a theatre, which was called the Théâtre du Marais. The newcomers, it is true, obtained their rights only by agreeing to pay the group at the Hôtel de Bourgogne a royalty of a crown, in the currency of Tours, for each performance. They were highly successful in spite of the tribute levied, and their prosperity continued when, several years later, they removed to another theatre, which was constructed, according to a chronicler, " in a tennis-court above the sewer in the old Rue du Temple."—*Le Dictionnaire du théâtre*, by Arthur Pougin (Paris, 1885), p. 198.

F

The Hôtel de Bourgogne was the first regular theatre ever established in Paris.

The Brotherhood of the Passion had just moved into the Hôtel de Flandre, in 1545, when they received an order to leave from François I, who desired to raze a number of the surrounding houses. They then purchased the Hôtel de Bourgogne, which was situated at the corner of the Rue Française and the Rue Mauconseil. The building was vacant at the time, and had fallen into decay since the death of Charles le Hardi, the last Duke of Bourgogne, who had been killed at the siege of Nancy. The Brotherhood set about converting the house into a theatre, in which they presently began to produce their plays, and over the door they placed the symbols of the Passion as their personal device, which was still to be seen as late as 1763.

The Brotherhood gave up their dramatic activities after twenty-five or thirty years and rented their theatre to a company of professional players, who soon succeeded in making a reputation for themselves, and drew large crowds to their performances. It was then that the Hôtel de Bourgogne acquired its famous reputation which lasted for an entire century; and from this beginning was born the French theatre, which produced the first great French actors. There the plays of Jodelle were first performed . . . and later the works of Routron, Corneille, and Racine.

In the early days of the Hôtel de Bourgogne the coarsest farces were combined with tragedies and plays of the most serious *genre*. It was during this period that the three famous *farceurs*, Gaultier Gargouille, Gros Guillaume, and Turlupin appeared. Their real names were Hugues Guèru, Robert Guérin, and Henri Lapauze, and they were the delight and rage of Paris for nearly half a century. They performed in serious plays under the more elegant sobriquets of Flechelles, Lafleur, and Belleville.

In his *Galerie historique des acteurs du théâtre français* Lemauzurier gives the following details concerning the Hôtel de Bourgogne:

> The stage was built, like all theatres of the time, in a tennis-court, which was oblong and doubtless appropriate for the game for which it was constructed, but not at all for theatrical spectacles. The proprietors had not even taken the trouble to change the shape of the hall. At one end a

platform was erected in imitation of the proscenium of the ancients. Two or three window-frames on either side, a painted canvas for a back-drop, a few strips of blue paper on the ceiling to represent clouds, formed the usual scenic decoration, which served for palace or prison, forest or garden. When it was necessary to indicate a change of scene a curtain was lowered, or else drawn to one side, and this took place ten or twelve times during the performance of one piece.

Along the walls... was built a gallery of two or three tiers, supported by beams, and it was so arranged that one half of the spectators could not see the actors except from the side. Therefore they who occupied the first boxes, which were considered the best seats, were, in reality, too far removed from the stage and could appreciate little of what took place unless their sight and hearing were perfect. One had a better view from the parterre; but there one had not only to stand but to endure other inconveniences which made the place objectionable. One contemporary author describes it thus:

"The pit is highly inconvenient because of the crowd. It is filled with a thousand knaves who mingle with respectable folk and sometimes give offence to them. They provoke a quarrel over nothing, whip out their swords, and constantly interrupt the play. At their quietest they never cease to talk, shout, or whistle; and because they pay nothing for admittance and come there only for lack of anything better to do, they scarcely care to listen to what the players have to say."

The Hôtel de Bourgogne was, together with the Théâtre du Marais, the true cradle of the Comédie Française, and it afterward housed the Italian comedy until as late as 1783.—*Le Dictionnaire du théâtre*, by Arthur Pougin (Paris, 1885), pp. 422–425.

G

Of his [Gherardi's] life we know but few facts which can be relied upon apart from his theatrical career. Francesco Bartoli would have him a Ferrarese who "was a clever actor in the part of the Innamorato," but a later writer (Professor Rasi, author of *I Comici italiani*), weighing all the evidence, sets Bartoli's information regarding him aside as erroneous, and states him to have been the son of a certain Giovanni Gherardi of Spoleto, himself an actor of considerable talent, who made his first appearance at Paris in 1677 in the play *Arlechin Berger de Lemnos* under the name of Flautino, which he selected on account of the numerous wind instruments which he knew how to imitate with his mouth. In fact his talent for music was evidently a marked one, since, as Robinet, in a rhymed letter of January 5, 1675, tells us, he could give forth,

de son seul gosier
un concert de flûtes entier!

and was also skilful with the guitar as is recorded in a verse beneath his portrait by Bonnart:

Avec sa guittare touchée
plus en maître qu'en écolier
il semble qu'il tienne cachée
une flûte dans son gosier.

Skilled as he was alike in music and acting, this elder Gherardi won considerable popularity and applause, and his association with the Comédie Italienne would have probably been of long duration had he not been, on account of his "depraved habits," first imprisoned and then expelled from France.

Of this debonnaire but disreputable person and of his wife Leonarda Galli was born in the little town of Prato, in Tuscany, on November 11, 1663 (according to the *Bibliografia Pratese*), a son who received the name of Evaristo, and who, after concluding his studies in philosophy, made his *début* at the Comédie Italienne in Paris on October 1, 1689, playing the part of Arlecchino in Regnard's play *The Divorce*, which had been acted for the first time at the Hôtel de Bourgogne on the 17th of March, 1688, with Domenico Biancolelli in the cast. . . .

Gherardi continued to act at the Comédie Italienne until its suppression in 1697, and died suddenly on August 31, 1700, from a blow on the head received in a fall during a performance with Thorillière and Poisson at Saint-Maur, where he had been to offer a copy of his book *Le Théâtre italien* to Monsignore. . . .

Thus really all that we know of this actor is summed up in a very few, though sufficient, facts . . . his birth, parentage, death; the number of years he spent at the Comédie Italienne, the name of the mask under which he played, and then . . . that which contains all, sums up all the rest and brings us nearer to the man himself . . . the work by and in which he lives.—*The Mask*, vol. iii, pp. 165–166.

H

It was in or about the year 1675 that Luigi Riccoboni, celebrated upon the stage under the name of "Lelio," was born at Modena, being the son of a Venetian actor, Antonio Riccoboni, who played the part of Pantalone in the company of the Duke of Modena in 1670, and who, still in the service of the same Duke Alfonso, visited London and acted there in 1679. The first appearance of Luigi Riccoboni on the stage was in the part of the "Innamorato," but the name which he then adopted was Federico, and he only changed afterwards to Lelio at the instance of the Directress of the Company, Diana, the wife of Giovan Battista Constantini, who thought the latter name more "theatrical."

He seems to have married twice. His first wife was Gabriella Gardelini ("Argentina"), who was step-sister to Francesco Materazzi, the "Dottore" of the Company, but she died very young, leaving no children, and Luigi Riccoboni, left a widower, then married Elena Virginia Balletti, an actress who was celebrated under the name of Flaminia.

In Luigi Riccoboni we see the beginnings of the decline of that splendid period of the great Improvisatori, of Andreini, Pasquati, Biancolelli, Martinelli, Barbieri, Fiorelli and those who had rendered the *commedia dell' arte* so justly famous, since he believed himself to be "reforming" the theatre by introducing, instead of improvised comedies, the written works of the poets, such as the *Sofonisba* of Trissino, the *Œdipus* of Sophocles and many more.

This experiment in the literary drama seems to have been successful enough at Modena, but fortunately Venice, to which city he next took his company, remained faithful to its Arlecchinos, its Dottores, and its Pantalones, and Riccoboni, disappointed and discouraged, had to renounce his purpose.

It was at this time that he decided to accept an invitation which he had received from France to form a company of Italian actors for Paris under the patronage of the Regent, the Duke of Orleans, hoping to realise there the dreams which had been so rudely disappointed in his native land. But for a second time he had to submit, and renounce his literary dramas, since, even before the opening of the theatre, the Parisians plainly manifested their intention of having only such plays as they had been familiarised with by the Italian companies which had visited Paris in previous years. . . .

In June 1733 Riccoboni, together with his wife and son, became a naturalised French subject, and in April 1727 he obtained permission to absent himself for two months and go to act in England, while two years later leave was granted him to retire from the stage with his wife and son with an annual pension of one thousand francs. He withdrew to Italy, but after two years spent at Parma, he returned to Paris, where he died on December 6, 1753, at the age of seventy-eight, being referred to in his death certificate as "un ancien ufficiel du roi."—*The Mask*, vol. iii, pp. 175–176.

THE ITALIAN COMEDY

I

Gillot, Claude. A French artist born at Langres 1673, died in Paris 1722. Having begun his studies under his father, himself a painter, he was sent to continue them in Paris under Jean Battiste Corneille, a historical painter ; but the boy, endowed with keen imagination and impatient of the course of study laid down for him, preferred to escape from the studio and, wandering about the streets and squares, study from life and especially from the actors who performed in the public places, and his work chiefly represents popular scenes and burlesque adventures. He was the master of Watteau. He also directed the scenery and costumes at the Opera, and published the *Livre d'ornements, de trophées, cul-de-lampe, et dessins* and *Le Théâtre italien*, a volume of scenes from plays, some of which are reproduced in *The Mask.—The Mask*, vol. iii, p. 162.

J

This Italian word [*lazzi*] . . . serves to designate all sorts of burlesque pleasantries either in words, play on words, action, grimaces, grotesque gestures, etc. . . . The *lazzi* are characterized if not by coarse humour at least by a certain vulgarity ; it is comedy without distinction, real buffoonery which has little wit to it, but inevitably gives an effect of surprise and laughter. The comedians of the Hôtel de Bourgogne in the old days, as well as Turlupin and the like, were famous for their *lazzi* ; Molière did not disdain to employ them in his wonderful comedies, and more than one actor since has owed a part of his reputation to them.—*Le Dictionnaire du théâtre*, by Arthur Pougin (Paris, 1885), p. 467.

This word, meaning " knots " (*lazzi* being the Lombardian expression for the Tuscan *lacci*), is used to denote the scenes wherein the buffoons interrupt the story with irrelevant pranks —scenes of a kind which Shakespeare frequently wrote for his clowns in order to relieve the tensity of his plots, and which in England were called " jigs."—*Goldoni : a Biography*, by H. C. Chatfield-Taylor (Duffield and Co., New York), pp. 92–93.

K

The Harlequin was Tomasso Antonio Vicentini, known as Thomassin. He was born at Vicenza about 1683. At an early age he joined a company travelling through Italy and played tragic parts. It is also said of him that at Rome, where the appearance of women on the stage was forbidden, he acted the parts of young princesses to much applause. For some reason unknown to us, he forsook tragedy for comedy and became a Harlequin, in which character he soon acquired a considerable reputation. He made his first appearance on the 18th of May, 1716, in *L'Inganno Fortunato*, an Italian piece known in French as *L'Heureuse Surprise*. . . .

When the number of spectators at the Hôtel de Bourgogne began to thin, partly because they could not understand plays presented in Italian, and perhaps more so on account of the revival of certain old French pieces, the grossness of which had caused them to be omitted from the repertory of the old company, Thomassin still found favour with the public and helped to revive the waning interest.

He had a brilliant career. Agile, gay, and always original, he would set the house in roars of laughter by some inimitable display of buffoonery, then, passing almost imperceptibly from comedy to tragedy, he would cause the same public to shed tears of sorrow—no light achievement when it is remembered that his face was covered by a mask. . . . Thomassin died on the 19th of August, 1739, and was buried in the church of Saint-Laurent.—*The History of Harlequin*, by Cyril W. Beaumont (C. W. Beaumont, 1926), pp. 56–57.

L

ARLEQUIN

Adio, Signor Giove.

JUPITER

D'où vient que Mercure est monté sur mon aigle? N'a-t-il pas des ailes aux talons pour voler?

ARLEQUIN

Hélas! Seigneur Jupiter, mes ailes ne peuvent plus me servir, perchè passando per una strada, una servanta m'a vuidé un pot de chambre dessus, et me les a tellement mouillées que se non fossi tombé per bonhor sur un tas de fumier, Mercurio si saria rotto il collo; ecosi ho trova la vostra aquila dans l'écurie, au râtelier, et je m'en suis servi per far tutte le commissionni dont je suis chargé.

JUPITER

Et bien, j'ay quelque chose à te dire. Descens et prens la forme d'un berger.
(*La machine disparaît et on voit Arlequin dans son habit naturel et monté sur un âne.*)

M

Carlo Antonio Bertinazzi, called Carlin, ... was born at Turin on the 2nd of December, 1710. He was the son of Felice Bertinazzi, an officer in the army of the King of Sardinia, and Giovanna Maria Gti. He was only three years old when his father died, but his mother gave him a thorough education which included fencing and dancing.

At fourteen he became an ensign, but conceiving a distaste for the military profession, and the death of his mother having freed him of family ties, he resigned his commission and became an actor.

Having studied his art for some time, he played the part of Harlequin with considerable success at theatres in Bologna and Venice. He was soon acclaimed one of the best players of the day, and the Italian comedians at Paris, being anxious to fill the gap created by the death of Thomassin, invited him to join them. Carlin arrived in Paris early in the year 1741, and on the 10th of April he made his bow before the Parisian public. Since he spoke little French, he selected Riccoboni's piece *Arlecchino Muto per Forza* for his first appearance. The day appointed was also that of the reopening of the theatre, which according to custom had been closed during the Easter fortnight. ...

Carlin made an excellent impression, and in the year following he became a permanent member of the company, pleasing alike with the excellence of his miming and the charm of his dancing. He had an extraordinary prescience in divining the public taste, and the most solemn spectator was soon reduced to smiling at his sallies. He possessed the rare merit of appearing always different and always excellent. And like Thomassin, he could make the audience laugh one moment, and cry the next. ...

Carlin was a well-informed man on many subjects; he played several musical instruments, both painted and engraved well, and wielded a skilful pen—witness his piece *Les Métamorphoses d'Arlequin*. ... Goldoni, speaking of Carlin in his *Memoirs*, declares that he

> was in high estimation for his propriety of behaviour, celebrated as a Harlequin, and in the possession of a reputation which raised him to a level with Domenique and Thomassin in France, and Sacchi in Italy. Nature had endowed him with inimitable graces; his figure, his gestures, his movements, possessed every one in his favour. For his action and talents he was admired on the stage, and for his private character he was beloved in society.

The pieces with which his name is inseparably associated are *Coraline Magicienne*, *Les Fées Rivales*, *Le Prince de Salerne*, and *Les Vingt-six Infortunes d'Arlequin*, all by Veronese; the two anonymous pieces, *Coraline Esprit Follet* and *La Joute d'Arlequin*; and, in particular, *Le Fils d'Arlequin Perdu et Retrouvé*, by Goldoni.

Carlin died at Paris following an attack of apoplexy on the 6th of September, 1783.—*The History of Harlequin*, by Cyril W. Beaumont (C. W. Beaumont, 1926), pp. 58–61.

N

BIANCHI, GIUSEPPE. An actor who flourished about the middle of the seventeenth century under the name of Capitano Spezzaferro. The Frères Parfaict tell us that, during the two years (1668–69) during which the famous Scaramuccia (Tiberio Fiorillo) was, by permission of the Court, absent in Italy, his place in Paris was taken by a new and most able Italian actor whose talent was such as to cause his celebrated predecessor to be but little missed; and they add that on Fiorillo's return this actor, Bianchi, surrendered the part of Scaramuccia and took again that of the Captain, which he seems to have played previously in 1645.—*The Mask*, vol. iii, p. 161.

O

FERRARA, DUKE OF, ERCOLE I. Born 1431. Died 1505. It was in Ferrara, under his rule, that the splendour of the ancient Italian dramatic performances was revived, and, beginning with a representation in 1486 of the *Menecmi*, performances were given at his Court, with the co-operation of Ariosto, Boiardo, Strozzi and many others, of most of the plays of Terence and Plautus as well as of more modern works

Some idea of the richness of the scenery and costumes is conveyed in the letters of Ercole's daughter, Isabella d'Este (wife of the Duke Francesco of Mantua), written from her father's Court at Ferrara to her husband on the occasion of her brother's marriage with Lucrezia Borgia. —*The Mask*, vol. iii, p. 126.

PICTORIAL SUPPLEMENT

Publisher's Note

The plates in this Pictorial Supplement have been reproduced from the *Recueil Fossard*, a rare collection of sixteenth-century engravings which Duchartre first published himself in 1928 (Duchartre et Van Buggenhoudt, Paris). The *Recueil* was compiled for Louis XIV by a certain M. Fossard, but remained unpublished and unknown until it was rediscovered by M. Agne Beijer in the early twentieth century in the uncataloged reserves of the Museum of Stockholm, Sweden (see Translator's Note, p. 5).

Duchartre makes frequent reference to the *Recueil* throughout *The Italian Comedy*, and has incorporated seven of the forty-two plates into his text. The remaining plates are reproduced in this supplement. Included in this supplement also are plates from another document (in the Bibliothèque Nationale, Paris) called *Compositions de rhétorique de M. don Arlequin*, which was published together with the *Recueil* and which gives a curious treatment of the subject of Harlequin during the Renaissance (see p. 125).

RECUEIL.

DE.

Plusieurs fragments des premieres comedies Jtaliennes qui ont esté representees en France sous le regne de Henry 3

Où lon uoit les differents Caracteres qu'ils donnoient a leurs Acteurs, et les intrigues de leurs pieces meslées de bouffonnerie, & de beaucoup de licences.

AVEC.

Les habillemens de tous leurs personnages tant serieux, que comiques dont les plus considerables estoient le seig.r Leandre, la Dona Cornelia, Fracisquine Harlequin, le seig.r Dottor, Pantalon, & Zani qui ont esté les Originaux, & les modelles des autres Comediens qui ont paru en suitte sous les regnes de Henry 4e et Louis 13 et

LOUIS LE GRAND.

Le tout graué en plusieurs estampes dont il y a quelques vnes d'enluminées

Et mis en ordre par le Sieur Fossard

Ordinaire de la Musique,

DU ROY.

Carl G. Tessin.

Agnan.
La Laictiere.
Harlequin.
Verrier traiſtre & larron, puis q̃ tu ne veux rẽdre
Mon alleſne qu'as priſe ainſi que bien ie ſçay,
Ie te feray le ſon de ceſte flute entendre,
Et dancer à ton dan pour premier coup d'eſſay.
Dancerai-je touſiours, que veut dire ceci?
Mes œufs ſõt tous caſſez, & mõ lait eſt par terre
Maudit ſoit le Berger cauſe d'vn tel ſouci,
Et de ſa flute auſſi le ſon qui me fait guerre. ij.
Ne ſone plus (Berger) humblemẽt ie t'en prie,
Ie te ren ton alleſne & me delaiſſe en paix,
Mes verres ſont rompus, dõt par grãd' faſcherie
Me faudra demeurer pauure pour tout iamais.

La bonne mere Guillemette.
Agnan Magiſter.
Peronne.
Mon fils tu ès ja grãd, tu deurois te cognoiſtre,
Et ſage te monſtrer pour vn iour te pouruoir,
Ne cours dõc point apres la fille de ton maiſtre,
Il la faut courtiſer autrement pour l'auoir.
Ma mere laiſſez moy, ie veux baiſer Perõne,
Car elle m'a donné vn ſoufflet pour faueur,
Aproche mon ſoulas, ne t'enfuis ma mignõne,
Par la mort d'vn étron tu as raui mon cœur.
Vous ne me tenez pas Magiſter de village,
Puis que ie vous ay peu le dernier coup donner,
Ma foy vous eſtes trop éueillé pour voſtre aage,
A dieu dõc Magiſter, il m'en faut retourner. iij

Peronne.
Iulien le débauché.
Mathieu Bouclon.
Mes cousins, pour certain le Magister se vãte,
Que mourir luy conuient s'il ne iouït de moy,
Dix escus ie vous donne, & à l'heure presente,
Faictes luy quelque tour sans luy causer émoy.
Cousine asseurez vous que dedãs ce iourd'huy
Il cognoistra que c'est de l'amoureux martire,
Car dessous vostre nom i'iray par deuers luy,
En femme déguisé, vous apprestant a rire.
De moy, sous vn habit de Negromancien,
Ie l'iray visiter en personne incogneuë,
Et soustiendray que i'ay par mon art le moyen,
De vous mettre en ses mains maintenãt toute nue.
iiij.

Agnan.
Mathieu Bouclon Philosophe.
Iulien déguisé en femme.
Le gourmand ancien, di-ie double mõsieur,
Fine-isope sçauant, ostez moy de tristesse,
Adoucissant Peronne où repose mon heur,
Car lors qu'elle me voit elle fait la diablesse.
Magister mon amy, par mon enchantemẽt,
Ie vous ay fait venir vostre dame en chemise
Voiez comme sa cuisse elle monstre gayment,
Preste à faire l'amour auec vous sans faintise.
Agnan mon doux souci, i'ay par charmes esté,
Contrainte de venir ores en ta presence,
Tien doncques ce bouquet gage de loyauté,
Et pren pareillemẽt de mõ corps iouïssance.
v

Agnan.
La bonne mere Guillemette.
Mathieu Bouclon.
Perõne ma douceur, puis q̃ ie tien maujoint,
C'est par necessité qu'il faut que ie vous sangle,
Ne faites la retiue on ne nous verra point,
Au meurdre, acourez tous, la vilaine m'ẽtrãgle.
Qu'est-ceci malheureux, veux-tu deshonorer
Vne fille de bien tant belle & tant honeste,
Frapons dessus voisin, plus n'en puis endurer,
Il a bien merité qu'on lui rompe la teste.
Tost laissez moy passer voisine Guillemette,
Ie veux du premier coup ce meschãt assommer
Il cõuient par fureur que sur luy la main mette,
Ma cousine il violle en faignãt de l'aymer. vj.

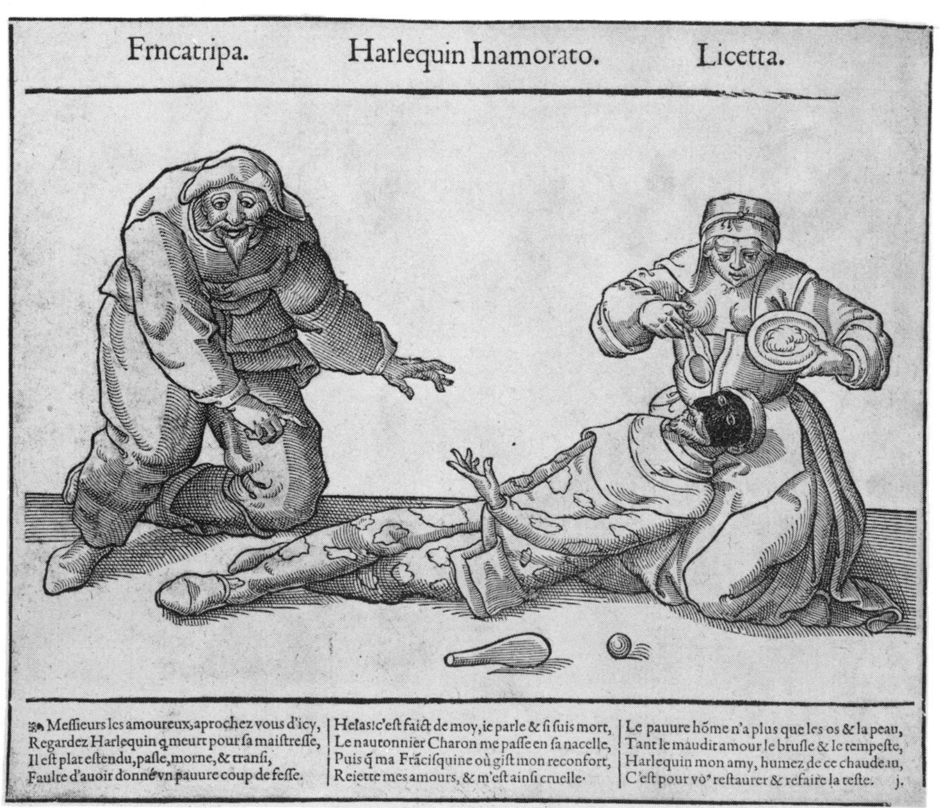
Frncatripa.
Harlequin Inamorato.
Licetta.
Messieurs les amoureux, aprochez vous d'icy,
Regardez Harlequin q̃ meurt pour sa maistresse,
Il est plat estendu, pasle, morne, & transi,
Faulte d'auoir donné vn pauure coup de fesse.
Helas! c'est faict de moy, ie parle & si suis mort,
Le nautonnier Charon me passe en sa nacelle,
Puis q̃ ma Frãcisquine où gist mon reconfort,
Reiette mes amours, & m'est ainsi cruelle.
Le pauure hõme n'a plus que les os & la peau,
Tant le maudit amour le brusle & le tempeste,
Harlequin mon amy, humez de ce chaudeau,
C'est pour vo' restaurer & refaire la teste. j.

Il Segnor Pantalon.
Zany.
Francisquina.
Zany mon Achilles, arretons ce gallant,
Ce mignõ Harlequin q̃ tranche ainsi du braue,
Ha, ie te feray veoir que ie suis plus vaillant,
Qu'vn tel double poltron qui n'a rien q̃ la baue.
Ie sçay bien (Pantalon) qu'estes vn second Mars,
Pour prendre cõtre vn mur finemẽt vne mouche,
Marchez donc le premier, car ie crain les hazars,
La cuisine vaut mieux cent fois q̃ l'escarmouche.
Receuoir il me faut Harlequin, q̃ vers moy
A desir tout armé maintenãt de se rẽdre, ij.
Pour en ma faueur seule auãcer vn tournoy
Où il veut ma beauté soutenir & deffendre.

Il Capitan Cocodrillo.
Harlequin deguisé.
La Donna Lucia.
Caché de mon manteau, ie sçauray le secret
De ce faux Harlequin q̃ soubs l'habit d'Horace,
Veult ioüir finement & entrer en la grace
De ceste Dame cy, qui l'estime discret.
Ie suis Cheualier & Seigneur estranger,
Arriué d'outre mer pour vo' veoir mà maistresse,
Iamais ne manquerez de biens ny de richesse,
Si voulez comme amy ceste nuict me loger.
Pour vous rendre (monsieur) en ce cas satisfaict
Veu que tãt vous m'aimez, vous aurez ioüissance
De ce que desirez, tout à vostre plaisance, iij.
Pour l'or & les presens, la femme beaucoup fait.

Il Segnor Horacio.
Harlequin,
Il Segnor Dotour.
Ie te tien, ie te tien, ô trahitre, ô inhumain,
Tu as pris mon habit, pour aller par faintiſe
Violer vne Dame, ou mon amour c'eſt miſe:
Sus ſus, c'eſt à ce coup q̃ mourras de ma main.
Pardonnez moy, Monſieur, hé ne me tuez pas,
Ie vous ren voſtre habit, ne ſoyez ſanguinaire,
Ou ſi de mes boyaux du boudin voulez faire,
Atẽdez ſ'il vous plait, que ſois vn peu plus gras.
Hola, Seigneur Horace, appaiſez la rancœur
Que portez à bon droit contre ce miſerable. iiij.
Vous voiez qu'il vous faict vne amẽde hõnorable,
Et qu'a genoux pardon il requiert de bon cœur.

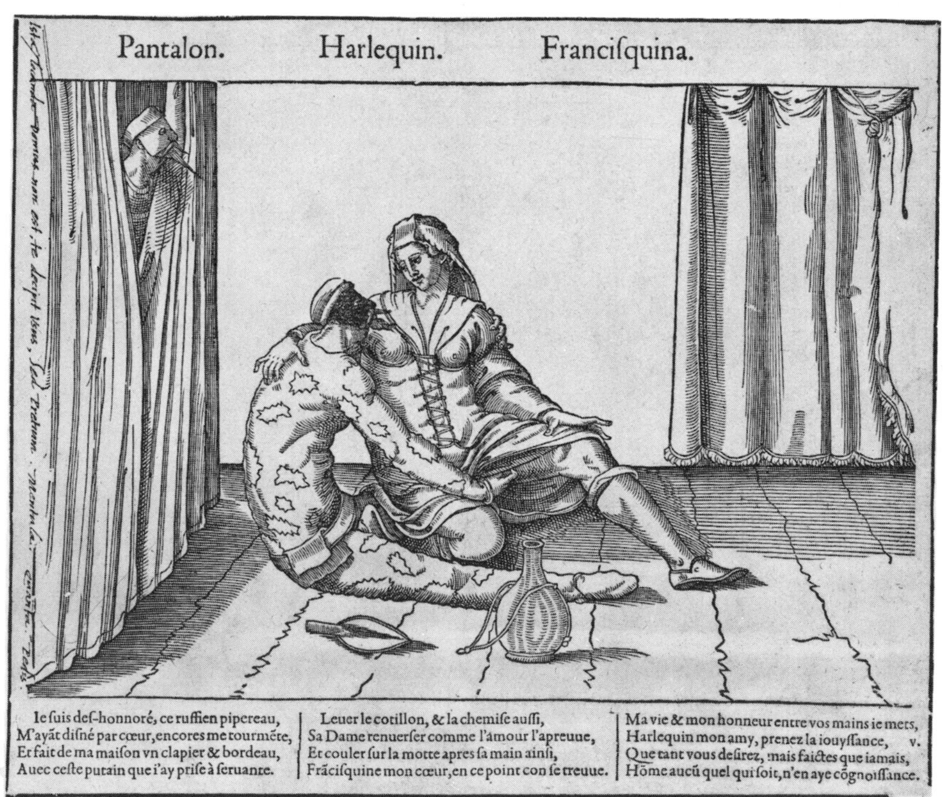
Pantalon.
Harlequin.
Franciſquina.
Ie ſuis deſ-honnoré, ce ruffien pipereau,
M'ayãt diſné par cœur, encores me tourmẽte,
Et fait de ma maiſon vn clapier & bordeau,
Auec ceſte putain que i'ay priſe à ſeruante.
Leuer le cotillon, & la chemiſe auſſi,
Sa Dame renuerſer comme l'amour l'apreuue,
Et couler ſur la motte apres ſa main ainſi,
Frãciſquine mon cœur, en ce point con ſe treuue.
Ma vie & mon honneur entre vos mains ie mets,
Harlequin mon amy, prenez la iouyſſance, v.
Que tant vous deſirez, mais faictes que iamais,
Hõme aucũ quel qui ſoit, n'en aye cõgnoiſſance.

Zany Corneto.
Harlequin.
La Dona Lucretia.
Ca, ça, deſpéchons nous puis qu'il ſe faut riper,
Que i'égorge quelqu'vn en ma forte colere:
Ie cours en vn combat comme apres vn ſouper,
Et ſuis grand Capitaine ainſi que feu mon pere,
Madame, ie vous prie puis que ie ſuis armé,
Que me laiſſiez aller contre mon aduerſaire,
Ie le feray mourir, ſ'il n'a le corps charmé:
Venez prendre plaiſir à me le voir deffaire.
Harlequin, ne bougez, voſtre paix ſe fera,
Ce iourd'huy de par moy, qui ſçay voſtre querelle,
Meſſerre Pantalon d'argent vous aydera,
Et ne hantera plus Franciſquine la belle.
vj.

Il Segnor Horacio.
Harlequin.
Puis que i'ay pour armet ce braue pot de fer,
Et ce harnois en dos, monté ſur mon aneſſe,
Ie veux cõme Hercules Aſſaillir tout l'éfer,
Soutenãt la beauté de ma chere Maiſtreſſe.
La belle Frãciſquine eſt mon cœur & mon bien,
C'eſt ma felicité, c'eſt ma ſeule eſperance,
Pour l'auoir i'emploiray mes amis, mon moyen,
Et ma force au ſurplus en tirant coup de lance.
Le trenchant de l'eſpee, apres ne manquera,
En cheualier errant, & de la table ronde,
Amoureux iuſqu'au cul: ſi bien que l'on dira,
Qu'il n'eſt qu'vn Harlequĩ pour triõpher au mõde.
J.

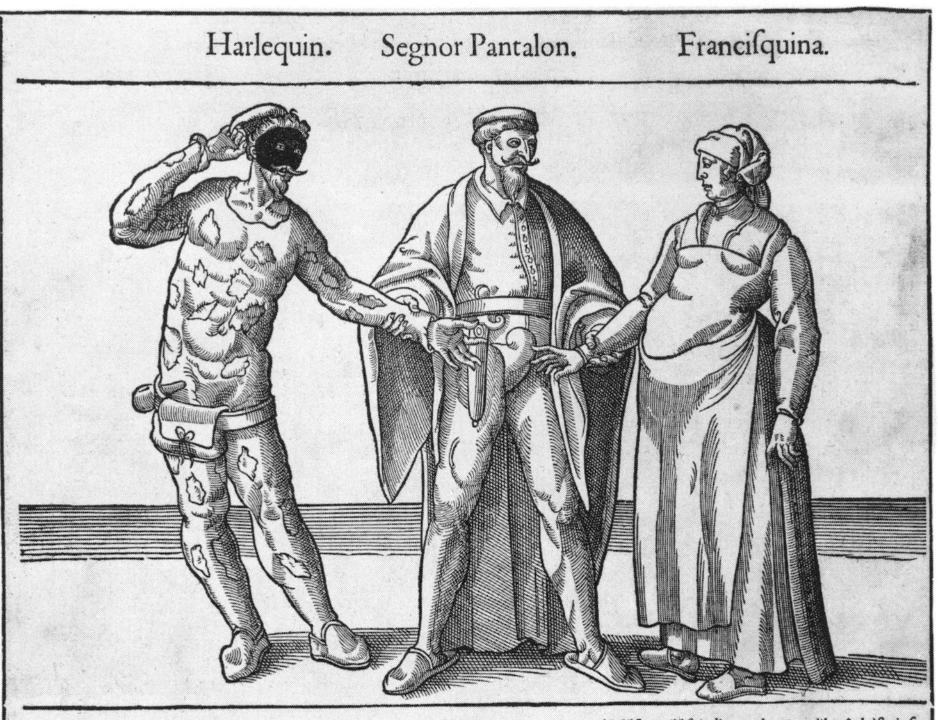

Puis, Seigneur Pãtalõ, qu'il vo⁹ plaiſt me dõner
La belle Franciſquine en loyal mariage,
Ie vous promets la foy de ne l'abandonner,
Tãt qu'au cul me tiendra ceſte amoureuſe rage.

Mettez les mains enſẽble, & puis vo⁹ iurerez,
Que ferez à iamais l'vn à l'autre fidelles:
Pour voſtre auancemẽt, de ma part vous aurez
Six curedẽs de rente, vn pot, & deux eſcuelles.

Mõſieur, i'ẽ ſuis d'accord, puis qu'il vo⁹ plaiſt ainſi,
Ce ſera pour couurir la faulte que i'ay faite:
Harlequin eſt bon drolle, & homme ſans ſoucy,
Ie le veux pour eſpoux, autre ie ne ſouhaite. ij.

Deſloyal Pantalon, ie me doy bien faſcher,
Tu m'as faict eſpouſer vne paillarde infame,
Elle vient maintenant d'vne fille accoucher,
Et il n'y-a qu'vn mois que ie l'ay priſe à femme.

I'en créue de deſpit, Ce pendãt (malheureux)
Huit enfans, tous à toy, ie t'aporte & ameine,
A fin de les nourrir en ce temps rigoureux:
Le pere doit ayder à ſes enfans en peine.

A Dieu pauure génin, tu te romps le cerueau,
Ie n'ay eu en ma vie auec ta femme affaire:
Si tu as voulu prendre & la vache & le veau,
Nourry les ſi tu veux, ie n'y ſçaurois que faire. iij.

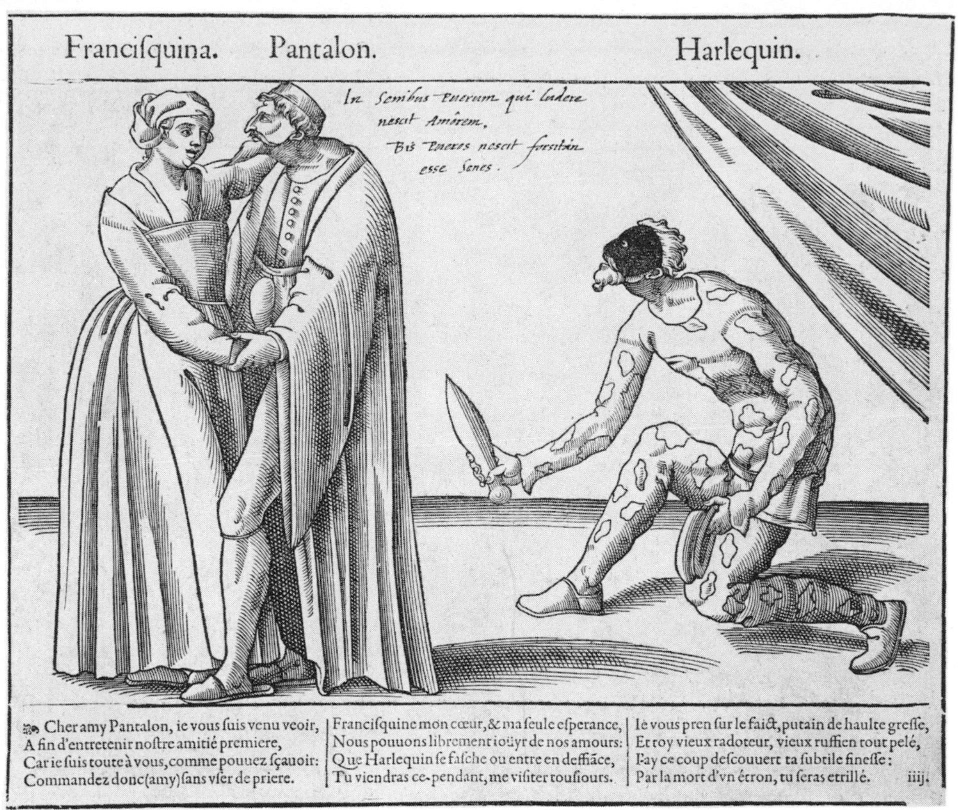
Francisquina.
Pantalon.
Harlequin.
In Senibus Puerum qui ludere nescit Amôrem,
Bis Pueros nescit forsitan esse Senes.
Cher amy Pantalon, ie vous suis venu veoir,
A fin d'entretenir nostre amitié premiere,
Car ie suis toute à vous, comme pouuez sçauoir:
Commandez donc (amy) sans vser de priere.
Francisquine mon cœur, & ma seule esperance,
Nous pouuons librement iouÿr de nos amours:
Que Harlequin se fasche ou entre en deffiãce,
Tu viendras ce-pendant, me visiter tousiours.
Ie vous pren sur le faict, putain de haulte gresse,
Et toy vieux radoteur, vieux ruffien tout pelé,
I'ay ce coup descouuert ta subtile finesse:
Par la mort d'vn étron, tu seras etrillé. iiij.

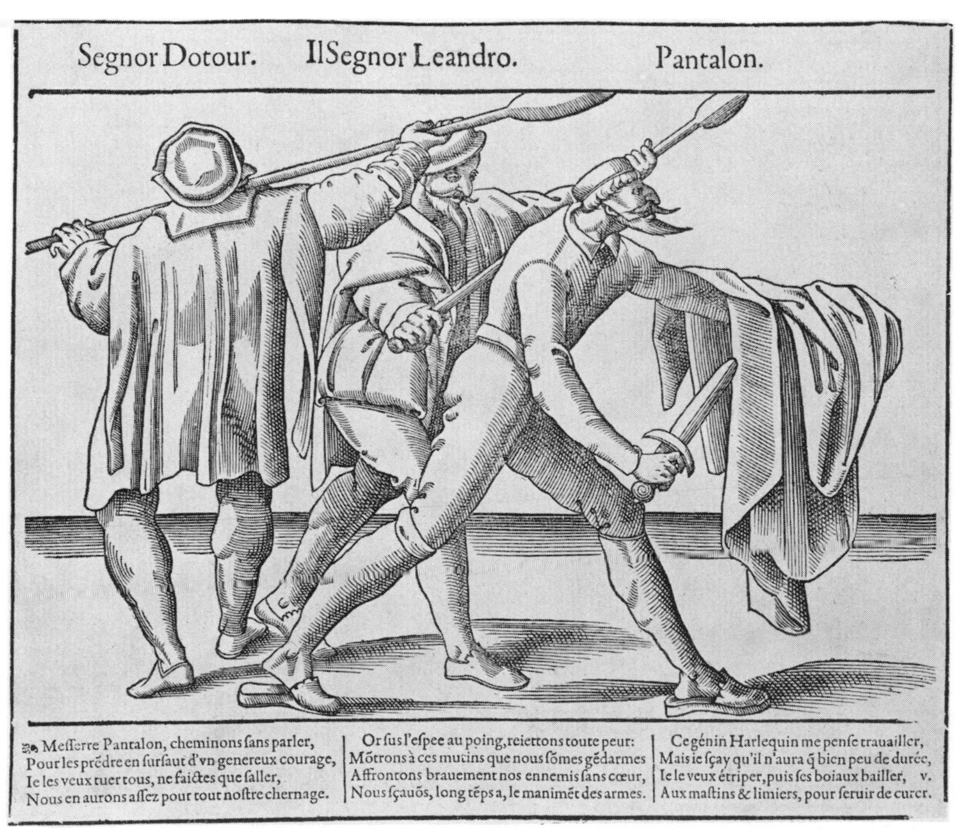
Segnor Dotour.
Il Segnor Leandro.
Pantalon.
Messerre Pantalon, cheminons sans parler,
Pour les prẽdre en sursaut d'vn genereux courage,
Ie les veux tuer tous, ne faictes que saller,
Nous en aurons assez pour tout nostre chernage.
Or sus l'espee au poing, reiettons toute peur:
Mõtrons à ces mutins que nous sõmes gẽdarmes
Affrontons brauement nos ennemis sans cœur,
Nous sçauõs, long tẽps a, le manimẽt des armes.
Ce génin Harlequin me pense trauailler,
Mais ie sçay qu'il n'aura q̃ bien peu de durée,
Ie le veux étriper, puis ses boiaux bailler, v.
Aux mastins & limiers, pour seruir de curer.

Il Segnor Pantalon.
Zany Cornetto.
Qui est ce grand soldat, qui s'arreste à mon huis,
Et qui de son mâteau bouche en ce point sa face?
C'est qlqu'vn qui me guette, il faut dõc si ie puis,
Voir si ie le congnois sans partir de la place.
Mes lunettes me font sçauoir asseurément,
Que c'est mon seruiteur, q viẽt à l'eschapée,
De faire la desbauche, & furieusement,
Porte en mauuais garsõ sa massacrãte espée.
Me voyla découuert, il ne s'en faudra rien,
Puis qu'il met à son nez ses deux grãds yeux de verre,
Ie les embreneray si iamais ie les tien, vj.
Deussay-je auecques luy viure tousiours en guerre.

La Donna Lucia.
Il Segnor Pantalon
Zany.
Impudent Pantalon, pense-tu captiuer
Par tes faquins propos, la fleur de ma ieunesse?
Non non, ioindre vn printãs auec vne viellesse,
Est faire vn feu flambant à la neige estriuer.
Ma mignõne, mon bien, mõ ame, & mon cœur doux,
De vostre pauure Esclaue oyez vne parole,
Ainsi que dict Zany, mon sçauant protecolle,
I'enrageray tout vif, si ne couche auec vous. ij.
Au diable le poltron, ie n'ay pas dict ainsi,
Voila pour tout gaster, ô la grande pécore,
Pantalon escoutez, recommencez encore,
Et de mieux haranguer prenez tost le soucy.

Harlequin.
Zany Corneto.
Il Segnor Pantalon.
O la belle chanſon, Pantalon chantons bien,
Si voulez eſgayer voſtre maiſtreſſe belle,
C'eſt le moyen certain pour en fin iouïr d'elle,
Qu'eſtre muſeau de chien, dy-ie muſicien.
Accordons nous tous trois, ſi bien & proprement
Que puiſſions l'endormir au doux ſon de ma lire,
Encor que comme vous ie n'aye apris à lire,
Ie ne laiſſeray pas de iouër brauement.
Courage (mes amis) ie chante le deſſus,
De ce plaiſant trio, compoſé pour madame,
La douceur de ma voix luy penetrera l'ame:
Mes paſſages ne ſont ni tortus ni boſſus.
j.

Philipin.
Harlequin.
Il Segnor Pantalon.
Viue, viue à iamais tout gentil biberon,
Qui cõme no⁹ aura d'iurõgner bõne enuie,
Harlequin, ruõs nous ſur ce gros macaron,
C'eſt le meilleur mãger q̃ gouſtay de ma vie.
Mon Philipin gaillard, mõ amy, mõ couillault,
Iamais il ne m'ennuye en vne bonne table,
Mais, auant que gouſter de ce macaron chault,
Ie m'en vay boire à toy de ce vin delectable.
Ah quelle cruauté, mes amis acourez,
Ces deux volleurs mētront toute en blãc ma cuiſine.
Ils boiront mon vin, ſi trop vous demeurez,
O trahitres, ô villains, il faut que vous ruine.
iij.

I· Honeruogt excudit
Le docteur est remply de si grande seiance
Quil luy fault arracher tous les motz de ses doigtz
Pantalon et Zany le sont a sa semblance
Dont ilz ont a tirer si fort comme tu vois

I. Honeruogt excudit
Pantalon despite de quelque menterie
Quil recoit de Zany secolere si fort
Que par grande furie il le veult mettre a mort
Mais Zany luy requiert en aulmone la Vie

Pantalon chez sa Dame en mulle veut aller
ni monte dessus qui le tourmente & picque
Dont Pantalon se plaint. mais Zani luy replique
Taistoy qui vit Jamais une mulle parler

La donna Cornelia.

Il Segnor Léandro.

Pantalon.

neur Pãtalon, on m'a voulu pourueoir,
met d'endurer des lunes de ma teſte,
t pourquoy i'ay voulu en cõmancer la feſte,
ar le bal couſtumier, cõme vous pouuez veoir.

Meſſerre Pantalon, ſi eſtes vertueux,
Affin de reiouir ceſte noble aſſiſtance,
Pẽdãt que ie iourray, faictes trois tours de dãce,
Et ne vous montrez point en rien deffectueux.

Sus ſus, iambes en lær, puis que dancer il fault,
Sonnez ſur voſtre Luth la bruſque millãnoiſe,
Ou quelq̃ aultre gaillarde, ou volte à la frãçoiſe
Ie caprioll eray plus d'vn pouce de hault. vj.

La Donna Isabella.

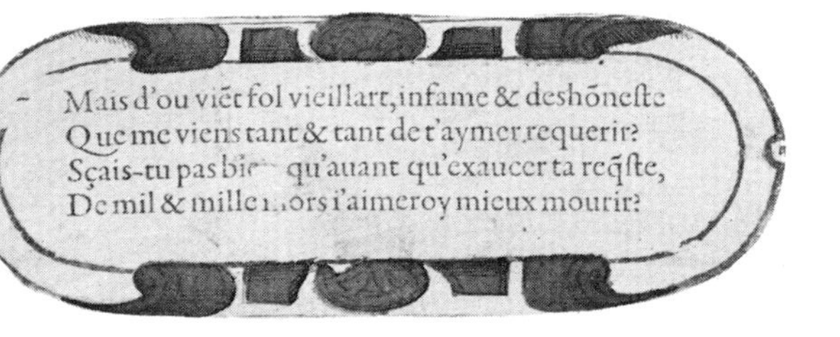

Pantalon Inamorato.

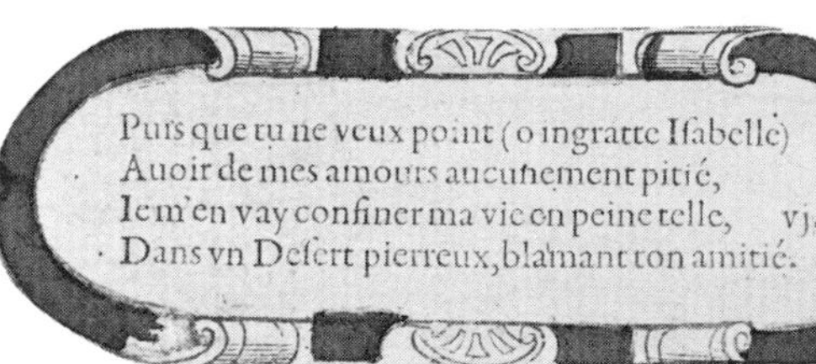

Segnor Pantalon.

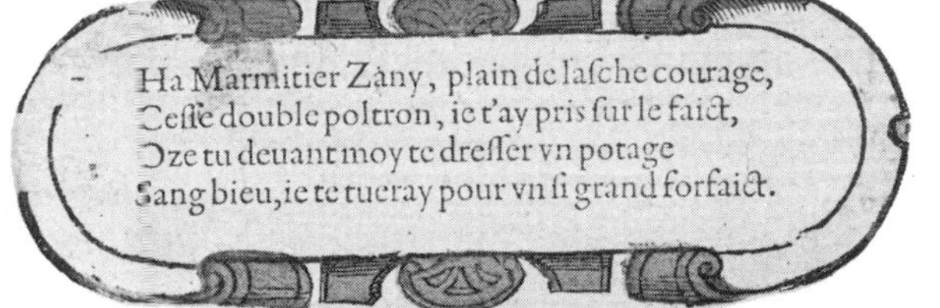

Zany Corneto.

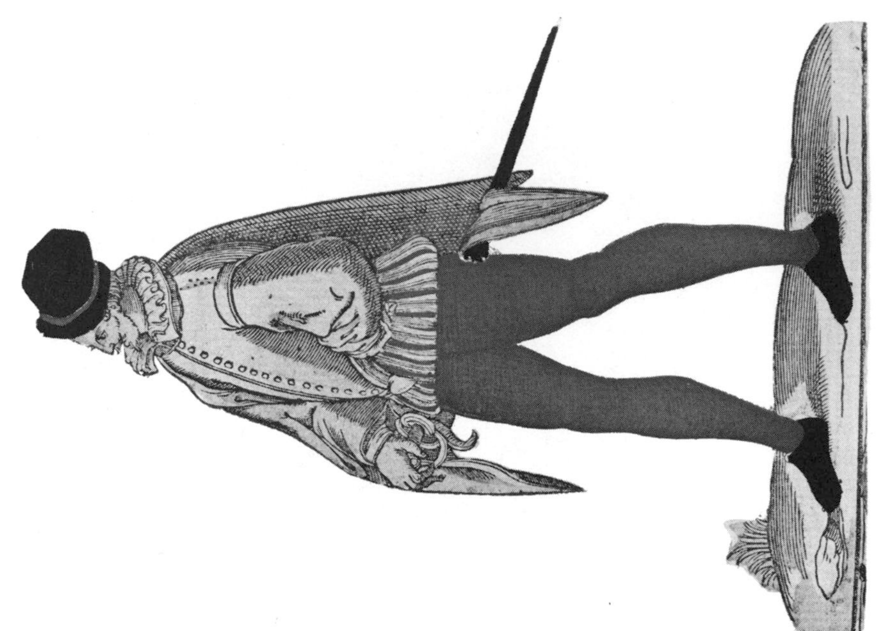
Il Signor Horacio.

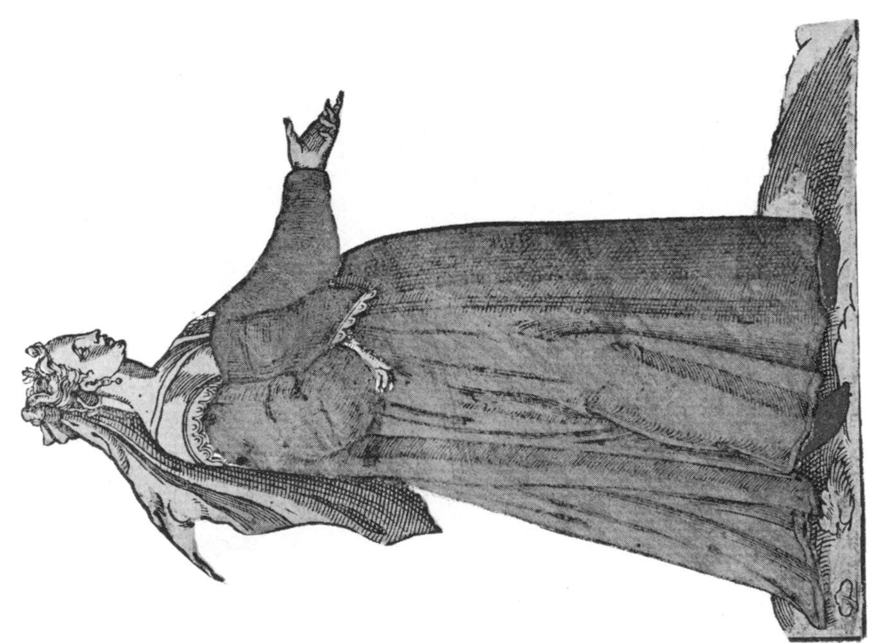
Francisquina.

HAREQUIN QUIN HAREQUIN
STEPHANEL
BOTTARGA.
SIBILOT.

FRANCATRIPA.
ZANY CORNETTO.
DOCTOR GRATIAN.
PANTALON DI BESONGNOSI
LA DONA ISABELLA
CAPITAN COCODRILLO

Comedie ou farce de six parsonnaiges.
H. Liefrinck excu.
Chenu viellardt est grand cocu et fort infame,
A qui les cornes met sa ieune belle dame.

COMPOSITIONS

DE RHETORIQVE.

De M.ʳ Don ARLEQVIN, Comicorum de ciuitatis Noualensis, Corrigidor de la bonna langua Francese & Latina, Condutier de Comediens, Connestable de Messieurs les Badaux de Paris, & Capital ennemi de tut les laquais inuenteurs desrobber chapiaux.

ARLECHIN.

IMPRIME' DELA' LE BOVT DV MONDE.

AL MAGNANIMO Monſieur, Monſieur HENRY de BOVRBON, premier bourgeois de Paris, chef de tuts les Meſſieurs de Lyon, Conte de Mommeillan, Chaſtellan du fort de ſanta Caterina, Gouuerneur de la Breſſa, Pretentor del Marquiſat de Saluces, Armiral de la mer de Marſeille, maiſtre de la moitié du pont d'Auignon, & bon amy du maiſtre de l'autra moitié, Conſeiller ſouuerain au Conſeil de guerra contre les Plamontois, Gratieuſiſsimo courreur de bague, Cappitaine general de

France & de Nauarre, Despensier liberal de canonades, Terreur de Sauoyard, Spauente de Spagnols, Colonel des soldats, qui sont en Sauoye, Secretaire Secret du plus secret Cabinet de Madama MARIA DI MEDICI, Reina du Louure, Grand Thresorier des Comediens Italiens, & Prince plus que tut autre digne d'estre engraué en Medaille tant de moy desiree, & plus vltra,

SALVT,

ET

A Madama,
Madama sa femme autant.

5

Ha REINE, *Colana,*	ROY *Medaglia,*
Quantumque donné moy,	*per la morbiu,*
Autrement m'en iray cert'	*in Itaglia.*

ET HARLEQVIN DONNERA A V. M.

Un mezo (C.) *Niente,*
Con un (O.) *Niente entiero,*
Accompagnato con un (RE.)

ARLECHIN

LIVRE PREMIER DE RHETORIQVE.

Quantumque la chaine & la Medaglia,
Pour la monstrer à ces Messieurs d'Itaglia.

50 COMP. DE RHETOR

Fradeli à menenuo con Arlechin
A guadagnar vn poco di quatrin.

SONGE.

Ie mi ſuis inſomniato ce matin,
Qu'vn Facquin d'importanza
Mi tiroit par la panza,
Et mi diſoit, Monſieur Arlequin,
Habebis medagliam & colanam.
Ie reſpondis en dormant,
Si non me burlat opinio:
Piaccia à Iddio
Di farci vedere il maturo parto
Di queſte pregne ſperanze.
Per la mia foy en ſongeant au guadagno
Io parlo Toſcolagno.

SONET IN ottaua rima.

Vient, void & vince, el grand Cesar Roman,
Cosi ha faict HENRY Roy de BOVRBON,
Qu'a prins la Bressa, le Fort, & Mommeillan
Plus facilment, que manger maccaron.

A moy, qui suis Arlequin Sauoian
Me semble bien qu'HENRY a grand raisor
De far' que Carlo li tienna parole,
De luy rendre Salux & Carmagnole.

Que venga la verolè
A son conseil, qui l'a mal conseillé,
Qu'est causa qu'Arlequin est ruiné.

Ah sacra Majesté,
Fais moy doner tout astheure pour streina
La medaglia, attachee à vna grossa chaina.

Bibliography

I DESIRE to thank Mr Gordon Craig, M. Henry Prunières, and especially M. A. G. Bragaglia for their kindness in aiding me with the compilation of the references which follow. I also wish to say that M. Luigi Rasi's notable work *I Comici Italiani* was of the greatest assistance to me. His three volumes, which he modestly calls "dictionaries," are a truly admirable proof of his great learning and industry.

Although several critics have suggested that I should provide an exhaustive bibliography with the present volume, I have been disinclined to do so for two reasons—namely, that the task has already been adequately accomplished by other hands, and that I have in no sense aimed at mere erudition in my work. The list herewith has been verified with the aid of M. Bragaglia. I have, at the same time, drawn upon the bibliographies of M. Rasi and of M. Miclascefsky (M. Constant Mic), whose book was translated into French from the Russian and published in 1927.

ADEMOLLO, A.: *Una Famiglia di comici italiani nel sec. XVIII* (Florence, 1885).

—— *I Teatri a Roma nel sec. XVII* (Rome, 1888).

ADRIANI, P.: *Selva overo zibaldone di concetti comici raccolti dal P. D. Placido Adriani di Lucca* (1734) (Manuscripts of the Communal Library of Perugia, A, 20).

AGRESTI, A.: *Studii sulla commedia italiana del sec. XVI* (Naples, 1871).

ALBERT, M.: *Les Théâtres de la foire (1660–1789)* (Paris, 1900).

ALIONE, G. G.: *Commedia e farse carnevalesche nei dialetti Astigiano, Milanese e Francese misti con latino barbaro, composte sul fine del sec. XV* (Milan, 1865).

ALLACCI, L.: *Dramaturgia* (Rome, 1666).

ALLEN, P. S.: "The Medieval Mimus," *Modern Philology*, viii, January and July 1910.

D'AMBRAS: *Napoli Antica* (1889).

DE AMICIS, V.: *La Commedia popolare latina e la commedia dell' arte* (Naples, 1882).

—— *L'Imitazione latina nella commedia italiana del sec. XVI* (Florence, 1897).

D'ANCONA, A.: *Origini del teatro italiano* (2 vols. Florence, 1877, and Turin, 1891).

—— "I Dodici mesi dell' anno nella tradizione popolare," *Archiv. per le Tradiz. Popolari*, vol. ii, 1883.

—— "Due Farse del sec. XVI," *Scelta di curiosità letterarie*, No. 187 (Bologna, 1882).

—— *Lettere di comici italiani del sec. XVII* (Pisa, 1893).

ANDREINI, F.: *Le Bravure del Capitano Spavento, divise in molti ragionamenti in forma di dialogo di Francesco Andreini da Pistoia, Comico geloso* . . . (Venice, 1607). Incomplete French translation, by J. de Fontenes (Paris, 1633).

—— *Nuova aggiunta alle bravure del Capitano Spavento, detto Francesco Andreini* . . . (Venice, 1614).

—— *Ragionamenti fantastici posti in forma di dialoghi rappresentativi.*

ANDREINI, G.-B.: *Teatro Celeste, nel quale si rappresenta come la Divina bontà habbia chiamato al grado di beatitudine e di Santità Comici penitenti, e martiri* . . . (Paris, 1624).

—— *Lo Specchio, composizione sacra e poetica; nella quale si rappresenta al vivo l'imagine della comedia, quanto vago, e deforme sia allor che da Comici virtuosi, e viziosi rappresentata viene* . . . (Paris, 1625).

ANDREINI, I.: *Lettere della Signora Isabella Andreini, Padovana, Comica gelosa e Academica Intenta, nominata l'Accesa* (Venice, 1607).

—— *Contrasti Scenici.* Fragments of some of the writings of Signora Isabella Andreini, collected by F. Andreini and brought out by F. Scala (Venice, 1625).

—— *Le Rime d'Isabella Andreini* (Naples, 1696).

ANIELLO SOLDANO: *La Fondazione, e origine di Bologna, cavata dalle sue etimologie, recitata per prologo di comedia in quella città da Aniello Soldano, detto Spacca Strummolo, Napoletano* (Bologna, 1610).

—— *Fantastiche et ridicolose etimologie, recitate in commedia da Aniello Soldano* (Bologna, 1610).

APPOLINAIRE, G.: *Le Théâtre italien, avec une étude sur le théâtre italien en France par Ch. Simon* (Paris, 1910)

Argomento e scenario della commedia, intitolata "Non puo essere, overo custodire una donna è fatica senza frutto," da representarsi nel carnevale dell' anno 1682, nel Palazzo dell' eccellentiss. Sig. Marchese del Carpio, Ambasciatore di S. M. C. (Rome, 1682).

D'AURIAC, EUGÈNE: *Théâtre de la Foire.* A collection of the plays presented at the Fairs of Saint-Germain and Saint-Laurent (Garnier Frères, Paris, 1878).

BARBIERI, N.: *La Supplica, discorso famigliare di Nicolo Barbieri, detto Beltrame, diretta a quelli che scrivendo, o parlando trattano de comici trascurando i meriti delle azzioni virtuose* (Venice, 1634, and Bologna, 1636).

—— *L'Inavertito overo Scappino disturbato e Mezzettino travagliato, di Nicolo Barbieri detto Beltrame* (Turin, 1629, and Venice, 1630).

BARETTI, G.: *La Frusta letteraria di Aristarco Scanabue* (Venice, Ancona, 1763–65; Florence, Sansoni, 1897).

—— *An Account of the Manners and Customs of Italy* (2 vols., London, 1769).

—— "Carlo Gozzi and his Plays," *The Mask*, vol. iii, 1910–11.

BARTOLI, A.: "Scenari inediti della commedia dell' arte." Contributed to the *History of the Italian Popular Theatre* (Florence, 1880).

BARTOLI, F.: *Notizie Istoriche de' comici italiani che fiorirono intorno all' anno 1540 fino a giorni presenti* (Padua, 1781).

BARTOLI, P.: *La Schiava, comedia nuova e ridicolosa. Nuovamente posta in luce, ad instantia d'ogni spirito gentile* (Scenario). (Pavia, 1602.)

BARTOLOMEI, G.: *Didascalia, cioè la dottrina comica di Girolamo Bartolomei, già Smeducci* (3 vols., Florence, 1658 and 1661).

BASCHET, A.: *Les Comédiens italiens à la cour de France sous Charles IX, Henri III, Henri IV et Louis XIII* (Paris, 1882).

BAUMGARTEN, J.: *La France qui rit* (2 vols., Kassel, Kay, 1880).

BEAUMONT, CYRIL W.: *The History of Harlequin* (C. W. Beaumont, London, 1926).

BEIJER, AGNE: *Recueil de plusieurs fragments des premières comédies italiennes qui ont été représentées en France sous le règne de Henry III. Recueil, dit de Fossard, conservé au musée national de Stockholm, présenté par Agne Beijer, conservateur du musée national de Drottingholm, suivi de compositions de rhétorique de M. Don Arelequin présentées par P.-L. Duchartre* (Duchartre et Van Buggenhoudt, Paris, 1928).

BELIVACQUA, E.: *Giambattista Andreini e la compagnia dei "fedeli"* (Turin, 1894).

BERNARDIN, N. M.: *La Comédie italienne en France et les théâtres de la foire et du boulevard, 1570–1791* (Paris, 1902).

BERNERI: *Meo-Patacca. Poème en dialecte populaire* (Rome, 1685).

BERTELLI, F.: *Il Carnevale italiano mascherato ove si veggono in figura varie inventione di capritii* (Venice, 1642) (Iconography).

BERTOLDO: *Ragionamento fra il re e Bertoldo.* Popular edition, illustrated with woodcuts. Eighteenth century (?). (Neither publisher, place, nor date given.)

BERTOLOTTI, A.: *Musici alla corte dei Gonzaga in Mantova dal sec. XV al XVIII* (Ricordi, Milan, n.d.)

(BIANCHI, L.): *Cento e quindici conclusioni in ottava rima del Plusquamperfetto Dottor Gratiano Partesana da Francolin, comico Geloso* (Siena, 1606; Verona and Mantua, 1585?).

BIANCOLELLI, P.: *Nouveau Théâtre italien* (Antwerp, 1713).

Bibliografia della cronistoria dei teatri d'Italia (Leghorn, 1896).

BOCCHINI, B.: *Raccolta di tutte le opere di Bartolomeo Bocchini, detto Zan Muzzina . . .* (Modena, n.d., 1665?).

—— *La Corona maccheronica* (Bologna, 1660).

BOHM, A.: "Fonti plautine del Ruzzante," *Giorn. stor. d. lett. ital.*, xxix, 1897.

BONFIGLI, L.: *Un Capitolo in morte di Simone da Bologna, comico Geloso.* Reproduction of the edition of 1585. (Arezzo, 1907.)

BORROMEO, C.: *Sentimenti di S. Carlo Borromeo intorno agli spettacoli* (1759).

—— *Traité contre les danses et les comédiens* (Paris, 1664).

BIBLIOGRAPHY

BOZIO, Z.: *Il Teatro dialettale veneziano e l'opera di Luigi Sugana* (Rome, Milan, 1905).

BRAGAGLIA, A. G.: *I Comici Italiani maestri di teatro in Francia. L'Esame* (April, 1925).

—— *La Maschera mobile* (Franco Campitelli, Foligno, 1926).

BROADBENT, R.: *A History of Pantomime* (London, 1901).

DE BROSSES: *Le Président de Brosses en Italie.* Informal letters written from Italy in 1739 and 1740. (Second edition, 1858.)

BROUCHARD, C.: *Les Origines du théâtre de Lyon* (Lyons, 1865).

BRUNI, D.: *Fatiche comiche di Domenico Bruni, detto Fulvio, comico di Madama Serenissima Principessa di Piemonte* (Paris, 1623.)

—— *Prologhi di Domenico Bruni, detto Fulvio, Comico di Madama,* etc. (Turin, 1621, and Paris, 1623).

—— *Dialoghi fatti in diverse occasioni ad istanza delle sue compagne Flaminia, Delia, Valeria, Lavinia e Celia.* Manuscript in the library of L. Rasi in Florence.

—— *Prologhi di D. Bruni, comico confidente, detto Fulvio.* Forty prologues. Manuscript of the seventeenth century in the Brera at Milan.

BRUSCAMBILLE: *Les Fantaisies de Bruscambille, contenant plusieurs discours, paradoxes, harangues et prologues facétieux. Faites par le sieur des Lauriers, comédien* (Paris, 1612).

—— *Les Nouvelles et Plaisantes Imaginations de Bruscambille, en suite de ses fantaisies* (Bergerac, 1615).

—— *Facétieux Paradoxes de Bruscambille, et autres discours comiques* (Rouen, 1615).

BURCKHARDT, J.: *Die Kultur der Renaissance in Italien* (ninth edition, Basel, 1860). Authorized English translation published by George G. Harrap and Co., London, 1929.

BYRN: *Comici italiani alla corte di Polonia e di Sassonia.*

CALLOT, J.: *Balli di Sfessania, etc.* (Iconography).

CALMO, A.: *Lettere piacevole* (1572). See also ROSSI, V.

CAMERINI, E.: *I Precursori del Goldoni* (Milan, 1872).

—— "La Commedia dell' arte alla corte di Baviera nel sec. XVI e i tipi comici," *Nuovi profili letterari* (vol. iii, Milan, 1876).

CAMINNECI, G.: *Brevi cenni storici, biografici, artistici delle maschere siciliane in Palermo* (Palermo, 1884).

CAMPARDON, E.: *Les Spectacles de la foire . . . depuis 1595 jusqu'à 1791* (2 vols., Paris, 1877).

—— *Les Comédiens du roi de la troupe italienne pendant les deux derniers siècles* (Paris, 1880).

CAMPARDON, E., and CONGNON, A.: *La Vieillesse de Scaramouche.* Unpublished documents, 1690–94.

CANTU, C.: *Cicalamento in canzonette ridicole . . .* (Florence, 1646).

Canzonette, di echo. Contains *Le Nozze del Zane.* (No date or place of publication; sixteenth century.)

CAPRIN, G.: "La Commedia dell' arte al principio del sec. XVIII," *Rivista teatrale italiana,* February–August 1905.

CARAVELLI, V.: *Tradizioni drammatiche popolari.* Critical gossip.

CASAMARCIANO, A.: *Gibaldone de soggetti da recitarsi all' impronto. Alcuni proprii e gl'altri da diversi. Raccolti di D. Annibale Sersale Conte di Casamarciano.* Ninety-three scenarios. Manuscript in the National Library, Naples.

—— *Gibaldone comico di varii suggetti di comedie, ed opere bellissime copiate da me Antonio Passanti detto Oratio il Calabrese per comando dell'ecc^mo Sig. Conte di Casamarciano* (1700). Ninety scenarios. Manuscript in the National Library, Naples.

CASANOVA, J.: *Mémoires* (Paris, 1843). (English trans. by A. Machen, Dover reprint, 3 vols., 1961.)

CECCHINI, P. M.: *Brevi Discorsi intorno alle comedie, comedianti, e spettatori, dove si comprende quali rappresentationi si possono ascoltare et permettere* (Vicenza, 1614, Naples, 1616, and Venice, 1621).

—— *Lettere facete e morali* (Venice, 1622).

—— *Frutti delle moderne comedie et avisi a chi le recita, di Pier-maria Cecchini, nobile Ferrarese, tra comici detto Frittellino* (Padua, 1628).

—— *Discorso sopra l'arte comica con il modo di ben recitare, di Pier Maria Cecchini, comico Acceso, detto Frittellino.* Manuscript in the Library of Turin.

CELLER, L. (Leclerc): *Les Décors, les costumes et la mise en scène au XVIIe siècle (1615–80)* (Paris, 1860).

—— *Caractères populaires au théâtre* (Paris, 1870).

DEL CERRO, E.: *Nel Regno delle maschere* (Naples, Perella, 1914).

DE CHARNI: "Lettres historiques sur la nouvelle comédie italienne," *Mercure de France*, May 1740 *et seq.*

CHASLES, PH.: *Études sur l'Espagne et sur les influences de la littérature espagnole en France et en Italie* (Paris, 1847).

CHATFIELD-TAYLOR, H. C.: *Goldoni: a Biography* (Duffield and Co., New York, 1913).

CIAMPI, I.: *Studio sulla commedia italiana nel sec. XVII* (Rome, 1856).

—— *Le Rappresentazioni sacre nel medio evo in Italia considerate nella parte comica* (Rome, 1865).

CINELLI, G.: *Bibliotheca volante* (Modena, 1695).

COCCHI, G.: *Studio sulle maschere italiane* (1891).

COCCHI, S.: *La nova Maschera Milanese* . . . (1890).

COLLÉ, CH.: *Journal historique* (1751 ?).

Commedia d'un villano e d'una zingara che da la ventura . . . da recitare in maschera.

Compositions de Rhétorique. See DUCHARTRE, P.-L., and also *Recueil.*

CONSTANTINI, A.: *La Vie de Scaramouche* (Paris, 1695 and 1876). Italian translation (Venice, 1726).

Contrasto di bravura, fra il Capitano Delvvio e Zan Badil (Ferrara and Bologna, 1613).

Contrasto del fortunao et del Zani in ottava rima, con alcune stanze in lingua bergamasca del magnar del Zane (1576).

CORBONI, P.: *Cristoforo Colombo nel teatro.* (Scenario.) (Milan, 1892.)

CORTESE, G.: *Il Dramma popolare in Roma nel periodo delle origini e suoi pretesi rapporti con la commedia dell' arte* (Turin, Baglione, 1897).

CORYAT, T.: *Coryat's Crudities* . . . (3 vols., London, 1611 and 1776).

COTOLENDI, C.: *Arlequiniana, ou les bons mots, les histoires plaisantes et agréables recueillies des conversations d'Arlequin* (Paris, 1694 and 1708).

CRAIG, GORDON: "The Characters of the Commedia dell' Arte," *The Mask*, January 1912.

—— "The Commedia dell' Arte Ascending," *The Mask*, October 1912.

CREIZENACH, W.: *Geschichte des neueren Dramas* (4 vols., Halle, 1893, 1911).

CROCE, B.: *I Teatri di Napoli, secolo XV–XVIII* (Naples, 1891).

—— *Pulcinella e il personaggio del napolitano in commedia* (Rome, 1899).

—— *Lo Spagnolo nelle commedie.* Taken from the *Acts of the Pont. Acad.*, vol. xxvii. (Naples.)

—— "Un Repertorio della commedia dell' arte," *Giorn. stor. d. lett. ital.*, xxxi, 1898.

—— "Una nuova Raccolta di scenari," *Giorn. stor. d. lett. ital.*, xxix, 1897.

CROCE, G. C.: *Bravure tremende del Capitano Belerofonte Scarabombardone da Rocca di Ferro* (Bologna, 1629).

—— *Bravate, razzate et arcibulate dell' arcibravo Smedola* (Bologna, 1628).

—— *Indice universale della libraria, o studio del celebratissimo arcidottore Gratian Furbson de Fraculin* . . . (Bologna, n.d.).

CUNLIFFE, J.: "The Influence of Italian on English Drama," *Modern Philology*, vol. iv, 1907.

DECOMBE, L.: *Les Comédiens italiens à Rennes au XVIIIe siècle* (Rennes, 1900). (Room 410, Bibliothèque Nationale, Paris.)

DESBOULMIERS, J. A. J.: *Histoire anecdotique et raisonnée du théâtre italien, depuis son établissement en France jusqu'à l'année 1769, contenant les analyses des principales pièces et un catalogue de toutes celles, tant italiennes que françaises, données sur ce théâtre avec les anecdotes les plus curieuses de la vie et des talents des acteurs et des actrices* . . . (7 vols., Paris, 1769).

DESPOIS, E.: *Le Théâtre français sous Louis XIV* (fourth edition, Paris, 1894).

Dialogo in versi in furbesco fra Scatarello e Campagnolo, assassini da strada (no date or place of publication).

Dialogue between Louis le Petit and Harlequin le Grand, A (London, 1705 ?).

DIETERICH, A.: *Pulcinella, pompeianische Wandbilder und römische Satyrspiele* (Teubner, Leipzig, 1897).

DOSSON, S.: *Les Sujets et les personnages de la comédie nationale à Rome* (Paris, 1891).

DRACK, MAURICE: *Le Théâtre de la Foire, la comédie italienne et l'opéra-comique.* A collection of selected plays given from the end of the seventeenth century up through the early years of the nineteenth century. (Librairie de Firmin-Didot et Cie, Paris, 1889.)

DRIESSEN, O.: *Der Ursprung des Harlekin* (Berlin, 1904).

BIBLIOGRAPHY

DUCHARTRE, P.-L.: *Les Compositions de rhétorique de M. Don Arlequin* (Duchartre et Van Buggenhoudt, Paris, 1928).

FABIANI, G.: *Memoria sopra l'origine ed istituzioni delle principali Academie della città di Siena, detti gl' Intronati, dei Rozzi e dei Fisiocritici . . .* (Venice, 1757).

FAINELLI, V.: " Chi era Pulcinella ? " *Giorn. stor. d. lett. ital.*, liv, 1909.

FALCONI, C.: *Le Quattro Principali Maschere italiane, nella commedia dell' arte e nel teatro del Goldoni* (Rome, 1896).

FERRARI, G.: *La Scenografia* (Hoepli, Milan, 1902).

FERRETTI, E.: *Le Maschere italiane nella commedia dell' arte e nel teatro di Goldoni* (Rome, 1904).

FICORONI: *De Larvis Scenicis et figuricis comicis* (1754). (Iconography.)

FIORENTINO, P. A.: *Comédies et comédiens* (1867).

FIORILLO, S.: *Il Mondo conquistato di Silvio Fiorillo, detto il Capitan Mattamores, comico* (Milan and Bologna, 1627).

FLECHSIG, E.: *Die Dekoration der modernen Bühne in Italien von den Anfangen bis zum Schluss des XVI Jahrh.*, Part I. (B. Schluze, Dresden, 1894).

FLERES, U.: " Ancora del Capitano Fracassa," *Giorn. " Capitan Fracassa,"* 1880.

FORNER, K.: *Le Canzonette de Mistro Rigo Forner et le stanze di un medico Schiavon che si chiama Mistro Damian.* Contains " Discorso in ottava rima che un ciarlatano indirizza al popolo per vendere le sue frottole." (Venice, 1547.)

FOURNEL, V.: *Curiosités théâtrales anciennes et modernes* (1859).

FOURNIER, E.: *L'Espagne et ses comédiens en France au XVIII*[e] *siècle.*

FRANCIA, L.: " Alcune novelle del Decameron illustrate nelle fonti," *Giorn. stor. d. lett. ital.*, xlix, 1907.

FRANCIOSINI, L.: *Rodomontades espanolas—traduz. in francese e in italiano da Lorenzo Franciosini—cavate da commentari spaventevolissimi, terribilissimi et invincibili capitani, amazzamori Cocodrillo e Scheggia brocchieri* (Milan, 1643).

FRIZZI, A.: *Cinquanta Maschere italiane illustrate nei loro costumi* (1888).

Frottola d'un padrone, e d'un servo. Intitolata Zanin da Bologna (1577).

GABBRIELLI, G. See SIVELLO.

GABRIEL, F.: *Pazzia di Scapino con spropositi pazzeschi et canzoni burlevoli, data in luce da me Federico Gabriel, in Bologna.* (N.d.).

GALIANI, F.: *Storia di Pulcinella . . .*

GALLAND: *Au Pays des illusions* (eighteenth and nineteenth centuries).

GANDINI, A.: *Cronistoria dei Teatri di Modena* (Modena, 1873).

GARZONI, T.: *La Piazza universale di tutte le professioni del mondo e nobili et ignobili* (Venice, 1585; 1615, and 1665). (Discorso XV: "De formatori di spettacoli in genere, e de' ceretani e ciurmatori massime.")

GASPARY, A.: *Geschichte der italienischen Litteratur* (2 vols., Berlin, 1885 and 1889). Italian translation (Turin, 1887–91).

GAZEAU, M.: *Les Fous et les bouffons* (Paris, 1882).

Generici brighelleschi consistenti in sortite di scena, discorsi di bravura, moti satirici, proverbi, sentenze, dialoghi, alfabeti estrati da vari comici autori, particolarmente dal A. Zanone per uso della commedia italiana (Milan, n.d.).

—— *Generici, consistenti in moti faceti, sentenze, dialoghi* (1635).

—— *Generici ai dilletanti alla maschera di Truffaldino* (Venice, 1835).

—— *Generici per la maschera d'Arlecchino . . . raccolti da diversi comici che vestirono il detto personaggio* (Milan, n.d.)

DU GÉRARD, M.: *Table alphabétique et chronologique des pièces représentees sur l'ancien théâtre italien depuis son établissement* (1750).

GHERARDI, E.: *Le Théâtre italien, ou le recueil général de toutes les comédies et scènes françaises jouées par les comédiens italiens du roi, pendant tout le temps qu'ils ont été au service.* With copper-plate engravings at the head of each comedy, printed tunes, and notes at the end of each volume. (First edition, 1694; second edition, Paris, 1741, 6 vols.)

DI GIACOMO, S.: *Cronaca del teatro San Carlino* (Naples, 1895).

GIANNINI, G.: *Teatro popolare lucchese* (Turin and Palermo, 1895).

—— *Canti popolari della montagna lucchese* (Turin, 1889).

GIGLÏ, G. (?): *Vocabulario Gratianesco in Mss. d. Bibl. Vitt. Em.* (Sessor Collection, 587).

GILLOT, C.: *Le Théâtre italien* (Iconography).

Goethes Gespräche (W. v. Biedermann edition, Leipzig, 1889–91).

GOLDONI, C.: *Mémoires de M. Goldoni pour servir à l'histoire de sa vie et à celle de son théâtre, dédiées au roi* (Paris, 1787). Italian translation (3 vols., etc., Venice, 1788). See also CHATFIELD-TAYLOR, H. C.

GOTHEIN: *Die Culturentwicklung Süditaliens.*

GOZZI, C.: *Memorie inutili, a cura di G. Prezzolini* (Bari, 1910). Freely translated by P. de Musset, Paris, 1848.

—— *Memoirs of Count Carlo Gozzi.* Translated into English by J. A. Symonds . . . with essays on Italian impromptu comedy, Gozzi's life, the dramatic fables, and Pietro Longhi, by the translator (2 vols., London, 1890).

—— *Le Fiabe di Carlo Gozzi a cura di Ernesto Masi* (2 vols., Bologna, 1885). *A cura D. Ciampoli.* Contains "L'amore delle tre melarance." (2 vols., Lanciano, 1913.)

—— "I Contratti rotti." Opere, iv, 35. (Scenario.)

GRAF, A.: "Arlecchino," *Giorn. stor. d. lett. ital.*, ix, 1886, p. 48.

GRAZZINI, A. (Il Lasca): *Le Rime burlesche edite ed inedite* (*C. Verzone*) (Florence, Sansoni, 1882). Contains "Canto carnascialesco de Zanni e magnifici."

GRIMM, F.: *Correspondance littéraire, philosophique, et critique, 1753–92* (Edition Tourneux, Paris, 1877–82).

GUEULETTE: *Traduction du scenario de J. Dominique Biancolelli et avis au lecteur, contenant les noms, les rosles, les naissances, les débuts, les morts et les faits principaux qui concernent les comédiens italiens, qui ont paru en Italie et en France, depuis 1577, jusqu'en la présente année 1750 ; et les années qui suivront. Par Mr. G. 2e partie. Traduction du scenario ou du recueil des scènes que Joseph Dominique Biancolelli jouait en habit d'Arlequin dans les pièces italiennes de son temps, rédigé et écrit de sa main.* Contains 173 scenarios. Manuscript finished before 1760. (Library of the Paris Opera.)

GUEZONI, G.: *Il Teatro italiano nel secolo XVIIIe.*

GUILLEMOT, J.: "Le Théâtre italien de Gherardi," *Revue Contemporaine*, May 1866.

—— "La Comédie dans le vaudeville," *ibid.* li, 1866.

HIPPERN, C.: *Le Théâtre à Rome.*

HUGUENET, P.: *Mimes et Pierrots* (Paris, 1889).

Infermità, testamento e morte di Francesco Gabrielli, detto Scappino (Verona, 1638). *Propugnatore*, May–June 1880.

INGEGNERI, A.: *Della Poesia rappresentativa et del modo di rappresentare le favole sceniche* (Ferrara, 1598).

JAL, A.: *Dictionnaire critique de biographie et d'histoire. Errata et supplément pour tous les dictionnaires historiques* . . . (second edition, Paris, 1872).

JARRO, G. (Piccini): *L'Epistolario d'Arlecchino* (T. Martinelli, Florence, 1895).

—— *L'Origine della maschera di Stenterello* (Florence, 1898).

JORIO, A.: *La Mimica degli antichi investigata nel gestire napolitano* (Naples, 1832).

KLEIN, J. L.: *Geschichte des Dramas*, vol. iv (Leipzig, 1866).

KLINGER, O.: *Die Comédie Italienne in Paris nach der Sammlung von Gherardi* (Strasburg, 1902).

LAMBRANZI, G. (di Venetia): *Nuova e curiosa scuola de balli theatrali. Prima parte, continente cinquanta balli di diverse nationi, e figure theatrali con i loro vestimenti, si che, come si deve contenera nelle positure di questi balli . . . con le arie, e con pieno, e necessario avvertimento, come ogn'uno ha da contenersi in simili balli . . . da Gregorio Lambranzi, maestro de balli francesi, inglesi, ridiculi e sery in aria ed à terra e compositore de balli theatrali, disegnati, e intagliati da G. G. Puschner, in Norimberga, 1716.* Italian and German text.

LEE, VERNON (Violet Paget): *Studies of the Eighteenth Century in Italy* (London, 1880, and Chicago, 1908). *Il Settecento in Italia* (Milan, 1882).

—— "A Survival of the 'Commedia,'" *The Mask*, vol. iii, 1910–11.

LEES, D. NEVILLE: "A Biographical Note on Evaristo Gherardi," *The Mask*, 1910–11.

LEVI, C.: *Saggio di bibliografia degli studi critici su C. Gozzi* (extract from *Rivista d. archivi e biblioteche*, 1906) (Florence, n.d.).

—— "Il Signor Brighella," *Natura ed Arte.* English: *The Mask*, July, 1912.

BIBLIOGRAPHY

LISONI, A.: *Drammatica italiana nel sec. XVII* (Parma, 1898).

LOCATTELLI, B.: *Della Scena de sogetti comici et tragici di B. L. R.* (2 vols., Rome, 1618–22). (103 scenarios and two speeches: 1. "Si Mostra esser necessario le facetie a la vita humana: et faceto chiamarsi il Comico"; 2. "Si Mostra il Comico essere l'Accademico virtuoso, le reppresentationi et Comedie del quale si possono ascoltare e permettere, et non quelle dell' Histrione infame". Manuscript in the Royal Casanatense Library at Rome. Segn. F, iv, 12–13, Cod. 1211–12.

LOEHNER, E.: "Carlo Goldoni e le sue memorie," *Archivio veneto*, xxiii, parte 1.

LOMBARDO, G. D.: *Nuovo Prato di prologhi di Gio. Donato Lombardo da Bitonto, detto il Bitontino* (Venice, 1618).

LOVARINI, E.: "Notizie sui parenti e sulla vita del Ruzzante," *Giorn. stor. d. lett. ital.*, xi, 1888.

LUCAS. H.: *Les Types comiques étrangers qui ont servi à la comédie de Molière et de Regnard*, in Baumgarten's *La France qui rit* (Kassel, 1880).

DE LYDEN, E.: *Ceci est l'Histoire d'Arlequin*, in Baumgarten's *La France qui rit* (Kassel, 1880).

LYONNET, HENRY: *Le Théâtre en Italie.*

—— *Les Théâtres hors de France; Pulcinella et C°* (1901).

MADDALENA, E.: "Uno Scenario inedito," *Sitzungsberichte der K. Akad. der Wissenschaften* (Vienna, Phil.-Hist. Klasse, cxliii, 1901).

MAGNIN, C.: "Teatro celeste. Les commencements de la comédie italienne en France," *Revue des Deux Mondes*, December 1847.

—— *Histoire des marionnettes en Europe, depuis l'antiquité jusqu'à nos jours* (Paris, 1852 and 1862).

MAGRINI, G. B.: *I Tempi, la vita e gli scritti di C. Gozzi, aggiunt; le sue annotazioni inedite alla Marfisa Bizzarra* (Benevento, 1883).

MANTZIUS, K.: *Skuespilkunstens Historie* (Copenhagen, 1897–1907). English translation: *A History of Theatrical Art in Ancient and Modern Times*, vol. ii (London, Duckworth, 1903).

MANZONI, L.: "Libro di carnevale dei secoli XV e XVI," *Scelta di curiosità letterarie*, clxxxii (Bologna, 1881).

MARASCA, A.: *Comici dell' arte secondo le notizie istoriche di Fr. Bartoli* (Rome, 1911).

MARAZIN, J.: *Le Théâtre des boulevards et la comédie improvisée* (Limoges, 1886).

MARCELLO, BENEDETTO: *Il Teatro alla moda, satiro contra il teatro* (1722).

MARCHINI-CAPASSO, O: *Goldoni e la commedia dell' arte* (second edition, Naples, 1912).

Maridaz over sermo da fé in maschera a una sposa, in lengua bergamasca . . . (no date or place of publication).

MARTELLI, P. J.: *Lettera a G. B. Recanati in Seguito del teatro italiano di Pier-jacopo Martello* (Bologna, 1723).

(MARTINELLI, T.): *Compositions de rhétorique de Mr Don Arlequin.* Imprimé delà le bout du monde (Lyons, 1601). Only copy extant in the Bibliothèque Nationale, Paris (Rés. Y 2. 922).

MARTUCCI, G.: "Un Comico dell' arte," *Nuova Antologia*, xlviii, 1884.

—— An unpublished scenario, *Nuova Antologia*, 15 maggio, 1885.

Mascherata et capriccio del confuso Accademico Sprezzato con alcune passate da zingara (Viterbo, 1623).

MASI, E.: *Sulla Storia del teatro italiano nel sec. XVIII* (Florence, 1891).

The Mask, 1910 *et seq.*: Articles by G. Craig, Ph. Monnier, M. Scherillo, and others.

MAZZI, C.: *La Congrega dei Rozzi di Siena nel sec. XVI, con appendice di documenti, bibliografia e illustrazioni concernenti quella ed altre accademie e congreghe senesi* (2 vols., Florence, 1882).

Mémoires historiques et critiques d'Amsterdam (November 1722). A letter in verse from the Italian Comedians to the Bishop of Montpellier.

MERCEY, F.: "Le Théâtre en Italie: Stenterello," *Revue des Deux Mondes*, xxi, 1840.

—— "Les quatre Masques du théâtre italien," *Revue des Deux Mondes*, xxxiii.

Mercure de France, 1716–47.

DU MÉRIL: *Origines latines du théâtre moderne* (Paris, 1849).

MERLINI, D.: *Saggio di recerche sulla satira contro il villano* (Turin, 1894).

MERULA, A.: *Capitoli e publicatione del fansoso e trionfante sposalicio dell' invitto capitano Marchione Pettola, bravo napolitano* (Bologna, n.d.).

MÉZIÈRES, A.: *Prédécesseurs et contemporains de Shakespeare* (Paris, 1863 and 1894).

MEZZABOTTA, E.: *Il Congresso delle maschere* (1885).

MIC (MICLASCEFSKY), CONSTANT: *La Commedia dell' arte* (Éditions de la Pleïade, Paris, in 4to, 1927).

—— *La Commedia dell' arte* (Petrograd, 1914).

MIGNON, MAURICE: *Études de littérature italienne. . . . La Comédie Italienne de la Renaissance, Carlo Goldoni, Giovanni Pascoli* (Paris, 1912).

MINTURNO, A.: *L'Orte poetica nella quale si contengono i precetti eroici, tragici comici, satirici . . .* (1564, and Naples, 1725).

MOLAND, L.: *Molière et la comédie italienne* (Paris, 1867).

—— *Les Méprises, comédies de la Renaissance racontées* (Paris, 1869).

MOLMENTI, P.: *La Storia di Venezia nella vita privata* (3 vols., Venice, 1906). German translation by Bernardi (Hamburg, 1886).

MONNIER, PH.: *Venise au XVIIIe siècle.*

MORTIER, ALFRED: *Ruzzante* (Paris, J. Peyronnet, 1925).

Motti arguti allegorici alla maschera del Brighella (Verona, 1839).

MOUNTFORD: *The Life and Death of Dr Faustus made into a Farce by Mr Mountford, with the Humours of Harlequin and Scaramouche* (London, 1697; O. Francke, Heilbronn, 1886).

MURRAY, J.: *The Influence of Italian upon English Literature during the Sixteenth and Seventeenth Centuries* (Cambridge, 1886).

MUSARD, M.: *Les Parades des boulevards ou entretiens bouffons entre Paillasse et Cassandre, enrichi de lazzis d'Arlequin, contés jadis à Lelio par le célèbre Carlin sur le théâtre de la comédie italienne* (Paris, 1810).

MUSSI, N.: *La Maschera e il teatro* (1895).

NAPOLI-SIGNORELLI, P.: *Storia critica de'teatri antichi e moderni* (6 vols., Naples, 1787, 1790).

NERI, A.: "Una commedia dell' arte." *Giorn. stor. d. lett. ital.*, i, 1883.

—— "Scena illustrata," *ibid.*, August, 1887.

—— "L'Antonazzi," *Gazzetta Letteraria*, May 11 and 18, 1889.

NERUCCI, G.: "Arlecchino," *Giornale di erudizione di Firenze*, vii, 1898.

Nouveau théâtre italien ou recueil des comédies représentées par les comédiens italiens, Le (Paris, 1733).

Nuova scelta di villanelle et altre canzoni ingeniose, et belle . . . con un dialogo del patron et del zane . . . (no date or place of publication; sixteenth century).

Nuova scelta di villanelle di diversi autori con la canzone de Caterinon con la Tognina, raccolte da Zan Cazamoleta. (Turin, n.d.; end of the fifteenth century?)

Opera nuova nella quale si contiene un insonio, che ha fatto il Zanni Bagotto in lingua bergamasca . . . (1576).

Opera nuova, nella quale si contiene il maridazzo della bella Brunettina, sorella di Zan Tabari Canaja de Val Pelosa . . . (Brescia, 1582).

D'ORIGNY: *Annales du théâtre italien* (Paris, 1788).

OTTONELLI, D.: *Della Christiana moderatione del teatro . . . libro detto l'istanza per supplicare à signori superiori che si moderi christianamente il teatro dall'oscenità e da ogni altro eccesso nel recitare. . . .* (Florence, 1646).

OURRY: *Histoire de Polichinelle* in Baumgarten's *La France qui rit* (Kassel, 1880).

PAGLICCI-BROZZI, A.: *Il Teatro a Milano nel sec. XVII* (Milan, 1891).

PARDI, A.: *Le Stupende, forze e bravure del Capitano Spezza Capo, et Sputa Saette* (Padua, 1606).

PARFAICT, C. and F.: *Dictionnaire des théâtres de Paris contenant . . . les extraits de celles [pièces] qui ont été jouées par les comédiens italiens depuis leur établissement en 1716 . . .* (7 vols., Paris, 1756).

—— (Gueulette) "Histoire du théâtre italien," in *Dictionnaire des théâtres*, vol. viii (Paris, 1756).

—— *Histoire de l'ancien théâtre italien, depuis son origine en France, jusqu'à sa suppression en l'année 1697, suivie des extraits ou canevas des meilleures pièces italiennes qui n'ont jamais été imprimées* (Paris, 1753 and 1767).

Parodies du nouveau théâtre italien, avec les airs gravés, Les (7 vols., Paris, 1731 and 1738).

PELLIZZARO, G. B.: *La Commedia del sec. XVI e la novellistica anteriora e contemporanea in Italia* (Vicenza, 1901).

PERRENS, F.: *Histoire de la littérature italienne* (Paris, 1867).

PERRUCCI, A.: *Dell' arte rappresentativa, premeditata, e dall' improviso. Parti due Giovevole non solo a chi si diletta di rappresentare; ma a' predicatori, oratori, accademici e curiosi. Del dottor Andrea Perrucci* (Naples, 1699). Very rare. Rome, Casanatense Library; Florence, Library of L. Rasi . . .

BIBLIOGRAPHY

PETRACCONE, ENZO: *La Commedia dell' arte. Storia, tecnica, scenari* (Riccardo Ricciardi, Naples, 1927).

PETRAI, G.: *Maschere e burattini* (Rome, 1885).

—— *Lo Spirito delle maschere* (Turin and Rome, 1901).

PICOT, E.: *Pierre Gringoire et les comédiens italiens* (Paris, 1878).

—— " Le Monologue dramatique dans l'ancien théâtre français," *Romania*, xvi, 1887.

Pompe funèbre d'Arlequin, mort le dernier jour d'Aoust 1700, La (Paris, 1701).

PLAN, PIERRE-PAUL: *Jacques Callot, Maître Graveur.* Nouvelle édition révue et réduite, ornée de 96 estampes et d'un portrait (G. Van Oest et Cie, Brussels and Paris, 1914).

PORTIOLI, A. (?): *Epistolario d'Arlecchino* (Strenna Mantovana, 1871).

POUGIN, A.: *Dictionnaire historique et pittoresque du théâtre* (Paris, 1885).

Prologo: *Nuova Antologia* (December 15, 1884).

PRUNIÈRES, HENRY: *L'Opéra italien en France avant Lulli* (Paris, 1913).

PUBLIUS SYRUS: *Publii Syri mimi sententiæ.*

QUADRIO, F. S.: *Della Storia e della ragione d'ogni poesia* (7 vols., Bologna and Milan, 1739–52).

RABANY, CHARLES: *Le Théâtre et la ville en Italie au XVIII*[e].

RAO, C.: *L'Argute e facete lettere* . . . (Pavia, 1573).

RAPPARINI: *Arlichino* (Heidelberg, 1718).

RASI, L.: *I Comici italiani. Biografia, bibliografia, iconografia* (3 vols., Lumachi, Florence, 1897–1905).

—— *Catalogo generale della raccolta drammatica italiana di Luigi Rasi* (Florence, 1912).

RAYNAUD, G.: *La Mesnie Hellequin.* Romanic studies dedicated to Gaston Paris. (Paris, 1891).

RE, E.: " Scenarii modenesi " (Bibl. Estense Modena), *Giorn. stor. d. lett. ital.*, lv (1910).

—— " La Commedia veneziana e il Goldoni," *Gior. stor. d. lett. ital.*, lviii (1911).

Recueil de plusieurs fragments des premières comédies italiennes qui ont esté représentées en France sous le règne de Henry 3 (*Recueil Fossard*). See also BEJER, AGNE.

REINHARDTSTOETTNER, K.: *Die plautinischen Lustspiele in spätere Bearbeitungen* (Leipzig, 1880).

—— " Über die Beziehungen der italienischen Litteratur zum bayrischen Hofe und ihre Pflege an demselben," *Jahrb. f. mün. Geschichte*, i, 1887.

RENIER, R.: *Appunti sul contrasto fra la madre e la figliuola bramosa di marito.* In Msc. nuziale Rossi-Teiss (Trento, 1897).

—— " Arlecchino," *Fanfulla di domenica*, xxvi, 1904.

RENNERT, H.: *The Spanish Stage in the Time of Lope de Vega* (New York, 1909).

RICCI, C.: *I Teatri di Bologna nei secoli XVII e XVIII* (Bologna, 1888).

RICCOBONI, F.: *L'Art du théâtre* (Paris, 1750). Italian translation (Venice, 1762).

RICCOBONI, L.: *Histoire du théâtre italien depuis la décadence de la comédie latine, avec un catalogue des tragédies et comédies italiennes imprimées depuis l'an 1500 jusqu'à l'an 1660, et une dissertation sur la tragédie moderne* (Paris, 1728 and 1730). The edition of 1730 is much more complete.

—— *Dell' arte rappresentativa, capitoli sei* (London, 1728).

—— *Nuovo teatro italiano che contiene le comedie stampate e recitate dal S. L. Riccoboni, detto Lelio.* Italian-French. (3 vols., Paris, 1733.)

—— *An Historical and Critical Account of the Theatres in Europe, viz., the Italian, Spanish, French, English, Dutch, Flemish, and German Theatres, in which is contained a Review of the Manners, Persons, and Characters of the Actors ; intermixed with many Curious Dissertations upon the Drama* . . . (London, 1741).

RICH, J.: *Companion to the Latin Dictionary.*

RIGAL, E.: *Le Théâtre français avant la période classique, fin du XVI*[e] *et commencement du XVII*[e] *siècle* (Paris, 1901).

ROMANO, E.: *I Contrasti fra Carnevale e Quaresima nella letteratura italiana* (Pavia, 1907).

ROMANO, R.: *Prima Raccolta di bellissime canzonette musicali e moderne . . . per il Sig. Remigio Romano* (Pavia, 1625). In four parts. A collection of Spanish, Bergamask, etc., farces.

ROSSI, N.: *Discorsi sulla commedia* . . . (Vicenza, 1589).

ROSSI, V.: *Le Lettere di Messer Andrea Calmo . . . con introduzione ed illustrazioni di V. Rossi* (Turin, 1888).

—— *I Suppositi dell' Ariosto ridotto a scenario di commedia improvisa* (Bergamo, 1895).

ROSSI, V.: "Una Commedia di G. B. della Parta ed un nuovo scenario, l'Astrologo," extracted from *Rend. d. R. Istit. Lombardo*, second series, vol. xxix (Milan, 1896).

LE ROUSSEAU, F.: *A Chacoon for a Harlequin with all the Postures, Attitudes, Motions of the Head and Arms, and Other Gestures proper to this Character. Being the First that ever appeared in this Gust* (London, 1730 ?).

RUBIERI, E.: *Storia della poesia popolare italiana* (Florence, 1877).

SAINT-NON, ABBÉ DE (1730–91): *Choix de quelques morceaux des peintures antiques d'Herculanum, extraits du Musée de Portici* (Paris). (Iconography.)

SAND, M.: *Masques et bouffons. Comédie Italienne* (2 vols., Paris, 1860).

SARTI, C. G.: *Il Teatro dialettale bolognese* (Bologna, 1894).

SCALA, F.: *Il Teatro delle favole rappresentative, overo la ricreazione comica, boscareccia, e tragica; divisa in cinquanta giornate* . . . (Venice, 1611). Fifty scenarios. The following are the titles:

(1) "Li Due vecchi gemelli, comedia." (2) "La Fortuna di Flavio." (3) "La Fortunata Isabella." (4) "Le Burle d'Isabella." (5) "Flavio tradito." (6) "Il Vecchio geloso." (7) "La Creduta morta." (8) "La Finta pazza." (9) "Il Marito." (10) "La Sposa." (11) "Il Capitano." (12) "Il Cavadente." (13) "Il Dottor disperato." (14) "Il Peregrino fido." (15) "Lo Specchio." (16) "Li Due capitani simili." (17) "Li Tragici successi." (18) "Li Tre fidi amici." (19) "Li Due fidi notari." (20) "Il Finto negromante." (21) "Il Creduto morto." (22) "Il Porta-lettere." (23) "Il Finto Tofano." (24) "La Gelosa Isabella." (25) "Li Tappeti Alessandrini." (26) "La Mancata fede." (27) "Flavio finto negromante." (28) "Il Fido amico." (29) "Li Finto servi." (30) "Il Pedante." (31) "Li Due finti Zingani." (32) "Li Quattro finti spiritati." (33) "Il Finto cieco." (34) "Le Disgrazie di Flavio." (35) "Isabella astrologa." (36) "La Caccia." (37) "La Pazzia d'Isabella." (38) "Il Ritratto." (39) "Il Giusto castigo." (40) "La Fortunata prencipessa, tragedia." (41–42) "Gli avvenimenti comici, pastorali e tragici, opera mista." (43) "L'Alvida, opera regia." (44) "Rosalba incantatrice, opera heroïca." (45) "L'Innocente Persiana, opera reale." (46–48) "Dell' Orseida, opera reale, parte I, II, III." (49) "L'Arbore incantato." (50) "La Fortuna di Foresta, prencipessa di Moscou, opera regia."

SCENARIOS: *Raccolta di scenari più scelti d' istrioni, divisi in due volumi.* Contains 100 scenarios and 100 illustrations in colours. (Manuscript in the Corsini Library, Rome. Segn.: Cod. 652. 45. C. 6.)

—— *Raccolta di drami, commedie, oratorii e scenari di varii autori.* Contains 2 scenarios. (Manuscript in the Corsini Library, Rome. Segn.: Cod. 976. 45. F. 1.)

—— *Codice Barberiniano contenente un gruppo di nove scenarii*, xliv, 256. (See VALERI, A. *Scenarios of B. Locatelli*, p. 9.)

—— Forty-eight scenarios. Casanatense Library, Rome. (See DE SIMONE BROUWER, F. Another collection, etc.) Manuscripts No. 4.302–No. 4.186. Casanatense, Rome.

—— Fifty-one scenarios. Civic Museum, Venice. (See ROSSI, V. *I Suppositi*, etc.)

SCHERILLO, M.: *La Commedia dell' arte in Italia. Studi e profili.* (Turin, 1884.)

—— *La Commedia dell' arte.* "La Vita italiana nel seicento" (Florence, 1897).

—— "The Commedia dell' arte. Capitan Fracassa. The Genealogy of Pulcinella," *The Mask*, vol. iii, 1910–11.

—— *La Commedia dell' arte. Conferenza* (Milan, Trèves, n.d.).

—— "Die Atellanen und das heutige Volkslustspiel Neapels," *Das Ausland* (Munich, 1884), No. 16.

SCHLEGEL, A. W.: *Vorlesungen über dramatische Kunst und Literatur* (3 vols., Heidelberg, 1805–11).

SCHÜCKING (LEWIN, L.): "Studien über die stoffischen Beziehungen der englischen Komödie zur italienischen bis Lilly," *Studien zum englischen Philologie*, vol. ix (Halle, 1901).

SEMAR, JOHN: "Biographical Notes to the 'Commedia dell' Arte,' 'Capitan Fracassa,'" *The Mask*, 1910–11.

SENIGAGLIA, G.: *Capitan Spavento* (Florence, 1899).

SERLIO, S.: *Libri d'architettura* (Venice, 1560). (*Il secondo libro di prospettiva.*)

Sermo da far in maschera ad una sposa in lingua bergamasca . . . (no date or place of publication).

SFORZA, G.: "I Comici italiani del sec. XVI e XVII e la moralità del teatro," *Gazzetta letteraria*, anno xiv, Nos. 15–19.

SIMON, C.: See APPOLINAIRE, G.

BIBLIOGRAPHY

DE SIMONE BROUWER, F.: "Due scenari inediti del sec. XVII," *Giorn. stor. d. lett. ital.*, xviii, 1891.

—— *Capitan Fracassa* (Naples, 1900).

—— "Ancora una raccolta di scenari," *Rendic. d. accad. d. Lincei, classe di scienze morali, stor. e filolog*, Series V, vol. x (Rome, 1901).

SIVELLO (GABBRIELLI, G.): *Maridazzo di M. Zan Frognocola con Madonna Gnigniocola alla bergamasca con il suo baletto alla romana et altre bizarie, composte dal Sivello* (Venice, 1618).

SMITH, W.: *The Commedia dell' Arte. A Study in Italian Popular Comedy* (New York, Columbia University Press, 1912).

SOLERTI, A.: *Ferrara: la corte estense nella seconda metà del sec. XVI.* Città di Castello (second edition, 1899).

—— *Gl' albori del melodramma* (3 vols., Milan, Palermo, Naples, 1904).

—— *Musica, ballo e drammatica alla corte medicea dal 1600 al 1637* (Florence, 1905).

SOLERTI, A., AND LANZA, D.: "Teatro ferrarese nella seconda metà del sec. XVI," *Giorn. stor. d. lett. ital.*, xviii, 1891.

DE SOMMI, L.: *Dialoghi.* Manuscript in the National Library, Turin (1565 ?).

Sontuos tirà da Narcis, da cantar pr' intermez in temp d' Carneval (Bologna, 1752).

SOUBIES, A.: *Almanach des Spectacles (1752–1815)* (Paris).

Spaventose hiperboli del gran Capitano Coviello, Le (Venice, 1725).

STIEFEL, A.: "Lope de Rueda und das italienische Lustspiel," *Zeitschr. f. romanische Philologie*, xv, 1897.

STOPPATO, L.: *La Commedia popolare in Italia.* Saggi (Padua, 1887).

SYMONDS, J. A. See GOZZI, C.

TABARIN: *Œuvres complètes* (Paris, 1858).

—— *Inventaire universel des œuvres de Tabarin* (Paris, 1623).

TALPI, P.: *Al Duttour comic; tirà souvra particular divers, da dir dov s' vol* (Bologna, 1738 and 1872).

Théâtre des boulevards ou recueil des parades (3 vols., Mahon, 1756).

TINGHI, C.: *Diario di Ferdinando I e Cosimo II, gran Duca di Toscana scritto da Cesare Tinghi, suo aiutante di camera, da' 22 luglio, 1600.* Manuscript in the National Library, Florence.

TIRABOSCHI, A.: *Vocabolario dei dialetti bergamaschi antichi e moderni* (second edition, Bergamo, 1873).

TOLDO, P.: "Un Scenario inedito della commedia dell' arte," *Gior. stor. d. lett. ital.*, xlvi, 1905.

—— "Di Alcuni scenari inediti della commedia dell' arte e della loro relazione col teatro di Molière," Royal Academy of Science, Turin, Acts xlii, 1907.

—— "Études sur le théâtre de Regnard," *Revue d'histoire littéraire de la France*, x, 1.

—— *L'Œuvre de Molière et sa fortune en Italie* (Turin, 1910).

TOMADONI, S.: *Nuove Pazzie dell dottore* (Venice, 1689).

TORRACA, F.: *Il Teatro italiano nei sec. XIII, XIV, XV* (Florence, 1885).

DELLA TORRE, A.: *Studi sulla origine della commedia dell' arte.* Manuscript in the Library of L. Rasi, Florence.

TRAGIENSE, L. (BIANCHI): *De i Visj e de difetti del moderno teatro, e del modo di correggerli, e d' emendarli.* Ragionamenti VI . . . (Rome, 1753).

DU TRALAGE, J. N.: *Notes et documents sur l'histoire des théâtres de Paris* (1880).

TRAUTMANN, K.: "Italienische Schauspieler am bayrischen Hofe," *Jahrb. für münchener Geschichte*, i, 193 (Munich, 1887.)

TROIANO, M.: *Discorsi delli trionfi, giostre, apparati, e delle cose più notabili, nelle sontuose nozze dell' Illustr. et eccell. Sig. Duca Guglielmo . . ., nell' anno 1568 . . . di Massimo Trojano da Napoli* (Monaco, 1568).

URBANI: *Maschere in Venezia* (1877).

VALENTINI, F.: *Abhandlung über Comödie aus dem Stegreif und die italienischen Masken. . . .* With 20 coloured engravings (Berlin, 1826). German-Italian text.

VALERI, A. (CARLETTA): "Un Palcoscenio del seicento," *Nuova Rassegna* (Rome, 1893).

—— *Gli Scenari inediti di Basilio Locatelli* (Rome, 1894).

—— "Chi era Pedrolino ?" *Rassegna bibliografica*, iv, 1896.

VALERINI, A.: *Oratione d' Adriano Valerini veronese in morte della divina Signora Vicenza Armani, comica eccellentissima* . . . (Verona, 1570).

Vanto del Zani, dove lui narra molte segnalate prove che lui ha fatto nel magnar. (N.d.; sixteenth century.)

VERALDO, P.: *Mascherate et capricci dilettevoli, recitativi in comedie et da cantarsi in ogni sorte d' istromenti, opérette di molto spasso, di Paulo Veraldo romano* (Venice, 1672).

WESSELOFSKY, A.: "Arlichino e Aredodesa," *Giorn. stor. d. lett. ital.*, xi.

DE WISMES: *Un Portrait de Molière en Bretagne. Étude sur quelques comédiens, farceurs et bouffons français et italiens au XVIIe siècle* (Nantes, n.d.).

XAVERY, G. J.: *Aardige Versameling van Koorde-danssers, springers en postuurmaakers* (Amsterdam. n.d.) (Iconography.)

—— *Het nieuw geopend italiaans toneel* (Amsterdam, 1710 ?). (Iconography.)

ZAN CEPELLA: *Genealogia di Zan Capella, fatta in una bellissima matinata alla sua cara innamorata, detta D. Bertolina* (no date or place of publication).

ZANETTI, Z.: *La Medicina delle nostre donne, studio folk-lorico.* Città di Castello (1892).

ZANNONI, A.: *Raccolta di vari motto arguti, allegorici, e satirici ad uso del teatro, di Atanasio Zannoni, comico* (Venice, 1787).

ZENATTI, A.: "Una Raccolta di scenari della commedia dell' arte," *Rivista crit. d. lett. ital.* (May, 1885).

ZERBINI: *Atti d. Ateneo di scienze, lettere ed arti a Bergamo. VIII, 1887, seduta d. 28 marzo, 1886.*

SUNDRIES

Documents concerning the Marionettes. Manuscripts of the Commedia dell' Arte, Nos. 306, 592, 812. Foundation V. E. (Biblioteca Vittorio Emanuele, Rome).

Galerie Théâtrale, vol. ix (Bibliothèque Nationale, Paris).

"Illustrazione Italiana," *Milan Review*, March 1884, p. 135; 1889, p. 96; 1877, p. 115.

Les Amours de Pantalon et d'Arlequin. Illustrated scenario. Engravings by Shübler. (Bibliothèque Nationale, Paris.)

Pulcinella Comedies. Manuscripts Nos. 66–71, Foundation V.-E., Rome.

Revista Storica Italiana, vol. x, p. 522.

Revista Teatrale Italiana, vol. i, p. 163; vol. ix, pp. 20, 48, 144; vol. x, p. 19.

Scenes from the Life of Pulcinella. Series of 103 sepias by Tiepolo (property of Mr Richard Owen).

Index

INDEX

INDEX

INDEX